D0872269

THE ECONOMICS OF INDUSTRIAL STRUCTURE CONDUCT AND PERFORMANCE

To Diana Leigh

The Economics of Industrial Structure Conduct and Performance

DOUGLAS NEEDHAM

BSc(Econ.), MA(Econ.), PhD(Econ.)
Head, Department of Economics,
James Madison University, Virginia;
Formerly at State University of New York, Brockport

St. Martin's Press
New York

For information write:
St. Martin's Press, Inc., 175 Fifth Avenue, New York N.Y. 10010

Printed in the United States of America

Library of Congress Catalog Card Number 77-93897

ISBN 0-312-23665-4

First published in the United States of America in 1978

PREFACE

This book is a complete revision and extension of *Economic Analysis and Industrial Structure*, published originally in 1969, and is intended to provide the reader with an up-to-date and forward-looking treatment of the current state of knowledge in the field of industrial organization. The greater length of this book reflects a considerable expansion in coverage and depth of treatment of individual topics and, since only a few portions of the original book have remained intact here, a new title seemed appropriate.

The book focuses upon the role of business firms in influencing, and being influenced by, industrial structure and with the consequences of this relationship for economic performance in the economy as a whole. In contrast to most other industrial organization texts, where emphasis is upon industrial structure as a determinant of pricing behavior, this book presents a more balanced analysis emphasizing that many structural features, such as product differentiation and entry barriers, for example, are themselves under the control of firms. The resulting relationship between product pricing and other aspects of firms' behavior, and the implications of this relationship for public policy, receive greater emphasis than in other available texts. This is aided in the revised edition by a much improved exposition of the nature of the interdependence which exists between different facets of a firm's behavior.

Throughout the book major emphasis is placed upon developing an analytical framework linking firms' behavior and industrial structure, thereby providing the reader with an analytical peg upon which to hang his or her empirical knowledge. Without this it is impossible for the student of industrial organization to understand, interpret, or evaluate the stream of statistical studies of industrial structure–behavior relationships which pours forth steadily in the journals. References to empirical studies are included, but descriptive and statistical data are entirely omitted from the text. Similarly, those sections of the book which deal with public policy are not concerned, in the main, with the detailed provisions of laws affecting industrial behavior and structure, nor with the way in which these laws have been applied in particular cases; they concentrate, instead, on equipping the reader with a clear understanding of the relevance and limitations of economic analysis in providing a rationale for laws governing pricing, advertising, the exchange of information, mergers, and other aspects of firms' behavior.

While the book covers the same subject-matter as other industrial organization texts, there is another major difference of emphasis in addition to those already mentioned: the book focuses on the firm rather than on the industry, and on the determinants of the behavior of a firm's decision-makers. This approach, aided by a number of relatively recent developments in the economics literature and the results of my own research, permits the use of a unifying analytical framework which remedies at least three important deficiencies present in the existing industrial organization literature: first, the lack of an adequate theoretical framework linking industrial structure and behavior. Major emphasis in the existing literature is on structure–performance relationships, such as studies of seller concentration and industry profitability. In contrast, the conduct or behavior link in the structure–conduct–performance trilogy, which deals with the mechanism by which structure and behavior are related, is relatively neglected. This lack of attention to firms' behavior is largely responsible for the inconclusive nature of much of the theorizing and empirical research in the field of industrial organization to date, since it leads to the omission of many relevant variables which influence firms' behavior apart from industrial structure. The as yet unresolved issue of *why* seller concentration and industry profitability are observed to be positively associated is a notable example. It is also significant that neither the textbook literature of industrial organization nor price theory contains a satisfactory theoretical framework which includes all the determinants of a firm's optimal pricing behavior including market share, price-elasticity of market demand, and rival firm reactions. This particular defect is remedied in Chapter Three of the book. The analytical framework developed and utilized throughout the book shows clearly the relationship between various dimensions of industry structure and behavior. The reasons for the inherent complexity of these relationships and the resulting implications for firms' behavior are clarified, a step which is essential in furthering one's understanding of structure–performance relationships and in devising and interpreting statistical studies in the field of industrial organization.

Second, the existing industrial organization literature concentrates excessively on pricing behavior. The same expository framework which is used in the book to explain the determinants of optimal pricing behavior can readily be broadened to include non-price aspects of firms' behavior. As a result, the reader is encouraged to develop a more balanced view of the importance of pricing decisions in industrial behavior. Price is not always the most important of the many characteristics of a product which influence buyer behavior, price reactions by a firm's rivals are not always the most likely competitive response, and empirical studies of managerial behavior have revealed that businessmen often rate pricing decisions low on their priority list.

Third, the existing industrial organization literature lacks an adequate theoretical framework linking pricing and non-price aspects of firms' behavior. Price determination and non-price dimensions of firms' behavior are generally treated separately in the economics and business literature alike. While such a partial-equilibrium approach may be satisfactory as a teaching and learning device, the two aspects of behavior are inextricably related, since each simultaneously influences buyer and rival seller behavior. The book demonstrates clearly the manner in which pricing and other decisions are related and opens up a number of significant opportunities for extending our understanding of the relationship between industrial structure and aspects of industrial behavior other than pricing. While many of the ingredients which are combined in the approach adopted in the book can be found scattered through the more recent journal literature, nowhere are they synthesized into a unified and logically coherent analytical framework showing clearly the links between industrial structure and behavior.

The book is intended to serve not only as a basic text for upper-level undergraduate and first-year graduate courses in Industrial Organization for economics students and lawyers specializing in antitrust law and firms' behavior, but also as a serious contender for adoption in business-administration program courses which deal with the relationship between different facets of a firm's internal operations and with the implications of external constraints, including competitors' reactions and public policies, for optimal policies of the firm. Managerial texts used in business courses which deal with individual decisions relating to production, pricing and advertising generally fail to take adequate account of the interdependence which exists between these different decisions. On the other hand, by neglecting to analyze sufficiently the behavioral link between industrial structure and performance, and by concentrating excessively on pricing decisions, industrial organization texts have in the past eliminated themselves from this market. By providing a relatively simple yet comprehensive analytical framework encompassing all of the major determinants of optimal levels of a firm's decision variables, and using operational concepts such as market shares and elasticities which the reader can easily comprehend and relate to the real world, it is hoped that this book will offer the business student a good deal more than the price-theory texts which typically serve as the microeconomic portion of most business-administration programs.

Although familiarity with elementary price-theory concepts would be helpful to the reader, previous exposure to an undergraduate price-theory course is not required, since I have tried to make the book a self-contained treatment of the current state of knowledge in the field of industrial organization. Mathematical exposition is occasionally used in the body of the text, but only to summarize earlier verbal or diagrammatic exposition, or to convey concisely a few important relationships. Diagrams supplement the verbal exposition wherever they are useful in aiding the reader's understanding. When used as a graduate text the book should be supplemented extensively by articles from the journal literature. Up-to-date bibliographies are provided at the end of each chapter to assist readers who wish to pursue further the matters dealt with in the text.

I wish to thank David S. B. Inglis, Editor-in-Chief at Holt, Rinehart and Winston Ltd, without whose persistence the book would not have been published, and Lee E. Preston, who managed to sustain my interest in completing the book over a period of several years. Permission to reprint portions of two articles which originally appeared in the *Journal of Industrial Economics* is also gratefully acknowledged.

JANUARY 1977   *Douglas Needham*

CONTENTS

CHAPTER ONE

FIRMS, OBJECTIVES, AND INDUSTRIAL STRUCTURE

1. Nature of Firms, and the Structure–Conduct–Performance Relationship

The theory of industrial organization deals with the relationship between industry structure and firms' behavior, and with the implications of this behavior for economic performance and aggregate satisfaction in the economy. A precise definition of the term 'firm' is difficult, for there are many concepts of the firm. From an accounting point of view, for example, a firm is a collection of assets and liabilities; from a legal point of view a firm is either a sole proprietorship, a partnership, or a company with a separate legal existence from its owners. Professor F. Machlup (reference (44) in Recommended Readings) believes that there are at least 21 concepts of the firm. A firm is also an organization of individuals related through a more or less complex hierarchical system of authority and responsibility over different aspects of the firm's operations. For a more recent survey of developments in the theory of the firm see Cyert and Hedrick (17).

Although a firm has many characteristics, all have one thing in common: they are the result of decisions made by people controlling the operations of the firm and are related to each other through the decision-making process. The choice of what to produce, for example, influences the type of assets and liabilities a firm will acquire; the choice of legal form may influence the supply of funds available to the firm and the overall level of its operations. The firm in the sense of a decision-making unit is of primary relevance to anyone seeking to explain the determinants of various characteristics of business enterprises and the relationship between these characteristics, because these are the result of a decision-making process.

Any decision implies choice between alternatives. A firm's decision-makers control the level of a number of decision variables such as methods and scale of production, advertising, and research and development activities, as well as the prices and other terms of sale of the firm's products. The process of choosing between alternative levels of these decision variables and implementing such choices is usually referred to as the behavior, or 'conduct', of the firm. The extent to which the levels of decision variables selected by a firm's decision-makers achieve various concepts of economic efficiency, including allocative, technical and distributive efficiency, is referred to as 'economic performance'. The central hypothesis of industrial organization theory is that there exists a systematic

1

relationship between 'industrial structure' and a firm's conduct, and therefore, between industrial structure and economic performance.

The term industrial structure is used to refer to a number of characteristics of the productive activities of a firm or group of firms which comprise an industry. These characteristics include cost conditions, seller concentration, vertical integration, diversification, product-differentiation activities and entry barriers. Cost conditions describe the relationship between the cost of producing a particular product or service and alternative rates or volumes of output of that product or service. Seller concentration refers to the number and size distribution of rival sellers. Vertical integration refers to the extent to which successive production processes are performed within a single firm, and diversification refers to the extent to which a firm produces different kinds of output which are not vertically related to each other. Product-differentiation activities, such as advertising and research and development activities, are used by firms to attempt to differentiate their products from those of rival sellers either physically or in the minds of buyers. Entry barriers are obstacles confronting potential entrants into an industry. A more detailed consideration of the nature and significance of these and other features of industrial structure will be provided in subsequent chapters.

The general manner in which structural features are linked to the behavior of a firm's decision-makers can be summarized quite briefly as follows: the effect of any set of decision variables on the firm's revenues and costs will depend on the behavior of buyers and other sellers. Buyers' behavior depends on their objectives, usually taken to be the maximization of personal satisfaction, and on constraints such as income, tastes and information concerning available goods and services and terms of sale. Firms can influence buyer behavior by altering some of these constraints and, therefore, the choice-set confronting the buyer. However, the effect of a particular firm's activities on its revenues depends also on the behavior of other sellers, because this also influences the choices confronting buyers and, therefore, buyer behavior. In addition, the level of rival sellers' demands for inputs may influence the level of a firm's costs by affecting input prices. In deciding upon the level of its various decision variables, a firm's decision-makers will therefore treat the factors underlying the behavior of buyers and other sellers as constraints, and the perceived nature of these constraints will influence the levels of decision variables selected by the firm's decision-makers. The structural features referred to in the preceding paragraph may influence the nature of some of the perceived constraints confronting firms' decision-makers, thereby in turn affecting the optimal level of decision variables and the resulting economic performance of the firm.

In discussing the structure–conduct–performance hypothesis, economists have traditionally placed emphasis on the causal flows operating from structure to conduct. Causation may, however, run both ways, not only from structure to conduct but also from current conduct to resulting implications for structure at a future point in time. If so, two simultaneous relationships will exist between structure and conduct; moreover, the resulting relationship between these factors will then be dynamic in character, implying a process which involves changes in structure and conduct through time. There may also be causal flows running from economic performance to conduct, structure, or both, as a result of antitrust or similar restrictions on firms' behavior. For example, due to departing from required standards of economic performance, firms in a particular industry may be enjoined from particular kinds of conduct; alternatively they may be 'restructured' because of a legally enforced change in the number of firms operating in the industry.

Few economists would argue with the structure–conduct–performance hypothesis; the real issue concerns the precise nature of the relationship or relationships if there are simultaneous underlying causal flows linking conduct, structure and performance. The nature of these relationships in theory and the empirical evidence bearing on the nature of such relationships in practice will be discussed extensively in subsequent chapters. First, however, it is appropriate to examine the nature and significance of decision-maker objectives since the exact nature of these objectives will influence firms' behavior independently of the nature of the constraints faced by firms' decision-makers.

2. Nature of Firms' Objectives

As already noted in the preceding section, the level of a firm's sales revenues depends on the level of the firm's own decision variables and on characteristics of buyer and rival seller behavior. Similarly, the level of the firm's total costs depends not only on the levels of the firm's own decision variables but also on the technological relationships between inputs and outputs and on factors influencing input prices such as rival sellers' behavior. The relationship between a firm's total revenues or total costs and the various factors which influence revenues and costs may be viewed as constraints. Given their perceptions of the manner in which buyer and rival seller behavior influence these constraints, a firm's decision-makers must choose between alternative levels of each of the firm's decision variables, since different levels of decision variables will imply a different outcome in terms of the firm's total revenues and costs. The firm's decision-makers will select, from all the feasible alternatives, that combination of variables under their control which best achieves their objectives.

An objective, or goal, is an intent to achieve some outcome. The outcome which is sought by a firm's decision-makers may relate to a single aspect of the firm's operations, such as profit, or sales, or growth: such goals might be termed unitary goals. Alternatively, the goals pursued by a firm's decision-makers may involve multiple goals, in the sense of a desired outcome involving a number of aspects of the firm's operations, such as certain levels of profits *and* sales *and* growth, for example. For a more detailed discussion of the concept of decision-maker objectives and organizational goals, see L. B. Mohr (48).

Instead of attempting to list the infinity of possible objectives which a firm's decision-makers might pursue, several of the objectives considered to be of major importance in influencing business behavior will be described in this section. For more detailed treatment of these objectives, the reader is referred to the writings of Baumol (5, 6, 7), Baumol and Stewart (9), Cyert and March (18), Lanzillotti (38) and Williamson (72, 73) listed at the end of this chapter. Section 3 will deal briefly with the influence of the precise timing of outcomes of alternative courses of action and the existence of uncertainty regarding outcomes on the behavior of firms' decision-makers. Section 4 will then deal with the implication of different objectives for decision-maker behavior.

The first objective to be considered, that of maximizing profits, has for long occupied pride of place in economic analysis of the behavior of firms. The word 'profit' has many different meanings in everyday usage. In economic analysis, profits are the difference between the total revenues from the sale of a firm's output(s) and the total costs of the inputs required to produce and market those outputs. A distinction is usually drawn in economic analysis between economic profit and 'accounting profit' as measured by traditionally accepted methods of business bookkeeping. In the case of economic profit, the relevant costs to be deducted from the firm's total revenues in arriving at a profit figure are the 'opportunity cost' of the inputs, which is defined as the highest return an input could earn in alternative uses outside the firm, whereas accounting profit generally measures input costs by the actual money expenditures made on inputs. Thus, for example, accounting profit includes the wages which an owner-manager could earn by selling his services elsewhere, and also includes the interest which owners of a business could earn elsewhere on the funds they have invested in the business; since these should be included in the relevant total costs measure of the firm, economic profit excludes these two items. The logic of the distinction is fairly straightforward: unless input costs are measured by their opportunity costs, or earnings in alternative uses, the resulting profit figure will overstate the excess of the value of their use in current activities over their value in alternative uses, and could even result in a situation in which the resources continue to be used for one activity when an alternative use would yield greater return to the owners.

The objective of profit maximization is not quite the same thing as maximizing the profit from a given level of total outlay or investment, although this is a necessary condition for profit maximization and is what many people have in mind when thinking of maximizing profits. Profit maximization also encompasses the determination of the optimal level of total cost, or investment outlay itself. Maximizing the difference between the total revenue and total costs of a particular productive activity, (TR − TC), is clearly not the same as maximizing the rate of profit expressed as a fraction of the total costs or the rate of return on expenditure (TR − TC)/TC. Maximizing this last expression is equivalent to maximizing the *average* rate of profit per unit of total cost or outlay. Even if (TR − TC) increases when a particular productive activity is expanded (TR − TC)/TC, the rate of return on expenditure, will fall as long as the increase in TC necessary to increase profits exceeds the resulting increase in profits itself. In these circumstances, failure to expand the level of the activity implies forgoing a net increase in profits, or increment of wealth, for the owners. Profit maximization as previously defined implies maximization of the level of the owners' wealth. This can be increased as long as the marginal or incremental profits, defined as the change in TR minus the change in TC, are positive even though the average profit rate on total expenditures may be reduced. In fact, profit maximization as defined implies setting the marginal profit equal to zero, for only if this condition is satisfied can owners' wealth not be increased by an increase in the level of the productive activity in question. Even when the revenue and cost concepts are capitalized in a manner to be indicated in the next section, profit maximization implies setting the marginal profit return on the investment equal to zero, not maximizing the ratio of total profit to total investment, or average profit return on investment.

Even in those cases in which the objective of a firm's decision-makers is not maximization of profits, the desire to make some profits will nonetheless usually enter into the decision-maker's objectives for one or both of the following reasons. First, making some profits may be necessary to enable the decision-maker to achieve some other objective: an example discussed in more detail later is the need to make profits in order to grow in size. Second, a firm's decision-makers will generally have to meet a profit constraint in the form of some minimum benefits to the owners of the firm. This constraint may take the form of a required level of paid-out profits to owners which is necessary in order to permit management to remain in control. If dividends fall below a certain level, control may be lost because existing shareholders either replace the managers or alternatively sell out to new owners who in turn might install a new management in the hope that the latter would distribute higher dividends. The profit constraint need not necessarily involve paid-out profits, however; if profits are retained in the business, thereby increasing the firm's net assets and profit-earning potential, owners may experience benefits in the form of capital appreciation of their ownership claims such as shares in the firm.

Rather than attempt to maximize profits, a firm's decision-makers may seek to maximize sales revenue, subject to the constraint that profits equal or exceed a certain amount. A number of reasons have been advanced by various economists to explain why a firm's decision-makers should be more concerned with sales revenues than with profits. For example, it is sometimes argued that the prestige or remuneration of professional managers who control the operation of firms in which ownership is divorced from control may be linked more closely with sales than with profits. If executive rewards are more highly correlated with sales than with profits this may motivate managers to produce and market levels of output larger than those which maximize profits. However, the evidence obtained to date in a number of empirical studies of the determinants of executive compensation and its association with profits versus sales is conflicting.

Even if decision-makers do pursue maximum sales revenue subject to a profit constraint, the crucial question is what determines the minimum acceptable amount of profit and how far does it depart from the maximum feasible level of profit? In the early literature dealing with this objective, it was assumed that the profit constraint was imposed externally by the capital market and the need to pay owners a return comparable with that paid by other firms in the economy. The level of the constraint therefore depended on the determinants of economy-wide rates of return on industrial assets. Apart from such an externally imposed constraint in the form of a minimum profit constraint necessary to prevent loss of control by the present decision-makers, it can also be shown that in a multiperiod analysis in which the decision-makers' objectives are maximization of the present value of sales revenue, the profit constraint may be generated automatically by the need to finance growth of sales revenue. See the analysis of growth maximization objectives in section 4 of this chapter.

A desire to maximize the discounted present value of either profits or sales revenue accruing from a firm's operations may result in growth. Growth is, in these circumstances, a means towards achieving another objective rather than an end itself. However, a desire to maximize the growth rate of some aspect of the firm's operations is itself another possible objective. A number of variations of this objective are possible, depending upon whether the growth rate of paid-out profits, sales revenue, total assets, net assets, or some other aspect of the firm is to be maximized. In the case of growth objectives, the desire to make some profits is inherent in the objective itself, because profits are necessary in order to finance growth internally or to obtain additional outside finance. This applies whether the objective is to maximize the growth rate of profits, sales revenue, or net assets. However, as the analysis contained in section 4 of this chapter will demonstrate, the level of profits which maximizes growth need not be the maximum attainable level of profit.

Decision-makers may pursue other objectives which are variations on the theme of profit, sales revenue, or growth-rate maximization. For example, instead of attempting to maximize sales revenue subject to a profit constraint a firm may wish to maximize profits subject to a self-imposed constraint in the form of a desire to achieve a certain level of sales revenue. The sales revenue constraint may be imposed by a desire on the part of the firm's management to prevent the firm's market share from falling in absolute or relative terms. Alternatively, the firm may wish to maximize profits or sales revenue subject to achieving a certain growth rate of the firm's net assets or owners' wealth.

Instead of attempting to maximize profits, or sales revenue, a firm's decision-makers may attempt to maximize their own personal satisfaction, pursuing 'managerial utility maximization' as the objective has come to be termed in the literature. Managerial utility may depend on factors such as the leisure and income of the decision-maker, and on the personal satisfaction which he derives from his job, either directly from his decision-making activities or indirectly from the prestige, status, or self-esteem associated with these activities. These determinants of the level of his personal satisfaction may, in turn, be dependent on one or more facets of the firm's operations, such as profits, sales, levels of particular inputs, or growth rates of some aspects of the firm. However, for reasons to be explained later, the pursuit of managerial utility maximization will not, in general, lead either to profit maximization or to sales revenue maximization, even where profit and sales enter directly into the managerial utility function.

Aspects of the firm's operations, such as profit and sales revenue, can enter into the objective function of a managerial utility maximizer in two distinct ways: they may either enter as unconstrained variables which affect the level of his satisfaction or alternatively they may be restricted or constrained to specific levels which must be achieved. Such constraints on the actual level of profits, or sales, or other variables may either be self-imposed by the decision-maker himself, or may be imposed by forces external to the decision-maker himself. The first case would be exemplified by a situation in which a manager himself sets a restriction on the minimum profit return on investment he wishes the firm to achieve; an example of the second case would be where the minimum profit return is set by market forces which dictate that in order to attract capital the firm must earn a return comparable to comparably risky investment.

The managerial utility maximization hypothesis is compatible with an infinity of possible variants, depending on which variables enter the manager's utility function, and the nature of the constraints he faces. It is a more plausible description of reality than the profit maximization or other behavioral hypotheses since it recognizes that decisions are made by individuals, and goes deeper into the reasons why particular facets of the firm's operations may be selected as the criteria for decisions. Analysis of firms' behavior based upon the managerial utility maximization hypothesis has come to be referred to as 'managerial' theories of the firm. It is important to recognize that there are innumerable possible variants of this hypothesis, with different behavioral implications. Profit maximization, sales-revenue maximization and other objectives can be shown to be special cases of this general hypothesis.

The present section may be summarized briefly, as follows: the 'objective function' or 'maximand' of a firm's decision-makers may involve one or more aspects of the firm's operations, and may in addition involve constraints on the specific levels of some of the variables entering into the decision-makers' maximand. Before we proceed to investigate some of the implications of different objectives which decision-makers may pursue, a brief digression is appropriate in order to examine two characteristics of the alternatives confronting all decision-makers which expand the number of possible variants of any particular objective. The first characteristic is the time period considered relevant by the decision-maker and the available methods of comparing outcomes that occur in different time periods. The second characteristic is connected with the implications of uncertainty surrounding the results of any particular course of action.

3. Timing and Uncertainty of the Outcomes of Decisions

It must be emphasized that any given objective, whether involving profit, sales revenue, growth or managerial utility, applies to a specific time period which the decision-maker in question considers to be relevant in his decision-making. Objectives may differ merely in respect of the length of the time period considered relevant. Profit-maximizing objectives which apply to time periods of different lengths, for example, are capable of leading to differences in behavior even though all other relevant considerations confronting the decision-makers are the same.

Given the total length of time period considered relevant by a decision-maker, and whatever the objective he pursues, the results of any particular set of decision variables he selects will usually be spread over a number of time periods extending into the future. For example, currently produced output will take some time to reach the market, and the effect of current advertising activities on buyer behavior will also be spread over a number of time periods. Similarly, the decision to use particular inputs need not imply that all outlays, or costs, are current; a type of capital equipment which requires maintenance at specific intervals of time is an example. In order to compare the revenues and costs associated with a particular course of action, and more importantly in order to choose between alternative courses of action which result in dissimilar streams of revenues, costs or other relevant outcomes through time, a decision-maker must be able to compare outcomes occurring at different points in time. This can be achieved by transforming anticipated future revenues, costs or other relevant outcomes into an equivalent 'present value' by means of a process usually referred to as 'discounting'. Discounting is simply the opposite of the more familiar practice of 'compounding', which illustrates how a sum of money, C, grows to equal $C(1 + i)$ after one period, $C(1 + i)^2$ after two periods, and $C(1 + i)^n$ after 'n' periods when the interest rate which can be earned is 'i' per period. The discounted present value, P, of an amount of receipts or outlays, V, which is expected to occur 'n' periods into the future, is defined as follows:

$$P = V.\left(\frac{1}{1 + r}\right)^n$$

where the fraction $1/1 + r$, called the 'discount rate', reflects the decision-maker's own relative evaluation of current versus future receipts or outlays. The discount rate may be related to the rate of interest at which the decision-maker can borrow or lend additional funds. For example, if a firm can borrow or lend any amount of money at an interest rate i, $1/1 + i$ will be the appropriate discount rate to use in calculating the discounted present value of the future anticipated receipts associated with alternative courses of action such as investment projects that might be undertaken by the firm. The present value of any future anticipated stream of revenues is equivalent to the amount of money which, if invested currently at the discount rate, would yield exactly the same stream of future revenues. Using the interest rate at which a firm can lend or borrow money to find the present value of the stream of anticipated income associated with an investment project will, therefore, be appropriate because unless the resulting present value exceeds the cost of the resources used in the project, it automatically follows that the firm can obtain a larger stream of future revenues by lending the investment outlays at the market interest rate instead of undertaking the investment project in question. Alternatively, if the firm is borrowing the money to undertake an investment project, if the present value of the anticipated future income from the project is less than the present value of the costs, this implies that the project will not earn sufficiently to repay the amount borrowed plus interest. If the interest rate which a firm must pay for borrowed funds rises with the amount borrowed, the marginal interest rate on borrowed funds, not the average interest rate, is relevant in determining the appropriate discount rate.

The rate at which a firm can lend or borrow money need not always be relevant in determining the appropriate discount rate used to evaluate and compare the future consequences of alternative courses of action, however. In certain circumstances the appropriate discount rate may instead be related to the anticipated rate of return on alternative uses of the firm's existing resources. This might be the case, for example, where a firm must choose between alternative investment projects which all yield a positive net present value when market interest rates are used in the discounting process. Moreover, the choice of discount rate for comparing alternative courses of action can affect the relative ranking of each alternative. At first, this may sound confusing and the reader may ask how the mere choice of a discount rate can affect the relative desirability, from the point of view of a decision-maker's objective, of actions whose anticipated consequences are given. The explanation is that the comparison of the discounted present value of net income associated with different projects employs an implicit assumption. This important implicit assumption is that the future net revenues associated with each project are reinvested at the discount rate being used, up to the terminal date of the longest-lived project which is being compared. This rather complicated sounding proposition can be demonstrated very simply by the following example, which involves a comparison of two projects, both incurring an expenditure of $100 in the current period, and one project yielding a return of $110 after one period and the other yielding $120 after two periods.

	Cost	Period 1	Period 2
Project 1	$100	$110	
Project 2	$100		$120

Clearly, the outcome of these two projects can only be meaningfully compared if some assumption is made about what happens to the receipts from Project 1 between the end of the first and second periods. The present-value calculation implicitly assumes that these proceeds could be reinvested at the discount rate which is being used in the discounting process, and shows the present value of the resulting terminal values of each stream. In the above example, a discount rate of approximately ten per cent or less will rank the present value of Project 2 above that of Project 1, while higher discount rates will rank the present value of Project 1 above that of Project 2. This is because, at discount rates of ten per cent and above, and assuming reinvestment of the $110 proceeds of Project 1 for one period at the discount rate, the terminal value of the stream of outcomes of Project 1 will exceed the outcome of Project 2. Under the same assumptions, the terminal value of Project 1 will be less than that of Project 2 at discount rates below ten per cent. The reinvestment assumption is responsible for the possibility that project rankings may be affected by the discount rate used.

It should be emphasized that although the preceding discussion of discounting has been applied to firms' revenues and costs, it is equally applicable to outcomes expressed in terms of decision-maker utility. In such cases, the relevant discount rate to be used in transforming future anticipated utility levels into equivalent 'present value' utility equivalents is the ratio between the decision-makers' evaluation of the relative utility of present and future outcomes. This ratio equals the number of units of a future outcome which are 'equivalent' to a unit of the same present outcome in terms of the utility yielded to the decision-maker. For a useful selection of articles dealing with the net present value and alternative methods of comparing events occurring at different points in time, the reader is referred to the writings of Beenhakker (10), Mishan (47), Ramsey (57), Solomon (66) and Turvey (69) listed in the Recommended Readings.

Next we consider briefly the implications, for decision-makers' objectives, of the existence of uncertainty about the future. Some of these implications are dealt with in the articles by Frankel (25), Leland (40) and Malmgren (45). The profits, or any other outcome which enters into a decision-maker's objective function, which are anticipated in any future period as the result of a given pattern of current behavior are not a single-valued variable in the presence of uncertainty about the future. Rather, the decision-maker's estimate of the outcome of his current actions may take the form of a probabilistic estimate, a range of possible values of the outcome, each associated with a probability assigned by the decision-maker himself, denoting the confidence with which he expects the outcome to take on that particular value. In these circumstances, any particular objective, such as profit maximization, for example, takes on new variations depending on which characteristic of the probability distribution of possible profit outcomes enters into the maximand of the decision-maker. The relevant profit concept for one decision-maker may, for example, be the mathematical expectation of profits, which is the sum of each possible outcome multiplied by its probability. Alternatively, the decision-maker may instead be concerned with the dispersion of possible outcomes around the mean, or may consider some composite characteristic of the probability distribution involving a combination of these and other characteristics of the probability distribution as the relevant decision criterion. In these instances, it cannot be argued that any particular measure of profits is more appropriate than others; the decision-maker will adopt the measure he considers most appropriate, and behavior will be influenced by the measure chosen. The implications of uncertainty for objectives other than profit maximization are similar; in each case, in the presence of uncertainty several variations are possible depending upon which characteristics of the probability distribution of possible outcomes are considered an appropriate index of the variable to be maximized by the decision-maker in question.

4. Implications of Alternative Objectives for Firms' Behavior

This section outlines briefly the basic elements involved in a firm's decision-making process, and the implications of different objectives for optimal levels of the firm's decision variables. See the references by Azariadis, Cohen and Porcas (3), Brown and Revankar (11), Crew (15), Encarnacion (22), Ferguson (24), Hawkins (31), Heal and Silberston (32), Johnson (34), Osborne (55), Shepherd (61), Shubik (62), Solow (67) and Williamson (71) for more detailed analysis of the implications of different objectives for firms' behavior. In order to gain perspective over a firm's decision problems, it is useful to think of the relationship which describes how the firm's total revenues are related to levels of its own decision variables, rivals' decision variables and relevant buyer characteristic as an equation. The same is true of the relationship between the firm's total costs and those factors which affect the level of the firm's costs, including technological input—output relationships and input prices. The objective function of the firm's decision-makers is an additional equation, representing the relationship between the outcome intended by the decision-makers and various aspects of the firm's operations, such as profit, sales revenue or specific input levels. In some cases, the intended outcome may be directly related to some aspect of the firm's operations; an example is the intention to maximize profits. In other cases, the intended outcome may be related only indirectly to the firm's operations; an intention to maximize managerial utility where managerial utility is partially dependent on the firm's profits is an example.

The task of the decision-makers is to select values of the firm's decision variables which maximize the level of the objective function, subject to the constraints represented by the revenue and cost functions, and any additional constraints that may confront the decision-makers. The values of decision variables which maximize the objective function while simultaneously satisfying all relevant constraints are referred to as 'optimal' values of the firm's decision variables. A set of necessary conditions which must be fulfilled in order for the level of a firm's decision variables to be optimal can be derived from the objective function and constraints facing the firm. These necessary conditions are equivalent to a set of equations which must all be simultaneously satisfied in order for a firm's decision variables to be at optimal levels. Because the precise form of the necessary conditions depends on the decision-makers' objective function and on all the relevant constraints it follows that the optimal levels of each decision variable which satisfy the necessary conditions will in turn depend on the objectives and all constraints facing other firms' decision-makers. Therefore, given the constraints, it follows that the nature of decision-maker objectives will play an important part in influencing the optimal levels of the firm's decision variables.

Two related points of importance require emphasis at this stage: first, it is the *perceived* form of the constraints confronting decision-makers which influence their behavior. The nature of all the relevant relationships confronting the firm will rarely be known with certainty by a decision-maker; his perceptions of the nature of the relationships are relevant in determining his behavior. Secondly, although the optimal values of a firm's decision variables are simultaneously determined by the objective function of the firm's decision-maker(s) and the nature of the relevant constraints as perceived by the decision-makers, and are interrelated, this should not be taken to imply that the firm's *actual decision process* involves simultaneous solution of the decision problem in order to determine optimal values of all decision variables. There are two major reasons why simultaneous solution of a firm's decision problems to find the optimal levels of all the firm's decision variables will not generally occur in practice. First, the cost of obtaining and transmitting all the relevant information necessary to permit simultaneous solution of the firm's overall decision problem may be prohibitive or, alternatively, may be so high relative to the resulting contribution toward attaining the decision-makers' goals that obtaining this information is not worth while. In other words, the problem of how much of the firm's resources to invest in information-gathering activities is itself an aspect of the firm's decision problem. Second, even if information on the precise nature of all relevant relationships could be obtained at low cost, limitations on the problem-solving capacity of individual decision-makers could prevent simultaneous solution of all aspects of the firm's decision problem from being feasible.

Given the perceived constraints confronting a firm's decision-makers the nature of their objectives will influence the precise nature of the necessary conditions which must be met in order for decision variables to be at optimal levels. This will in turn affect the levels of the firm's decision variables which are optimal in the sense of satisfying all the necessary conditions simultaneously. The manner in which different objectives affect decision-makers' behavior will now be illustrated by comparing the behavior of profit, sales revenue, growth and managerial utility maximizers. The Appendix to this chapter offers a more rigorous derivation of the conclusions reached in the text, together with some conclusions of wider applicability.

The output level of a profit and sales-revenue maximizer may be compared with the aid of Figure 1–1. The total revenue, or sales, associated with different output levels of the firm is represented by curve TR, and total costs by curve TC. The firm's profit, which equals the difference between total revenue and total cost, is shown at different output levels. A profit-maximizing firm will produce output level Q_p, the level which maximizes the firm's profit. At this output level, the vertical distance between TR and TC is maximized, and the slope of TR, usually referred to as marginal revenue, equals the slope of TC, which is referred to as marginal cost. However, since TR is still increasing (marginal revenue is positive) at that output level, a sales-revenue maximizer will expand output up to the level of Q_s, where further expansion of output would decrease profits below the minimum acceptable level.

In a multiperiod setting, the reason why an intent to maximize the *present value* of sales revenue will lead a firm's decision-makers to produce a larger output level than will an intent to maximize the present value of profits is not immediately obvious. Why, it may be

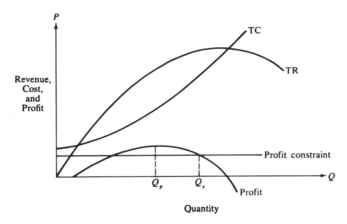

Figure 1–1. A single-period constrained sales maximization model.

asked, should the firm deliberately sacrifice current profits, which can be used to finance future expansion in the scale of the firm's operations and sales revenues, in order to expand current sales beyond the profit-maximizing level? The explanation, in brief, is as follows. The present value of a firm's sales revenue depends upon the size of current sales revenue and on the rate at which this level of sales revenue grows through time. The latter rate depends on the current profits of the firm, because these provide the means to finance expansion of the firm's sales revenues in the future, either internally or by attracting additional investor capital. Increasing the level of the firm's current output to the level which maximizes current profits increases both the level of current sales revenue and the rate at which the firm's operations and revenues can grow. It must, therefore, increase the present value of the firm's sales revenues. If output is increased above the profit-maximizing level, the rate at which sales revenue can grow through time is reduced, but the resulting increase in the level of current sales revenue will imply an increase in the present value of sales revenue. Therefore, a maximizer of the present value of sales revenue will produce a larger output level than a profit maximizer.

The contrast between profit and sales-revenue maximization in a multiperiod setting can be further illuminated with the aid of Figure 1–2. The bottom half of the diagram, below the horizontal axis which represents levels of current sales revenue (hereafter abbreviated to S_c) is simply Figure 1–1 'turned on its side'. In the top half of the diagram the vertical axis represents growth rate of current sales revenue (hereafter abbreviated to g). Curve OM depicts, for an individual firm, the maximum attainable g at different levels of S_c. As the levels of current output and S_c are increased, profits and, because profits are required to finance growth, the maximum attainable g increase and reach a maximum at level of current sales S_p, then decline as sales are pushed beyond the level which maximizes current profits. Eventually, at a level of S_c involving zero profits, the maximum attainable growth rate is zero.

In order to demonstrate that a maximizer of the present value of sales revenue (hereafter abbreviated to P_s) will produce a larger scale of output than a profit (and growth-rate) maximizer, it is necessary to introduce into the diagram 'iso-present value' lines. It was pointed out earlier that, given the discount rate of the decision-maker, the present value of sales revenue, P_s, depends upon the level of current sales revenue and the growth rate of that revenue. An 'iso-present value' line will be defined as the locus of combinations of S_c and g which (given the decision-maker's discount rate) yield a constant level of P_s.

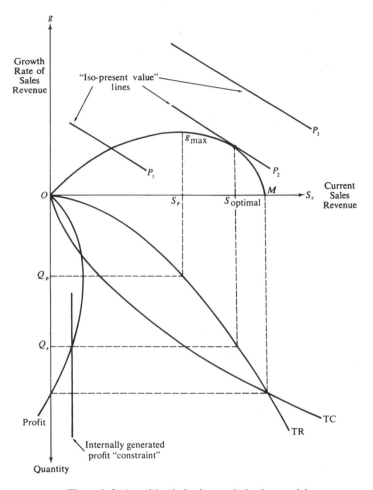

Figure 1-2. A multiperiod sales maximization model.

Holding S_c at any particular level, an increase in g will tend to increase P_s; similarly, holding g constant at a particular level, an increase in S_c will tend to increase P_s. It follows that higher levels of S_c must be combined with smaller levels of g in order to yield a constant level of P_s; that is, an iso-present value line as defined above must slope down from left to right in the top half of Figure 1–2. It must be noted that without further information, the precise shape of an iso-present value line is not known; it may be convex, concave or a straight line. However, all that is required in the present context is the negative slope. There will be an iso-present value line for every different value of P_s, such as P_1, P_2, and so on, higher subscripts indicating higher values of P_s.

Diagrammatically, the problem of a firm which desires to maximize the present value of sales revenue is to select a point on OM which yields the greatest P_s, which amounts to getting on to the highest possible iso-present value line. Such a point will be one where an iso-present value line just touches, or is tangent to, OM; if the point involved an intersection between an iso-present value line and OM, this would automatically imply that a move to another point on OM could increase P_s. If, as has been argued above, iso-present value lines slope down from left to right, it follows that the point of tangency must lie on that portion of OM which is negatively sloped, that is, to the right of S_p. The point must therefore involve a level of current output and sales revenue larger than the profit-maximizing level. A profit (or growth-rate) maximizer will, as argued earlier, select an output and sales revenue level which maximizes profits in the current period, that is, level Q_p and S_p in Figure 1–2.

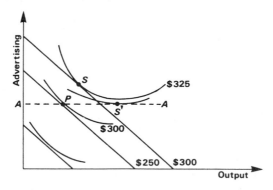

Figure 1–3. Optimal advertising–output levels under alternative objectives.

The conclusion that a sales-revenue maximizer will produce a larger output level than a profit maximizer if both face the same cost and demand conditions is subject to an important qualification. Assuming that the cost and demand conditions are the same for both firms implies that *the level of all other decision variables which influence demand for a firm's product*, such as advertising, for example, are the same for a profit maximizer and a sales-revenue maximizer. The pursuit of different objectives will usually imply differences in the levels of these other decision variables, however, and in such circumstances it can be shown that a profit maximizer may produce a *larger* output level than a sales-revenue maximizer. These propositions can be clarified with the aid of Figure 1–3. Each of the U-shaped lines represents alternative combinations of advertising expenditure and output which will yield a particular level of total revenue to a firm. The reason for the U shape is as follows. A reduction in advertising expenditure will reduce demand for the firm's product and total revenue at any price charged by the firm. In order to keep total revenue unchanged, the reduction in advertising must therefore be accompanied by (i) a reduction in price and a rise in quantity demanded if the price-elasticity of demand for the firm's product exceeds unity or (ii) a rise in price and reduction in quantity demanded if price-elasticity of demand is less than unity.* Since at any given level of advertising outlay, price-elasticity of demand will exceed unity at low levels of output, and will be less than unity at high levels of output, this results in the U shape of the total revenue lines.

---

*Price-elasticity of demand is defined as follows:

$$\frac{\text{proportionate increase in quantity of a firm's product demanded}}{\text{proportionate change in the price of the product}}$$

When price-elasticity of demand exceeds unity, a reduction in price of a firm's product results in a more than proportionate increase in quantity demanded, thereby increasing the total revenue earned from sales of the product. Conversely, when price-elasticity of demand is less than unity, a reduction in price accompanied by a less than proportionate rise in quantity sold implies a reduction in total revenue. See Chapter 3 for a detailed analysis of the relationship between price-elasticity of demand and a firm's optimal pricing policy.

Each of the parallel straight lines sloping down from left to right represents alternative combinations of advertising outlay and output which can be obtained for a given total outlay on inputs by the firm. The straight lines reflect the assumption that total production costs increase proportionately with output level, so that a reduction of a given size in advertising outlay permits the same increase in output to be produced irrespective of the initial output level. The particular conclusions we seek to demonstrate would not be significantly altered, however, even if production costs did not vary in proportion to output and these lines were curved.

The highest total revenue that can be earned for any particular total outlay on advertising and production activities will be indicated by the point of tangency between the particular total outlay line and one of the total revenue curves. Both a profit maximizer and a sales-revenue maximizer will wish to maximize the total revenue they earn from their total outlays on inputs. They will generally select different total outlay levels, however. Specifically, the profit maximizer will select, from all available tangency points open to him, that which maximizes the *difference* between the TR and TC; in contrast the sales-revenue maximizer will select the highest level of TR, subject to meeting the minimum necessary level of profit he must make. In Figure 1–3 these points are shown by P and S respectively. At P, profits are equal to ($300 − 250), but at S profits are lower at ($325 − 300). The tangency points also indicate the optimal allocation of expenditure between advertising and output. In Figure 1–3 the sales-revenue maximizer has both a higher level of output and a higher level of advertising than the profit maximizer. This is not the only possibility, however, as Figure 1–4 indicates. The profit maximizer may have a higher output level and lower advertising level than the sales-revenue maximizer or, alternatively, a lower output level and higher advertising level. The underlying explanation for these differences consists of the precise manner in which advertising affects the demand conditions confronting a firm, and in particular the marginal revenues associated with different output levels.

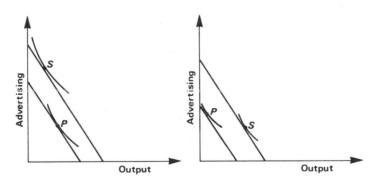

Figure 1–4. Optimal advertising–output levels under profit and sales maximization.

The earlier analysis which concluded that a profit maximizer will produce a smaller output level than a sales-revenue maximizer can also be related to Figure 1–3. That analysis is equivalent to a choice between alternative output levels along a horizontal line such as AA indicating alternative levels of output at a particular advertising level. Clearly, moving to the right along such a line up to point S' increases the firm's total revenues; and if this is the only way to change the firm's total revenues, it leads to the conclusion that a sales-revenue maximizing firm will produce a larger level of output than a profit maximizer.

The preceding analysis and conclusion is equally applicable to decision variables other than advertising which influence demand conditions for firms' products. A related qualification of the proposition that sales-revenue maximizing firms will produce larger output levels than profit-maximizing firms is connected with the firm's diversification opportunities. If a firm could diversify instead of expanding output of a single product beyond the profit-maximizing level, it could expand its sales revenues without reducing profits; this is clearly a superior alternative to increasing sales revenues at the expense of reduced total profits. The only circumstances in which diversification would be impossible could be where entry barriers exist into other industries.

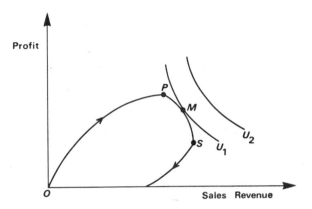

Figure 1–5. Optimal profit–sales combinations under alternative objectives.

The output levels of profit, sales revenue and managerial utility maximizers may be conveniently compared with the aid of Figure 1–5. If the profit–sales revenue combinations associated with each output level in Figure 1–1 are plotted, the result is locus $OPSO$ in Figure 1–5. This shows that as output is increased, profits and sales revenue both increase at first (segment OP), profit then declines while sales revenue continues to increase (segment PS), and eventually sales revenue also declines together with total profits (segment SO). This locus signifies the constraint representing all feasible profit–sales revenue combinations open to the firm's decision-makers. A profit maximizer will select point P, a sales-revenue maximizer will select S if there is no profit constraint and some other point on segment PS if constrained by the need to make a certain level of profit. The point selected by a managerial utility maximizer will depend on the satisfaction he derives from profits and sales respectively. Provided that profits and sales both yield positive increments of satisfaction to the decision-maker, combinations of profit and sales revenue yielding a particular level of satisfaction must slope down from left to right, indicating that increases in profit must be accompanied by reductions in sales revenue in order to keep the decision-maker at the same level of satisfaction. This is shown by the indifference curves labeled U_1, U_2 in Figure 1–5 where curves lying above and to the right imply higher levels of total satisfaction. The highest level of satisfaction attainable from alternative profit–sales revenue combinations will be where one of the indifference curves of the decision-maker is tangent to the constraint locus $OPSO$, such as M. If the indifference curves slope down from left to right, as they must if increases in profit and sales revenue both yield positive increments of satisfaction to the decision-maker, the tangency point must be somewhere on segment PS of the constraint locus. The managerial utility maximizer will therefore produce an output level which differs from the profit and (unconstrained) sales revenue maximizer. Only if the decision-maker derived no satisfaction from sales revenue, in which case his indifference curves would be horizontal lines because the slope of the indifference curves equals the ratio of the marginal satisfaction yielded by increments of profits and sales revenue respectively, would he select P. Similarly, if profits yielded no satisfaction to the decision-maker, his indifference curves would be represented by vertical straight lines, and point S would maximize his satisfaction.

The preceding examples have demonstrated that the levels of decision variables such as output and advertising selected by decision-makers confronted by a particular set of constraints will differ depending on their objectives. This reflects the fact that *different objectives will usually change the form of the necessary conditions which must be satisfied in order for decision variables to be at optimal levels.* In the process it was demonstrated that the effect of different objectives on the level of a particular decision variable depends in part on the implications of those objectives for levels of other decision variables. Predictions concerning the output levels of the firm's decision variables under different objectives must take interdependence between different decision variables into account. As the comparison of the profit and sales-revenue maximizing firms with advertising as a variable indicated, the nature of this interdependence depends on the precise form of the constraints – in particular the precise manner in which total revenues are related to advertising and output levels – and a number of different outcomes are possible.

Although the optimal levels of a firm's decision variables will generally differ depending on the firm's objectives, this should not be taken to imply that all aspects of the firm's behavior will be changed by the pursuit of different objectives. Some aspects of the firm's behavior may be similar under entirely different objectives. For example, some necessary conditions which relate to the manner in which the firm *combines* its inputs or decision variables, as opposed to the overall level of those decision variables, may not be changed. A prominent example is the necessary condition for minimizing the total cost of producing a particular output level. This condition is that the ratio of the marginal products of each pair of inputs used by the firm be equal to the ratio of their marginal costs to the firm. If this condition is not met, the firm can change its input mix and produce its existing output level at lower total cost. Profit, sales revenue, and managerial utility maximizers of the variety discussed in this section will all wish to minimize the total cost of producing the different output levels they selected. If they were not minimizing the total cost of the selected output level they could, respectively, increase profits, sales revenue or total satisfaction by doing so. As is proved rigorously in the Appendix of this chapter, only if managerial utility depends directly on one of the firm's inputs will minimization of total cost not be necessary in order to maximize the manager's satisfaction. This case will be examined in more detail later in the chapter dealing with cost conditions.

In addition to the conditions which are necessary in order for total costs of producing any given output level to be minimized, the conditions which are necessary to enable a firm to be maximizing the total revenue from a given total outlay on inputs, such as advertising and production, for example, may similarly be invariant under a variety of objectives. These conditions, sometimes referred to as the 'Dorfman–Steiner' condition after two economists who contributed a seminal paper on the subject, will be dealt with in some detail in Chapter 5 in the sections dealing with optimal advertising policy. In the present context it is sufficient to point out that maximizing the total revenue from a given outlay on inputs is not only necessary in order to maximize profits, but also in order to maximize total revenue or to maximize managerial utility when managerial utility depends on profits and sales revenue. If total revenue could be increased by a change in the firm's input mix, without changing total costs, this would simultaneously increase total revenue, profits and also managerial utility.

5. Inferring Firms' Objectives from Observed Behavior

Because firms' behavior depends partly on the objectives pursued by the firm's decision-makers, economists interested in explaining and predicting various aspects of firms' behavior have naturally been interested in attempting to determine the nature of the objectives actually pursued by firms in practice by resorting to empirical evidence relating to firms' behavior. To date, such attempts have not met with a high degree of success for a number of reasons which will be outlined in this section. For a selection of studies which attempt to infer the nature of firms' objectives, see Grabowski and Mueller (27), Hall (29), Lewellen and Huntsman (41) and Mabry and Siders (43).

First, analysis of the behavior of decision-makers pursuing different objectives frequently predicts that some aspects of behavior will be identical; a prominent example already mentioned in the preceding section is the necessary condition for minimizing the total costs of any particular output level. In such circumstances, these facets of a firm's behavior are no guide to the exact nature of the objectives actually pursued by the firm's decision-makers; attention must be focused instead on other facets of firms' behavior which do differ under different objectives.

Second, even where different predictions are associated with the pursuit of different objectives, several problems are involved in testing these predictions by resorting to empirical evidence relating to decision-maker behavior. Decision-makers' expectations current at the time decisions were made may not be fulfilled by subsequent events; in such cases the observed results of the decision-makers' behavior will not correspond to intended results, and it is the latter which are relevant if one is seeking to determine the nature of decision-makers' objectives. The fact that marginal revenue associated with a particular decision variable is observed to differ from the marginal cost, for example, is quite compatible with an intention to maximize profits combined with an inaccurate estimate of the marginal revenue or marginal cost associated with different levels of the decision variable in question.

Even where a decision-maker's expectations are fulfilled, behavior depends not only on the decision-maker's objectives, but also on the perceived nature of the constraints which he considers to be relevant to his own decision. Differences in the form or number of constraints will generally change the conditions that are necessary in order to maximize the decision-maker's objective function and, therefore, the behavior of the decision-maker. In other words, to predict how a decision-maker will behave under any particular objective we need to know the constraints he faces, or considers relevant. Any prediction concerning behavior under different objectives automatically carries an explicit or implicit assumption regarding the constraints confronting the decision-maker. Conversely, in comparing observed behavior of decision-makers against behavior predicted under different objectives, the predicted behavior is necessarily based on explicit or implicit assumptions concerning the nature of the relevant constraints. If the constraints that are implicitly considered to be 'relevant' by the observer were not in fact relevant in determining the behavior observed, incorrect inferences will be drawn regarding the decision-makers' objectives. For example, if a constraint on available investment funds prevents a profit-maximizing firm from expanding the levels of its decision variables to the point where marginal revenue and marginal cost are equal, rejection of the profit-maximization hypothesis on the grounds that decision-makers were observed not to equate marginal revenue and marginal cost of their decision variables would be an error. In circumstances in which the observer's notion of relevant constraints confronting a decision-maker are incorrect, all that attempts to infer firms' objectives from observed behavior are accomplishing is forcing the observer's value judgement of what constraints are 'relevant' into the analysis.

A third type of problem must be mentioned. The conclusions and predictions resulting from traditional comparative static analysis of decision-maker behavior relate to optimal values of the relevant decision variables. Unless empirical observations relate to a period during which the values of a firm's decision variables are at optimal levels, it is impossible to test the predictions of analyses which are concerned with equilibrium levels of decision variables. There are at least two reasons why observed levels of decision variables may not be at optimal levels. First, the firm's decision-makers may not solve the firm's overall decision problem simultaneously, for reasons already mentioned in an earlier section. Instead it may adopt an iterative and possibly decentralized process of solving the overall decision problem. During this process, there is no reason why optimal conditions and relationships between the firm's decision variables associated with the pursuit of a particular objective need be met. Moreover, one cannot assume that a sufficiently long period of observation of a firm's reactions following some disturbance will solve the problem by allowing the firm's decision variables to settle down at optimal levels. Changes in perceived constraints, and therefore in the optimal levels of the firm's decision variables, will occur with the passage of time. The use of an iterative decision process by the firm introduces another problem connected with attempts to infer firms' objectives from observed behavior; namely, the distinction between the 'intermediate' goals, or objectives of the firm's decision-makers, and the 'ultimate' goals. Certain decision-making rules of thumb may be adopted, for example, which link particular decision variables to the attainment of particular targets during the disequilibrium process of converging towards the levels of the firm's decision variables which solve the firm's overall decision problem. The nature of the firm's overall objectives may be difficult or impossible to infer from such rules of thumb.

As the preceding remarks suggest, inferring the nature of decision-maker objectives from observed behavior is exceedingly difficult. Yet some attempt must be made if one is concerned with predicting aspects of behavior which do vary with different objectives. It is also clear that information on the nature of the relevant constraints is just as important in enabling accurate predictions of firms' behavior to be made. Moreover, as the next section indicates, there may be some relationship between the nature of a firm's objectives and some of the constraints confronting firms' decision-makers.

6.   Separation of Ownership and Control

A question which has interested economists concerned with the behavior of firms is whether there is a systematic relationship between a firm's objectives and the degree of separation of ownership and control. The main reason for expecting such a relationship to exist is that when ownership and control are separated, the objectives of the decision-makers controlling the firm's operations will not coincide with those of the owners. The objective of the owners is usually assumed to be profit maximization, while the objectives of hired managers may be managerial utility maximization, which, as explained in an earlier section, does not usually lead to profit maximization. The argument that hired managers will not act as profit maximizers ignores the possibility that the existence of constraints on the behavior of hired managers may prevent them from departing very far from profit-maximizing behavior. The threat of dismissal by disgruntled shareholders is one such constraint, and the threat of purchase of the firm's shares and takeover by other managements who see an opportunity for profit when the value of the firm's shares is below its potential level as a result of low profits is another. The existence and effectiveness of such constraints on the behavior of hired managers largely depends on the availability of information regarding the extent to which hired managers' behavior deviates from attainable profit-maximizing behavior. Such information may be available to only a few knowledgeable shareholders, for example, and transmission of the information to other shareholders may be costly. On the other hand, if the firm operates in an industry with other firms facing similar demand and cost conditions, the managers of the latter may possess adequate knowledge to recognize non-profit-maximizing behavior and opportunities for profitable takeover. This constraint will, however, be weakened whenever competing managers' objectives are not profit maximization.

Whether the so-called 'market for corporate control' is an effective constraint on the behavior of hired managers, forcing them to act in a profit-maximizing manner, can only be established by resorting to the facts. The majority of empirical studies seem to indicate no significant difference in the profitability of owner-controlled and manager-controlled enterprises (see the articles by Hindley (33) and Kamerschen (36, 37), for examples). This is consistent with the hypothesis that constraints on hired managers exist and are effective. Before concluding that this is the only logical interpretation, however, an aspect of the problem which has been neglected until relatively recently should be noted. This concerns the nature of the constraints, and the resulting behavior, of *owner-managers themselves*. The automatic assumption that profit-maximizing behavior will be the rule in the case of owner-managers may be premature, particularly when it is recognized that profit-maximizing behavior uses the owner's time, which is limited and has alternative uses in the form of leisure activities or alternative hired employments yielding the owner money income which may even exceed the profit income he can attain by being an owner-manager. If, like hired managers, an owner's objective is utility maximization, and his utility depends on leisure, income and other factors, it does not necessarily follow that profit maximization will be optimal behavior for an owner-manager. In a recent article E. O. Olsen, Jr (54) investigated the circumstances under which utility maximization by owner-managers will result in profit-maximizing levels of output produced. His analysis demonstrates that while utility maximization will result in profit maximization by owner-managers whose firms sell in perfectly competitive markets, for owner-managed firms that sell in imperfectly competitive markets utility maximization will not generally result in profit maximization! In firms selling in imperfectly competitive markets, neither owner-managers nor hired managers may maximize profits; moreover, if hired managers are confronted by additional constraints which are not present for owner-managers, hired managers may even produce output levels closer to profit-maximizing levels than owner-managers! For example, owner-managers may indulge a preference for leisure and sacrifice some potential profit income while hired managers may be prevented from doing so by the type of shareholder or takeover threat constraints previously discussed.

The question of whether a firm's objectives are related to certain constraints, such as the degree of separation of ownership and control, can be extended to other aspects of the firm. For example, since an organization typically consists of a number of individuals, each with control over one or more of the firm's decision variables, instead of an 'objective function' which is related to the preferences of a single individual, there are in reality a number of objective functions for different decision-makers, each of which may be viewed as an additional constraint in the firm's overall optimization problem. Moreover, the precise form of the internal organization of the firm, including the allocation of decision-making tasks between individuals and the system of rewards and penalties associated with the performance of these tasks, will influence the precise form of the constraints confronting each decision-maker and the resulting levels of the firm's decision variables which are 'optimal' in the sense of maximizing the constrained objective function of the firm's decision-makers. Viewed in this light *the issue of what objectives a firm pursues cannot be divorced from the nature of the firm's internal organization,* including the allocation of tasks between decision-makers and the penalties and rewards confronting individual decision-makers within the organization.

Another point related to the previous one is the possibility that the exact nature of the firm's objective function may change over time with changes in personnel, or with changes in the internal allocation of decision-making functions and so on.

As already noted in an earlier section, in the presence of uncertainty regarding the precise nature of the external constraints confronting the firm, a firm's decision-makers may use rules of thumb, according to which particular decision variables are assigned to the task of achieving certain intermediate goals or targets. See the references by Baumol and Quandt (8) and Day (21) for examples of such rules of thumb. The targets and even the decision rules themselves may be revised through time as information concerning the nature of the external constraints confronting the firm is accumulated as a result of feedback of results from earlier decisions, in an effort to achieve certain 'ultimate' objectives, such as profit maximization, for example. Even if the precise form of all the external constraints confronting a firm could be determined, the costs of transmitting this information to all the various decision-makers involved in the decision process may be prohibitively high. A decentralized decision process may be used instead, with specific decision-makers being assigned responsibility for certain sub-goals, or targets, in the firm's overall decision problem. This results in an iterative process of adjustments in individual decision variables without regard to their 'side effects' on the targets of other departments or decision-makers. However, provided the process is dynamically stable and converges towards the levels of the firm's decision variables which solve the firm's overall decision problem optimally, this approach may be far less costly than transmitting to all decision-makers sufficient information necessary to enable them to take into account the implications of their own actions for all other aspects of the firm's operations. Even if the information were not costly, the problem-solving capacity of individual decision-makers might be too limited to solve the resulting problem. For any or all of these reasons, firms frequently use intermediate 'targets' or sub-goals in their decision-making. Obviously, this greatly complicates the problem of inferring a firm's 'ultimate' objectives from observed behavior.

7. Relevance of Profit-Maximizing Behavior

Since a good deal of economic theory concerning the behavior of firms is based on the assumption that firms attempt to maximize profits, it is appropriate to consider why this remains the central behavioral hypothesis underlying the theory of industrial behavior despite the fact that decision-makers may pursue a variety of other objectives. See F. Machlup (44) for more on this point. In addition, its relevance for the behavior of non-profit organizations may be questioned, and is considered in the next section.

In defense of the profit-maximization hypothesis, several points may be made. The first is that the resulting predictions concerning some aspects of firms' behavior may be identical to those associated with the pursuit of other objectives. For example, cost-minimizing behavior is necessary in order to achieve a wide variety of objectives. In these circumstances the use of profit maximization will yield the same predictions regarding aspects of behavior which are related to cost minimization as would the use of the other behavioral hypotheses. Similarly, one may be interested in the sign of the response of a firm's decision variables to a change in some aspect of the firm's environment, such as a change in the price of its inputs, or tax rate, rather than in the precise magnitude of the resulting changes in the levels of the firm's decision variables. The sign of the response of some decision variables may be the same under profit maximization and a variety of different objectives, even though the magnitude of the response may differ depending on the precise nature of the objectives being pursued.

For dealing with those aspects of a firm's behavior which are the same under other objectives, the use of profit maximization as a behavioral hypothesis is quite appropriate; in these circumstances it is not necessary to know the precise nature of the objectives pursued by the firms whose behavior one is predicting. On the other hand, if one is concerned with predicting aspects of firms' behavior which analysis shows will differ significantly under different objectives, it may be necessary to obtain information on the nature of the objectives actually pursued by the firms one is dealing with. The problems of attempting to infer the nature of firms' objectives from observed behavior have already been mentioned in an earlier section. There is as yet surprisingly relatively little empirical evidence to indicate that firms' behavior is inconsistent with the pursuit of maximum profits. In part, this may reflect the difficulty of inferring firms' objectives from observed behavior rather than the underlying behavior itself. However, many economists argue that the test of a theory is its predictive ability rather than its realism, and that since observed behavior appears to be as consistent with the predictions yielded by the profit-maximization assumption as with alternative behavioral hypotheses, its continued use is justifiable. In part it may also be due to the fact that many aspects of behavior which are of concern are identical under different objectives.

Another reason why observed behavior may be consistent with that predicted by profit maximization is that constraints confronting firms' decision-makers may prevent their behavior from departing very far from profit-maximizing behavior, even though their personal objectives may not coincide with profit maximization. For emphasis on this point see J. T. Wenders (70).

The preceding discussion implicitly assumes that the purpose of analysis utilizing profit maximization is the prediction of firms' behavior in practice. This is not the only purpose, however. In price-theory courses in economics, where one of the major purposes is to teach the student logical reasoning processes, the use of profit maximization as a behavioral hypothesis will not make a great deal of difference to the development of the student's logical capabilities, and the student who acquires these capabilities will be aware that alternative behavioral hypotheses may yield different conclusions.

The use of profit maximization as a behavioral hypothesis in price-theory and other economics courses may also be justified on other grounds. It can be shown, as will be indicated in more detail in Chapter 10, that if firms attempt to maximize profits, under certain conditions this will result in an optimum allocation of resources in the economy as a whole. Understanding the reasons underlying this conclusion provides a standard of reference and is a prerequisite for analyzing the consequences, for resources allocation and aggregate satisfaction in the community as a whole, of the pursuit of other objectives. In other words, in this context, economic analysis indicates certain consequences, for the economy as a whole, of the pursuit of profit maximization; it does not claim that firms actually do pursue maximum profits as a goal.

Before concluding this section, a final point should be emphasized. It is undoubtedly true that knowledge of the nature of decision-makers' objectives in practice would permit improved prediction of firms' behavior and formulation of public policies influencing firms' behavior. This should not be permitted to obscure the fact that the same is true of knowledge of constraints confronting firms' decision-makers. Differences in the number, form or size of the constraints confronting a decision-maker can result in very different optimal relationships between the decision variables under his control. There is no a priori justification for elevating objectives above other determinants of decision-maker behavior in importance. As already noted several times, appropriate constraints on decision-maker behavior may prevent that behavior departing significantly from profit-maximizing behavior irrespective of the personal objectives of the decision-maker.

8. Behavior in Non-Profit Organizations

The behavior of non-profit organizations, such as hospitals, educational institutions and government departments, can be explained in terms very similar to those applicable to industrial firms, since the relevant factors are the objectives and constraints facing decision-makers in such organizations. There are, moreover, many similarities between the factors determining the behavior of non-profit organizations and industrial firms, and differences between the two types of organizations may often be more apparent than real, for reasons explained in this section. For a selection of articles dealing with behavior in non-profit organizations, see Clarkson (13), Davies (19), Lee (39), Newhouse (50) and Niskanen (52) listed in Recommended Readings.

Decision-makers in non-profit institutions must, like decision-makers in industrial firms, make choices between alternative input mixes and output levels of the organization, and must also often decide upon levels of information-creating activities which are analogous to the advertising activities of firms. In making such choices, decision-makers in non-profit organizations will be confronted by a number of constraints which are remarkably similar to those confronting a firm's decision-makers. For example, cost conditions describing the relationship between the total cost of the non-profit organization's activities and the characteristics of the services it provides will be determined, like those of a firm, by a production function relating inputs and outputs and by input-supply conditions which determine input prices. Similarly, the difference between the 'revenue conditions' confronting firms and non-profit organizations is more apparent than real. The latter may not obtain all, or any, of their revenues from prices charged for output; instead they may result from budget allocations to the organization. However, the budget allocation decision will usually be based upon considerations related to the quantity and/or quality of the services provided by the organization, as perceived by those persons making the budget allocations. This is little different, in principle, from the industrial firm, where buyers are willing to 'allocate' revenue to the firm on the basis of the quantity and quality of the output provided.

In addition, both types of organization will face a budget constraint relating total costs and total revenues. For the non-profit organization the budget constraint may merely require that total outlays by the organization not exceed total revenues, which is analytically equivalent to a zero profit constraint in an industrial firm; in contrast, industrial firms will usually be required to make a positive amount of profit. However, although the precise level of the profit constraint will influence the optimal levels of an organization's decision variables, it will not itself affect the form of the conditions that are necessary in order to achieve particular objectives pursued subject to a profit constraint, for reasons explained in more detail in the Appendix to this chapter. Due to the existence of the budget constraint, the behavior of a non-profit organization's decision-makers may, therefore, be very similar in many respects to that of industrial decision-makers pursuing similar objectives.

We turn next to the objectives pursued by decision-makers in non-profit organizations, which influence their decisions concerning alternative input and output levels, subject to constraints such as those previously outlined. Decisions in both types of organization will usually involve a number of decision-makers whose objectives must be reconciled: trustees, administrators and doctors in hospitals, for example; shareholders, top management, and sales, production and personnel decision-makers in industrial firms, for another example. In choosing between alternative input and output levels profit maximization is clearly not the objective which decision-makers in non-profit organizations seek to achieve. Many economists, however, would probably agree that it is also rarely the objective of decision-makers in industrial firms. In fact, there are no obvious reasons why the people who make decisions in non-profit institutions and industrial firms should have objective functions which are inherently different. In both cases, the personal satisfaction of the decision-maker will depend on his leisure and income, and may be affected directly or indirectly by aspects of the organization's operations such as the quantity and quality of its output(s), the size of the budget or revenues of the organization, and levels of specific inputs used by the organization. Another aspect, the difference between the organization's revenues and expenditures, is less likely to enter the personal maximand of decision-makers in non-profit organizations, but will nonetheless enter indirectly as a budget constraint as was previously noted.

The other aspects of an organization's operations are equally likely to enter the objective function of decision-makers in firms and non-profit institutions, varying in emphasis with individual decision-makers themselves rather than with the nature of the organization per se. There are, for example, no reasons why 'quality' aspects of output should be any more important in influencing non-profit decision-makers than profit-making enterprises. The exact meaning of the term 'quality' is not always clear in much of the literature. As will be indicated in more detail in Chapter 2, which deals with cost conditions, output has many dimensions, and 'quality' is usually meant to refer to some characteristic of an organization's output other than the rate and volume of its output. These characteristics depend on the level of the organization's inputs; any increase in input levels which involves changes in the characteristics of the organization's output other than an increase in the output level of the organization may be classed under the heading of 'quality' change. Quality may, therefore, be viewed in terms of the quantity and nature of the inputs per unit of output, as opposed to the level of output itself. Since an organization can increase expenditure on inputs which change its output level, or on other kinds of inputs, every organization faces a trade-off between quantity and quality of its output. The optimal quantity/quality combination will be achieved when a marginal increment of expenditure on quantity and quality yield equal contributions to the decision-maker's objectives. For profit and total revenue maximizers, this will be where the marginal contribution of expenditure on quantity and quality to the organization's revenues are equal, per dollar of expenditure; for utility maximizers where quantity and quality directly influence the satisfaction of the decision-maker, it will be the combination which yields equal marginal contributions to the satisfaction of the decision-maker. These combinations may differ, resulting in differences in decision-maker behavior. However, the point is that one type of behavior is no more likely to occur in non-profit organizations than industrial firms. On the contrary, behavior in the two types of organization may sometimes exhibit identical characteristics. For example, the behavior of a bureaucrat whose objective is maximization of the size of his department's budget allocation may be similar in many regards to that of the sales-revenue maximizing decision-makers in a firm. Other examples connected with the behavior of hospitals may be similarly cited. If hospital administrators place a value on certain types of input which is independent of the input's contribution to the quantity or quality of the service provided by the hospital in treating disease, it can be shown that the hospital administrator will use more of the inputs than is compatible with minimizing the total cost of providing the desired quantity/quality combination of treatment provided by the hospital. There is a close similarity between this situation and the behavior of a managerial utility maximizer who derives satisfaction from some of his firm's inputs, notably plush office space and pretty secretaries, independently of their contribution to the firm's output.

To summarize: the same body of analysis which is relevant to the behavior of industrial enterprises is also relevant to the behavior of decision-makers in non-profit organizations. That body of analysis indicates that the objectives of the decision-makers and the constraints confronting them are the crucial determinants of behavior, and it is differences in these factors to which we must turn in order to explain differences in behavior between the two types of organization. From the preceding discussion it is clear that one is likely to find as many similarities as differences between the behavior of firms and non-profit organizations.

Appendix

This Appendix deals with the implications of the pursuit of different objectives for decision-maker behavior more rigorously than the discussion in the body of the text. As was indicated in the text, each of the constraints confronting a decision-maker, and the decision-maker's objective function, may be viewed as an equation. From these equations, a set of necessary conditions can be derived which must be fulfilled if decision variables are to be optimal in the sense of achieving the highest value of the decision-maker's objective that is feasible, given the constraints he faces. This set of necessary conditions is also a set of equations, the solution to which yields the optimal values of decision variables. In what follows we shall outline a set of typical constraints facing a firm's decision-makers and, by introducing a generalized objective function, indicate the consequences for decision-maker behavior of the pursuit of different objectives. In the process, a number of general conclusions concerning the factors influencing optimal behavior will be demonstrated and emphasized.

Consider a decision-maker who is faced by the following constraints:

(a) A production function relating inputs and outputs $q_s = q(L, K)$: The quantity of output produced, q_s, depends on the amount of labor, L, and capital, K, employed.

(b) Input-supply functions indicating that the price of labor is w per unit and the price of capital is r per unit, and that these prices are independent of the total amount of labor and capital used by the firm.

(c) A demand function $q_d = q(p, A, Z)$: the quantity of output demanded, q_d, depends on the price of the product, p, advertising expenditures, A, and a set of variables Z related to rival suppliers' behavior and buyers' behavior, which are outside the decision-maker's control. The reader should note that the subsequent analysis and conclusions are equally applicable to any other type of outlay which, like advertising, affects the demand for a firm's product such as quality-increasing expenditures or R&D outlays, for example.

(d) The equilibrium condition $q_d = q_s$, which indicates that output demanded is met from current production, not from inventories.

(e) Sales revenue equals price times quantity sold: $R = pq$.

(f) The budget constraint $\pi = pq - wL - rK - A$: profit, π, equals the difference between total sales revenues and total costs of the firm's inputs, labor, capital and advertising.

(g) The decision-maker is assumed to have an objective function, or maximand, of the general form $U(\pi, R, q, A, L, K)$; that is, his personal satisfaction depends, potentially, on all aspects of the firm's operations.

Maximizing the objective function $U(\pi, R, q, A, L, K)$ subject to the constraints (a) to (f) is equivalent to maximizing the following constrained objective function:

$$G = U(\pi, R, q, A, L, K) + \lambda_1[q - q(KL)] + \lambda_2[q - q(p, A, Z)] + \lambda_3(\pi - pq + wL + rK + A) + \lambda_4(R - pq)$$

where $\lambda_1, \lambda_2, \lambda_3, \lambda_4$, called 'Lagrange multipliers', represent the effect on the level of the decision-maker's satisfaction, U, of a change in the level of the corresponding constraint.

By taking the partial derivative of the constrained objective function G with respect to each of the variables under the decision-maker's control, and setting the resulting expressions equal to zero, a set of necessary conditions for maximizing the objective function is obtained. The necessary condition relating to each decision variable shows the sum of all the direct and indirect effects of a change in that decision variable on the decision-maker's satisfaction. The direct effects of a change in the decision variable on the decision-maker's satisfaction are represented below by the terms 'U' accompanied by a subscript denoting the decision variable, while the indirect effects on his satisfaction are obtained by multiplying the effect of the change in the decision variable on each constraint by λ, the effect of a change in the level of the constraint on the decision-maker's satisfaction.

The resulting set of necessary conditions obtained in the preceding example are as follows:

(1) $\dfrac{\partial G}{\partial \pi} = U_\pi + \lambda_3 = 0$

(5) $\dfrac{\partial G}{\partial A} = U_A - \lambda_2 \dfrac{\partial q}{\partial A} + \lambda_3 = 0$

(2) $\dfrac{\partial G}{\partial R} = U_R + \lambda_4 = 0$

(6) $\dfrac{\partial G}{\partial L} = U_L - \lambda_1 \dfrac{\partial q}{\partial L} + \lambda_3 W = 0$

(3) $\dfrac{\partial G}{\partial q} = U_q + \lambda_1 + \lambda_2 - \lambda_3 p - \lambda_4 p = 0$

(7) $\dfrac{\partial G}{\partial K} = U_K - \lambda_1 \dfrac{\partial q}{\partial K} + \lambda_3 r = 0$

(4) $\dfrac{\partial G}{\partial p} = -\lambda_2 \dfrac{\partial q}{\partial p} - \lambda_3 q - \lambda_4 q = 0$

As already explained, each necessary condition will be an equation, the precise form of which depends on the nature of the equations representing the objective function and constraints facing the decision-makers from which it was derived. There will be 'n' necessary conditions for n decision variables. Because the λs are also variables whose optimal levels are unknown, there will, therefore, be more variables than the 'n' necessary conditions relating to the decision variables. However, by taking the partial derivative of the constrained objective function G with respect to each of the 'm' λs, this yields 'm' additional necessary conditions in the form of the 'm' original constraint equations, as the reader can easily verify There will, therefore, be a total of $n + m$ equations in the $n + m$ decision variables and λs. If the precise form of the original constraint equations and the decision-maker's objective function $U(\pi, R, q, A, L, K)$ are known, the precise form of the $n + m$ necessary conditions will also be known, and this will permit the set of necessary conditions to be solved to yield the $n + m$ optimal values of the decision variables and λs.

Several important propositions follow from the preceding analysis:

Proposition 1

The precise *level* of any constraint will itself affect the *optimal levels* of a firm's decision variables, because it will influence one of the equations in the set of necessary conditions. The precise level of a constraint will not, however, affect the necessary conditions which relate to each of the decision variables. When two or more of the necessary conditions relating to individual decision variables are combined, this yields necessary conditions which must be met in order for the two or more decision variables to be optimally combined; these conditions will be referred to as *optimal input-mix* conditions. In contrast to the optimal conditions governing the level of individual decision variables, these optimal input-mix conditions will not be affected by changes or differences in the level of constraints facing a firm's decision-makers.

Proposition 2

A change or difference in the *form*, as opposed to the level, of a constraint will not only affect the optimal levels of a firm's decision variables, but will also change the necessary condition for each decision variable which enters into the constraint in question. This, in turn, will imply a change in the firm's optimal input-mix conditions, except in the case of (i) decision variables which do not enter into the constraint in question, or (ii) decision variables which enter into the constraint but whose necessary conditions are changed in exactly the same manner by the change in the form of the constraint. Even in these last two cases, it must be remembered that the optimal levels of the decision variables will generally be changed, even if the optimal manner in which they are combined is not changed.

Proposition 3

Given the form and level of the constraints confronting a firm's decision-makers, the precise form of the decision-makers' objective function $U(\pi, R, q, A, L, K)$ will determine the nature of the necessary conditions that are appropriate and, therefore, the optimal levels of the firm's decision variables. The influence of different objectives on the firm's behavior can, therefore, be determined by examining the consequences of varying the form of the objective function on the necessary conditions relating to different decision variables. Again, a number of generalized results emerge, including the following: (i) Different objective functions will not change the necessary conditions for those decision variables which do not enter directly into the decision-makers' objective function. (ii) Although the nature of the necessary conditions relating to individual decision variables and, therefore, optimal levels of the decision variables may be affected by the nature of the objective function, the *optimal input-mix* conditions relating to particular decision variables need not be changed.

The preceding propositions will now be illustrated by reference to some prominent examples found in the literature of price theory and industrial organization:

Example I: Optimal Levels of Productive Inputs, Labor and Capital. The necessary condition which must be met in order for labor input to be at an optimal level, shown on page 25, in this Appendix, is as follows:

(6) $\dfrac{\partial G}{\partial L} = U_L - \lambda_1 \dfrac{\partial q}{\partial L} + \lambda_3 W = 0$

From necessary condition (3) $\lambda_1 = [(\lambda_3 + \lambda_4)p - \lambda_2 - U_q]$

And from necessary condition (4) $- \lambda_2 = (\lambda_3 + \lambda_4)q \left| \dfrac{\partial q}{\partial p} \right.$

Substituting for λ_1 and λ_2 in (6) above yields

$U_L - [(\lambda_3 + \lambda_4)p + (\lambda_3 + \lambda_4)q\dfrac{\partial p}{\partial q} - U_q]\dfrac{\partial q}{\partial L} + \lambda_3 W = 0$

or $W = \left(p + q\dfrac{\partial p}{\partial q} \right)\dfrac{\partial q}{\partial L} \cdot \left(\dfrac{\lambda_3 + \lambda_4}{\lambda_3} \right) + \dfrac{U_q}{\lambda_3} \cdot \dfrac{\partial q}{\partial L} + \dfrac{U_L}{\lambda_3}$

Which may be expressed alternatively as follows:

(6a) $W = \left[(\text{Marginal Sales Revenue}) \cdot \left(\dfrac{U_\pi + U_R}{U_\pi} \right) + \dfrac{U_q}{U_\pi} \right] \cdot (\text{Marginal Product of Labor}) + \dfrac{U_L}{U_\pi}$

If a firm's decision-makers derive no direct satisfaction from the firm's output, sales revenue, or labor, $U_q = U_R = U_L = 0$, and the above optimal condition indicates that the quantity of labor should be expanded until the extra sales revenue resulting from the added output produced by a marginal unit of labor equals the marginal cost of labor to the firm, which in this example equals the wage w. This will maximize the firm's profits, which in these circumstances is the only aspect of the firm's operations which yields satisfaction to the decision-makers and which is affected by the quantity of labor hired. In contrast, when a firm's decision-makers derive direct satisfaction either from the level of output produced ($U_q > 0$) or from the level of sales revenue ($U_R > 0$) or from the level of labor input ($U_L > 0$), the preceding optimal condition implies that the marginal cost of labor to the firm should exceed the resulting marginal revenue. In other words, the optimal level of labor input will exceed the level which maximizes the firm's profits.

Necessary condition (7), which must be met in order for capital inputs to be at an optimal level, can similarly be shown to be equivalent to the following condition:

$r = \left(p + q\dfrac{\partial p}{\partial q} \right)\dfrac{\partial q}{\partial K} \cdot \left(\dfrac{\lambda_3 + \lambda_4}{\lambda_3} \right) + \dfrac{U_q}{\lambda_3} \cdot \dfrac{\partial q}{\partial K} + \dfrac{U}{\lambda_3}$

or (6b)

$r = \left[(\text{Marginal Sales Revenue}) \cdot \left(\dfrac{U_\pi + U_R}{U_\pi} \right) + \dfrac{U_q}{U_\pi} \right] \cdot (\text{Marginal Product Capital}) + \dfrac{U_K}{U_\pi}$

The implications of the pursuit of different objectives for the optimal level of capital input are the same as those already discussed in the case of labor, and will not, therefore, be repeated. However, conditions (6a) and (6b) can be combined in order to obtain the following optimal input-mix condition:

$$\dfrac{w}{r} = \dfrac{\left[\text{MR} \cdot \left(\dfrac{U_\pi + U_R}{U_\pi} \right) + U_q/U_\pi \right] \cdot \text{MPP}_L + U_L/U_\pi}{\left[\text{MR} \cdot \left(\dfrac{U_\pi + U_R}{U_\pi} \right) + U_q/U_\pi \right] \cdot \text{MPP}_K + U_K/U_\pi}$$

The preceding condition must be met in order for labor *and* capital inputs to be simultaneously at optimal levels. From this condition, several important conclusions are apparent:

(i) When a firm's decision-makers derive no satisfaction directly from the level of labor or capital inputs themselves, $U_L = U_K = 0$, and the above condition requires that

$$\frac{w}{r} = \frac{MPP_L}{MPP_K}$$

which, in words, states that the ratio of marginal costs of labor and capital inputs must be equal to the ratio of the marginal physical products of the two inputs. This condition in turn is necessary in order that a firm's output be produced at minimum feasible total cost. In other words, irrespective of whether a firm's decision-makers pursue profit, sales revenue, or output maximization goals, or managerial utility maximization where managerial utility depends on any aspects of the firm's operations other than the level of labor or capital inputs, minimizing the total cost of producing the firm's selected output level will be necessary in order to achieve any of those goals.

(ii) When a firm's decision-makers derive direct satisfaction *either* from labor inputs utilized by the firm ($U_L > 0$) or from capital inputs ($U_K > 0$), the above optimal input-mix condition implies that $w/r \neq MPP_L/MPP_K$. Minimizing the total cost of producing the firm's output level will not be optimal from the point of view of the firm's decision-makers. Instead, when $U_L > 0$, the firm's decision-makers will use more labor and less capital than the cost minimizing combination, to produce the firm's output. The opposite will be true ($U_K > 0$).

(iii) When a firm's decision-makers derive direct satisfaction from both labor and capital inputs utilized by the firm, so that U_L and U_K are both positive, optimal combinations of labor and capital will result in cost minimization only if U_L and U_K, the marginal utility of labor and capital to the firm's decision-makers, are proportional to the marginal products of the respective inputs.

Example II: Optimal Output Levels.   The necessary condition which must be met in order for a firm's output to be at an optimal level was earlier shown to be

(3) $U_q + \lambda_1 + \lambda_2 - \lambda_3 p - \lambda_4 p = 0$

From necessary condition   (1) $\lambda_3 = U_\pi$
''   ''   ''   (2) $\lambda_4 = U_R$

''   ''   ''   (4) $\lambda_2 = \dfrac{-(\lambda_3 + \lambda_4)}{\dfrac{\partial q}{\partial L}}$

''   ''   ''   (6) $\lambda_1 = \dfrac{\lambda_3 W + U_L}{\dfrac{\partial q}{\partial L}}$

Substituting for λ_1, λ_2, λ_3 and λ_4 in necessary condition (3) yields

$$U_q - U_R p = U_\pi p + \left(\frac{U_\pi + U_R}{\dfrac{\partial q}{\partial p}}\right) q - \left(\frac{U_\pi w + U_L}{\dfrac{\partial q}{\partial L}}\right)$$

(i) When a firm's decision-makers derive satisfaction from profits, but no satisfaction either from the firm's output level, labor inputs or sales revenue, $U_q = U_L = U_R = 0$, and the above condition reduces to

$$0 = U_\pi \left[(p + q\frac{\partial p}{\partial q}) - w \bigg/ \frac{\partial q}{\partial L} \right]$$

which may be expressed alternatively as follows:

$0 = U_\pi$ (Marginal Revenue $-$ Marginal Cost)

which indicates the familiar profit-maximizing condition requiring that marginal revenue from an output-level change equal the resulting marginal cost. Since $MR = p(1 - 1/E_d)$, where E_d represents the price-elasticity of demand for the firm's product, defined as $(-)\dfrac{\partial q}{\partial p}\cdot\dfrac{p}{q}$, the profit maximizing output-level condition may also be expressed in the following form:

$$\frac{P - MC}{P} = \frac{1}{E_d}$$

which will be used extensively in the discussion of firms' pricing behavior contained in Chapter 3.

(ii) If a firm's decision-makers derive satisfaction from both profits and sales revenue, condition (3a) reduces to

$$0 = (U_\pi + U_R)\left(p + q\frac{\partial q}{\partial p}\right) - U_\pi w \left/ \frac{\partial q}{\partial L}\right.$$

which may be expressed alternatively as follows:

$$0 = (U_\pi + U_R)\,(\text{Marginal Revenue}) - U_\pi\,(\text{Marginal Cost})$$

The last form of this condition clearly implies that MR < MC at an optimal output level. In the limiting case in which decision-makers derive no satisfaction from profits, $U_\pi = 0$ and the optimal output-level condition is

$$0 = U_R\,.(\text{Marginal Revenue})$$

which implies expanding output until MR = 0.

It is appropriate in the present connection to remind the reader of the discussion contained in the body of Chapter 1 which indicated that producing an output level where MR < MC as occurs under sales-revenue maximization does not necessarily imply producing a larger output level than under profit maximization. The reason is that the magnitude of MR at any given output level will depend on the level of a firm's advertising, which will generally differ under profit and sales-revenue maximization.

(iii) When $U_q = U_R = 0$, but decision-makers derive satisfaction from labor inputs in addition to profits, $U_L > 0$ and condition (3a) reduces to

$$0 = U_\pi(\text{MR} - \text{MC}) + U_L \left/ \left|\frac{\partial q}{\partial L}\right.\right.$$

which implies that at the optimal output level MR < MC. A similar conclusion applies if the firm's decision-makers derive satisfaction from capital inputs in addition to profits.

Example III: Optimal Advertising Levels. If demand for a firm's product depends not only on the price charged, but also on other factors under the firm's control such as advertising expenditure levels, the firm must not only determine the optimal price and resulting output level at a particular level of advertising outlays, but also the optimal level of advertising expenditures itself. The necessary condition which must be satisfied in order for a firm's advertising to be at an optimal level was earlier shown to be

$$(5) \quad 0 = U_A - \lambda_2\frac{\partial q}{\partial A} + \lambda_3$$

Assuming, purely for expositional convenience, that a firm's decision-makers derive satisfaction only from the results of advertising, such as profits or sales and not from the advertising itself, $U_A = 0$.

From necessary condition (4) $\lambda_2 = (\lambda_3 + \lambda_4)q\dfrac{\partial q}{\partial A}$

while $\lambda_3 = U_\pi$ and $\lambda_4 = U_R$, as indicated by necessary conditions (1) and (2). Substituting for $\lambda_2, \lambda_3, \lambda_4$ in (5) yields

$$(5a) \quad 0 = (U_\pi + U_R)q\frac{\partial q}{\partial A} + U_\pi\frac{\partial q}{\partial p}$$

When multiplied by p/q, (5a) becomes

$$0 = (U_\pi + U_R)p\frac{\partial q}{\partial A} + U_\pi\frac{\partial q}{\partial p}\cdot\frac{p}{q}$$

$$\text{or (5b)} \quad p\frac{\partial q}{\partial A} = \left(\frac{U_\pi}{U_\pi + U_R}\right)\frac{\partial q}{\partial p}\cdot\frac{p}{q}$$

which may be expressed alternatively as follows:

$$\text{Marginal Revenue}_{\text{Adv.}} = \left(\frac{U_\pi}{U_\pi + U_R}\right) \cdot E_d$$

where E_d is the price-elasticity of demand for the firm's product. When $U_R = 0$ the marginal revenue from a firm's advertising must equal the price-elasticity of demand for the firm's product; this optimal condition is usually referred to as the 'Dorfman–Steiner' condition, following a seminal article by R. Dorfman and P. O. Steiner dealing with optimal advertising policy. The Dorfman–Steiner condition can also be expressed in terms of the firm's advertising-elasticity of demand as follows: multiplying both sides of (5b) by $A/p \cdot q$, the ratio of the firm's total advertising to sales revenue yields

$$\frac{A}{q} \cdot \frac{\partial q}{\partial p} = \left(\frac{U_\pi}{U_\pi + U_R}\right) E_d \cdot \frac{A}{p \cdot q}$$

The expression on the left-hand side of the equality symbol is the advertising-elasticity of demand for the firm's product, E_a, defined as the ratio between the proportionate change in quantity of the firm's product demanded and a proportionate change in the level of the firm's advertising expenditures. When $U_R = 0$, the optimal advertising condition may, therefore, be expressed as follows:

$$\frac{E_a}{E_d} = \frac{A}{pq}$$

Since the optimal output-level condition for the firm was earlier shown to be $P - MC/P = 1/E_d$, the optimal advertising condition is also equivalent to

$$\frac{(P - MC)}{P} \cdot E_a = \frac{\text{Advertising}}{\text{Sales}}$$

The reader is reminded that the Dorfman-Steiner condition applies to profit maximizing decision-makers; optimal advertising conditions differ when decision-makers derive satisfaction directly either from advertising itself or from sales revenues. On the other hand, the Dorfman–Steiner condition is equally applicable to decision-makers who derive satisfaction from output itself instead of, or in addition to, deriving satisfaction from profits.

Further Extensions

The analysis contained in preceding sections of this Appendix may be extended in two important ways:

(1) Introduction of Rival Firms' Reactions. To this point it was explicitly assumed that characteristics of buyer and rival firms' behavior which influence the demand for an individual firm's product, indicated by the term Z in the constraint which represents the firm's demand function, are not affected by the level of the firm's own decision variables. If, as often occurs in practice, the behavior of a firm's rivals depends to some extent on the level of the firm's own decision variables, this will change the form of some of the necessary conditions outlined on page 25 of this Appendix. Specifically, those necessary conditions which apply to decision variables which affect rivals' behavior will contain additional terms which indicate the effect of a change in the decision variable on rivals' behavior multiplied by the resulting effect of changes in rivals' decision variables on demand for the firm's product. This will obviously affect the optimal levels of a firm's decision variables, and may also influence some of the input-mix conditions, such as the Dorfman–Steiner condition which must be satisfied in order for the level of two or more of the firm's decision variables to be at optimal levels in relation to each other. Prominent examples of the influence of rivals' reactions on optimal levels of a firm's decision variables will be discussed in Chapter 3 dealing with optimal pricing behavior and Chapter 4 dealing with optimal levels of advertising and similar decision variables.

(2) Dynamic Aspects of Firms' Behavior. Whether incorporating the influence of rival firms' reactions or not, necessary conditions such as those outlined on page 25 of this Appendix represent conditions which must be satisfied if a firm's decision variables are to be at optimal levels. By adding 'adjustment rules' which indicate *the manner in which a firm's decision variables will be changed when the firm's necessary conditions are not met* and decision-makers' objectives are therefore not being achieved, one obtains dynamic implications which describe how the firm's decision variables will change through time. The resulting path of the firm's decision variables through time will depend on the precise manner in which individual decision variables are changed in response to failure to achieve the necessary conditions, including the directions and relative speeds of change of the decision variables. There are many possible alternative sets of 'adjustment rules' and each will imply a different

dynamic path of the firm's decision variables through time. Some adjustment rules will result in convergence of the firm's decision variables towards optimal levels, and others will not. One of the problems facing any firm is that of discovering and adopting a set of adjustment rules which, given the firm's environment, will result in rapid convergence of the firm's decision variables towards optimal levels. In the absence of information concerning the precise nature of all the constraints facing a firm, and therefore regarding the precise form of the necessary conditions which must be met in order for the firm's decision variables to be at optimal levels, selecting appropriate adjustment rules may be a process of trial and error, with changes in the adjustment rules in response to feedback of results obtained by using specific adjustment rules. The adjustment rules actually present in a firm will generally be related to characteristics of the firm's internal organization, including the manner in which responsibility for specific decision variables is allocated among different members of the organization.

RECOMMENDED READINGS

1. Alchian, A. A., The basis of some recent advances in the theory of management of the firm, *Journal of Industrial Economics*, November 1965.
2. Archibald, C. G., Qualitative content of maximizing models, *Journal of Political Economy*, February 1965.
3. Azariadis, C., Cohen, K. J. and Porcas, A., A partial utility approach to the theory of the firm, *Southern Economic Journal*, April 1972.
4. Baldwin, W. L., The motives of managers, environmental restraints, and the theory of managerial enterprise, *Quarterly Journal of Economics*, May 1964.
5. Baumol, W. J., On the theory of expansion of the firm, *American Economic Review*, December 1962.
6. Baumol, W. J., *Economic Theory and Operations Analysis*, 3rd ed. (Englewood Cliffs, N. J.: Prentice Hall, Inc., 1965), Chapter 13.
7. Baumol, W. J., *Business Behavior, Value and Growth*, rev. ed. (New York: Harcourt, Brace & World, Inc., 1967).
8. Baumol, W. J. and Quandt, R. E., Rules of thumb and optimally imperfect decisions, *American Economic Review*, March 1964.
9. Baumol, W. J. and Stewart, M., On the relevant theory of the firm. In *The Corporate Economy: Growth, Competition and Innovation Potential* (New York: McMillan, 1971), Chapter 5.
10. Beenhakker, H. L., Discounting indices proposed for capital investment evaluation: a further examination, *Engineering Economist*, April–May 1973.
11. Brown, M. and Revankar, N., A generalized theory of the firm: an integration of the sales and profit maximization hypothesis, *Kyklos*, Vol. 24, No. 3, 1971.
12. Ciscel, D. H., Determinants of executive compensation, *Southern Economic Journal*, April 1974.
13. Clarkson, K. W., Some implications of property rights in hospital management, *Journal of Law and Economics*, October 1972.
14. Cox, S. R. and Shauger, D., Executive compensation, firm sales, and profitability, *Intermountain Economic Review*, Spring 1973.
15. Crew, M. A., X-theory vs. management discretion theory, *Southern Economic Journal*, October 1971.
16. Cyert, R. M. and Cohen, K. J., *Theory of the Firm: Resource Allocation in a Market Economy* (Englewood Cliffs, N. J.: Prentice Hall, Inc., 1965), Part 3.
17. Cyert, R. M. and Hedrick, C. L., Theory of the firm: past, present and future; an interpretation, *Journal of Economic Literature*, June 1972.
18. Cyert, R. M. and March, J. G., *A Behavioral Theory of the Firm* (Englewood Cliffs, N. J.: Prentice-Hall, Inc., 1963).
19. Davies, D. G., The efficiency of public and private firms: the case of Australia's airlines, *Journal of Law and Economics*, April 1971.
20. Davies, J. R., On the sales maximization hypothesis: a comment, *Journal of Industrial Economics*, April 1973.
21. Day, Richard, H., Profits, learning and the convergence of satisficing to marginalism, *Quarterly Journal of Economics*, May 1967.
22. Encarnacion, J., Constraints and the firm's utility function. *Review of Economic Studies*, April 1964.
23. Feinberg, R. M., Profit maximization vs. utility maximization, *Southern Economic Journal*, July 1975.
24. Ferguson, C. E., The theory of multidimensional utility analysis in relation to multiple-goal business behavior; a synthesis, *Southern Economic Journal*, October 1965.
25. Frankel, N., Pricing decisions under unknown demand, *Kyklos*, Vol. XXVI, 1973.
26. Furbotn, E. G. and Pejovich, S., Property rights and economic theory: a survey of recent literature, *Journal of Economic Literature*, December 1972.

27. Grabowski, H. and Mueller, D. C., Managerial and stockholder welfare expenditures, *Review of Economics and Statistics*, February 1972.
28. Hall, M., On the goals of the firm, *Quarterly Journal of Economics*, February 1966.
29. Hall, M., Sales revenue maximization: an empirical examination, *Journal of Industrial Economics*, April 1967.
30. Haverman, R. and Bartolo, G. D., The revenue maximizing oligopoly model: comment, *American Economic Review*, December 1968.
31. Hawkins, C. J., On the sales-revenue maximization hypothesis, *Journal of Industrial Economics*, April 1970.
32. Heal, G. M. and Silberston, A., Alternative managerial objectives: an exploratory note; and Seton, F., the geometry of managerial objectives: a supplementary note, *Oxford Economic Papers*, July 1972.
33. Hindley, B., Separation of ownership and control in the modern corporation, *Journal of Law and Economics*, April 1970.
34. Johnson, H. L., *Graphic Analysis of Multiple-goal Firms: Development, Current Status, and Critique*. Occasional Paper 5, Center for Research College of Business Administration, Penn State University, April 1966.
35. Kafoglis, M. Z. and Bushnell, R. C., The revenue maximizing oligopoly model: comments, *American Economic Review*, June 1970.
36. Kamerschen, D. R., The influence of ownership and control on profit rates, *American Economic Review*, June 1968.
37. Kamerschen, D. R., Further thoughts on separation of ownership and control, *Rivista Internazionale di Scienze, Economiche e Commerciali*, February 1973.
38. Lanzillotti, R. F., Pricing objectives in large companies, *American Economic Review*, December 1958.
39. Lee, M. L., A conspicuous production theory of hospital behavior, *Southern Economic Journal*, July 1971.
40. Leland, H. E., Theory of the firm facing uncertain demand, *American Economic Review*, June 1972.
41. Lewellen, W. G. and Huntsman, B., Managerial pay and corporate performance, *American Economic Review*, September 1970.
42. Lin, W., Dean, G. W. and Moore, C. V., An empirical test of utility vs. profit maximization in agricultural production, *American Journal of Agricultural Economics*, August 1974.
43. Mabry, B. D. and Siders, D. L., An empirical test of the sales maximization hypothesis, *Southern Economic Journal*, January 1967.
44. Machlup, F., Theories of the firm: marginalist, behavioral, managerial, *American Economic Review*, March 1967.
45. Malmgren, H. B., Information, expectations and the theory of the firm, *Quarterly Journal of Economics*, August 1961.
46. McGuire, J. W., Chui, J. S. Y. and Elbing, A. O., Executive incomes, sales and profits, *American Economic Review*, September 1962.
47. Mishan, E. J., A proposed normalisation procedure for public investment criteria, *Economic Journal*, December 1967.
48. Mohr, L. B., The concept of organizational goal, *American Political Science Review*, June 1973.
49. Monson, R. J., Chui, J. S. and Cooley, D. E., The effect of separation of ownership and control on the performance of the large firm, *Quarterly Journal of Economics*, August 1968.
50. Newhouse, J. P., Toward a theory of nonprofit institutions: an economic model of a hospital, *American Economic Review*, March 1970.
51. Ng, Y. K., Utility and profit maximization by an owner-manager: towards a general analysis, *Journal of Industrial Economics*, December 1974.
52. Niskanen, W. A., Nonmarket decision making: the peculiar economics of bureaucracy, *American Economic Review*, May 1968.
53. Norris, R., The modern corporation and economic theory. In *The Corporate Economy: Growth, Competition and Innovation Potential* (New York: Macmillan, 1971), Chapter 9.
54. Olsen, E. O., Jr, Utility and profit maximization by an owner-manager, *Southern Economic Journal*, June 1973.
55. Osborne, D. K., On the goals of the firm, *Quarterly Journal of Economics*, November 1964.
56. Pfouts, R. W., Some cost and profit relationships in the multi-product firm, *Southern Economic Journal*, January 1973.
57. Ramsey, J. B., The marginal efficiency of capital, internal rate of return, and net present value: an analysis of investment criteria, *Journal of Political Economy*, September–October 1970.
58. Reeder, J. A., Corporate ownership and control: a synthesis of recent findings, *Industrial Organization Review*, Vol. 3, 1975.
59. Rosenberg, R., Profit-constrained revenue maximization: note, *American Economic Review*, March 1971.
60. Sandmeyer, R. L., Baumol's sales-maximization model: comment, *American Economic Review*, December 1974.

61. Shepherd, A. R., Sales maximization and managerial effort, *Nebraska Journal of Economics and Business*, Spring 1971.
62. Shubik, M., Objective functions and models of corporate optimization, *Quarterly Journal of Economics*, August 1961.
63. Simon, H. A., Theories of decision-making in economics and behavioral science, *American Economic Review*, June 1959.
64. Simon, H. A., New developments in the theory of the firm, *American Economic Review, Papers and Proceedings*, May 1962.
65. Smyth, D. J., Sales maximization and managerial effort: note, *American Economic Review*, September 1969.
66. Solomon, E., The arithmetic of capital budgeting decisions, *Journal of Business*, April 1956.
67. Solow, R. M., Some implications of alternative criteria for the firm. In *The Corporate Economy: Growth, Competition and Innovation Potential* (New York: Macmillan, 1971), Chapter 10.
68. Sorensen, R., The separation of ownership from control and firm performance: an empirical analysis, *Southern Economic Journal*, July 1974.
69. Turvey, R., Present value vs. internal rate of return: an essay in third best, *Economic Journal*, March 1963.
70. Wenders, J. T., What is profit maximization? *Journal of Economic Issues*, September 1972.
71. Williamson, John, Profit, growth and sales maximization, *Economica*, February 1966.
72. Williamson, O. E., Managerial discretion and business behavior, *American Economic Review*, December 1963.
73. Williamson, O. E., *The Economics of Discretionary Behavior: Managerial Objectives in a Theory of the Firm* (Englewood Cliffs, N. J.: Prentice-Hall, Inc., 1964).

CHAPTER TWO

COST CONDITIONS

Meaning and Determinants of Cost Conditions

The term 'Cost Conditions' is usually used to refer to the relationship between different levels of a firm's output of a particular product or service and the cost of producing that product or service. For reasons to be explained in this chapter, the term really covers a variety of different aspects of a firm's operations, all of which are related but which should be clearly distinguished in the interests of clear thinking and good decision-making.

The total costs of producing any particular output level of a product or service are simply the sum of the costs of the various inputs used. In conventional economic analysis it is assumed that the inputs used to produce any particular product are combined in a manner which minimizes the total cost of producing any particular level of output. The total cost of producing a particular level of output then depends upon existing knowledge concerning feasible input–output relationships, usually referred to as 'technology', and also upon the prices of the various inputs involved in the production process. The relationship between technology, input prices, and the minimum total cost of producing

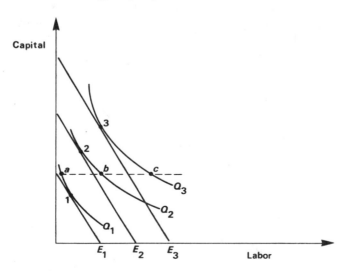

Figure 2–1. Determinants of cost-minimizing input levels.

various output levels is summarized diagrammatically in Figure 2–1. Each of the curved lines labeled Q_1, Q_2, Q_3, usually termed 'isoquants', indicates alternative combinations of two inputs, L and C, which can be used to produce a particular output level. The exact position and slope of each of these lines depends on available 'technology' as determined by existing knowledge concerning input–output relationships; the negative slope of each line reflects the fact that, usually, a particular output level may be produced by substituting more of one input for less of the other. Each of the straight lines labeled E_1, E_2, E_3 indicates alternative combinations of the two inputs which can be purchased with a constant amount of expenditure, or outlay, on inputs. The position of each such line will depend on the absolute level of input prices; the slope will depend on the ratio of the prices of the inputs. The constant slope of the equal-expenditure lines reflects the assumption that the prices of the inputs remain unchanged irrespective of the amount of each input purchased by the firm. This assumption is made merely for expositional convenience and in the present context could easily be relaxed without changing the nature of the conclusions derived from the analysis. Diagrammatically, relaxing this assumption would merely mean that the equal-expenditure lines were either convex or concave to the origin of the diagram.

The total-cost minimizing method of producing any particular output level is represented diagrammatically by the input combination where an equal-expenditure line is tangent to the isoquant representing the output level in question. Choice of any other input combination yielding the same output level would require a larger total expenditure on inputs, reflected by an equal-expenditure line lying above the level associated with the cost-minimizing input combination.

The series of tangency points 1, 2, 3, indicate the combination of inputs which minimize the total cost of various alternative output levels. The resulting minimum total cost of producing output level may be plotted, resulting in a relationship such as that indicated in Figure 2–2. The relationship between total cost and output implies, in turn, a relationship between output and two other cost concepts: the average cost and marginal cost of output. Average cost is simply the total cost of any particular level of output divided by the number of units of output produced; diagrammatically it is depicted by the slope of a line from the origin of Figure 2–2 to the point on the total cost curve corresponding to the output level in question. Marginal, or incremental, cost is the change in total cost associated with a change in the level of output; diagrammatically, it is represented by the slope of the total cost curve in Figure 2–2 at any particular output level. Average and marginal cost will be the same only when the relationship between total cost and output is a straight line through the origin of Figure 2–2.

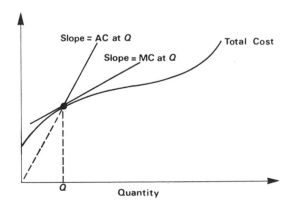

Figure 2–2. Relationship between total, average and marginal cost.

Short-Run Versus Long-Run Cost Conditions

A distinction is drawn in conventional economic analysis between short-run and long-run cost conditions. Long-run cost conditions describe the relationship between the different output levels and total, average, or marginal cost which is implied by the tangency points 1, 2, 3, in Figure 2–1. In contrast, short-run cost conditions describe the relationship between different output levels and total, average, and marginal cost in a situation in which the amount of one of the inputs involved in the production process cannot be varied for some reason. In terms of Figure 2–1, this implies that alternative output levels must be produced with input combinations such as a, b, c, involving the same amount of one of the inputs. These input combinations will generally involve a higher level of total cost than would be experienced if both inputs were variable and the cost minimizing method of producing any particular output level depicted by product combination 1, 2, 3, could be adopted. This conclusion follows from the fact that the expenditure line through input combinations a, b, c, intersects the isoquants, implying that the ratio of input prices is not equal to the ratio of the marginal contribution of each input to output. This, in turn, implies that it is possible to reduce the total cost of producing the same output level by increasing the amount of one input and reducing the other in such a manner as to leave output unchanged. Only one of the combinations a, b, c will generally involve tangency between an isoquant and an expenditure line, indicating that one of the optimal short-run input combinations corresponds to the input combination which would also be used in the long run where all inputs could be varied. This means that short-run cost curves will generally lie above long-run cost curves for all output levels except one; at that particular output level, where long-run and short-run costs are equal, the amount of the input which is 'fixed', or invariable in the short run, corresponds to the level of the input which would minimize the total cost of producing the output level in question even when the input is variable.

Although short-run cost curves will generally lie above the long-run cost curve corresponding to the same output levels, the precise shape of short-run cost curves will be determined by the relationship between total cost and output level implied by points a, b, c. The U-shaped short-run average and marginal cost curves of elementary economic theory result from the assumption of first increasing and then eventually diminishing marginal physical productivity associated with increases in the amount of a variable input combined with a fixed input. This assumption can also be depicted diagrammatically in terms of Figure 2–1. Assuming that increases in output-levels implied by moves from a to b to c points are proportionate, increasing and then diminishing marginal productivity would be reflected by first diminishing, then increasing, distances between the points a, b, c. These distances represent the increases in the amount of the variable input necessary to increase output by proportionate amounts; diminishing distances therefore imply that the marginal productivity of the variable input is increasing, while increasing distances imply that marginal productivity is decreasing. In addition to eventually diminishing marginal productivity of the variable input, the U-shape of short-run average and marginal cost curves may be accentuated by increases in the price of variable inputs as the quantity purchased by the firm increases. In this last case the isocost lines of Figure 2–1 will not be linear.

Whether short-run cost curves are U-shaped in practice can only be ascertained by empirical investigation. Evidence concerning the shape of short-run cost curves suggests that while average variable cost decreases at first in some industries, in many other industries the average variable cost curve is approximately horizontal, up to a level of output associated with the capacity output of the fixed input in question, followed by sharply increasing unit costs. The conditions resulting in such observations need not always correspond to the assumptions made in elementary price theory, namely that a fixed input is being combined with increased amounts of variable input, and that the state of technological knowledge confronting all firms is the same. The services of fixed capital equipment, for example, may be variable so that the amount of fixed input per unit of variable input is not in fact being decreased. More will be said later concerning the problems associated with estimating cost conditions.

Economies and Diseconomies of Scale

The precise form of the long-run relationship between cost of production and level of a firm's output which is implied by the points 1, 2 and 3 in Figure 2-1 is governed by what are termed economies and diseconomies of scale. See A. Silberston (23) for a useful survey article dealing with economies and diseconomies of scale. These terms are used to refer to influences which cause long-run average cost (hereafter referred to as LRAC) to decline, or to increase, as the output level of a particular product or service increases. In terms of Figure 2-1, these influences will determine whether proportionate increases in output levels associated with points such as 1, 2 and 3 require proportionate, less than proportionate, or more than proportionate, increases in total costs.

Simple geometric relationships between the material required for the construction of certain items of equipment and the equipment's capacity may account for declining long-run average costs as the level of output of some products increases. The amount of material required for constructing containers, for example, depends mainly upon the surface area of the container, whereas the capacity of the container depends on the volume enclosed. A storage tank is perfectly divisible in the sense that it can be built to any particular size specifications. However, the capacity of a storage tank will increase more than proportionately with increases in its surface area, and if the cost of the tank is proportional to surface area, unit storage costs will decline as tanks of larger and larger size are employed. Again, if a particular productive process requires liquid to be kept at a certain temperature, and heat loss is proportional to the surface area of the tank containing the liquid, the cost of keeping a unit of the liquid at a certain temperature will decline as the size of the tank is increased, because the cost of compensating for heat loss will increase less than in proportion to the capacity of the container. Another example of geometric relationships as a source of economies of scale concerns pipes. The capacity of a pipe depends on the cross-sectional area of the pipe, which increases more than proportionately with increases in the pipe's circumference – the chief determinant of material requirements used in the pipe's construction. Apart from the economies of scale arising in circumstances in which an increase in capacity and output does not require a proportionate increase in material, the labor cost of constructing or installing items of fixed equipment often varies with the amount of material being worked, rather than with capacity of the equipment being installed. Therefore, these geometric relationships often save labor costs in addition to material costs.

It must be stressed that merely increasing the physical size of items of equipment does not inevitably lead to falling unit costs. Larger dimensions of a storage tank or pipeline may, for example, require stronger materials. Alternatively, a larger ship may require larger engines, and after some size is reached reductions in unit carrying costs attributable to larger dimensions may be offset by increased fuel costs per unit carried.

Apart from geometric relationships, a second source of economies of scale arises from the fact that some inputs are indivisible below a certain size. Some items of capital equipment required to perform certain operations, for example, do not come in small sizes. Up to the capacity output of minimum-sized indivisible inputs, the cost of these inputs per unit of output produced will fall as scale of output increases, and therefore LRAC will decline with increases in scale of output, assuming, of course, that other input costs per unit of output are constant, or do not increase sufficiently to increase the total unit cost of larger scales of output.

The influence of indivisibility of machinery on unit costs may be magnified where balancing of processes is involved. Suppose, for example, that production of a particular product involves three different processes performed respectively by indivisible machines with a capacity output of 1000, 500, and 750 units. Cost per unit of final product is minimized when 3000 units of output (or any multiple of this amount) are produced; this equals the least common denominator of the capacity outputs of each of the three machines. 3000 units of output requires 3, 6, and 4 machines respectively working at full capacity. At any smaller output level, the unit cost of producing the final product will be greater because at least one type of machine will be operating at less than capacity level.

Indivisibility of inputs is not confined to items of capital equipment. Human inputs may account for economies of scale. A manager may be able to supervise production of 1000 units of output as easily as 500. The fact that, up to a point, his salary is spread over more and more units of output is by itself not sufficient to explain declining *long-run* average cost; in addition, the managerial input must be indivisible in the sense that it is impossible to acquire a *different* manager to supervise smaller levels of output at proportionately lower salary than that paid to managers supervising larger output levels.

Another type of indivisibility which may result in declining LRAC with increases in scale of output concerns the division of labor. If, for example, two men produce more output when each specializes in one process than when both perform both tasks, the unit cost of output will be higher when total output produced is not sufficient to require the services of more than one man working full time. Unit costs would only remain constant if it were possible to hire two men, each working half time.

There are other examples of economies of scale. Whenever set-up costs are involved in a particular productive operation, such as fixing a die in a press, the set-up cost per unit of output diminishes with increases in the scale of output. In addition, longer production runs often make it possible to reduce unit costs by automating production and substituting capital for labor. Finally, optimal inventory levels are likely to increase less than proportionately with increases in the scale of a firm's output, resulting in a reduction in inventory cost per unit of output. The principle underlying so-called 'stochastic economies of scale' associated with inventories can be explained briefly, using the example of spare components kept on hand to take care of possible machinery breakdowns, as follows. Optimal component inventory levels per unit of output depend upon two characteristics of the probability distribution of expected component failures per unit of output: the mean probable number of failures per unit of output, and the variance of the expected number of failures per unit of output. If the failure of one component is independent of other such failures, then as scale of output increases and capacity is increased through duplication of machinery, the mean number of expected failures per unit of output remains unchanged, but the variance of expected failures per unit of output declines. Therefore, the optimum inventory of spare components per unit of capacity and output will decrease. The principle also applies to inventory levels of work-in-progress and finished goods kept, respectively, to meet random work-flow stoppages or variations in demand. Stochastic economies of scale can also apply to the size of the stand-by labor force needed to repair breakdowns in machinery and equipment.

The level of output at which unit costs are minimized is sometimes referred to as the minimal optimal scale of output. This terminology, as mentioned in Chapter 1, should not be interpreted to mean that the producer's objective is always to minimize the unit cost of producing and distributing his product. This objective only becomes a condition of survival in a purely competitive market, for in such a case the level of output which minimizes unit costs also maximizes (long-run) profits. In other market situations, however, unit cost minimization may conflict with the decision-maker's objectives. In Figure 2–3, for example, assuming that the decision-maker's objective is profit maximization, the optimal level of output is Q_1, which differs from the (average) cost-minimizing level of output Q_2.

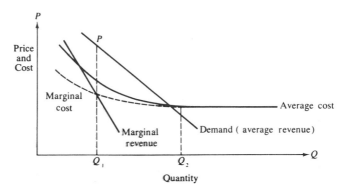

Figure 2–3. Profit-maximizing versus average cost-minimizing levels of output.

The empirical evidence contained in a number of studies listed at the end of this chapter suggests that there are economies of scale in the production of many goods and services, leading to a downward-sloping LRAC curve at low levels of output.

Turning now to diseconomies of scale, a number of hypotheses have been put forward purporting to explain why LRAC curves must eventually turn up. If, as a firm expands the scale of its output, the price which it must pay per unit of one or more of the inputs used by the firm increases, the unit cost of its output may increase; that is, rising input supply curves may be responsible for an upturn in the firm's LRAC curve. This is often referred to as a 'pecuniary' diseconomy of scale, in contrast to the 'technological' economies and diseconomies of scale which underlie disproportionate increases in total cost when input prices are unchanged.

A second class of argument involves the concept of managerial diseconomies of scale. In this context, it is not sufficient to point out that there is a physical limit to what a manager (or a fixed team of managers) can do. This may be relevant to explaining why short-run average cost curves turn up after some scale of output is reached, but in order to explain why long-run average cost curves turn up because of managerial diseconomies, it is necessary to explain why, for example, a proportionate increase in the scale of all inputs *including managerial inputs* causes the firm's total costs to increase more than in proportion to output.

One prominent explanation of why this may occur involves the concept of control loss. See the article by O. E. Williamson (35) on this subject. In all but the very smallest business organizations, the information upon which the top executive, or peak coordinator, must base his decisions, and the instructions based upon this information, must be transmitted across successive hierarchical levels. Such transmission results in a serial reproduction loss, or distortion, of the information and instructions, even though the objectives of people forming successive links in the hierarchical chain may not conflict in any way. Increasing the scale of a firm's output will increase the number of hierarchical levels over which information and instructions must pass, which exposes the data to further distortion and therefore results in a reduction in the *quality* of both the information reaching the peak coordinator and the instructions passed down to operating personnel. In addition, since the capacity of the peak coordinator for assimilating information and issuing instructions is limited, he can only acquire the additional information and issue the additional instructions, necessitated by an expansion in the scale of the firm's operations, by sacrificing some of the detail provided before the expansion (assuming he was initially fully employed). That is, the *quantity* of information received and transmitted per unit of output will be less after expansion than before.

This reduction in quality of data provided to the peak coordinator and in quality of instructions supplied to operating units made necessary by an expansion in the scale of a firm's output is referred to as control loss. Because of this phenomenon, it may be argued that the behavior of a firm's operating units will not correspond as closely to the peak coordinator's objective of minimizing costs as it did prior to expansion of the scale of the firm's output, resulting in an increase in the firm's unit costs as the scale of output is increased.

The reader is reminded that economies and diseconomies of scale refer to the behavior of unit costs in a given state of technological knowledge. A tendency for unit costs to rise as the result of control loss experienced as firms expand the scale of their output may be partially or totally offset by new technological developments which widen the information-processing capability and span of control of the firm's peak coordinator or his subordinates. That is, static limits to firm size may be constantly receding with the passage of time as new knowledge results in improvements in ability to coordinate and control the operations of large-scale enterprises.

Another class of arguments focuses upon uncertainty as a factor causing the LRAC curve associated with a firm's product to turn up after some scale of output is reached; see D. Schwartzman's article (20), for example. If one of the functions of management is that of adjusting a firm's operations to unpredictable variations in the demand and cost conditions confronting the firm, then the existence of any degree of uncertainty confronting a firm will give rise to the need for management and therefore cause the firm's LRAC curve to turn up due to the control loss phenomenon discussed in the preceding paragraphs. It is also undoubtedly true that the greater the degree of uncertainty regarding changes in conditions confronting a firm, the greater are likely to be the costs of dealing with uncertainty associated with gathering and organizing information concerning the firm's economic environment and making decisions which provide the appropriate instructions to subordinates. That is, more information will be required by management to assist in the detection of changes in conditions, and more frequent decisions will be required, as the degree of uncertainty confronting a firm increases. This is not, however, the same as saying that uncertainty causes increasing unit costs with increases in the scale of a firm's output; it merely explains why the cost of producing a particular level of output will be higher, the greater the degree of uncertainty confronting the firm producing the output. A crucial question is whether the degree of uncertainty itself is likely to vary with increases in the scale of a firm's output, either increasing and causing the LRAC curve to turn up earlier than it would otherwise do as a result of the control loss phenomenon, or decreasing and therefore postponing or offsetting the tendency for LRAC to turn up because of control loss. Fluctuations in the demand or cost conditions confronting an individual firm operating in a particular industry may result from changes in the demand or cost conditions confronting the industry as a whole, caused by influences external to the industry; alternatively, such fluctuations may occur because of changes in the behavior of the firm's rivals in the industry, even though the demand and cost conditions confronting the industry as a whole are unchanged. It can be argued that the degree of uncertainty associated with the activities of a firm's rivals in the industry will be smaller, the larger the proportion of industry output supplied by the firm and the smaller the number of rivals in the industry. Under conditions of monopoly, for example, this source of uncertainty will be completely absent. On the other hand, the larger the firm's output, relative to industry output, the greater will be the absolute impact on the firm of a change in the industry demand or cost conditions, and from this point of view it can therefore be argued that the degree of uncertainty confronting a firm increases as the scale of the firm's output increases. As this example indicates, purely a priori arguments concerning the relationship between the scale of a firm's output and the degree of uncertainty confronting the firm are rather inconclusive.

Empirical evidence accumulated thus far seems to be inconsistent, with an upturn in the LRAC curve associated with the product of most industries. There may be no upturn, or it may occur at a larger output level than that achieved by firms in practice. There is, as yet, no general agreement among economists as to whether the empirical evidence is consistent with constant costs (above a certain minimum scale of output) or continually declining LRAC. The reasons for disagreement concerning these matters revolve around problems encountered when an attempt is made to estimate cost conditions existing in various industries in practice. These matters will be treated further in the section entitled Estimating Cost Conditions.

In concluding this section it should be noted that the preceding discussion assumes that the state of knowledge concerning production methods, as reflected by the position and shape of the isoquants in Figure 2–1, remains unchanged. The factors influencing the shape and position of the LRAC curve associated with a particular state of technological knowledge and the efficiencies and prices of various inputs should be clearly distinguished from *dynamic* influences which affect the LRAC curve, possibly changing its position and shape, with the passage of time. For example, the efficiency of inputs in performing any particular operation may increase over time due to repetition and the phenomenon usually referred to as 'learning'. This will tend to lower the LRAC of producing any particular output level with the passage of time even though the state of technological knowledge and input prices remain unchanged. The resulting relationship between LRAC and time can be plotted and is referred to as a 'learning curve'. This relationship is conceptually distinct from the static LRAC curve previously discussed in this section. At any point in time, the currently available state of technology and input efficiencies underlying the static LRAC curve are outside the control of the decision-maker, but he can choose to operate any point on the LRAC curve. In contrast, the decision-maker cannot choose between different points on the 'learning curve', for different points on this curve refer to different points in time, which is outside the decision-maker's control. It should be added, however, that knowledge of the learning curve may influence a decision-maker's expectations about *future* cost–output relationships and may thereby indirectly influence the choice of current input-mix he selects.

Apart from the effect of changes in input efficiencies associated with learning, changes in the state of technological knowledge itself with the passage of time will of course influence the position and shape of the LRAC curve.

Variety of Output Dimensions

To this point, the concept of a firm's 'output level' has not been clearly defined. Following a seminal article by Armen Alchian (1), it is now generally recognized that the output level of any particular product or service has a number of dimensions, including, for example, the rate of output per period, the total contemplated volume of production, and the period in time during which the production is to take place. These different dimensions are often related in the sense that decisions concerning some of the dimensions will automatically determine others. For example, given planned volume and output rate per period, the total length of time during which production will take place is automatically determined (though not necessarily the exact timing, as emphasized by Whitin (32), who also stresses that there are many other facets of output in addition to the three dimensions already cited). Alternatively, given the planned time period during which production will take place, and the volume, the production rate per period is determined.

Although these different facets of a firm's output may be related, they are capable of varying in a number of different ways, and decisions to change one rather than another facet of the firm's output will usually have very different implications for the behavior of total cost of the firm's operations. For example, increases in the firm's output rate, ceteris paribus, will raise total cost and may do so more than proportionately due to rising input prices; on the other hand, an increase in volume may increase total cost less than proportionately, if no added set-up costs are required. In fact, many of the factors referred to as economies of scale are examples of the effect of increasing total volume on total costs, rather than output rate increases. As Hirschleifer has shown (11), volume and rate of output may both be increased. With proportionate increases in both, Hirschleifer concluded that total costs would on balance increase more than proportionately, resulting in U-shaped average and marginal cost relationships similar to those of conventional price theory. There is no reason to stop there, however; many dimensions of a firm's output plans could in principle be simultaneously varied, resulting in differences in observed effects on the firm's total costs. As a result, there is no such thing as 'the' total, average, or marginal cost relationship; there are many, one for each different dimension of output, and others for the various combinations in which output dimensions could be varied. In addition to the authors previously cited, see also D. Dewey's article (6) on this point.

Which output and associated cost concept is 'relevant'? The answer is the one which a *decision-maker* considers to be relevant in his decision-making. This may be related to the nature of the response the decision-maker expects to elicit from *buyers*, for a prime consideration in choosing between output levels is the influence on the firm's *revenues*, as indicated in more detail in the next chapter. Thus, for example, a decision-maker in electricity may consider potential volume demanded infinite, so the only relevant consideration is choice between alternative output rates per period. In contrast, in the case of a good which may be quickly obsolete, the relationship between volume and cost may be crucial.

The proposition that the nature of the marginal cost concept which is appropriate for decision-making can be ascertained only by reference to the objective function and constraints facing a particular decision-maker, including demand characteristics and available information, is emphasized by Turvey in an article dealing with the marginal cost concept appropriate for decision-making in the electricity generating industry (28). He argues that the marginal cost which is relevant to pricing decisions in this industry relates to a permanent increase in the rate of industry output, since tariff structures in the industry cannot be changed frequently and because consumer decisions usually involve the acquisition of durable complementary goods. Accordingly, the emphasis in Turvey's exposition is on the *timing* of output rate changes rather than on the volume or level of permanent output rates themselves. Permanent increases in the output rate can be postponed, thereby influencing the present value of the total costs of producing that output rate at any particular point in time. The associated marginal cost of a permanent output rate change is therefore the excess of (a) the present value in that year of total costs with a permanent output rate increase starting then, over (b) the present value in that year of total costs with the same permanent output rate increase postponed until the following year. Turvey's analysis is a valuable reminder that what is needed for decision-making in any particular industry is a cost model specific to that industry, incorporating the technological and demand constraints peculiar to that industry.

Allocating Costs Between Joint Products

If a firm produces a single product, the total cost of that product is simply the sum of the costs of the inputs used in its production. Most firms produce a variety of different products simultaneously. In such circumstances, if one is interested in determining the cost of one of the products, the problem arises of allocating the cost of inputs between the various products produced. Two cases may be distinguished in this connection: one is a situation in which particular inputs produce joint products whose proportions cannot be varied; an example would be the production of hides and beef from a cow. The other is a situation in which the proportion of different outputs produced from particular inputs can be varied; an example would be the production of different grades of lumber from a log.

Unfortunately, there is often much needless confusion and unnecessary mystique surrounding the problem of allocating joint costs, due to a combination of reasons which includes failure to specify the purpose of cost allocation, to recognize and specify the general principle which is applicable, and to distinguish between optimal and non-optimal situations (see Harris and Chapin (9), Littlechild (18), Walters (29) and Weil (30)). All these aspects will be dealt with below.

For purposes of determining the optimal level of a single decision variable, such as the level of a particular input or output, the general principle which is applicable is that the net effect of a change in the decision variable on the level of the decision-maker's constrained objective function be zero. For a profit-maximizing firm this requires that the effect of a change in the level of the decision variable on the firm's total revenue (marginal revenue) equal the effect on the firm's total cost (marginal cost). Only if this condition is met will it not be possible to increase the level of the firm's profit by selecting an alternative level of the decision variable in question.

Exactly the same principle is applicable in the case of simultaneous variations in a number of the firm's decision variables. That is, if it is possible to vary a number of the firm's decision variables simultaneously in such a manner that the firm's total revenue and total cost change by different amounts, the level of the firm's profits can be increased and the level of its decision variables will not be optimal. The condition which is necessary in order for a profit-maximizing firm's decision variables to be at optimal levels is therefore as follows:

$$\Sigma(MR_i - MC_i) = 0, \text{ or } \Sigma MR_i = \Sigma MC_i$$

where MR_i and MC_i represent the effect of a change in the ith decision variable on the level of the firm's total revenue, and total cost, respectively. This condition simply states that the algebraic sum of the effects of simultaneous changes in a number of decision variables on the firm's profit must be zero or, what is equivalent, that the algebraic sum of the effects of changes in each decision variable on total revenue equal the algebraic sum of their effects on total cost. This principle is compatible both with changes in decision variables in the same, or in opposite, directions.

The preceding condition may be rewritten as follows:

$$MR_i = \Sigma MC - (\Sigma MR_i - MR_i)$$

which states that for the level of any individual decision variable to be optimal, the effect of a change in that decision variable on the firm's total revenue must equal the difference between the effects of any simultaneous changes in all decision variables on the firm's total costs and the effect of any simultaneous changes in all *other* decision variables on the firm's total revenue. The expression on the right-hand side of the equality sign can be interpreted as the 'marginal opportunity cost' of a change in the ith decision variable when a number of decision variables are changed simultaneously.

The meaning of the marginal opportunity cost of a change in one of the decision variables can be easily understood in the case in which two decision variables, say two types of output, are changed in such a manner that the firm's total costs remain unchanged. In this case, the marginal opportunity cost of an increase in the ith output level is equal to the expression

$$(MC_i + MC_j) - MR_j$$

where MC_j and MR_j are negative and the expression in brackets is by definition zero. The marginal opportunity cost of the increase in output of i is therefore the marginal revenue from output j which is forgone by increasing i. In this case, the optimal condition therefore requires that MR_i be equated with MR_j; if they are not equal the firm can obviously increase its total revenue from a given expenditure on inputs, and therefore its profits, by changing the proportion of its total output allocated to i and j. This condition is therefore relevant in determining the firm's optimal output proportions in circumstances in which these proportions can be varied.

If changes in i and j output in opposite directions do not leave the firm's total cost unchanged, the above principle remains applicable and yields an appropriate measure of the marginal opportunity cost of changes in one of the output levels which must be equated with the marginal revenue associated with that decision variable if the decision variable is to be at an optimal level.

The preceding principle is also applicable in the case of joint products which must be produced in fixed proportions. Assuming, again for expositional convenience, that there are two joint products, i and j, MR_i and MR_j will in this case both be of the same sign, and the effect of the changes in i and j on total cost will be the marginal cost of the combined joint products. The marginal opportunity cost of the change in each output level is given by the following expressions:

$$MC_i = \Sigma MC \text{ (joint marginal costs)} - MR_j \text{ (marginal revenue associated with increases in other products)}$$

$$MC_j = \Sigma MC - MR_i$$

The appropriateness of the above marginal cost concept for each product may be demonstrated by focusing upon the reason for allocating joint costs, which is to yield optimal decisions concerning the level of the firm's decision variables. If decisions concerning joint products are centralized, in the sense that the decision-maker has information concerning the demand for both products, then allocation of the joint marginal cost between the products is unnecessary; the optimal condition simply requires that the total marginal cost of the joint products equal the sum of the marginal revenues associated with each product. However, if decisions concerning each joint product are decentralized, a marginal cost concept for each individual product will in general be necessary in order to prevent decisions regarding the level of one of the joint products from resulting in a situation which is not optimal from the point of view of both products. The preceding marginal opportunity cost concept for each product is appropriate for the following reasons: when MR_i is less than the marginal opportunity cost of i according to the above definition, this is the signal for the level of output i to be expanded. This will automatically increase the level of output j also, which is desirable since MR_j will also automatically be less than the marginal opportunity cost of output j, and the effect of increasing output i (and j) on the firm's total cost will be less than the effect of the increase in both types of output on the firm's total revenues. In other words, a decision regarding the output level of one of the joint products based on a comparison of that product's marginal revenue and marginal opportunity cost as defined above will lead to decisions which are optimal from the point of view of both products.

Apart from decentralized decisions concerning individual joint products, another situation in which it would be necessary to obtain a marginal cost concept for individual joint products is where a producer is confronted by an opportunity to 'buy in' one of the joint products. In these circumstances, the net effect on the firm's profits which is forgone by buying one of the joint products instead of producing both joint products is equal to the marginal cost of the joint products minus the marginal revenue associated with the other product, which is the marginal opportunity cost concept defined above. Another reason frequently advanced for allocating costs between joint products is the need for accounting data. In this connection it should be noted that accounting data rarely utilize marginal cost data, which are appropriate for decision-making purposes; rather, it is the average or total cost data that are recorded. However, if marginal cost data are to be recorded, it follows from the preceding optimality condition that when the output level of the joint products is less than optimal, the marginal opportunity cost of product i will be less than the marginal revenue associated with i, and since the same condition will be true of product j, the actual marginal cost of the joint products will be above the sum of the marginal opportunity costs of the two products as previously defined.

Failure to distinguish between optimal and non-optimal output levels of joint products can also lead to incorrect inferences concerning the appropriate marginal cost concept for each product. In an optimum situation, the marginal opportunity cost of each joint product, as previously defined, will necessarily equal the marginal revenue associated with that product. The inference should not be drawn, however, that the appropriate marginal cost concept for each individual product is its *own* marginal revenue; rather, it is the marginal cost of the joint products minus the marginal revenue associated with the *other* joint product(s).

The problem of determining optimal input and output levels in the case of joint products, and the distinction between the fixed and variable output-proportion cases can be demonstrated diagrammatically. Assuming that the demand for the different products is independent, to find the optimal output level of joint products produced in fixed proportions the appropriate procedure is to sum the marginal revenue curves for each product *vertically* in order to find the output level where the sum of the marginal revenues equals the marginal cost of the joint products, and then to set prices for each product to equate demand for each product with the optimal quantity. This procedure is demonstrated in Chapter 11 in connection with peak-load pricing, which may be regarded as a particular instance of the joint-product costing and pricing problem. In contrast, where output proportions are variable, the situation is analytically equivalent to that of determining the allocation of a discriminating monopolist's output between different markets. As demonstrated in Chapter 3, in this case the marginal revenue curves associated with each product (market) are summed *horizontally* in order to find the overall output level which equates marginal revenue in each market to the marginal cost of production.

Before concluding this section, it is necessary to emphasize that the appropriate marginal cost concept for decision-making depends on the objective of the decision-maker. The preceding analysis deals with profit-maximizing levels of joint products. If the decision-maker's objective were not profit maximization, the optimum principle, that the sum of marginal effects of changes in decision variables on the decision-maker's objective must be zero, remains unaltered. However, the marginal effects on the decision-maker's objective will no longer be differences between marginal revenue and marginal cost; if welfare maximization is the objective, for example, the marginal demand price of output rather than the marginal revenue is the appropriate variable to insert in the optimum condition, for reasons to be explained in Chapter 10. Despite this, the principle for calculating the marginal opportunity cost of a single decision variable remains unaltered and yields the following expression:

Marginal opportunity cost$_i$ = MC (joint marginal cost) − D-price$_j$

which must be equated with the demand-price of output i in order for the level of i (and all joint outputs) to maximize aggregate welfare.

Cost-Minimization, X-Efficiency, and Managerial Utility Maximization

To this point, the preceding discussion of the factors which underlie the relationship between the total, average and marginal cost of a firm's product and alternative output dimensions has assumed that the total cost of producing any particular output level was minimized. This section outlines two types of reasons why a firm's total costs might not be the minimum level feasible in the light of existing knowledge concerning production technology and input-supply conditions. The first type of reason to be discussed is associated with the theory of 'X-efficiency' and the second with the theory of managerial utility maximization.

The term 'X-inefficiency', originally coined by H. Leibenstein (14), is now used generally as an alternative to the term 'technical inefficiency' to describe a situation in which a firm's total costs are not minimized because the actual output from given inputs is less than the maximum feasible level. As Leibenstein has pointed out in a number of articles, if one considers the motivations of the individual inputs combined in a firm, output maximization will not generally maximize the satisfaction of the human inputs involved. Even where the income earned by human input is directly related to the output it produces, the level of an individual's satisfaction depends on other things also. Some of these, like a leisurely pace of work, are negatively correlated with the individual's output, so that an optimum allocation of an individual's time will rarely involve maximization of output per unit of time spent working for the firm. For the same set of human inputs purchased and the same knowledge of production techniques available to a firm, a variety of output levels is possible, depending on the preferences and constraints outside the firm confronting the individuals in question, and the preferred behavior of the inputs will not generally maximize the output level of the firm. The formal system of financial rewards, promotions, and conditions warranting dismissal within the firm may be used to modify the behavior of the inputs towards output-maximizing behavior; such a system, however, will necessarily entail monitoring and policing costs in order to attempt to enforce the desired types of behavior and to prevent the effort levels of individual inputs from dropping gradually towards levels which increase the satisfaction of individual inputs involved in the production process. Only if policing costs were zero would it be optimal for managers to ensure output maximization from given inputs. Policing costs will exceed zero, however, since managers themselves rarely have detailed knowledge of production processes necessary to attempt to define precisely job descriptions for every individual in the firm, and the acquisition of such knowledge would be very costly. Even if such information were available, moreover, extremely close supervision is also usually costly and resented by employees. In principle, policing activities should be expanded until the marginal effect on reducing total cost of producing a particular output level equals the marginal cost of policing activities; this optimal condition will result in a situation in which total production costs are not minimized, but exceed minimum levels by an amount equal to the total cost of policing activities.

The theory of X-inefficiency consists of recognizing that, even if cost-minimization is an objective of a firm's higher-level decision-makers, this will conflict with the objectives of operatives, and requires monitoring and policing costs to offset a tendency for the total costs of a particular operation to exceed the minimum feasible level. A different reason why a firm's total costs may not be minimized is that cost-minimization may conflict with the objectives of a firm's higher-level decision-makers themselves. In certain circumstances, outlined below, the objective of managerial utility maximization referred to in Chapter 1 may result in a failure to attempt to minimize the total costs of the firm's operation.

If managerial utility depends on profits, sales revenue, or growth, cost-minimization will be a condition which is necessary in order to maximize managerial utility. This proposition is easy to understand, for if costs are above the minimum level necessary to perform a particular set of operations, a reduction in total costs will increase the profits resulting from that operation. This, in turn, would either permit sales revenue to be increased at an unchanged profit level, or would permit growth to be increased by expanding the supply of investment funds available to the firm.

In contrast, if managerial utility depends on the level of one of the firm's inputs, it can be shown that the total cost of performing the firm's operations will tend to be higher than is necessary due to the existence of an incentive for managers to use excessive amounts of the input in question. In his original exposition of this 'staff-preference' model of managerial behavior, O. E. Williamson (33, 34) assumed that the inputs in question affected the level of the firm's total revenue rather than the output level of the firm, and showed that the managerial utility maximizer will use more of the input than maximizes the firm's profits. The same argument and conclusions are applicable within the context of the analytical framework used in this chapter without the need to introduce revenue conditions, however, as will now be demonstrated.

Consider one of the isoquants in Figure 2–1, indicating alternative combinations of two inputs which can be used to produce a particular output level. Since output is unchanged at all such points, the total revenue obtained from the sale of that output is also unchanged at all points on the curve. The profits earned by the firm from the production of that output level then depend solely on the total cost of the output level which, given the input prices faced by the firm, depends on the method of production, or input combination, used by the firm. Starting at an input combination on the isoquant above and to the left of the cost-minimizing input combination, and moving down the curve to the right, total costs will fall and profits rise until the cost-minimizing input combination is reached. If one continues to move down the isoquant to the right, the total cost of producing the output level will rise again, and profits will fall. The resulting relationship between the level of one of the inputs, say the input on the horizontal axis of Figure 2–1, and the firm's profits, can be plotted as in Figure 2–4. Point x corresponds to the cost-minimizing level of that input in Figure 2–1.

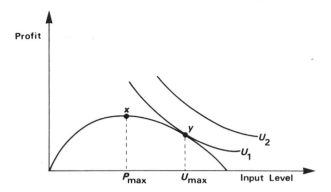

Figure 2–4. Optimal input level under profit- and managerial-utility maximization.

If a manager derives no satisfaction directly from the input in question, it follows that alternative combinations of profits and levels of the input yielding the manager a particular level of satisfaction would be represented by horizontal lines in Figure 2–4. Successively higher lines represent higher profit levels, and therefore higher satisfaction. The satisfaction-maximizing level of the input is x, which maximizes profits.

In contrast, if the manager derives some satisfaction directly from the input, the lines, or 'indifference curves', which represent alternative combinations of profit and input levels yielding a particular level of satisfaction must slope down from left to right indicating that higher profits must be offset by lower input level in order to leave the level of the individual's satisfaction unchanged. In these circumstances, the satisfaction-maximizing level of the input will be y, involving more of the input than minimizes the total cost of producing the firm's output. Point y corresponds to a point to the right of the minimum-cost input combination associated with a particular output level in Figure 2–1.

Although an incentive exists for a manager who derives satisfaction directly from some of the inputs used by the firm to use more of that input than is compatible with minimizing the total cost of the firm's operations, whether the manager is able to indulge this preference depends on whether any constraints exist which might prevent him from doing so. Since profits from the firm's operations are lower than they could be, owners' interests clearly conflict with those of the manager, giving rise to an incentive for owners to replace the manager. Alternatively, managers of other firms whose utility does not depend on input levels may perceive an opportunity to take over the firm and make a gain. In the limiting case in which a manager is constrained to make maximum profits or lose control of the firm he manages, he will select point x in Figure 2–4; the reason could be depicted diagrammatically by a 'profit constraint'. To the extent that information regarding the manager's failure to minimize total costs of the firm's operations is not available to the owners or managers of other firms, or sanctions are weaker, the height of this profit constraint will be lower, implying that the manager is able to select a level of the input above x and, ultimately, if no external constraints on the manager's behavior exist, to select y itself. It is important to distinguish the rationale for the incentive for a manager to fail to minimize total costs from the actual ability to do so, which depends on the nature and strength of external constraints facing the manager. The latter, and therefore the incidence of failure to minimize total cost for reasons connected with managerial utility maximization, may be very different for industrial firms, whose shares are marketable, and hospitals, for example.

Up to this point, the X-inefficiency and managerial utility maximization reasons for failure of firms to minimize the total costs of their operations have been distinguished. As the discussion in the preceding paragraph suggests, they are really very closely related, since the X-efficiency concept may be extended to explain why, when there is conflict between the interests of owners and the behavior of managers, it may not 'pay' the owners to remove managers even though it is evident that the managers fail to minimize costs and maximize profits. The explanation may be that whatever policing actions the owners take in an effort to make managerial behavior correspond closer to cost minimization and profit maximization would involve them in extra costs and/or expenditure of effort, and in some circumstances this would on balance lower the owners' utility level despite the increased profits resulting from such action. In this context, the X-efficiency theory is merely being extended to deal with the relationship between managers and owners, instead of the manager–worker relationship to which it was originally applied. See Blois (4), Crew, Jones-Lee and Rowley (5), Leibenstein (14, 15, 16) and Shelton (21), who deal with the subject of X-efficiency.

Estimating Cost Conditions

There are three main methods of attempting to estimate the cost conditions associated with the production of a particular type of product or service. These methods attempt to answer the following question: given the state of technology and knowledge, how do costs of producing a given product vary with the level of output? First, there is statistical cost analysis, which uses information regarding the actual cost of producing output in firms producing different levels of the output in question. Second, the technological studies or engineering estimates method uses estimates of what the costs of producing different levels of output would be, even though these output levels are not in fact being produced. The third method, the survival technique, employs data on shares of industry output contributed by different-sized firms in order to infer the shape of the cost curve. For examples of studies dealing with the statistical cost method of estimation, see Johnston (13) and Benston (3); for articles on the technological studies method, see Bain (2) and Haldi and Whitcomb (8); and for studies of the survival technique, see Saving (19), Shepherd (22), Stigler (26) and Weiss (31).

The method used will often be dictated by the information available. Thus, for example, the first method requires a reasonably large number of firms producing the product in question while the third method requires at least two firms, and if these requirements are not satisfied, method two is the only alternative available.

The first method encounters problems associated with the valuation of fixed capital assets. The outlay on these inputs, which is a cost of production, is by convention spread over a number of periods in the firm's accounts. Even though different firms use identical capital equipment, the capital input cost figure in any accounting period may reflect differences in the depreciation methods used by different firms. Not only the methods used, but the time period over which the cost of equipment is spread, may differ from firm to firm, reflecting differences in estimates of how long the equipment will last physically or economically, and therefore in the appropriate period over which the cost should be spread. The relevant consideration, if one is concerned with estimating the *long-run* average cost of producing a product, is the cost of new equipment embodying the most efficient known methods of production, not the cost of old equipment. The capital equipment used by firms in an industry may not represent the most efficient known methods of producing a particular level of output. This might result, for example, from different firms' entering the industry at different historical points in time when technical knowledge differed. In these circumstances, statistical cost analysis will not yield an estimate of the relationship between unit cost and scale of output *using the most efficient known methods.*

Even if firms use the same depreciation methods and their equipment embodies the latest technological knowledge, firms may be producing scales of output with capital equipment which does not minimize the long-run average cost of producing those output levels. That is, a firm may be in a position of short-run equilibrium only, waiting for its existing equipment to wear out before replacing the equipment with equipment that will reduce the cost of producing its existing level of output. In these circumstances, statistical cost analysis will confuse short-run with long-run average cost conditions. This is perhaps the most serious deficiency of the statistical cost study method; cross-section data concerning the cost of producing a particular kind of output in different sized firms will inevitably reflect short-run costs unless every firm in the industry is in a position of long-run equilibrium. The requirement that all firms be in a position of long-run equilibrium will hardly ever be satisfied in practice. In addition, one cannot assume that the observed short-run costs of producing a particular level of output in a large number of firms of equal size will be evenly distributed around the long-run cost of producing that output level. This will in fact be impossible, because it follows from the definition of long-run cost that the short-run cost of producing a particular output level can exceed but cannot possibly be less than the long-run cost of producing that output level.

The second method of estimating cost conditions, the technological studies method, is sometimes criticized on the grounds that the cost figures obtained by using this method are hypothetical. However, if one is interested in knowing what the cost of output levels which differ from the one currently being produced would be (and such information is indispensable to optimizing behavior, that is, knowing whether one can achieve one's objectives any better) that is precisely the information required by the decision-maker. It is not the hypothetical nature of the data that is to be criticized; rather, the difficulty of obtaining *accurate* hypothetical information, particularly estimates of distribution and other nonproduction costs.

The first and second methods of estimating cost conditions are complicated by the presence of multiproduct firms, that is, firms which produce a number of different products. In such cases, the cost of inputs that are used to produce more than one product must be apportioned between the products in order to provide an estimate of the cost of individual products. As with a single-product firm, the relevant cost to a multiproduct firm of one product is its marginal cost; however, accounting cost data are often based upon a more or less arbitrary allocation which does not reflect marginal cost accurately.

The third method, referred to as the survivor or survival technique, proceeds to estimate the shape of the long-run average cost curve for the product of a particular industry in the following manner. The firms in an industry are grouped into size classes, and the share of industry output (or some other index of size) accounted for by each size class at two or more points in time is compared. The shape of the long-run cost curve is inferred by assuming that changes in the share of industry output of any size class are related to the average cost of producing and distributing the product in that size class. Size classes experiencing an increase in the share of industry output are assumed to have minimum average costs. Size classes experiencing a declining share of industry output are assumed to be relatively inefficient, that is, are assumed to have higher unit costs. It has been further assumed in some studies employing this technique that the more rapid the rate at which a size class loses its share of the industry's output, the higher the unit cost of production in that size class relative to the cost of production in firms whose share is increasing. It does not necessarily follow, however, that those sizes which are experiencing a falling share of industry output have higher costs than those firms experiencing increases in share. Firms experiencing reductions in the share of industry output may be just as efficient but may face slightly different economic environments which prevent them from growing as rapidly as other firms; alternatively, the objectives of such firms may involve lower growth rates than other firms having the same unit costs.

The fundamental postulate of the survival principle is that competition between different-sized firms sifts out the more efficient enterprises, and that the firms which survive best will be those operating at lower average costs. It is essential, therefore, that firms used in a study employing the survival principle be competing in the same market; otherwise, the eliminating mechanism will be absent. There must be no barriers, based upon spatial distance or product differentiation, which prevent competition. Also, the technique may not yield an accurate estimate of the shape of the LRAC curve if there are factors dampening the elimination process, such as price agreements or collusive agreements to restrain competition.

The survival technique can indicate only the shape of the LRAC curve showing the size of firm, or range of firm sizes, where cost per unit of output is lowest; it cannot, as can the other two methods, indicate the precise level of unit money cost at any particular scale of output.

Although the survival technique has been used to yield an estimate of the shape of the LRAC curve in certain industries, it must be emphasized that unless technology has remained constant over the period to which the study refers, such an interpretation of the results may be invalid. Rather than reflect relative efficiency in the static sense of the average cost of producing different levels of output in an environment in which technological information is the same for all firms, the technique may instead reflect the relative efficiency of different-sized firms in producing and in taking advantage of new knowledge. Unit costs may be lower, and the share of industry output may be growing faster, because firms of a certain size are more efficient in producing and using new knowledge. For example, it is possible to visualize circumstances in which there are no economies of scale in the static sense of lower unit cost at larger scale of output, yet in which the survival technique will yield an L-shaped cost function, indicating that, up to a certain size, larger firms are more efficient in the use of resources to add to knowledge, improve products, and reduce costs through technical innovation.

A number of economists have attempted to infer the shape of the long-run average cost curve associated with individual products from information about the growth rates of different-sized firms; see, for example, the article by Hymer and Pashigian (12). Under this approach, firms in an industry are grouped into size classes according to some index of size, such as assets, the growth rate of each firm's assets over a specified period of time is calculated, and the shape of the long-run average cost curve is inferred by assuming that the average growth rate of firms in each size class and unit costs in that size class are inversely related.

Before proceeding to outline the evidence revealed by this approach, it is appropriate to consider the rationale of such a method. In what circumstances do larger growth rates indicate lower unit cost? At any level of industry price, the profit rate on capital investment will be greater for firms with lower unit cost. Growth of a firm's operations requires funds to finance expansion, and profits largely determine the amount of funds available for expansion because profits are necessary either to finance expansion internally or to obtain outside finance. Therefore, the maximum attainable growth rate will be related to the profit rate, which, given industry price, depends upon unit cost.

Although maximum attainable growth rates will be related to the height of unit cost, it does not necessarily follow that actual growth rates will be so related. Even if their unit costs are the same, firms with different objectives may grow at different rates, as explained in Chapter 1. That is, differences in actual growth rates between firms may reflect different objectives rather than differences in unit cost. Therefore, if the objectives of different-sized firms are different, their growth rates need not reflect differences in the unit cost of production. It is not essential, if relative growth rates of different-sized firms are to reflect differences in unit cost, that all firms aim at growth maximization; what does seem to be required is that firms of different sizes pursue the same objective, which may be maximization of either growth, profits, sales revenue, or some other variable. This is a strict requirement indeed, and one might well doubt whether it is likely to be satisfied in practice. However, even though different firms in any size class pursue different objectives, provided that the objectives resemble those pursued by firms in any other size class, the average growth rates of different-sized firms may tend to reflect differences in unit cost rather than differences in objectives.

A considerable amount of empirical evidence suggests that there is no difference between the average growth rates of different-sized firms; see the articles by Hymer and Pashigian (12), Simon and Bonini (24) and Singh and Whittington (25). Some economists have argued that such evidence is inconsistent with the existence of diseconomies of scale. If there were diseconomies of scale, expansion of a firm beyond a certain size in a given market would lead to higher unit cost and lower profit margins. The large firms in an industry would grow more slowly than small firms in the industry. The evidence suggests that this does not happen, hence the inference is that diseconomies of scale do not exist, at least up to the scales of output reached by firms in practice.

There is disagreement among economists as to whether the statistical evidence regarding average growth rates is consistent with constant or continually declining unit costs as scale of output increases. It must be emphasized that the constant cost hypothesis is not that costs are constant at all levels of output; proponents of the hypothesis acknowledge that economies of scale exist at low levels of output in many, if not most, industries. The question at issue is whether, beyond some minimum scale of output, unit costs are constant or continue to decline as scale of output increases.

The argument that the existence of similar average growth rates for different-sized firms implies constant unit costs, at least beyond some minimum scale of output, has been challenged by the following argument, originally formulated by S. Hymer and P. Pashigian (12). If cost curves are continually falling, smaller firms in an industry will have smaller unit profits and will tend to be driven out of the industry. On the other hand small firms will have an incentive to expand and realize economies of scale. The small firm has, it is argued, a greater probability of decline because of high unit costs than does the large firm, and at the same time a greater probability of faster growth because of the incentive to realize cost savings through increased size. Therefore, it is claimed, the dispersion in growth rates should be higher for small firms than large firms, but there is no reason why the average growth rates should differ.

It is appropriate to mention several points concerning the logic of the preceding argument. First, it is not entirely clear why the incentive to expand should be greater for small than for large firms, if costs are continually declining as hypothesized. Why, if unit costs can be reduced by expanding further, should large firms have less incentive to expand than smaller firms? Second, the argument seems to deny the dependence of growth upon profits; even if the incentive to expand is greater for small firms than large, profit rates and therefore the *means* to grow, in the form of internal funds or additional external finance, will be smaller in the case of small firms, preventing them from growing faster than large firms.

In an effort to resolve the issue of whether costs are constant or continually declining,

Hymer and Pashigian focus attention upon the dispersion of firms' growth rates around the average growth rate of any size class. Their empirical evidence indicates that there is smaller variability in the growth rates of large firms than small (see also A. Singh and G. Whittington (25) for similar conclusions). That is, although average growth rates of different-sized firms are equal, the dispersion of the growth rates of firms in any size class about the average growth rate in that size class declines with increasing size of firm. Again, the question is whether this evidence is more consistent with constant costs above a minimum scale of output, or continually declining costs as scale of output increases.

If costs were constant at all output levels, there would be no reason to expect the variability of growth rates of different-sized firms to differ. This conclusion remains valid even if diversification reduces the variability of profits (and hence growth rates), because small firms could diversify as much as large firms without experiencing higher unit costs. Therefore, the evidence concerning dispersion of growth rates certainly seems inconsistent with constant costs at all levels of output. It is not, however, inconsistent with the existence of constant costs above a minimal scale of output, for the following reasons. If economies of scale exist at low levels of output, small firms would not be able to diversify as much as large firms without experiencing higher unit costs in individual product markets. If diversification reduces the variability of profit and growth rates, the existence of economies of scale up to some minimum level of output, resulting in lower degrees of diversification by small firms than by large, will result in declining variability in growth rates of larger firms, even though costs are constant above the minimum level.

Declining dispersion of growth rates as size of firm increases is compatible with the existence of constant unit costs above some minimum scale of output and also with continually declining unit costs. Although Hymer and Pashigian (12) argue persuasively that the observed reduction in dispersion is not as rapid as one would expect if costs were constant, the issue of which hypothesis is best supported by the facts remains unresolved for the present.

In view of the difficulties associated with estimating cost conditions, it is hardly surprising that empirical evidence has not yet produced general agreement regarding the shape of the LRAC curve existing in industries in practice. No matter which method of estimation is employed, however, statistical evidence seems inconsistent with the existence of diseconomies of scale in most industries within the range of firm sizes encountered to date. Similarly, all the enumerated methods of estimation indicate that economies of scale exist in many, if not most, industries. Disagreement centers around the question of whether economies of scale are exhausted beyond a certain scale of output, resulting in an L-shaped long-run average cost curve, or whether they continue indefinitely. The evidence based upon statistical cost, technological study, and survival technique methods of estimation generally support the first view; evidence based upon the growth rate approach is inconclusive and can be interpreted as supporting either the first or the second view. In any event, the U-shaped LRAC curve traditionally presented in economics textbooks does not seem to be encountered in practice.

Significance of Cost Conditions for Firms' Behavior

Cost conditions influence firms' behavior in a number of ways. The level of a firm's output of a particular product is influenced *directly* by the nature of the cost conditions associated with producing and distributing that product. Given the demand conditions confronting the firm, and the firm's objectives, cost conditions determine how much output the firm will produce.

The question of whether the LRAC curve associated with a particular product turns up after some scale of output has been reached is intimately bound up with the question of whether there exists some limit to the size of individual firms. If there are no diseconomies of scale in producing individual products, there is nothing to prevent a firm from expanding until it supplies the total market for an individual product. Downward-sloping market demand curves for individual products will impose a limit upon the size of a firm's operations in any individual market; that is, it will become unprofitable to expand the scale of the firm's output beyond a certain level since price will ultimately fall below unit cost. Since firms are not, however, restricted to the sale of a single product, but can diversify and expand by producing other products, downward-sloping market demand curves alone cannot impose a limit upon the firm's size. Total revenue will expand at the same rate as output provided that the firm is not forced to cut its prices in individual markets in order to expand. Only if the firm's total costs increase at a faster rate than output – that is, if there are diseconomies of scale – will there be a limit to the size of the firm in the long run. It must be added that even in the absence of diseconomies of scale there may be a limit to firm size at any point in time, a limit imposed by the need to obtain funds for expansion, combined with a limitation on the supply of funds available to the firm in any subperiod. That is, the need for capital to finance expansion may set a limit to the size of the firm at any given point in time, even in the absence of diseconomies of scale, but there will be no limit in the long run unless diseconomies of scale exist.

Economies and diseconomies of scale help determine whether there are few or many firms producing a particular kind of output, that is, the degree of seller concentration in a particular industry. Given industry demand conditions for a particular product, if existing firms in the industry compete on a price basis, only the firms with unit costs below industry price can survive; if unit costs depend upon scale of output, the number of firms in the industry will therefore be influenced by economies and diseconomies of scale. If firms compete on a nonprice basis, through advertising, style changes, or other strategies, this shifts up the unit cost curves of all firms and, given industry price, economies and diseconomies of scale will, again, influence the number of firms producing the total industry output demanded at a particular price.

Cost conditions may also influence the level of the firm's output *indirectly*, by influencing entry barriers into the firm's industry and hence demand conditions confronting the group of firms established in the industry. The demand conditions for a firm's product depend upon the reactions of firms already established in the industry and potential entrants into the industry. As will be explained in Chapter 7, entry barriers, which influence the behavior of potential entrants, depend to a large extent upon cost conditions associated with the product of the industry.

Finally, the degree of diversification in a firm, or industry, is influenced by the cost conditions governing the production of individual types of output, as explained in Chapter 9.

RECOMMENDED READINGS

1. Alchian, A. A., Costs and outputs. In Abramovitz, M. (Ed.) *The Allocation of Economic Resources* (Palo Alto, California: Stanford University Press, 1959). Reprinted in Breit, W. and Hochman, H. M. (Eds.) *Readings in Microeconomics* (New York: Holt, Rinehart and Winston, Inc., 1968).
2. Bain, J. S., Economies of scale, concentration, and the conditions of entry in twenty manufacturing industries, *American Economic Review*, March 1954. Reprinted in Heflebower, R. B. and Stocking, G. J. (Eds.) *Readings in Industrial Organization and Public Policy* (Homewood, Ill.: Richard D. Irwin, Inc., 1958); published under the sponsorship of the American Economic Association.

3. Benston, G. J., Multiple regression analysis of cost behavior, *The Accounting Review*, October 1966.
4. Blois, K. J., A note on X-efficiency and profit maximization, *Quarterly Journal of Economics*, May 1972.
5. Crew, M. A., Jones-Lee, M. W. and Rowley, C. K., X-theory versus management discretion theory, *Southern Economic Journal*, October 1971.
6. Dewey, D., The ambiguous notion of average cost, *Journal of Industrial Economics*, July 1962.
7. Goldschmidt, H. J., Mann, H. M. and Weston, J. F. (Eds.) *Industrial Concentration: The New Learning* (Boston: Little, Brown & Co., 1974), Chapter 2.
8. Haldi, J. and Whitcomb, D., Economies of scale in industrial plants, *Journal of Political Economy*, August 1967.
9. Harris, W. T. and Chapin, W. R., Joint product costing, *Management Accounting*, April 1973.
10. Hart, P. E., The size and growth of firms, *Economica*, February 1962.
11. Hirschleifer, J., The firm's cost function: a successful reconstruction? *Journal of Business*, July 1962.
12. Hymer, S. and Pashigian, P., Firm size and rate of growth, *Journal of Political Economy*, December 1962.
13. Johnston, J., *Statistical Cost Analysis* (New York: McGraw-Hill, Inc., 1960).
14. Leibenstein, H., Allocative efficiency vs. X-efficiency: *American Economic Review*, June 1966.
15. Leibenstein, H., Comment on the nature of X-efficiency, *Quarterly Journal of Economics*, May 1972.
16. Leibenstein, H., Competition and X-efficiency: reply, *Journal of Political Economy*, May–June, 1973.
17. Leibenstein, H., Aspects of the X-efficiency theory of the firm, *Bell Journal of Economics*, Autumn 1975.
18. Littlechild, S., Marginal cost pricing with joint costs, *Economic Journal*, June 1970.
19. Saving, T. R., Estimation of optimum size of plant by the survivor technique, *Quarterly Journal of Economics*, November 1961.
20. Schwartzman, D., Uncertainty and the size of the firm, *Economica*, August 1963.
21. Shelton, J. P., Allocative efficiency vs. X-efficiency: comment, *American Economic Review*, December 1967.
22. Shepherd, W. G., What does the survivor technique show about economies of scale? *Southern Economic Journal*, July 1967.
23. Silberston, A., Economies of scale in theory and practice, *Economic Journal*, March 1972, supplement, pp. 369–391.
24. Simon, H. A. and Bonini, C. P., The size distribution of business firms, *American Economic Review*, September 1968.
25. Singh, A. and Whittington, G., *Growth, Profitability and Valuation: A Study of United Kingdom Quoted Companies*, University of Cambridge Department of Applied Economics Occasional Paper 7 (Cambridge: Cambridge University Press, 1968).
26. Stigler, G. J., The economies of scale, *Journal of Law and Economics*, Vol. 1, 1958.
27. Stigler, G. J., The xistence of X-efficiency, *American Economic Review*, March 1976.
28. Turvey, R., Marginal cost, *Economic Journal*, June 1969.
29. Walters, A. A., The allocation of joint costs with demands as probability distributions, *American Economic Review*, June 1960.
30. Weil, R. L., Allocating joint costs, *American Economic Review*, December 1968.
31. Weiss, L. W., The survival technique and the extent of suboptimal capacity, *Journal of Political Economy*, June 1964.
32. Whitin, T. M., Output dimensions and their implications for cost and price analysis, *Journal of Business*, April 1972.
33. Williamson, O. E., Managerial discretion and business behavior, *American Economic Review*, December 1963.
34. Williamson, O. E., *The Economics of Discretionary Behavior: Managerial Objectives in a Theory of the Firm* (Englewood Cliffs, N. J.: Prentice-Hall, 1964).
35. Williamson, O. E., Hierarchical control and optimum firm size, *Journal of Political Economy*, April 1967.

CHAPTER THREE

PRICING BEHAVIOR

The first section of this chapter summarizes the main elements of conventional price theory, the second section develops the formal relationship between a firm's pricing behavior and the firm's market share, price-elasticity of market demand, and rivals' reactions, and the third section stresses the analytical irrelevance of the number of firms in conventional price theory. The two following sections deal, respectively, with price discrimination and multi-product pricing, and the final section with pricing behavior in practice.

Conventional Price Theory

In that branch of economic theory which concerns itself with the determination of product prices, the individual firm is assumed to be confronted by demand and cost conditions which are outside the firm's control. The price charged for the firm's product, and the level of the firm's output, are determined by these two sets of conditions, plus the firm's objective, which is usually assumed to be profit maximization. Given the firm's objective and cost conditions, the firm's pricing behavior will depend upon the demand conditions confronting the firm. These are depicted diagrammatically by a demand curve which shows the quantity of output the firm expects to sell at different alternative prices. It must be emphasized that the relevant demand curve reflects the expectations of the producer. The nature of such a curve depends upon the type of market in which the firm sells. Selling markets are usually classified into four different types. The market types are pure competition, monopoly, monopolistic competition and oligopoly.

Pure competition is a market situation in which a large number of firms sell an identical product, and in which no firm is large enough to influence the market price by its output decision. Monopoly exists when there is a single seller of a product that has no close substitutes. Monopolistic competition is a market situation in which there are many firms selling differentiated varieties of a particular product, that is, the products of individual firms are not perfect substitutes for each other, and in which the actions of a single firm will have no appreciable effect on other firms. An oligopolistic market situation is one in which the number of producers is small enough for the policy decision of a single seller to affect the other firms noticeably, and in which each firm considers how its rivals will react to its own policies. The products of different firms in an oligopolistic industry can be either identical or differentiated.

The essential difference between these four market situations lies in the nature of the demand conditions confronting the individual firm, and can be briefly summarized as follows. In the purely competitive market situation, the individual firm assumes that the market price will be unaffected by its output decision – the firm's demand curve is horizontal at the prevailing market price. In the case of monopoly, the firm's demand curve is the market demand curve, that is, the demand curve facing the seller is the aggregate demand curve for that good and slopes down from left to right. In the model of monopolistic competition, each firm is confronted by a downward-sloping demand curve. The demand curve is sloped down because of product differentiation and the attachment of some consumers to particular varieties of the general class of product, which permits an individual seller to raise price relative to competitors' prices without losing all of his customers and to lower price relative to competitors' prices without attracting all or most of their customers. Furthermore, the demand curve reflects the firm's assumption that other firms will not notice, and therefore will not react to its own policy decisions by changing their prices. In contrast to monopoly, however, there are a large number of firms producing close substitutes for any individual firm's product. If each firm finds it profitable, on the basis of assuming that other firms will not change their strategies in response to its own decision to lower the price of its product, this will be true of all firms in the group. As a result, the demand curve indicating quantities which the firm will *actually* sell at different alternative prices will have a steeper slope at the existing price than the anticipated demand curve. There are, in other words, two distinct demand curves for each firm in monopolistic competition. One of these curves, labeled *dd* in Figure 3–1(c) shows the quantities the firm expects to sell at various alternative prices if all other firms in the group hold their prices constant. This is the demand curve used by the firm in making its price and output decision, because each firm believes that other firms will not change their prices in response to its own actions. The other demand curve, labeled *DD* in Figure 3–1(c), shows the quantities which the firm will actually sell if all firms in the group change their prices simultaneously. Curve *dd* is sometimes referred to as an 'other-prices-constant' demand curve, and *DD* as an 'other-prices-changing' demand curve. Figure 3–1 depicts the

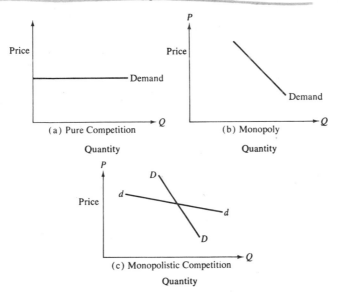

Figure 3–1. Demand conditions in alternative market situations.

demand conditions confronting a firm in pure competition, monopoly, and monopolistic competition.

In the case of oligopolistic market situations, the demand conditions confronting the individual firm depend upon the firm's assumptions regarding the way in which other firms will react to its own policies, and there are numerous alternative possibilities. There is, therefore, no demand curve diagram which is typical of oligopoly.

Price theory compares and contrasts the price–cost and price–output relationships that result in each market situation. Monopolization of a purely competitive industry, for example, results in a higher price and lower level of industry output, assuming that cost and total market demand conditions do not change. There is no single equilibrium industry price–quantity combination in monopolistic competition. Since the products of individual firms are not perfect substitutes for each other, there may be more than one price involved in a group equilibrium situation. That is, different equilibrium prices may exist for different varieties of the same class of goods. Despite this, it is possible to compare the price–output combinations of individual firms in such a market situation with the behavior of a 'monopolist'. Indeed, it is necessary to show that there is a difference (apart from the presence or absence of entry barriers, to be mentioned later) between the behavior of an individual firm in monopolistic competition, and a monopolist, in order to justify separate classification. The difference between the individual firm in monopolistic competition and monopoly (apart from a difference in entry conditions) can be illustrated by considering the short-run equilibrium price–quantity situation of the individual firm in these two types of market structure. In both cases, the firm assumes that its actions will not lead to reactions by other firms. In the case of monopoly, this assumption is justified, for the product has by definition no close substitutes. Any adjustments by firms in *other* markets do not affect the market demand curve. In contrast, in monopolistic competition, although each firm expects its actions to go unnoticed because of the large number of competitors, other firms do not behave as each individual firm anticipates. The actual demand curve confronting the firm in monopolistic competition is steeper in slope than the demand curve used by the firm in arriving at its price–output decision. In equilibrium, the optimal price–quantity combination selected by the monopolistic competitor will equate the marginal cost of production with the marginal revenue associated with the subjective demand curve showing the quantities the firm expects to sell at different prices if other firms' behavior remains unchanged. Since the actual demand curve, showing quantities the firm could sell at different prices if other firms pursue similar policies, is steeper than the subjective demand curve at the selected optimal price–quantity combination, actual marginal revenue must be less than the subjective marginal revenue at that quantity of output. Each individual firm in the group could increase its own profits, and therefore total industry profits, by producing a smaller level of output of each variety of the product.

Oligopolistic market situations are many and varied. As already explained, the common characteristic of these models is that a firm makes some explicit assumptions about the reactions of other firms to its own strategies. The firm's pricing behavior will depend upon the precise nature of these assumptions, and the resulting equilibrium industry price, or set of prices if the products of individual firms are differentiated, can range from a purely competitive price to a monopoly price.

The different market situations of conventional price theory are contrasted with respect to the different price–marginal cost relationships that result in each case. We shall return to analyze the significance of such relationships for resource allocation in Chapter 10. Apart from the price–marginal cost relationship, a further distinction is usually made between the different market situations according to the conditions of entry existing in each case. In pure competition and monopolistic competition, entry is assumed to be easy. In monopoly and oligopoly, entry is assumed to be barred. Conditions of entry affect the relationship between the equilibrium price and average cost of products marketed. The significance of entry barriers is analyzed in greater detail in Chapter 7.

Pricing, Elasticity of Demand, Market Share, and Rivals' Reactions

The preceding section outlined the four types of market, and the associated pricing behavior, which characterize conventional price theory. It was pointed out that the difference between these market types, and the resulting pricing behavior, was the result of different demand conditions confronting the typical firm in each market situation. This section demonstrates that the demand conditions confronting any firm, and therefore the firm's pricing behavior, depend on the firm's market share, the price-elasticity of total market demand for the firm's product, and the reactions of rival sellers. The analysis will then be utilized to demonstrate that the distinction between the market types of conventional price theory does not depend on the number of firms in each market situation.

A condition which must be fulfilled in order for a firm to maximize its profits is that the effect of a change in any of its decision variables on the firm's total revenues and total costs must be equal. This is the familiar marginal-revenue-equals-marginal-cost condition encountered repeatedly in price theory. A change in the price of the firm's product will change the quantity of the firm's product demanded, and a profit-maximizing price will be achieved when the marginal revenue (MR) and marginal cost (MC) of output are equal.

It is easy to show* that the firm's $MR = P(1 - 1/E_d)$, where P represents the price of the firm's product, and E_d represents the 'price-elasticity of demand' for the firm's product, which is formally defined as the percentage change in quantity demanded as the result of a price change, divided by the percentage price change. The formula for the price-elasticity of demand may therefore be written as follows:

$$\frac{\text{Percentage change in quantity demanded}}{\text{Percentage change in price}} = \frac{(\Delta Q/Q)}{(\Delta P/P)} = (-)\frac{\Delta Q}{\Delta P}\cdot\frac{P}{Q} = E_d$$

where Δ stands for a 'small change', and the minus sign in brackets is used to turn the resulting number into a positive number since $\frac{\Delta Q}{\Delta P}$ will be negative in sign, reflecting the fact that price reduction will increase the quantity demanded, and vice versa. A diagrammatic interpretation of the firm's price-elasticity of demand is possible; it represents the inverse of the slope of the firm's demand curve multiplied by the ratio of price to quantity demanded at any point on the firm's demand curve.

Substituting the above expression for MR into the profit-maximizing condition yields the following expression:

$$P(1 - 1/E_d) = MC, \text{ or alternatively, } \frac{P - MC}{P} = 1/E_d$$

This last expression indicates that the profit-maximizing relationship between a firm's

---

$$*MR = \frac{d\,(\text{Total Revenue})}{dQ} = \frac{d(P.Q)}{dQ} = P + Q\frac{dP}{dQ} = P(1 + \frac{Q}{P}\frac{dP}{dQ}) = P(1 - 1/E_d)$$

price and marginal cost will depend on the price-elasticity of demand for the firm's product. It will now be shown that the price-elasticity of demand for the firm's product depends, in turn, on three other factors, namely the elasticity of total market demand for the product in question, the firm's market share, and the reactions of rival sellers anticipated by the firm. The relationship between these various factors may be illustrated with the aid of Figure 3–2. A firm's share of total market demand for the product in question at any price, such as P, equals the ratio of demand for its product (Q_f) to total market demand (Q_m) at that price. Given the firm's market share, the price-elasticity of demand for the firm's product at P depends on the slope of the firm's demand curve at the price–quantity combination PQ_f. If the firm's rivals maintain their output unchanged in response to a reduction in the price of the firm's product, the increase in quantity of the firm's product demanded will equal the increase in total market demand resulting from such a price cut, because equilibrium in the market will require that the firm supply all the resulting increase in a market demand. In these circumstances, the slope of the firm's demand curve will equal that of the market demand curve. Alternatively, if the firm expects rival sellers to increase the quantity of output they produce in response to a price reduction initiated by the firm, the slope of the firm's demand curve will be less than that of the market demand curve, while if the firm's rivals are expected to reduce their output level the slope of the firm's demand curve will be greater than that of the market demand curve. Rivals' reactions therefore determine, in part, the price-elasticity of the firm's demand curve. Finally, it is also clear from the diagram that, whatever the anticipated reaction of the firm's rivals, the slope of the firm's demand curve, and therefore the elasticity of demand for the firm's product, will be greater, the more price-elastic is total market demand. See A. C. Johnson and P. Helmberger (16), whose article deals with price-elasticity of market demand as an element of market structure; and see J. R. McKean and R. D. Peterson (23) who also stress the reactions of a firm's rivals as an independent influence on the price-elasticity of demand for a firm's product and pricing behavior.

The formal relationship between a firm's price-elasticity of demand, its market share, market elasticity of demand, and rivals' reactions, is indicated by the following expression:*

$$E_d = \frac{E_m}{S_f}(1 + E_s \cdot S_r)$$

and the relationship between the firm's profit-maximizing price and marginal cost is therefore represented as follows:

---

* This relationship may be derived as follows:

$$E_d = (-)\frac{\Delta Q_f}{\Delta P_f} \cdot \frac{P}{Q_f} = (-)\frac{(\Delta Q_m - \Delta Q_r)}{\Delta P} \cdot \frac{P}{Q_f}$$

where the expression $\dfrac{\Delta Q_m - \Delta Q_r}{\Delta P}$ can be positive (indicating that rivals' output increases less than the increase in market demand) or negative (indicating that rivals' output increases by more than the increase in market

demand) $\quad E_d = -\dfrac{\Delta Q_m}{\Delta P} \cdot \dfrac{P}{Q_f} + \dfrac{\Delta Q_r}{\Delta P} \cdot \dfrac{P}{Q_f}$

Since $Q_f = Q_m \cdot S_f$, while the elasticity of supply of rivals' output may be defined as $E_s = \dfrac{\Delta Q_r}{\Delta P} \cdot \dfrac{P}{Q_r}$

$$E_d = \frac{E_m}{S_f} + E_s \cdot \frac{Q_r}{Q_m \cdot S_f} \quad \text{or alternatively,} \quad E_d = \frac{E_m}{S_f} + \frac{E_s \cdot S_r}{S_f}$$

$$\frac{P - MC}{P} = \frac{1}{E_d} = \frac{S_f}{E_m + E_s \cdot S_r}$$

where E_m is the price-elasticity of total market demand, S_f and S_r are respectively the market shares of the firm and its rivals, and E_s stands for the elasticity of supply of rivals' output with respect to a change in the firm's price, which is defined as the percentage change in quantity of rivals' output occurring in response to the firm's price change, divided by the percentage price change. E_s can be negative or positive, depending on whether rivals increase, or reduce, their output levels in response to a price reduction by the firm.

The influence of price-elasticity of market demand, market share, and rivals' reactions on a firm's pricing behavior is indicated by the preceding expression. When there is only one firm serving the market (monopoly), the firm's price-elasticity of demand equals the price-elasticity of market demand. The optimal excess of price over marginal cost will depend on the elasticity of market demand, being lower the greater the price elasticity of market demand, which will depend on buyers' tastes and alternative options presented to buyers by producers of other products. Given the price-elasticity of market demand and the reaction of rival sellers in the market, anticipated by the firm, the optimal price–marginal cost relationship will depend on the firm's share of the market; the lower this share, the larger will be the P/Q_f component of the firm's elasticity of demand, the larger will be the firm's price elasticity of demand, and the lower the optimal excess of price over marginal cost. Thus, the lower a firm's market share, if AC = MC (or if AC and MC are linearly related), declining $P - MC$ per unit of output implies declining profit per unit of output. W. G. Shepherd has pointed out in several articles (see (31) and (32), for examples) that empirical data suggest that a firm's market share is a major determinant of its profit rate.

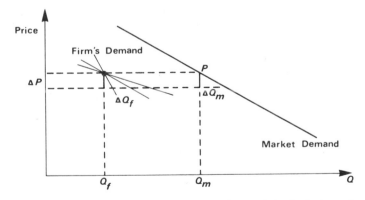

Figure 3–2. Market share, elasticity, rivals' reactions and the firm's demand.

As already mentioned, Figure 3–2 indicates that the greater the increase in rivals' output anticipated by the firm in response to its price reduction, the less elastic will be demand for the firm's product, and the higher will be the optimal excess of price over marginal cost. For expositional convenience it was assumed that the response of rivals was a quantity response. If rivals' products are identical, this would imply an associated price response. However, it may now be emphasized that the response could also take the form of changes in other decision variables, such as increased advertising, which affect buyer behavior and therefore influence the response of demand to the initiating firm's price change. The use of alternative competitive responses leaves the conclusions of the preceding analysis unchanged; whatever the exact nature of rivals' responses, it will influence the response of demand for a firm's product to a change in the firm's price. The analysis can also be applied to groups of firms producing dissimilar products. Although the concept of 'market demand' loses some of its precision in these circumstances, the total market demand at any particular set of prices charged by the various firms can still be obtained by adding together the demand for each firm's (dissimilar) product at those prices, and it remains true that the price-elasticity of demand for a single firm's product will depend on the elasticity of market demand, the firm's share, and the response of rival sellers.

The Number of Firms and Pricing Behavior

The analytical framework of the preceding section may be used to emphasize that the different equilibrium price–marginal cost relationships associated with the market types of conventional price theory depend not on differences between the number of firms in each of those market situations, but on different assumptions concerning rivals' reactions which are applicable in each case (see G. C. Archibald (2), for similar emphasis).

Perhaps the best way to demonstrate that the number of firms is analytically irrelevant is to show that the pricing behavior associated with each of the market types of conventional price theory is compatible with any number of firms. For example, Fama and Laffer (11) have shown that if a firm's rivals react by changing their output by an equivalent amount and in an opposite direction to that of the firm initiating a price change, market quantity and price will remain unchanged, and the demand curve confronting an individual firm will be horizontal as in the model of a perfectly competitive market irrespective of the number of firms present in the market. These authors indicate the conditions under which such a reaction would be optimal for rivals, stressing the absence of any clear-cut relationship between the number of firms and pricing behavior.

As another example, the pricing behavior characteristic of monopolistic competition can be obtained irrespective of the number of competing firms provided that each firm expects its rival(s) to maintain the level of their output constant. As already noted in the preceding section, this assumption (which is often referred to as the Cournot assumption, and in connection with entry-barrier theory as the Sylos postulate) implies that a firm's subjective demand curve is parallel to the market demand curve. This demand curve will be flatter, at any price–quantity combination sold by the firm, than the demand curve which indicates the quantity which the firm would sell at different prices assuming that all firms in the market act in the same manner. Each firm equates the marginal cost of producing its product with the marginal revenue expected to accrue to the firm if its rivals produce an unchanged level of output; since the elasticity of the subjective demand curve exceeds that of the actual demand curve, price exceeds marginal cost by less than would be necessary to maximize the group of firms' profits, as already explained in the first section of this chapter.

Assuming that a firm's market share is inversely related to the number of competing firms, an increase in the number of firms will shift the subjective demand curve facing any individual firm to the left in Figure 3–2. Provided that each individual firm continues to assume that its competitors will maintain their output constant in response to its own actions, the slope of the firm's subjective demand curve will not be changed, however. At any price, the elasticity of demand for the firm's product will be increased, because the firm's market share will be diminished, but the demand curve facing the firm does not become horizontal, as in a purely competitive model. Because the firm's demand curve continues to slope down, average revenue exceeds marginal revenue and the profit-maximizing price remains above marginal revenue and therefore above marginal cost, no matter how many firms are in the industry. To obtain the horizontal demand curve of pure competition it is necessary to change the firm's assumption about the policy of its rivals; what is required, instead of the assumption that rivals keep output constant, is the explicit assumption that each individual firm believes that changes in its output level will not alter price. These remarks emphasize that the distinction between pure competition and monopolistic competition depends not on numbers, but on the beliefs attributed to the firms involved in each situation. The example also demonstrates that product-differentiation is not required to achieve an equilibrium price–marginal cost relationship identical to that achieved in monopolistic competition models.

As a last example, it is possible, given the appropriate assumption by each firm regarding the reactions of its rivals to its own policies, to obtain a monopoly pricing solution irrespective of the number of firms serving a particular market. If each firm assumes that other firms in the market will imitate both its price and output strategy, with constant marginal costs identical for each firm and a linear total market demand curve, the equilibrium market price and output will be the same as that resulting under conditions of monopoly, irrespective of the number of firms in the market, as demonstrated in Chapter 7.

To summarize the argument of this section thus far; given the number of firms in a market, a different pattern of pricing behavior will result depending on the assumption made by an individual firm concerning the reaction of other firms in the group to its own actions. Conversely, given the belief about the reactions of its rivals, the behavior of a firm will be the same whether its rivals are one or many, and a particular industry pricing pattern is compatible with any number of firms. Whether a firm's pricing behavior is affected by the number or size distribution of its rivals in a particular market depends on whether, given the elasticity of market demand, the number or size distribution of rivals influences the firm's market share or the nature of the firm's anticipations regarding its rivals' reactions.

In an illuminating article (35), Professor Stigler has focused attention on the crucial importance for pricing behavior of a firm's anticipations regarding its rivals' reactions. If a group of firms selling in a particular market act in unison, charging the same price for their product, each firm's demand curve will be represented by a 'share-of-the-market' demand curve indicating the demand for the firm's product when all firms charge the same price. The optimal price and quantity for each firm will in these circumstances depend on the elasticity of its share-of-the-market demand curve, which in turn will depend on the elasticity of total market demand and the size of the firm's market share. If a firm is able to reduce the price of its product without its rivals emulating this move, the resulting increase in demand for the firm's product will be larger than that indicated by the share-of-the-market demand curve. This larger price-elasticity of demand implies a larger marginal revenue at any quantity sold by the firm, and this in turn implies a lower optimal price and larger optimal quantity for the firm than that associated with the share-of-the-market demand curve. For this reason, an incentive will always exist, for a firm which is party to a collusive agreement to maximize group profits, to cut the price of its product secretly. This incentive only disappears when immediate retaliation by other firms in the group would occur, so that the firm's effective demand curve is the share-of-the-market demand curve, or when detection of a price reduction incurs a penalty which the group is able to impose upon the price-cutter.

The reactions of a firm's rivals will depend on whether they are aware of the firm's price reductions. Information about the firm's behavior may be transmitted to rival firms via the resulting effects of the firm's price reduction on the distribution of buyers between firms in the market. Other things being equal, it may seem reasonable to expect that the magnitude of the absolute change in demand experienced by an individual firm as a result of another firm's actions will be smaller, the larger the number of firms in the market, and if the ease of detecting rivals' actions decreases with an increase in the number of rival sellers, this may affect the anticipations and behavior of individual firms selling in a particular market. However, the ability to detect rivals' moves will depend on many other factors in addition to the number of rival sellers in a market; for example, the degree of stability of total market demand, and the extent of buyer turnover between rival sellers, even when total market demand is unchanged, will also be relevant. Stigler (35) presents evidence which suggests that the number of rival sellers in a market is likely to be relatively unimportant in influencing the ease of detecting rivals' actions and therefore in influencing firms' behavior. Moreover, Stigler's analysis deals with the levels of price only; when other decision variables are introduced into the analysis of industrial behavior, a collusive monopoly solution must include the level of *all* decision variables of rival sellers which influence buyer behavior. The ease of detecting changes in some of those other variables, such as advertising or product quality changes, may be more difficult than that associated with price changes, with the result that collusive group solutions are likely to be more fragile. This is also stressed by W. Fellner's analysis of oligopoly (12).

Although there may be persuasive priority reasons why the number of firms selling in a market might influence the nature of an individual firm's assumptions regarding the reactions of other firms to its own policies, and therefore the firm's behavior, these hypotheses must be tested by reference to empirical data, which is dealt with in Chapter 6. It is important to remember, however, that a monopoly solution in a particular market is quite possible without any overt collusion between the rival sellers, and can be explained solely by the nature of the reactions of its rivals anticipated by an individual firm in the group.

Emphasis on the importance of rivals' reactions in determining a firm's behavior elevates oligopoly models to a place of central importance in any realistic analysis of industrial behavior. There are innumerable oligopoly models, one of each possible pattern of rivals' responses anticipated by a firm. Two aspects of these models should be distinguished: a particular pattern of anticipated rivals' responses is equivalent to an additional constraint confronting a firm's decision-makers, and the precise nature of this constraint will therefore influence the optimal levels of a firm's decision variables for reasons already explained in Chapter 1. It will also affect the values of different firms' decision variables which simultaneously satisfy the constrained objective functions of all the firms comprising a group. A different aspect of oligopoly models concerns their dynamic implications for the path of firms' decision variables through time when the values of those decision variables differ from the equilibrium levels which simultaneously satisfy the constrained objective functions of all firms in the group. The dynamic path of an oligopoly model, including whether or not the system will return to an equilibrium if initially in disequilibrium, depends on a combination of factors. In addition to each firm's expectations about the reactions of its rivals, the direction of changes in a firm's decision variables, and the relative speeds of change of different decision variables, are also relevant. Unfortunately, traditional analysis of oligopoly models in economics has, with few exceptions, dealt with models selected more for their mathematical tractability than with their empirical relevance. There has also been excessive emphasis on price and quantity reactions rather than changes in other decision variables, and on the dynamic stability of the resulting model.

Price Discrimination

The term 'price discrimination' is used to refer to the practice of selling the same kind of product or service at different prices to different buyers. This section outlines the rationale of price discrimination and its implications for a firm's pricing behavior; the implications of price discrimination for resource allocation and aggregate satisfaction in the community will be dealt with in Chapter 10.

In order to maximize profits, a firm must equate the MR and MC of its output. Assume, purely for expositional convenience, that a firm is confronted by two buyers (or groups of buyers) whose demand conditions are depicted diagrammatically by the demand curves D_1 and D_2 in Figure 3–3. If the firm charges the same price for its product to all buyers, the total quantity of its output demanded at any particular price will equal the sum of the quantities demanded in each market at that price, shown by the total demand curve D_T. The MR curve associated with D_T, shown by the dotted discontinuous line in Figure 3–3, shows the firm's MR at different output levels when prices are uniform in all markets, and the intersection of this curve and the firm's MC curve indicates the profit-maximizing output level of the firm when the same price is charged to all buyers. The profit-maximizing uniform price is P_u, and at that price the allocation of the optimal output level between the two markets is given by q_1 and q_2 respectively.

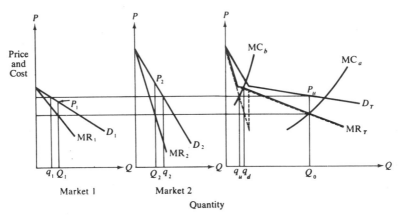

Figure 3–3. A price discrimination model.

If the MR associated with output sold to different buyers (or groups of buyers) is different, as depicted by the different height of the MR curve in each market at q_1 and q_2, it follows automatically that the firm could increase the total revenue it obtains from its output, and therefore its profits, by reallocating output from the market where MR is lower to the market where MR is higher. This can be achieved by raising the price to buyers in the market where MR is lower and lowering the price to buyers in the market where MR is higher, resulting in different prices charged to different buyers. In order to maximize profits, a firm faced by different buyers should therefore observe the following two rules in deciding on the level of its output and the prices charged to different buyers: Rule One is that any given level of output produced should be allocated between different buyers (markets) in such a manner as to equate the MR in each market. If MR differs between buyers (markets), a reallocation of the total output currently being sold in these markets is possible and this will increase total revenue and, therefore, because the total cost of that output level will be unchanged, the firm's profits. Rule Two is that the firm should produce a total level of output which equates its MR, which will be equal in all markets if Rule One is observed, to the MC of the product.

The determination of the optimal output level of the firm and the optimal prices in each market is depicted diagrammatically by horizontal summation of the marginal revenue curves in each market, MR_1 and MR_2, to obtain MR_T, which shows the firm's marginal revenue associated with different output levels when the allocation of output between different markets satisfies Rule One. The profit-maximizing level of total output is that output level which equates this marginal revenue with the marginal cost of output; for example, Q_0 if MC_a represents the marginal cost of producing the product. The optimal allocation of this output level between the two markets, and therefore the price to be charged in each market, follows automatically by observing Rule One; diagrammatically, the optimal allocation of output between markets is obtained by extending a horizontal line at the level where MR_T intersects MC_a until it intersects the marginal revenue curve in each market. Thus, in Figure 3–3, Q_1 and Q_2 are the profit-maximizing quantities in market 1 and market 2 respectively, while P_1 and P_2 are the respective optimal prices in each market.

In the example depicted by Figure 3–3, maximum profits are earned by charging a different price in each market. When charging a uniform price in each market, MR in each market will differ and therefore price discrimination will be profitable if at that price the price-elasticity of demand of different buyers is different. This can be demonstrated by referring to the following relationship between price, marginal revenue, and price-elasticity of demand:

$$\text{Marginal Revenue} = \text{Price}\left(1 - \frac{1}{\text{price-elasticity of demand}}\right)$$

If the price in each market is the same, it follows from the preceding relationship that marginal revenue in each market will differ unless the price-elasticity of demand of buyers in each market is identical at that price. It is also apparent from the preceding relationship that when the price-elasticity of demand differs in different markets, the optimal price in each market will depend on the elasticity of demand in each market; with two markets, price will be higher in the market where the price-elasticity of demand at the optimal quantity is lowest. Because marginal revenue associated with the optimal level of output sold in each market must be equal in order to maximize the firm's total revenue, the ratio of price to marginal revenue (and marginal cost) will be higher in the market in which the price-elasticity of demand is smallest at the optimal quantity. The last phase must be added in view of the fact that price-elasticity of demand usually varies along any given demand curve, and demand curves cannot be said to be more or less elastic without reference to a specific point on the demand curve.

Price discrimination will be *profitable* whenever the price-elasticity of demand of different buyers is different at a uniform price; whether it is *possible* for a firm to practice price discrimination depends on its ability to separate its total market into independent markets in order to prevent switching of buyers between markets or resale of the product between different markets. In diagrammatic terms, separation of markets means that each of the demand curves D_1 and D_2 in Figure 3–3 is independent of the price charged in the other market.

It is customary in economic analysis to distinguish between first-, second- and third-degree price discrimination, the distinction hinging on the degree to which a firm is able to separate the total market for its output. The example used in this section would be a case of third-degree price discrimination if each of the demand curves refers to a large group of buyers; second-degree price discrimination involves finer separation of markets and smaller groups of buyers; first-degree price discrimination, also often termed 'perfect discrimination', is the extreme case and occurs where the seller is able to separate his total market so effectively that he is able to extract the maximum possible amount of total revenue buyers are willing to pay for his output. In this last case, each unit of output sold is sold to a buyer at the maximum price that the buyer is willing to pay for the product. See R. Battalio and R. B. Ekelund (5) and D. L. White and M. C. Walker (37) for analyses of third- and first-degree price discrimination.

Price discrimination has also been classified in many other ways according to whether the markets served are distinguished from each other geographically, temporally, or on the basis of one or more of a variety of differences among individual buyers or groups of buyers, including differences in personality, income, socio-economic class, extent of use of the product, and other characteristics. These various classifications reflect mainly the different basis on which markets may be separated for purposes of price discrimination, and not differences in the principles which are applicable in each case; see, for example, K. G. Lofgren (20) and F. Machlup (22).

Although we are primarily concerned in this chapter with the implications of price discrimination for pricing behavior, it is appropriate to note at this stage its implications for the total output level of the firm. In the example depicted in Figure 3–3, if the firm's cost conditions are represented by MC_a, the optimal level of the firm's total output is the same whether the firm charges a uniform price or practices price discrimination; only the allocation of that output level between markets will differ. In other circumstances, however, the level of the firm's output may be either higher or lower with price discrimination than under uniform pricing. For example, if marginal cost conditions were depicted by MC_b in Figure 3–3, total output would be greater with price discrimination ($= q_d$) than with uniform pricing ($= q_u$).

The need for a firm to be able to separate the market for its product in order to permit price discrimination to be practiced has already been noted. A firm usually has some control over the degree of separation of the total market for its product. In such a situation, the decision of whether to discriminate on a price basis will involve comparing the additional profitability of price discrimination, compared to uniform pricing, with the costs of separating the market.

A relatively costless method of separating the market, available notably to firms producing a product with high transportation costs, consists of choosing to quote a delivered price rather than a factory, or mill, price. Under a delivered price system, the purchaser is quoted a price which covers transportation, and the seller assumes responsibility for transporting the product to the buyer. In contrast, under a mill price system the seller quotes a price which does not cover the cost of transporting the product from seller to buyer, and the buyer is left to arrange transportation.

The manner in which choice of a delivered price system, as opposed to a mill price system, can separate the total market of a seller, and permit the firm to discriminate between different geographical sectors of its market, can be illustrated by the following example. Consider a firm selling to two groups of consumers located in two different geographical areas A and B. For simplicity, assume that transportation costs between seller and each group of consumers are the same. Assume further, that conditions of demand for the product differ in each area and that elasticity of demand for the product at any particular price is less in area A than in area B. This means that if the firm were to charge the same price in both markets, the marginal revenue associated with the quantity sold in market B would be higher than the marginal revenue associated with the quantity sold in market A. That is, the firm could earn more profits by charging a higher price in A and a lower price in B, thereby causing a reallocation of output from A to B without changing the level of its total output. If the firm attempts to charge a different mill price to purchasers in the different areas, discrimination tends to be thwarted by resale from low-price to high-price consumers. Apart from the problem of attempting to prevent low-price purchases from being resold to the high-price area, discrimination will be difficult to implement because buyers will not willingly disclose their locations. A necessary condition for the practice of geographical price discrimination is knowledge of the location of prospective customers. Without this information the seller who wishes to discriminate does not know which of the two mill prices to quote to them. Consumers in the high mill-price area will not willingly disclose this fact, hoping thereby to get the lower mill-price quotation. The firm wishing to discriminate will be faced by the prospect of having to check customers' locations.

Delivered pricing reduces the profitability of resale because buyers at the low 'mill net return' (delivered price minus transportation cost) must take delivery in the low mill-price area. The mill net return received by the seller per unit sold in each market can differ by an amount equal to the cost of transporting the product between the two geographical areas before resale from low-price to high-price area becomes profitable. Also, since all prices are delivered prices, customers are forced to disclose their locations in order to obtain quotations.

Charging a delivered price need not mean that the seller actually performs the transportation itself; the seller may simply hire the services of some independent transportation firm. If the firm actually performs the transportation itself, the situation is a special case of separating the market by (forward) vertical integration, which is discussed in Chapter 8.

If a firm performs the transportation itself, the delivered price charged to buyers must cover the transportation cost in addition to the production cost of the product. In these circumstances, and in view of the fact that in general the transportation costs to different buyers may differ, it becomes necessary to elaborate further on the definition of price discrimination given at the beginning of this section, particularly the concept of the 'same kind of product or service'. Price discrimination may be defined more precisely as the practice of selling products at prices disproportionate to the marginal costs of the products. It follows from this definition that charging different buyers different prices for a product need not constitute price discrimination if the marginal cost of selling the product is different for different buyers. Thus, for example, a seller who sells a physically identical product to buyers located at different distances from the seller will not be discriminating in price if he charges delivered prices which differ by the difference in transportation cost between seller and each buyer. Conversely, price discrimination may occur even in the absence of a price differential between different buyers. This will be the case if different buyers of the same kind of product are charged identical prices, in a situation in which the seller incurs different production, selling, or transportation costs in serving them. In order to determine whether price discrimination is being practiced by a seller, it is obviously necessary to have information concerning not only the prices charged, but also the costs incurred by the seller in serving different buyers.

The points dealt with in the preceding paragraph have important implications for public policies relating to the practice of price discrimination which are sometimes ignored. In the United States, for example, Section 2a of the Robinson–Patman Act makes price discrimination illegal if it tends to lessen competition substantially. However, a prerequisite for finding an illegal price discrimination under Section 2a is the existence of a price difference resulting from sales by the seller of a particular class of goods at a lower price to one purchaser than to another. Unless a price difference between two buyers is established, the courts will not consider the further legal issue of whether the price discrimination may injure competitors, or tend to lessen competition substantially, or tend to create a monopoly. Hence the law will omit cases of price discrimination which occur whenever products with different marginal costs are sold at the same price.

Multiple Product Pricing

The analytical framework developed in the preceding section dealing with price discrimination may be extended to deal with the subject of pricing multiple products produced by a firm. For a selection of articles dealing with multiple product pricing see Bailey (3), Clemens (7), Coase (8) and Pfouts (27); market segmentation is dealt with by Barnett (4) and Smith (34). A moment's reflection will confirm that price discrimination may be viewed as a special case of maximizing profits by setting $MR = MC$ in each of the two or more markets, in circumstances in which the product sold in each market is the same, while demand in each of the different markets is independent of prices and quantities in other markets. When demand for different products is independent, the marginal revenue associated with output sold in any market equals $P(1 - 1/E_d)$ as already explained in the preceding section, and equating MR and MC therefore implies establishing the following relationship in each market:

$$\frac{P - MC}{P} = \frac{1}{E_d}$$

When the products sold in different markets are identical, and therefore have the same marginal cost, the optimal prices in each market will differ depending only on the price-elasticity of demand in each market, in the manner indicated in the preceding section. If the marginal cost of sales to buyers in different markets differs, optimal prices in different markets will obviously differ even when the price-elasticities of demand in different markets are the same, and such prices will not be discriminatory in the sense previously defined since they will be proportionate to marginal cost in each market. However, whenever the price-elasticities of demand in different markets at prices which are proportionate to marginal cost in each market are different, setting prices disproportionate to marginal costs in each market will be necessary to maximize profits, and will imply price discrimination according to the previous definition.

The discussion in the preceding section assumed that the products sold in different markets were physically identical; physical differentiation of products may, however, constitute a means of separating the total market confronting a seller in order to permit price discrimination to be practiced, and is the essence of some types of price discrimination found in practice. When the demand (and cost) conditions relating to different products are independent, the principles and diagrammatic procedures described in the preceding section would apply without any changes if each of the different products produced by the firm has the same cost conditions, which is obviously the case when the products are identical. When the cost conditions associated with different types of output differ, reflecting physical or other methods of differentiation, each type of output will have a different marginal cost curve in addition to its demand curve and the associated marginal revenue curve. If the demand (and cost) conditions associated with each product are independent of prices and quantities of other products, which as explained may be the *reason* for a firm's differentiating varieties of its output, the optimal level of each type of output and its price are depicted diagrammatically by the output level and price in each market which equates MR and MC in that market. The optimal relationship between price and marginal cost of each product will depend on the price-elasticity of demand in each market, as previously indicated.

When the demand or cost conditions associated with a product are influenced by the prices and quantities of other products, the preceding analysis of optimal pricing principles must be amended to reflect this interdependence.

If a firm changes the price and quantity of one of its products in these circumstances, the effects on the firm's total costs and total revenues depend also on the effects of this change on the demand and cost conditions associated with other products. If the firm maintains the quantities of all other products unchanged when it reduces the price and increases output of one product, the resulting effect on the firm's total revenue is given by the following expression:

$$MR_{Q_1} = P_1 + Q_1 \frac{dP_1}{dQ_1} + Q_2 \frac{dP_2}{dQ_1} + Q_3 \frac{dP_3}{dQ_1} \cdots Q_n \frac{dP_n}{dQ_1}$$

where the expressions $\frac{dP_i}{dQ_1}$ represent the effect on the price buyers are willing to pay for each of the products of the firm when Q_1 changes, so that each $Q_i \frac{dP_i}{dQ_1}$ expression represents the effect on total revenue earned by the firm from selling unchanged quantities of one of its other products. The $\frac{dP_i}{dQ_1}$ terms will be positive, and therefore MR_{Q_1} will be larger, when the demand for other products increases as Q_1 increases (complementary goods); they will be negative, and MR_{Q_1} will be smaller, when the demand for other products decreases as Q_1 increases (substitute goods). When demands for different products are independent, the $\frac{dP_i}{dQ_1}$ terms are zero, and $MR_{Q_1} = P_1 + Q_1 \frac{dP_1}{dQ_1}$, or $MR = P_1(1 - 1/E_d)$.

The above expression indicating the marginal revenue associated with a change in the output level of one product when there is interdependence between demands for a firm's products can be rewritten as follows:*

---

*Proof: Since E_i is defined as follows: $(-) \dfrac{dQ_i}{dP_i} \cdot \dfrac{P_i}{Q_i}$

$P_i + Q_i \dfrac{dP_i}{dQ_i}$ is equivalent to $P_i(1 - 1/E_i)$

The remainder of the expression for marginal revenue is the sum of terms such as $Q_j \dfrac{dP_j}{dQ_i}$, and since cross-elasticity of demand CE_{ij} is defined as $\dfrac{dQ_i}{dP_j} \cdot \dfrac{P_i}{Q_i}$ these terms may be rewritten as $\dfrac{Q_j P_j}{Q_i} \cdot \dfrac{1}{CE_{ij}}$ or alternatively as follows:

$$P_i \left(\frac{Q_j P_j}{Q_i P_i} \cdot \frac{1}{CE_{ij}} \right) \text{ or } P_i \left(\frac{1}{\dfrac{S_i}{S_j} \cdot CE_{ij}} \right)$$

$$MR_{Q_i} = P_i \left(1 - \frac{1}{E_i} + \frac{1}{\sum \frac{S_i}{S_j} \cdot CE_{ij}} \right)$$

where E_i stands for the price-elasticity of demand for the product in question, CE_{ij} stands for cross-elasticity of demand between the ith and jth products, which is defined as

$$\frac{\text{percentage change in quantity demanded of } j\text{th product}}{\text{percentage change in price of } i\text{th product}}$$

and S_i and S_j represent, respectively, the share of the firm's total revenue earned from the ith and jth products.

Equating the MR and MC associated with a particular product therefore implies establishing the following relationship for each product: $\dfrac{P - MC}{P} = \dfrac{1}{E_i} + \dfrac{1}{\sum \frac{S_1}{S_2} \cdot CE_{ij}}$

This expression indicates that when there is interdependence between the demands for different products, profit-maximizing prices depend not only on the price-elasticity of demand for each product (E_i), but also on the cross-elasticities of demand between the product and other products produced by the firm (CE_{ij}). If substitute relationships between the product and other products are dominant, the sum of cross-elasticities will be positive, implying that the optimal price of the product will be higher in relation to the

---

The marginal revenue expression as a whole is therefore equivalent to

$$MR_{Q_i} = P_i \left(1 - \frac{1}{E_i} + \frac{1}{\sum \frac{S_i}{S_j} \cdot CE_{ij}} \right)$$

It is appropriate to note at this stage that the preceding marginal revenue definition is based on the assumption that the firm maintains the quantities of all other products unchanged when demands for those products change, and implies price changes for the other products. If, instead, the firm maintains the prices of all other goods unchanged, and responds to the changes in demand for other products by varying its output, the appropriate definition of marginal revenue is as follows:

$$MR = Q_1 + P_1 \frac{dQ_1}{DP_1} + P_2 \frac{dQ_2}{dP_1} \cdots P_n \frac{dQ_n}{dP_1}$$

and the corresponding marginal cost concept is now

$$MC = MC_{Q_1} \cdot \frac{dQ_1}{dP_1} + MC_{Q_2} \cdot \frac{dQ_2}{dP_1} + \cdots MC_n \cdot \frac{dQ_n}{dP_1}$$

because total cost now changes not only due to changes in the quantity of output 1, but also due to changes in the levels of other output. It is not difficult to prove that when these MR and MC concepts are equated, optimal prices must satisfy the relationship already explained, i.e.

$$\frac{P - MC}{P} = \frac{1}{E_{d_i}} + \frac{1}{\sum \frac{S_i}{S_j} \cdot CE_{ij}}$$

marginal cost, and output will be lower, than when there is no interdependence. The reason is that marginal revenue associated with any level of output of the product will be lower, due to the reduction in demand for other products of the firm associated with the reduction in price and increase in output of the product in question. If complementary relationships between the product and other products dominate, the sum of cross-elasticities of demand will be negative, and the optimal price of the product will be lower in relation to marginal cost of the product, and output higher, than when there is no interdependence. The reason is that the marginal revenue associated with any level of output of the product will be higher, due to the increase in demand for other products of the firm associated with the reduction in price and increase in output of the product in question.

The determination of optimal prices and quantities when there is interdependence between the demand or cost conditions relating to different products can be depicted diagrammatically. If demands are interdependent, for example, the demand for one product will depend on the prices or quantities of other products produced by the firm. Assuming for expositional simplicity that the firm produces two products, X and Y, and that each product is produced at constant marginal cost; Figure 3–4 depicts the situation when the products are substitutes. In Figure 3–4(a) the higher, closely spaced curves are the demand curves of the products, say X, with a different curve for each amount sold (or price)

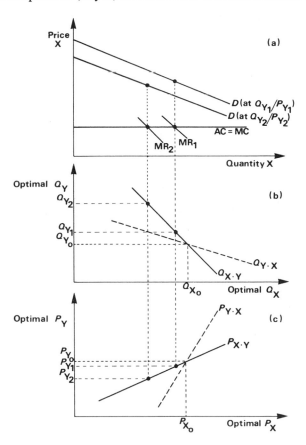

Figure 3–4. Substitute product relationships.

of the other product Y. The greater the amount of Y sold (or lower its price), the lower the demand for X at any given price. The lower, more widely spaced curves are the marginal revenue curves corresponding to each demand curve. Then for each output (price) of Y there will be an optimal output (and price) of X, indicated by the intersection of the appropriate marginal revenue curve for X with the product's marginal cost curve. In Figure 3–4(b) the optimal output levels of X at different output levels of Y are plotted, resulting in curve $Q_{X.Y}$. From the demand conditions for Y at different quantities of X, not shown here in order to conserve space, it is possible to derive an analogous curve, $Q_{Y.X}$, showing the optimal level of output of Y at different quantities of X. This curve is indicated by the dashed line in Figure 3–4(b). The shape of each of the curves in Figure 3–4(b) indicates that the optimal output of one of the products will be lower, the larger the output level of the other product. The intersection of these two curves at $X_0 Y_0$ indicates the level of each product which will maximize the firm's overall profits. In Figure 3–4(c) are plotted the optimal price of X at different prices of Y, resulting in curve $P_{X.Y}$, and the optimal price of Y at different prices of X, resulting in curve $P_{Y.X}$. The shape of these curves indicates that the optimal price of one of the products will be higher, the higher the price of the other product. The intersection of these two curves indicates the prices of the two products which will maximize the firm's overall profits.

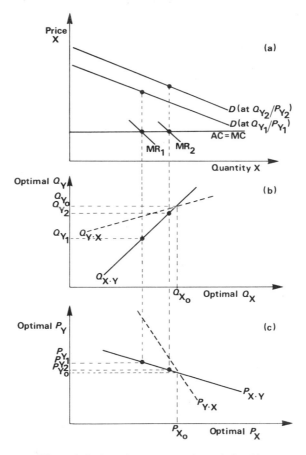

Figure 3–5. Complementary product relationships.

In the case of a complementary relationship between X and Y, the demand for each of the products would be greater at any price, the higher the quantity (or the lower the price) of the other product, and the slopes of the curves in Figure 3–4(b) and (c) would be reversed, as shown in Figure 3–5.

The implications of the existence of interdependence for the output levels and prices of the firm's products may be demonstrated by comparing the shapes of the curves in Figure 3–4(b) and (c) (for substitutes) or Figure 3–5(b) and (c) (for complements) with the shapes which the same curves would exhibit in the absence of interdependence. When there is no interdependence between the firm's products, the optimal output level of X does not depend on the quantity (or price) of Y, so that the curve $Q_{X.Y}$ is a vertical line as shown in Figure 3–6. Similarly, curve $Q_{Y.X}$ will be a horizontal line, indicating that the optimal output level of Y does not depend on the output level of X. In Figure 3–6(a) the corresponding curves when the products are substitutes are drawn in as dotted lines; and indicate that the output level of both products will be lower than when there is no interdependence. In Figure 3–6(b) the optimal price relationships are exhibited, and indicate that the price of each product will be higher when they are substitutes than when there is no interdependence. In Figure 3–6(c) and (d) the corresponding comparison for the case of complementary products indicates that the quantity of both products will be higher, and their prices lower, than when there is no interdependence. These results confirm the implications of the preceding algebraic analysis of optimal pricing relationships under interdependence. They also indicate that the greater the degree of substitutability (complementarity), the lower (higher) the output levels of the products.

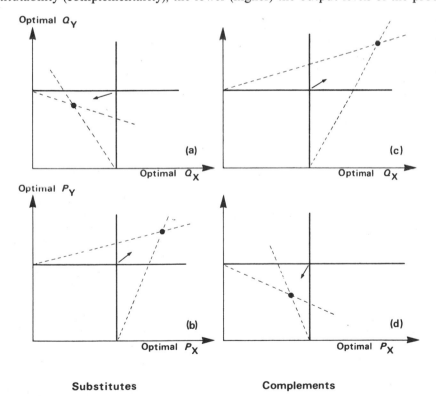

Figure 3–6. Optimal price quantity combinations with independence, substitutability and complementarity.

Interdependence between the costs of different products can also be indicated diagrammatically. Assuming for expositional simplicity that demands are independent, interdependence between costs implies that the marginal cost curve, rather than the demand curve and associated marginal revenue curve as before, depends on the level of output of the other product. Once again, the optimal level of one product will depend, therefore, on the output level of the other product. Figure 3–7 indicates the relevant diagrammatic results for the case where the marginal cost of one product is higher, the larger the output level of the other product. The major implication is that the optimal level of each output will be lower than when there is no interdependence; the opposite conclusion would have been obtained if the marginal cost of each product declined with increasing output levels of the other product.

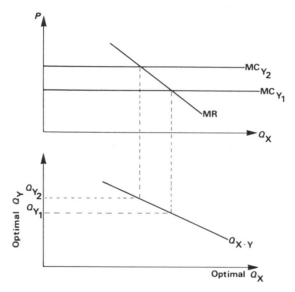

Figure 3–7. Cost interdependence.

The case of cost and demand interdependence is merely a combination of the two preceding cases and will not be developed here. Instead, the major implications, for optimal pricing, of the existence of interdependence between the demand or cost conditions relating to a firm's products will be underlined. First, as the preceding analysis clearly demonstrates, the optimal level of prices and outputs depends on the nature and degree of interdependence between the firm's products. Second, when there is interdependence, a change in the demand or cost conditions relating to one of the firm's products will imply a change not only in the optimal level of output and price of the product in question, but also in the price and output level of the firm's other products. This proposition may be easily understood by reference to Figure 3–4, for example. A change in the demand or cost conditions relating to one product, say X, will shift the curve $Q_{X.Y}$ (and also $P_{X.Y}$), reflecting the fact that the optimal level of output of X at any given level of output of Y is now changed. This will, however, change the intersection point of $Q_{X.Y}$ and $Q_{Y.X}$, (and the intersection of $P_{X.Y}$ and $P_{Y.X}$), implying that the optimal output level and price of the other product are changed also. It should be noted, however, that no generalizations are possible regarding the manner in which the change affects the optimal prices and quantities of the products. This depends on the relative slopes of $Q_{X.Y}$ and $Q_{Y.X}$

(and of $P_{X.Y}$ and $P_{Y.X}$), which in turn are determined by the magnitude of the interdependence between products in addition to whether they are substitutes or complements, and by the relative magnitudes of the price-elasticities of demand for each product.

Price Determination in Practice

Most empirical studies of firms' pricing behavior indicate that decision-makers do not appear to equate MR and MC in the manner prescribed by the conventional analysis of profit-maximizing pricing. For a selection of articles on the subject of price determination in practice, see Alfred (1), Laden (17), Lanzillotti (18), Ripley and Segal (29), Silberston (33) and Weston (36). The studies reveal that prices are generally determined by some variant of cost-plus, mark-up, or full-cost pricing, where the price of the product or service is calculated by adding to average variable cost (sometimes referred to as average 'prime' cost) a margin for overheads ('fixed' costs which do not vary directly with the level of output) and profit. The precise methods of calculating the mark-up over average variable cost vary widely between industries, between firms in a particular industry, and even between products within the same firm, for reasons which will be indicated below. There are two major reasons for the observed discrepancy between the pricing procedures utilized by firms in practice and the 'marginalist' principle of equating MR and MC propounded in conventional price theory. First, conventional price theory assumes profit-maximizing objectives and very simple constraints; second, it also presumes that decision-makers have knowledge of the precise nature of the cost and demand functions confronting them. The consequences, for firms' pricing behavior, of relaxing each of these assumptions will now be outlined briefly in turn.

On the first point, equating the MR and MC of a decision variable will be optimal only if the decision-maker's objective is profit maximization, and if no constraints exist in addition to those considered by conventional price theory which prevent attainment of this condition. As was noted in Chapter 1, the objective of 'profit maximization' itself has numerous variants, depending on the time period considered relevant by the decision-maker, the discount rate reflecting his relative evaluation of events occurring in different time periods, and the particular dimension of the decision variable in question which he considered to be relevant in his decision-making, such as output rate or volume, for example. Corresponding to each of these different variants of the profit-maximization objective, there is a different relevant marginal revenue and marginal cost concept. The difficulty of inferring decision-makers' objectives from behavior has already been referred to in Chapter 1; in the present context, the implication of the preceding point is that what appears to an observer to be failure to pursue profit-maximizing objectives may simply be a failure of the observer to comprehend the variables which the decision-maker considers to be relevant.

If decision-makers pursue objectives other than profit maximization, the optimal conditions which are necessary in order to achieve these objectives will not, in general, require equality between the MR and MC of a decision variable. A sales-revenue maximizer, for example, will expand the level of a decision variable to a level where the resulting addition to the firm's total revenue (MR) is less than the resulting addition to the firm's total cost (MC). The same is true of a managerial utility maximizer who derives satisfaction directly from the decision variable in question in addition to deriving satisfaction from the resulting effect on the firm's profits, for reasons explained in Chapter 1. Alternatively, decision-makers may attempt to maximize profits subject to some additional constraint(s) not present in conventional price theory. For example, if there is a limit on the supply of investment funds available to the firm which prevents the levels of all the firm's decision variables from being expanded to the profit-maximizing level, optimal levels of all decision variables will be achieved when MR exceeds MC by the same proportion for each decision variable.

Even when decision-makers' objectives differ from profit maximization, or where additional constraints are present which change the profit-maximizing relationship between the MR and MC of a decision variable from that found in conventional price theory, 'marginalist' principles will still be applicable in the sense that there will be a determinate optimal relationship between the MR and MC of a decision variable, which will depend on the precise nature of the decision-maker's objectives and constraints. Despite this, with very few exceptions, empirical studies of pricing behavior suggest that decision-makers do not think in a 'marginalist' way, nor behave even subconsciously in such a manner, when determining the prices of the products and services they sell. The reason, and probably the major reason why pricing practices appear to differ from the principles expounded in conventional price theory, is the existence of uncertainty concerning the precise form of the demand and cost relationships confronting decision-makers. In order to select the level of a decision variable, such as a price or output level, which equates MR and MC (or which establishes any other relationship between these concepts required by a decision-maker's objectives and constraints), the decision-maker must know what the MR and MC associated with that decision variable are. Since MC represents the effect of a change in the level of the decision variable in question on the firm's total costs, this requires knowledge of the technological input–output relationships and input prices which underlie total cost, at different levels of the decision variable. Similarly, MR represents the effect of a change in the level of the decision variable on the firm's total revenue. As explained in the second section of this chapter, for a firm producing a single product, the MR association with its output and price level depends on the price-elasticity of demand for the firm's product, which in turn depends on the firm's market share, the price-elasticity of market demand and, perhaps most important of all, the reactions of rival sellers to the firm's policies. For a multiple-product firm, the MR associated with the price and output of one of its products depends, in addition to these factors, also on the cross-elasticities of demand (and cost-interdependencies) between all its products.

Knowledge concerning the various factors underlying the MR and MC associated with a decision variable can be acquired by a firm's decision-makers prior to making a decision, but is costly to acquire and would have to be continually up-dated in the presence of changing demand and cost conditions. Instead, in the presence of uncertainty concerning the precise form of the demand and cost relationships confronting them, a firm's decision-makers generally adopt rules of thumb in their decision-making which are intended to enable the firm to approach the optimal levels of its decision variables through an iterative process while economizing on the costs of acquiring and transmitting information. For more on the nature of such rules of thumb see R. H. Day (9) and W. J. Baumol and R. E. Quandt (6). These rules, and the resulting iterative process, consist of a process of (i) formulating targets or goals relating to various aspects of the firm's operations, and operating procedures which define which of the firm's decision variables are to be varied, and how, in order to attempt to achieve these targets, and (ii) revising the targets, and sometimes the assignment of decision variables between targets, in the light of the resulting feed-back of information concerning the performance of the firm, in an effort to improve performance and move closer to levels of the firm's decision variables which are optimal. Several aspects of this process are particularly noteworthy, and will be emphasized briefly here.

One important feature of the preceding decision process is the assignment of decision variables to the task of achieving intermediate targets, or goals, rather than directly to the attainment of the firm's overall objectives, whatever they might be. Since different firms pursuing similar 'ultimate' goals, such as profit maximization, for example, may adopt different intermediate targets to which specific decision variables such as prices are assigned in an effort to implement the firm's overall objectives, it is not surprising that empirical studies of firms' pricing behavior reveal a variety of (intermediate) pricing goals existing in practice. This, of course, also greatly complicates the problem of attempting to infer a firm's ultimate objectives from its (pricing) behavior. It also enables one to understand why some types of behavior, which appear to be inconsistent with the pursuit of certain objectives when viewed from a static one-period point of view, may be quite consistent with that objective when viewed as part of a dynamic process of searching for values of decision variables which will achieve that objective.

A second important characteristic is the decentralized nature of the preceding decision process, which unless properly interpreted may appear inconsistent with the intrinsic interdependence between different activities of the firm. That is, the MR and MC associated with any particular decision variable generally depends on the level of the firm's other decision variables, so that the optimal levels of the firm's decision variables are interdependent and are jointly determined by the precise manner in which the demand and cost conditions of the firm are related to all the firm's decision variables. Despite this, the decision rules of thumb adopted by firms do not generally attempt to take account of all the interdependencies between decision variables. For example, the price of a particular product may be varied, in order to achieve a target rate of return on the product without regard to the resulting implications for the demand for other products, and the resulting implications for the firm's overall performance. Notwithstanding the failure to take the interdependence between different decision variables into account, in the sense of estimating the effects of changes in one decision variable on all aspects of the firm's operations, the resulting decentralized iterative dynamic decision process may converge upon those values of the firm's decision variables which are optimal when the relevant interdependencies are taken into account. In the process of convergence, however, the resulting changes in the level of individual decision variables in certain time periods may often appear to be moving away from, rather than towards, their optimal values, because the process of convergence to optimal values need not necessarily be direct, or asymptotic, and may involve 'overshooting' and an oscillatory time path of the firm's decision variables. This also greatly complicates the problem of inferring firms' objectives from observed behavior of the firm's decision variables.

A third feature of the decision process is the continuous revision of intermediate targets as the firm learns from experience and adapts to the information acquired. It is in the context of uncertainty that cost-plus pricing practices should be interpreted. These practices are not, like conventional price theory, a description of the conditions that are necessary in order for a firm's decision variables to be at optimal levels; they are, instead, a description of pricing processes which are an attempt to search for and establish the optimal levels of the firm's decision variables.

Cost-plus pricing practices can be quite consistent with 'marginalist' principles. For example, it was pointed out in the second section of this chapter that for a firm producing a single product, equating MR and MC implies establishing the relationship $(P - MC)/P = 1/E_d$. If the firm's total cost increases proportionately with proportionate increase in the level of output, MC = AC, and profit maximization requires that $(P - AC)/P = 1/E_d$. If a firm initially has no knowledge concerning its demand conditions, and therefore no knowledge of the level of price which will establish this relationship, it may simply vary the mark-up $P - AC$, observing the resulting changes in quantity sold and therefore the level of $1/E_d$, until the preceding optimal relationship is established. Alternatively, the firm may vary $P - AC$ without reference to the value of E_d, simply by referring to the resulting effects on the level of its profits. When reductions in $P - AC$ increase profits, implicitly MR exceeds MC, or $(P - AC)/P$ exceeds $1/E_d$.

Even if a firm's total cost does not increase proportionately with proportionate changes in the level of its output, so that AC and MC are not equal, there will still always be a systematic relationship between AC and MC. Establishing the relationship $(P - MC)/P = 1/E_d$ therefore automatically implies establishing a relationship between $(P - AC)/P$ and $1/E_d$, though not one of equality. When AC rises with output, MC will exceed AC so that the profit-maximizing level of $(P - AC)/P$ will exceed $1/E_d$, for example. The firm may use $P - AC$ in its decision-making rather than $P - MC$ simply because AC is easier to calculate or is used for other purposes, such as accounting purposes, and is readily available.

Contrary to first appearances, cost-plus pricing procedures do not ignore demand conditions. For one thing, unless the firm's AC does not vary with the level of output, the calculation of the average cost which is used to determine price itself presumes an estimate of the firm's total output level. Second, the magnitude of the margin or mark-up over average cost, which determines $P - AC$ may be either initially set, or later varied, on the basis of estimates of rival sellers' actions and the resulting implications for the level of demand for the firm's product. In this connection, it is interesting to note that in some circumstances the usual causal chain linking a firm's pricing to its rivals' reactions may be reversed. It was stressed in the second section of this chapter that the price-elasticity of demand for a firm's product, and therefore the optimal level of the firm's price and output, depend on the policies of rival sellers. In certain circumstances, however, the *method of price setting* used by a firm may itself make rivals' reactions more predictable and therefore help to determine indirectly the optimal level of the firm's price and output. For example, in some industries 'price leadership' is a feature of the price determination process, one firm setting price and others following suit. Provided the firm sets price at a level which will enable the other firms to earn acceptable profits, it may be reasonably secure in assuming that they will follow suit; in these circumstances the relevant cost used in the price-setting process is related to the AC of all firms in the industry, rather than that of the price leader itself. A similar situation is found in the context of 'limit pricing', or pricing to deter entrants, which is discussed in detail in Chapter 7. For reasons explained, there is a unique level of $P - AC$ in an industry which will deter entrant firms, and established firms may in certain circumstances set price in relation to AC at this level.

If a firm produces more than one product, the analysis contained in the preceding section indicates that generally the profit-maximizing $P - MC$ (and therefore optimal $P - AC$ which this implies) for each product depends not only on the price-elasticity of demand for the product, but also on the cross-elasticities of demand between the products. The determination of optimal prices and quantities in these circumstances was depicted diagrammatically, and is relevant in the present context. The existence of uncertainty concerning the precise form of the firm's demand conditions which determine the price- and cross-elasticities of demand for the firm's product at alternative levels of the firm's prices and output levels implies that the exact position and slopes of the curves such as $Q_{X,Y}$ and $Q_{Y,X}$, and $P_{X,Y}$ and $P_{Y,X}$ in Figure 3–4(b) and (c) and Figure 3–5(b) and (c) are not known by the firm's decision-makers, because these curves are the diagrammatic representations of alternative combinations of output levels, or price levels, of two products which satisfy the condition that MR = MC, and $(P - MC)/P = 1/E_i + 1/\Sigma \dfrac{S_i}{S_j} \cdot CE_{ij}$ for each product. This, in turn, implies that the optimal levels of price and

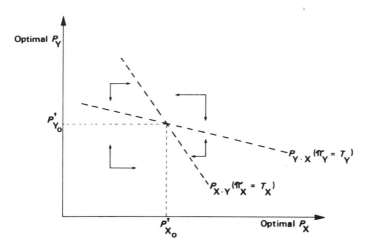

Figure 3–8. Convergent iterative pricing rules in the presence of uncertain demand conditions.

quantity of each product cannot be instantaneously determined by the firm's decision-makers. Instead, they may, for example, set target profit levels $\pi_X = T_X$ and $\pi_Y = T_Y$ for each product. The alternative price levels of both products which achieve these profit targets, which of course depend on the firm's unknown demand conditions, will be depicted diagrammatically by curves such as the dashed $P_{X \cdot Y}$ and $P_{Y \cdot X}$ curves in Figure 3–8, which apply to complementary products. If the price of each product is then varied independently in an effort to achieve the profit target assigned to the product, when the targets are not being achieved prices will move in the directions indicated by the arrows in Figure 3–8. As the directions of the arrows indicate, the resulting dynamic path of prices will converge toward the levels P_{X0} and P_{Y0}, which achieve the target profit levels set for each product simultaneously, despite absence of knowledge of the positions and shapes of these curves on the part of the firm's decision-makers. The firm may then vary the profit targets for each product, in an effort to improve the overall performance of the firm. This will shift the position of the dashed $P_{X \cdot Y}$ and $P_{Y \cdot X}$ lines, and the result may be to move the intersection point of these lines and therefore the equilibrium levels of the firm's decision variables closer to the optimal levels shown by the intersection of the $P_{X \cdot Y}$ and $P_{Y \cdot X}$ lines depicted in Figures 3–4 and 3–5. By such a process of target revision and observation of the results for the firm's overall profit performance, the firm's decision-makers seek to overcome the obstacle to optimal decision-making present whenever uncertainty exists concerning the demand and cost conditions confronting a firm.

The preceding discussion implies that price decisions, and price variations, are an important instrument used by firms in an effort to achieve the targets established at each stage in the firm's decision process. Empirical studies indicate, however, that top executives often do not concern themselves with pricing details; these are delegated to lower levels of management. This is easily explained in the context of the preceding outline of firms' decision processes; once targets are established by higher-level management, the routine task of varying decision variables to achieve these targets can be left to lower-level administrators. It is the choice of targets and the assignment of decision variables to targets which determine the resulting performance of the firm. Less consistent with the preceding discussion is the fact that casual observation, and numerous empirical studies of firms' pricing behavior, indicate that prices often remain unchanged for long periods of time, and often remain inflexible in the face of changes in demand and cost conditions. This may, however, simply reflect the fact that a firm has other decision variables in addition to prices, such as numerous dimensions of product quality or advertising which influence buyer behavior and the firm's total revenue and total cost. Variation of these other decision variables may sometimes be preferred by a firm's decision-makers to price variations for one or more of a number of reasons. The resulting effects on the firm's total revenue may be more predictable; a price reduction may increase or reduce the firm's total revenue, depending on whether the price-elasticity of demand for the firm's product is greater or less than unity in absolute magnitude, whereas increases in advertising expenditures, for example, will generally increase the firm's total revenue. Another reason may be that decision variables other than price are less difficult or costly to change, or may in certain circumstances be more effective in influencing buyer behavior and the firm's total revenue, or less likely to invite competitive retaliation by rival sellers. Changes in decision variables other than price may also be dynamically superior in terms of the speed and direction of approach of the firm's performance to desired results.

Partial-Equilibrium versus General-Equilibrium Analysis of the Behavior of the Firm

Conventional price theory focuses attention upon the determination of the price and level of output of a firm's product(s). It demonstrates that demand conditions indicating the quantity of the firm's product demanded at different prices, cost conditions depicting the relationship between the firm's output level and costs, and the firm's objectives together determine the optimal price and output level of the firm. The quantity of a firm's product demanded depends however on numerous other decision variables in addition to price, including product-quality dimensions and advertising variables, which influence buyer behavior, and the essence of much business behavior is a conscious attempt to influence the demand and cost conditions depicted in conventional price theory by spending money on activities, such as advertising, research and development which shape buyer preferences and add to the body of knowledge concerning production techniques and input–output relationships. If a firm can influence the demand and cost conditions for its product by varying the level of other decision variables such as advertising and R&D outlays, it is necessary to regard the conventional treatment of a firm's pricing behavior as a partial-equilibrium analysis of the firm's behavior, in contrast to a general-equilibrium analysis.

A general-equilibrium analysis of the firm deals with the determination of optimal levels of all the firm's decision variables, whereas a partial-equilibrium analysis focuses attention on the determination of optimal levels of a smaller number of its decision variables by assuming, either explicitly or implicitly, that the other decision variables not considered are already determined. Thus, conventional price theory implicitly assumes that all decision variables which influence the firm's demand and cost conditions, such as advertising and R&D outlays, have already been determined, and focuses upon the determination of the remaining decision variables, price and the level of the firm's output. This should not be permitted to obscure the fact that the optimal levels of all the firm's decision variables are interdependent and jointly determined by the precise form of the relationship between the firm's total cost, and total revenue, and *all* of the firm's decision variables. Thus, for example, while the level of MR and MC associated with the price of the firm's product(s), and therefore the optimal level of price, depends on the level of the firm's other decision variables, it is equally true that the MR and MC associated with other decision variables depend on the price of the firm's product(s). If a firm's decision-makers determine the optimal levels of some of the firm's decision variables simultaneously, in the manner illustrated in Chapter 4 in connection with advertising and price decisions, for example, one cannot then illustrate the determination of one of the decision variables in isolation, except in the context of a hypothetical partial-equilibrium analysis. Alternatively, decision-makers may adopt a decentralized approach to the determination of the firm's decision variables, attempting to reach optimal levels of each decision variable without regard to the interdependence between the various decision variables. This is equivalent to a partial-equilibrium approach to the firm's decision problem since it ignores the consequences of the optimal level of one decision variable for the optimal levels of other decision variables. Despite this, the resulting path of the firm's decision variables through time may converge to levels of all decision variables which are optimal.

A firm's decision-makers will not generally adopt a general-equilibrium approach to the firm's decision problem, which attempts to take the interdependence between all the firm's decision variables into account and to determine the optimal levels of all decision variables simultaneously, due to a combination of reasons. These include lack of knowledge of the precise form of the relationship between total revenue and total cost and all the firm's decision variables, and the limited problem-solving capacity of individual decision-makers which necessitates decentralized decision-making and which would involve costly transmission of information between decision-makers if a simultaneous approach to the determination of all decision variables were adopted. Even in these circumstances, however, most aspects of a firm's operations will still be closely related due to the fact that the funds available to a firm, in the form of its sales revenues and additional external finance, are limited at any point in time. The firm's decision concerning the level of its investment in current production activities, in advertising activities, and in R&D or other activities may be made by weighing the effects of spending its investment funds on one activity rather than on another, and by comparing the anticipated contribution of each activity to the decision-makers' objectives in the light of their own evaluation of how the different activities contribute towards these objectives. See D. Mueller (24) for empirical evidence indicating the simultaneity of many of a firm's decisions.

The inherent simultaneity of many of the firm's decisions necessitates a general-equilibrium approach to the behavior of the firm, rather than a partial-equilibrium approach. A complete understanding of the relationship between different aspects of a firm's behavior is essential in order to assist formulation of logically consistent public policy measures designed to influence business conduct. A policy which is designed to influence one aspect of the firm's behavior will very likely, as a result of this simultaneity, also influence other aspects of the firm's behavior. Public policy measures imposed without regard to the effect of the measures on all aspects of the firm's behavior may have side effects which, on balance, render the measures undesirable. For example, the profitability of R&D investment depends upon anticipated prices received for the resulting products. These prices depend, in part, upon the anticipated extent of price competition in the markets concerned. A policy designed to increase price competition in a particular industry might, in addition, reduce R&D investment and result in an undesirable reduction in the rate of new product introduction. In order to place firms' pricing behavior in perspective in relation to a broader view of firms' activities, Chapter 4 will deal with the determination of optimal levels of decision variables other than the level of product prices, and with the characteristics of optimal relationships between the price and quantity of a firm's output and other decision variables.

RECOMMENDED READINGS

1. Alfred, A. M., Company pricing policy, *Journal of Industrial Economics*, November 1972.
2. Archibald, G. C., 'Large' and 'small' numbers in the theory of the firm, *Manchester School of Economic and*

Social Studies, January 1959.

3. Bailey, M. J., Price and output determination by a firm selling related products, *American Economic Review*, March 1954.

4. Barnett, N., Beyond market segmentation, *Harvard Business Review*, January–February 1969.

5. Battalio, R. and Ekelund, R. B., Output change under third degree price discrimination, *Southern Economic Journal*, October 1972.

6. Baumol, W. J. and Quandt, R. E., Rules of thumb and optimally imperfect decisions, *American Economic Review*, March 1964.

7. Clemens, E., Price discrimination and the multiple product firm, *Review of Economic Studies*, Vol. 19, No. 1, 1951.

8. Coase, R. H., Monopoly pricing with interrelated costs and demands, *Economics*, November 1946.

9. Day, R. H., Profits, learning and the convergence of satisficing to marginalism, *Quarterly Journal of Economics*, May 1967.

10. Demsetz, H., Joint supply and price discrimination, *Journal of Law and Economics*, October 1973.

11. Fama, E. F. and Laffer, A. B., The number of firms and competition, *American Economic Review*, September 1972.

12. Fellner, W., *Competition Among the Few* (New York: Knopf, 1949).

13. Finn, T. J., The quantity of output in simple monopoly and discriminating monopoly, *Southern Economic Journal*, October 1974.

14. Frankel, M., Pricing decisions under unknown demand, *Kyklos*, Vol. 26, 1973.

15. Gallo, J., Oligopoly and price fixing: some analytical models, *Antitrust Law and Economics Review*, Fall 1970.

16. Johnson, A. C. and Helmberger, P., Price elasticity of demand as an element of market structure, *American Economic Review*, December 1967.

17. Laden, B. E., Perfect competition, average cost pricing, and the price equation, *Review of Economic Studies*, February 1972.

18. Lanzillotti, R. F., Pricing objectives in large companies, *American Economic Review*, December 1958.

19. Leftwich, R. H., *The Price System and Resource Allocation*, 3rd ed. (New York: Holt, Rinehart and Winston, Inc., 1966), Chapter 6.

20. Lofgren, K. G., The theory of intertemporal price discrimination: an outline, *Swedish Journal of Economics*, September 1971.

21. Machlup, F., Monopoly and competition: a classification of market positions, *American Economic Review*, September 1937.

22. Machlup, F., Characteristics and types of price discrimination. In Stigler, G. J. (Ed.) *Business Concentration and Price Policy* (Princeton, N.J.: Princeton University Press, 1955).

23. McKean, J. R. and Peterson, R. D., Demand elasticity, product differentiation and market structure, *Journal of Economic Theory*, April 1973.

24. Mueller, D., The firm's decision process: an econometric investigation, *Quarterly Journal of Economics*, February 1967.

25. Olson, M. and McFarland, D., The restoration of pure monopoly and the concept of the industry, *Quarterly Journal of Economics*, November 1962.

26. Pelzman, S., Pricing in public and private enterprises: electric utilities in the United States, *Journal of Law and Economics*, April 1971.

27. Pfouts, R. W., Some cost and profit relationships in the multi-product firm, *Southern Economic Journal*, January 1973.

28. Ranlett, J. G. and Curry, R. L., Jr, Economic principles: the monopoly, oligopoly and competition models, *Antitrust Law and Economics Review*, Spring 1968.

29. Ripley, F. C. and Segal, L., Price determination in 395 manufacturing industries, *Review of Economics and Statistics*, August 1973.

30. Robinson, Joan, *The Economics of Imperfect Competition* (London: Macmillan & Co. Ltd, 1933), Chapters 15 and 16.

31. Shepherd, W. G., The elements of market structure, *Review of Economics and Statistics*, February 1972.

32. Shepherd, W. G., Elements of market structure: an interindustry analysis, *Southern Economic Journal*, April 1972.

33. Silberston, A., Surveys of applied economics: price behavior of firms, *Economic Journal*, September 1970.

34. Smith, W. R., Product differentiation and market segmentation as alternate marketing strategies, *Southern Economic Journal*, October 1972.

35. Stigler, G. J., A theory of oligopoly, *Journal of Political Economy*, February 1964.

36. Weston, J. F., Pricing behavior of large firms, *Western Economic Journal*, March 1972.

37. White, D. L. and Walker, M. C., First degree price discrimination and profit maximization, *Southern Economic Journal*, October 1973.

CHAPTER FOUR

NON-PRICE BEHAVIOR

As already noted in the last section of Chapter 3, the level of price of a firm's product(s) is only one of many variables with which a firm's decision-makers must concern themselves. Other variables, such as advertising and numerous quality dimensions of the firm's output, influence the firm's total revenues via their effects on buyer behavior, and also affect the firm's total costs. The present chapter deals with the determination of optimal levels of decision variables other than the level of product prices, and with the relationship between optimal levels of price and non-price decision variables. The first three sections will indicate the principles that are generally applicable when considering non-price decision variables, using the determination of optimal levels of a firm's advertising as an illustration; later sections will then focus upon various aspects of some other non-price decision variables including durability, the frequency of style changes, and research and development decisions.

Optimal Levels of Non-Price Decision Variables

As in the case of pricing decisions, the optimal level of a non-price decision variable depends upon the nature of the decision-maker's objectives and on the constraints he is faced by, since these determine the exact form of the conditions which must be satisfied in order to maximize the level of the decision-maker's objective function while simultaneously satisfying all of the constraints which he faces. Thus, for example, a decision-maker who is faced by constraints indicating how the firm's total costs and total revenues are related to levels of the firm's decision variables must select levels of the firm's decision variables which equate the MR and MC associated with each decision variable in order to maximize the level of the firm's profits. On the other hand, if maximization of profit is not the decision-maker's goal, a different relationship between MR and MC will be optimal, and different levels of the firm's decision variables will therefore be required in order to achieve other goals. For expositional convenience only, the following discussion will assume that profit maximization is the objective of a firm's decision-makers; the only difference which the pursuit of other objectives would make to the analysis would be to change the optimal relationship between the MR and MC associated with each decision variable, not the factors which underlie these marginal revenue and cost concepts.

Advertising is a strategy influencing the shape or position of the demand curve for a firm's product, which as explained in the last chapter indicates the quantity of the firm's product buyers will demand at various alternative prices, without changing the physical characteristics of the product. In order to maximize profits, the firm's advertising must be at a level which satisfies the condition that the effect of a change in the level of advertising on the firm's total revenue (the marginal revenue from advertising) equals the resulting effect on the firm's total costs (the marginal cost associated with advertising). The MR associated with advertising equals the resulting change in the quantity of the firm's product demanded, multiplied by the current price, or $P \cdot \dfrac{\Delta Q}{\Delta A}$, where $\dfrac{\Delta Q}{\Delta A}$ represents the change in quantity demanded per unit change in the level of advertising. The resulting effect of the change in advertising on the firm's total cost will equal the increase in advertising outlays itself plus the increase in total production cost necessary to meet the increased demand for the product. The increase in total production cost resulting from a unit increase in the level of advertising outlays will equal the change in quantity demanded multiplied by the marginal cost of output, or $\dfrac{\Delta Q}{\Delta A} \cdot MC_Q$. Equating the marginal revenue and marginal cost associated with advertising therefore implies establishing the following relationship:

$$P \cdot \frac{\Delta Q}{\Delta A} = \frac{\Delta Q}{\Delta A} \cdot MC_Q + 1$$

Multiplying both sides of this expression by $\dfrac{A}{PQ}$ and defining

$$\frac{\Delta Q}{\Delta A} \cdot \frac{A}{Q} = \frac{\text{proportionate change in quantity demanded}}{\text{proportionate change in advertising outlays}} = E_a$$

as the elasticity of quantity demanded with respect to advertising, or advertising-elasticity for short, this can be expressed alternatively as

$$\frac{A}{PQ} = \frac{P - MC}{P} \cdot E_a$$

which indicates that the profit-maximizing advertising-to-sales ratio depends on $(P - MC)/P$, the proportionate excess of price over marginal cost of the firm's product, and E_a, the advertising-elasticity of demand for the firm's product.

Like the price-elasticity of demand for a firm's product, which was dealt with in section 2 of Chapter 3, the advertising-elasticity of demand for a firm's product, E_a, depends on the behavior of buyers and rival sellers. The expression $\dfrac{\Delta Q}{\Delta A}$, which represents the increase in demand for the firm's product in response to a unit increase in the level of the firm's advertising outlays, is in reality the net result of (i) the effect of a change in the firm's advertising on the demand for its product when rivals' advertising is unchanged, $\dfrac{\Delta Q}{\Delta A}$, plus (ii) the effect of a change in the firm's advertising on the (anticipated) level of its rivals' advertising $\frac{\Delta A_r}{\Delta A}$, multiplied by $\frac{\Delta Q}{\Delta A_r}$, the effect of a change in rivals' advertising levels on demand for the firm's product.*

The marginal revenue associated with a unit change in the level of a firm's advertising, previously represented by $P \cdot \frac{\Delta Q}{\Delta A}$, may therefore be expressed alternatively as follows:

$$\mathrm{MR}_A = P \cdot \left(\frac{\Delta Q}{\Delta A} + \frac{\Delta A_r}{\Delta A} \cdot \frac{\Delta Q}{\Delta A_r} \right)$$

When multiplied by $\frac{A}{PQ}$, the expression in brackets becomes

$$\left(\frac{\Delta Q}{\Delta A} \cdot \frac{A}{Q} \right) \cdot \frac{1}{P} + \left(\frac{\Delta A_r}{\Delta A} \cdot \frac{A}{A_r} \right) \cdot \left(\frac{\Delta Q}{\Delta A_r} \cdot \frac{A_r}{Q} \right) \cdot \frac{1}{P} \text{ or } \frac{E_A + E_{conj.} E_{Ar}}{P}$$

where $E_A = \dfrac{\text{proportionate change in demand for the firm's product}}{\text{proportionate change in the firm's advertising}}$

when rivals' advertising remains unchanged,

$E_{conj.} = \dfrac{\text{proportionate change in rivals' advertising}}{\text{proportionate change in the firm's own advertising}}$

and $E_{Ar} = \dfrac{\text{proportionate change in demand for the firm's product}}{\text{proportionate change in rivals' advertising}}$

Accordingly, since

$$\frac{A}{PQ} \cdot \mathrm{MR}_A = P \left(\frac{E_A + E_{conj.} E_{Ar}}{P} \right)$$

and $\dfrac{A}{PQ} \cdot \mathrm{MC}_A = \mathrm{MC}_Q \left(\dfrac{E_A + E_{conj.} E_{Ar}}{P} \right) + \dfrac{A}{PQ}$

the condition that the marginal revenue and marginal cost associated with the level of a firm's advertising must be equal requires that the following relationship be established:

$$\frac{A}{PQ} = \left(\frac{P - \mathrm{MC}_Q}{P} \right) \cdot (E_A + E_{conj.} E_{Ar})$$

This demonstrates that the profit-maximizing advertising–sales ratio depends both on buyer behavior and on rival seller behavior. When rival sellers do not change the level of their advertising in response to a change in the firm's advertising, $E_{conj.}$ is zero, and the

---

* This can be proved by straightforward application of differential calculus, as follows: if the quantity of the firm's product demanded depends on the level of price of the firm's product, and the level of its advertising, and also on the level of its rivals' advertising,

TR $= P \cdot Q \quad (P, A, A_r)$

and the marginal revenue

$$\frac{\partial (\mathrm{TR})}{\partial A} = P \cdot \frac{\partial Q}{\partial A} = P \cdot \left(\frac{\partial Q}{\partial A} + \frac{\partial A_r}{\partial A} \cdot \frac{\partial Q}{\partial A_r} \right)$$

resulting effect on demand for the firm's product depends only on E_A, which depends on the response of buyers to the advertising change. When rival sellers respond by changing the level of their advertising, $E_{\text{conj.}}$ will be positive if they increase the level of their advertising, and negative if they reduce the level of their advertising. E_{Ar} will be negative in sign, reflecting the fact that a rise in the level of rival sellers' advertising will reduce the demand for a firm's product at the current price. The optimal advertising–sales ratio of the firm will therefore be larger, the smaller the increase (or larger the decrease) in the level of rival sellers' advertising which is anticipated by the firm.

The factors which underlie a firm's anticipations regarding its rivals' actions, and the possibility that a relationship may exist between the number or size distribution of rival firms and the optimal levels of a firm's advertising, will be investigated in greater detail in Chapter 6. Some of the factors which will influence the extent of buyer response to a firm's advertising, and therefore the magnitude of E_A, will be discussed briefly in the third section of this chapter dealing with the firm's choice between alternative combinations of decision variables and competitive strategies.

Interdependence between Price and Non-Price Decisions

In the preceding section, when deriving the expressions for marginal revenue and marginal cost associated with a firm's advertising, it was assumed that the level of price of the firm's product remained unchanged. It is clear from the algebraic expression for the marginal revenue from advertising that the level of price will affect the magnitude of the marginal revenue from advertising, and will therefore influence the optimal level of advertising, where MR and MC of advertising are equal. In other words, simply equating the MR and MC associated with advertising will not maximize the firm's profits unless the level of the firm's product price is optimal in the sense that no other level of price can increase the firm's profits. Similarly, the MR associated with changes in the firm's product price depends on the level of the firm's advertising and the consequent shape and position of the firm's conventional demand curve. Again, simply equating the MR and MC associated with the level of product price will not maximize the firm's profits unless the firm's advertising is at an optimal level. The condition that the MR and MC associated with each of the firm's decision variables be equal must therefore be simultaneously satisfied for each of the firm's decision variables, in order for the level of the firm's profits to be maximized.

The preceding interdependence between the optimal level of a firm's product price and advertising can be demonstrated by combining the profit-maximizing pricing condition derived in section 2 of Chapter 3 with the profit-maximizing advertising condition derived in the preceding section of this chapter. Since profit-maximization requires that the MR and MC associated with the firm's price and output level be equal, and also that the MR and MC associated with advertising be equal, the two following conditions must be simultaneously satisfied:

$$\frac{P - MC_Q}{P} = \frac{1}{E_d}$$

and $\dfrac{A}{PQ} = \dfrac{P - MC_Q}{P} \cdot E_a$

This implies that $\dfrac{A}{PQ} = \dfrac{E_a}{E_d}$

or alternatively, when the factors underlying E_a and E_d are taken into account, that

$$\frac{A}{PQ} = \frac{(E_A + .E_{conj.} \cdot E_{Ar})}{\dfrac{E_m}{S_f} + \dfrac{E_r \cdot S_r}{S_f}}$$

This optimal condition relating to a firm's product price and advertising is usually referred to as the 'Dorfman–Steiner' condition in acknowledgement of a seminal article by those two economists (15) dealing with the optimal relationship between a firm's price and non-price decision variables. By showing that a firm's optimal advertising–sales ratio depends on the ratio of the advertising- and price-elasticities of demand for the firm's product, it demonstrates very clearly the interdependence between price and non-price decisions, because E_d depends on the level of price and on the response of demand for the firm's product to price changes. The second version of the Dorfman–Steiner condition noted above, incorporating the influence of buyers and rival sellers, also demonstrates another extremely important principle; namely, that the optimal level of a firm's advertising depends not only on the advertising reactions of rival sellers, but also on the price reactions of rival sellers. Thus, for example, even if a firm's rivals are not expected to respond to a change in its advertising by changing their advertising, the extent to which they react by changing *other* decision variables, such as their product prices, is relevant in determining the optimal level of the firm's advertising. A critical implication of this principle needs to be emphasized, for it is often overlooked in conventional theory and contemporary policy-oriented discussions of interfirm rivalry and 'competition'; it is that the lack of response in some decision variables such as price need not mean absence of 'competition' in the sense of high degrees of responsiveness of non-price decision variables to changes in rivals' policies. Moreover, it is clear from the preceding algebraic expression that high degrees of responsiveness of rivals' non-price decision variables influence the optimal level of a firm's prices even in the absence of interfirm price rivalry.

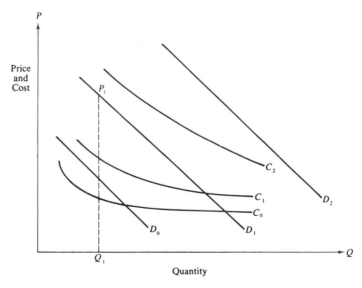

Figure 4–1. Simultaneous determination of price, output, and advertising levels.

The interdependence between a firm's price and advertising levels, and the joint determination of optimal levels of these decision variables can also be demonstrated diagrammatically, as illustrated in Figure 4–1. The demand curve labeled D_0 indicates the number of units of output the firm expects to sell at various alternative prices if it did not advertise. The average cost curve labeled C_0 indicates the average cost of production at different levels of output. If the firm can influence its demand curve by advertising, associated with each level of advertising there will be a different demand curve representing the demand conditions anticipated at that level of advertising outlay. For example, D_1 represents the demand conditions anticipated at a level of advertising outlays A_1; D_2 represents the demand conditions anticipated at a higher level of advertising A_2, and so on. Similarly, associated with each level of advertising there will be a different average total cost curve indicating the average cost of producing and distributing different levels of output of the firm's product. At a level of advertising A_1, for example, the firm's average total cost curve is C_1; it is obtained by adding a rectangular hyperbola representing the fixed level of advertising outlays A_1 vertically to C_0. The advertising outlays necessary to secure any given state of demand enter the firm's cost function as a fixed cost, that is, a cost which does not vary with the quantity of output. Therefore, the curve of average advertising costs will be a rectangular hyperbola, that is, average advertising cost multiplied by quantity of output is a constant.

In order to, say, maximize profits, the firm must compare the maximum profit (total revenue minus production and advertising cost) associated with each pair of demand and cost curves. This will involve selecting a price–output combination which maximizes profits from each pair of demand and cost curves. With an advertising level A_1, for example, the profit-maximizing price is P_1, at which the quantity sold is Q_1. Profits will be maximized by choosing a pair of demand and cost curves (that is, a level of advertising) and a price, which yield the maximum profits, subject to the constraint that the level of investment in production and advertising activities which are implied by this combination is no greater than the firm's available investment funds. The profits associated with any price depend upon the level of advertising and consequent position of the demand (and cost) curves; the profits associated with any given level of advertising depend upon the price charged at that level of advertising. The optimal level of advertising and optimal price (that is, optimal level of investment in current production activities) will be simultaneously determined. See N. S. Buchanan (6) for the same approach.

The previous example assumed that the firm was free to choose the price of its product. A similar analysis applies, however, if the price which a firm can charge is predetermined by conventional, oligopolistic, legal, or other considerations. The only difference that this makes to the previous example is that the firm must compare the profits associated with each pair of demand and cost curves when the price charged is the same in all circumstances. It still remains true that the optimal level of the firm's output, and optimal level of advertising outlays, are simultaneously determined.

The distinction between general and partial equilibrium analysis, referred to in the previous chapter, can also be illustrated using this example. If A_i is the optimal level of advertising outlays, one can assume that this is determined (hence the demand and cost conditions will be determined), and focus attention on the 'determination' of price using one demand curve and one cost curve. Likewise, if P_i is the optimal price, one can take this as given, and focus attention upon the 'determination' of the optimal level of advertising outlay as shown in Figure 4–2.

Neither of these partial-equilibrium approaches, however, shows the way in which price and the level of advertising are selected by the firm's decision-makers, if price and advertising level are simultaneously determined by comparison of the consequences of

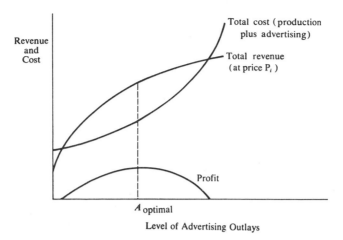

Figure 4–2. Partial equilibrium determination of advertising outlays.

price–advertising combinations where both decision variables vary. In practice, decision-makers in most firms will not adopt a simultaneous approach to the determination of all the firm's decision variables, for a variety of reasons which were already noted in the section of Chapter 3 dealing with price determination in practice. These reasons include lack of information on the precise form of the relationship between the firm's total revenue, and total cost, and all decision variables; the limited problem-solving capacity of individual decision-makers even if all relevant information were available; the costs of transmitting information between decision-makers when decisions are decentralized and interdependence exists between different decision variables. For one or more of these reasons, a firm's decision-makers may often use a process of decision-making which is essentially a partial-equilibrium approach to the determination of individual decision variables, attempting to approach the levels of the firm's decision variables which jointly maximize the firm's objective by this iterative decision-making process. This does not imply, however, that the firm's decision-makers are unaware of the interdependence between its price and non-price decision variables, and the nature of that interdependence will in any event affect the outcome of the firm's partial-equilibrium decision-making process in terms of the resulting path of the firm's decision variables and performance through time.

The Dorfman–Steiner condition itself indicates the relationship between a firm's advertising–sales ratio and the advertising- and price-elasticities of demand for the firm's product which must be established in order for the firm's price and advertising to be at optimal levels, not the absolute levels of the firm's price and advertising which will establish this relationship. The latter will depend on how buyer and rival seller behavior and therefore the relevant elasticities are related to different levels of the firm's decision variables. The preceding diagrammatic framework can, however, be employed to explain the logic of the argument, sometimes used by firms to defend their advertising activities, that advertising lowers the absolute level of product prices paid by buyers, and this argument will be analyzed briefly before concluding this section.

Since advertising increases the total cost of producing and distributing a particular product, total revenue must be higher to cover advertising outlays than it would have to be in their absence. However, average revenue (price) per unit of output sold need not increase in order to satisfy this condition. Total revenue is price multiplied by quantity sold, and if quantity sold increases, an increase in total revenue can be achieved without necessitating an increase in price. However, the fact that increased output increases production costs must be taken into account. If unit production costs are constant with increases in quantity produced, unit cost of production and distribution *must* increase with an increase in advertising, irrespective of the increase in quantity produced. This follows from the fact that unit advertising cost will be positive no matter how large the output. Therefore, to obtain a reduction in unit costs, unit production costs must *fall* with increases in the level of output.

It follows that, in order for advertising to lower price, advertising must increase the quantity sold *and* either unit profits must be reduced or unit production costs must decline with increases in output, as shown in Figure 4–3.

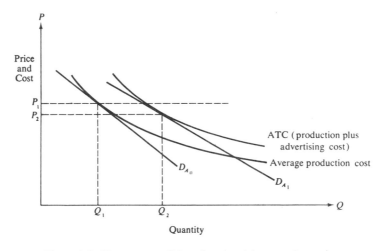

Figure 4–3. Necessary conditions for advertising to reduce price.

The argument that advertising reduces prices is invalid unless the aforementioned conditions are satisfied. If total industry demand for the advertised product remains unchanged, the demand for one firm's product can only expand at the expense of the demand for another firm's product. Any tendency for unit production costs to decline in one firm will be offset by the reverse tendency in firms experiencing a reduction in demand. In these circumstances, advertising can only lower industry price if some firms are driven out of the industry, enabling the surviving firms to reap economies of scale in production. If total industry demand for the advertised product increases as a result of advertising, it is possible for all existing firms to experience increases in demand for their individual products, permitting economies of scale in production to be reaped, and industry price to be lowered.

If one firm in a particular industry increases its advertising outlays, and other firms retaliate sufficiently to return the demand conditions confronting individual firms to the original state, advertising must simply raise the price of the product in question. In these circumstances, no single firm can afford to reduce its advertising efforts unilaterally, for it will thereby lose its share of the market. Although a reduction of advertising by all firms will simply reduce costs and increase industry profits at the existing industry price, firms may be unable to agree to this among themselves.

It should be emphasized that the presence of an increase in demand plus scale economies does not guarantee that advertising will lower price, merely that lower price is possible. The profit-maximizing price with advertising may be the same, higher, or lower, than the profit-maximizing price in the absence of advertising.

Finally, as will be explained in Chapter 10, the effect of advertising on price does not determine whether advertising is beneficial from the point of view of consumers, including purchasers of products whose prices may be reduced by advertising.

Optimal Combinations of Non-Price Decision Variables

The preceding analysis of the relationship between a firm's product price and advertising behavior can easily be extended to deal with the firm's choice between alternative combinations of non-price decision variables, since many of the principles involved are very similar. Advertising is only one of many non-price decision variables which influence the demand for the firm's product; later sections will consider other variables, including durability, the frequency of style changes, and research and development decisions. When considering these alternative strategies in isolation, however, it is important not to lose sight of the fact that they are all related, for reasons to be indicated in this section.

For a profit-maximizing firm the optimal principle is to equate the MR and MC associated with each of its decision variables simultaneously. In order to implement this prescription, a firm may compare the anticipated effects of spending a marginal increment of its investible funds on different non-price strategies, such as advertising, quality dimensions, or R&D activities. The magnitude of the marginal revenues associated with these alternative strategies, and therefore the levels of different decision variables selected by the firm's decision-makers, will depend on how demand for the firm's product(s) is affected by each strategy, and this in turn will depend on various characteristics of buyers and rival sellers in the market in which the firm sells. Whether a firm will consider engaging in R&D activities, for example, will be influenced by a set of conditions sometimes described under the heading of technological opportunity. In some industries, the broad advance of science and technology provides a continuous supply of exploitable new technical possibilities; in other industries, the prospect of R&D investment yielding significant new knowledge culminating in marketable products or cost-reducing processes is relatively limited. There may be little scope for differences in style in some industries; products which are the raw materials and inputs of other firms must often meet rigid specifications in terms of physical dimensions or chemical and other attributes, leaving little room for variety in style. Styling is more likely to be used as a market weapon in consumer good industries, where the product fulfills no simple technical function, but rather can satisfy many different sorts of personal needs or uses.

The anticipated return from advertising will likewise be influenced by the characteristics of buyers' information in the market in which a firm operates. See the article by G. J. Stigler (50) on this subject. Advertising is one of several possible methods of providing potential buyers with knowledge of the identity of sellers, the nature of the products offered, and the terms upon which they are offered. If buyers were already completely informed of these matters, advertising would not affect their behavior and therefore would not be a strategy considered by firms. The benefits of advertising, from the point of view of a firm, will therefore depend upon the amount of information a given level of advertising outlay provides to buyers. This, in turn, will be influenced by a number of factors connected with the nature of the firm's product. The effectiveness of advertising in providing information will depend upon the extent to which potential buyers bother to search for information.

The amount of search undertaken by an individual buyer will depend upon the benefits anticipated by the buyer as a result of searching for information, and upon the cost of this search. The benefits might, for example, consist of the saving in expenditure expected as a result of the search, while the cost of acquiring information is largely the opportunity cost of time spent on this activity. The anticipated benefits will tend to be greater, the larger the buyer's expenditure on the product; therefore, all other things being equal, one would expect advertising to yield greater returns in the case of products which occupy a relatively large fraction of a buyer's total expenditure. Another factor influencing the extent to which buyers search for information, and therefore the effectiveness of advertising, will be the frequency of purchase of a product by individual buyers. Given a stable and unchanging population of buyers, the amount of search per buyer will be greater the more infrequently the product is purchased, since there will be a greater need to refresh memories. Given a stable population of potential buyers in a market, and the amount of search undertaken per buyer, a given level of advertising will provide more information, and will therefore be more effective, the greater the turnover of buyers in the market. These factors influencing the effectiveness of a given amount of advertising apply even though the number of sellers in a market, the nature of their products, and the terms upon which these are offered remain unchanged. If technology, products, and terms are changing, the amount of information supplied to potential buyers by a given level of advertising will be greater, and in general, a given level of advertising will provide more information, and will be more effective, the greater the rate of change of these variables over time. There is in practice less advertising of producer goods than consumer goods. This difference may in part be accounted for by the fact that in the absence of advertising, producers are usually better informed than are consumers regarding the sellers and characteristics of the products they buy. Moreover, the turnover of buyers (and sellers) is likely to be less in the case of producer goods than consumer goods, while the frequency of purchase may be higher in the case of producer goods, resulting in a need for less information of the memory refreshing variety.

The expected returns associated with the different kinds of product differentiation strategy may differ in respect of the time lapse before they accrue. The returns from current R&D investment, for example, will probably be expected to accrue after a longer period than the return to current advertising outlays, for a long lag often occurs between the initiation of research project and the creation of something of marketable value. This does not, of course, create a general preference on the part of decision-makers for advertising (or style changes) as opposed to R&D investment as a competitive strategy. However, given the rate at which a decision-maker discounts the future, strategies yielding expected returns at more distant points in time must be more profitable relative to strategies yielding earlier expected returns, in order to induce the decision-maker to undertake the former.

Uncertainty will also play a part in influencing the firm's choice between different product differentiation strategies. The outcome of all activities, even current production activities, is uncertain; that is, the anticipated outcome of any strategy will take the form of a probability distribution of expected outcomes, rather than a single-valued magnitude. Although the expected profitability (that is, the mathematical expectation of profit) of different strategies may be similar, a firm may choose between them on the basis of other characteristics of the probability distribution associated with each strategy. The large variance of the profit probability distribution of an R&D project may cause a firm to prefer a strategy with a smaller variance of possible outcomes, for example.

The relative profitability of different types of product differentiation activity will be influenced by the firm's expectations regarding the behavior of its rivals. The extent to which it pays a firm to imitate its rivals' strategies is the subject of much current research and debate. In certain circumstances, the firm's optimal strategy is to imitate its rivals' actions. This can be demonstrated to be valid in circumstances in which only two firms compete, there is perfect knowledge on the part of sellers and buyers, and the behavior of buyers is hypersensitive. Hypersensitive behavior refers to a situation in which buyers react to the slightest difference between terms offered by different sellers; this is contrasted with threshold-sensitive behavior which occurs where buyers do not respond to differences in the terms offered by different sellers, even though fully informed of the existence of these differences, until terms differ by more than a certain amount. Increasing the number of firms, introducing imperfect knowledge on the part of buyers or sellers, or introducing threshold-sensitive behavior on the part of buyers can change the conclusion that a firm's optimal strategy consists of imitating its rivals. See, for example, the articles by N. E. Devletoglou (13, 14). Rather than engage in R&D investment like its rivals, for instance, a firm may rely upon advertising, and hope to keep abreast of new technological developments by licensing new products.

Apart from the current behavior of its rivals, the profitability of different strategies considered by a firm will depend upon the extent to which other firms react to such strategies. The profitability of any given strategy will be lower, the more immediate the anticipated reaction. The anticipated speed of reaction may, however, vary with the strategy used; rivals might be expected to obtain information regarding some types of strategy only after a longer lapse of time than in the case of other strategies or, even though information is received as fast, it may take rivals longer to fashion a reply. Decisions regarding expensive R&D projects, for example, may take longer than decisions to increase advertising outlays.

The preceding discussion of various factors underlying the effectiveness of different types of non-price strategy can be summarized quite briefly as follows: these factors determine the magnitude of the elasticity of demand for the firm's product with respect to the decision variable in question, which in turn influences the magnitude of the marginal revenue associated with that decision variable.

Thus far, the argument of the present section has stressed the interdependence between different non-price decision variables which arises because a firm's decision-makers must allocate their scarce investment resources between alternative types of non-price strategy. There is, however, another type of interdependence between different non-price decision variables which is exactly the same as that present between price and advertising already discussed in the preceding section. That is, the level of marginal revenue associated with one type of decision variable will generally depend also the level of other non-price variables; for example, the response of buyers to a change in some quality dimension of the firm's product may depend on the level of the firm's advertising, and the response of buyers to a change in the firm's advertising may depend on the nature of the quality dimensions of the firm's product. In these circumstances, the optimal levels of different non-price decision variables are interdependent in precisely the same manner that optimal levels of price and advertising were explained to be interdependent in the preceding section. The implications of that interdependence are also similar; for example, the optimal level of one type of decision variable will depend on the anticipated reaction of the firm's rivals not only in terms of that decision variable but also in terms of other decision variables.

Before concluding this section it is appropriate to stress that, like a firm's 'output', each type of non-price strategy has numerous dimensions. A firm's advertising, for example, may consist of a mixture of expenditure on different types of advertising media rather than expenditure on a single category of advertising activity. Buyers can be provided with information about a firm's products in a variety of ways including national or local advertising in newspapers and periodicals, T.V. and radio broadcasts, door-to-door salesmen, free samples and gift schemes, and inducements to retailers to display products in prominent positions. The reason why firms may adopt a mixture of these different advertising media is straightforward application of principles already covered; namely, buyer (and rival seller) behavior, and therefore the level of the firm's total revenue and total costs, may be influenced differently by different dimensions of a particular type of non-price strategy. Different advertising media may have different cost functions, for example, and if a given amount of information can be conveyed to potential buyers via any of these alternative media, the total-cost-minimizing media mix will be the one which equates the marginal cost of each medium. The profit-maximizing level of each advertising medium would be the one where its marginal cost equalled the marginal revenue associated with the firm's advertising activities. If the different advertising media also influenced buyer behavior and the firm's total revenue differently, the optimal principle would be to equate the marginal revenue and marginal cost associated with each advertising medium; in this case, the optimal marginal cost of different advertising media would not necessarily be equal. Once again, the optimal levels of different media will be interdependent if the marginal revenue associated with one medium depends on the level of other media, as would be the case, for example, where the level of a 'softening up' advertising campaign influences the magnitude of buyer response to a 'follow-up' campaign.

Durability

Durability is one of the many different characteristics of a firm's output. A firm's product yields a particular service to buyers, and the total amount of these services produced by the firm may be termed the volume of output on that service; durability refers to the number of units of service yielded by one unit of the firm's product, or, what is the same thing, the number of time periods during which the product yields a given quantity of service. For example, a firm which produces tires could sell tires which last 10, 20, or 30 thousand miles in order to provide buyers with a particular total number of car-miles of tire service. Volume of service, durability of product, and number of products produced are related as follows:

$$V = D \text{ (in units of service)} \cdot \text{Quantity of Product}$$

In addition to the problem of deciding the total volume of a particular service which they will sell to buyers, a firm's decision-makers must therefore also select the durability of their product in the sense of the number of units of service which the product will provide.

The subject of the determinants of the optimum durability of a firm's product, and in particular the comparison of optimum durability under competition and monopoly, has been controversial for some time. For major contributions to the debate see Coase (7), Douglas and Goldman (16), Kleiman and Ophir (25), Levhari and Peles (30), Levhari and Srinivasan (31), Martin (33), Parks (41), Swan (52, 53, 54), Swan and Sieper (55) and White (59). The majority of writers on the subject have concluded that a monopolist will tend to produce a good of lesser durability than would be the case under competition. However, in a number of recent articles, Professor P. Swan (52, 53, 54) has argued that these authors are mistaken, and that, for an important class of demand and cost relationships, firms will select the same degree of durability for their products irrespective of the degree of monopoly or competition even though the volume of output may be different under monopoly and competition. The reason he advances, in brief, is that firms will wish to minimize the total cost of providing any particular volume of service which they sell to buyers and, given demand, will select the degree of durability which minimizes this total cost. The optimal degree of durability will depend on the precise form of the firm's total cost function, and will, Swan argues, be identical even for firms producing different volumes of service, provided that the total cost function exhibits the characteristic which he postulates. This characteristic is that there are no heavy fixed costs in the production process.

Different writers on the subject of durability employ widely different analytical approaches, and their conclusions sometimes differ due to differences in the assumptions employed. Therefore, in order to place the debate in perspective, it is appropriate to view the relevant factors underlying durability decisions within the analytical framework which has been employed throughout this book. Consider, for example, a firm producing a particular service, and confronted by demand and cost conditions relating to the quantity of that service. The profit-maximizing volume of service will be where the MR and MC associated with the volume of service are equal. The durability of the firm's product, in the sense of the number of units of service which each unit of the product will provide, remains to be determined by the firm's decision-makers. To maximize profits, the firm must equate the MR and MC associated with variations in the degree of durability, and the degree of durability which will satisfy this condition will depend on how the firm's total revenue and total costs are affected by different degrees of durability. Assuming, for the moment, that demand conditions for the service, and therefore the firm's total revenue, are not affected by the degree of durability of the firm's product, the optimum degree of durability will depend solely on the effect of durability on the firm's total costs. The profit-maximizing firm will select that degree of durability of its product which minimizes the total cost of producing whatever volume of service it produces, or, what is the same thing, minimizes the unit cost of providing that volume of service. Provided that the same degree of durability also minimizes the total, and unit, cost of producing any other total volume of service, optimum durability will be independent of the volume of service produced by the firm, and will therefore be the same for firms facing different demand conditions, as under monopoly and competition. Professor Swan's argument noted earlier is therefore valid, given the critical assumptions that demand conditions are independent of the degree of durability and that the firm's cost function is such that the cost-minimizing degree of durability is the same for all volumes of service produced. If, however, the cost-minimizing degree of durability differs for different total volumes of service produced, the durability decisions of firms producing different volumes of service, such as monopolists and competitive firms, will differ.

There are other reasons, connected with the effect of durability on the demand conditions facing a firm, why optimal durability may differ for firms producing different volumes of service. Some of these reasons and the underlying principles will be outlined briefly next. In Chapter 3 it was pointed out that if the price-elasticity of demand of different buyers of a particular product or service differs at a particular price, a firm can earn higher total revenue from a particular quantity of its product or service by discriminating in price between buyers. In order for this to be possible, however, the different markets, or buyers, must be separated in order to prevent resale of the product or service between markets. For a monopolist facing the same demand conditions for a particular service as a competitive industry, the possibility of costless resale of the services of the product will prevent the monopolist from discriminating and charging a different price per unit of the service to different buyers. Conventional analysis concludes that the non-discriminating monopolist will charge a higher price, and produce a smaller quantity of the service, than a competitive industry facing the same cost and demand conditions. The influence of the relationship between durability and total cost on the durability of the product under monopoly and competition was outlined in the preceding paragraph. Even apart from the influence of cost considerations, however, Professor Coase (7) has argued that in order for a non-discriminating monopolist to obtain the monopoly price per unit of service, buyers at that price will have to be convinced that the monopolist will not subsequently attempt to sell additional units of service at a lower price. The more durable the product, the less easy it will be for buyers to benefit from the existence of a resale market for the service. Therefore, in order to convince buyers that he will not try to discriminate by subsequently offering the service at lower prices, Professor Coase argues that a monopolist may be obliged to offer buyers a less durable product than would be produced under competition.

Additional considerations arise where there is more than one market for the services of a durable product, and where discrimination in price between different buyers of the services is possible. In this connection, a number of different circumstances can be distinguished as follows: first (as the price-discrimination analysis in Chapter 3 indicates), if there are separate and independent markets for the services of a durable product, the total revenue from a particular volume of services will be maximized by charging different prices for the service in different markets in order to equate marginal revenue in each market, and profits will be maximized by equating marginal revenue in each market with the marginal cost of the service. Given the durability of the product, different quantities of service sold in different markets will imply different quantities of the durable product sold in each market. Assuming that market separation and demand conditions are not related to durability, the durability of the product sold in different markets will be the same, and will be that durability which minimizes the total cost of producing the volume of service which equates the MR and MC of the service. On the other hand, if market separation itself were related to durability, as would occur, for example, if the price-elasticities of demand for the service associated with buyers of different durabilities were different, and if resale of different durabilities entailed transactions costs, the durability of the product sold in each market would differ. In other words, rather than a single durability, there would be an optimal mix of different durabilities marketed by the firm in question. This optimal mix of durabilities would clearly be different from the single durability produced by a non-discriminating firm, whether a monopolist or a competitive firm.

Matters are complicated somewhat further when there is more than one market for the services of a durable product if the cost or demand conditions in each market are interdependent. For example, L. White has recently argued (59), in the context of the automobile industry and the division of the market for automobiles into markets for new and secondhand cars respectively, that the durability of new cars will be affected by this separation because the services of new and used automobiles are in joint supply. His argument is that if the price-elasticity of demand for the services provided by used cars is less than unity, so that the marginal revenue of used-car services is negative, an increase in total revenue from used-car sales can be achieved by reducing the supply of used-car services. Since new and used cars are joint products, and the supply of used-car services can only be altered independently of new car sales by varying durability, White argues that the durability of new cars will therefore be reduced by the automobile industry, compared to the situation which would obtain in the case of competition in the joint market for the services of new and used cars. In reply to this argument, Professor Swan (54) has argued that an alternative way of reducing the supply of services of used cars is to restrict the supply of new cars, by raising the price of new cars, and that the optimal solution for a monopolist may be to adopt this approach while leaving the durability of new cars at the same level as would be determined by competition. The validity of Swan's argument would appear to depend, however, on the price-elasticity of demand for new cars, and on an implicit assumption that the price of new cars was not initially at the profit-maximizing level. In any event, both White's and Swan's arguments ignore the influence of the possible existence of demand interdependencies between the services of new and used cars; when these are taken into account, the optimal level of new and used car services, and optimum durability, depend also on the cross-elasticities of demand between the services of new and used cars.

Without pursuing the analysis further, the preceding discussion should be sufficient to indicate that the determinants of the optimal degree of durability of a firm's product, and the comparison of durability decisions under different market structures, depend critically on the precise manner in which durability affects a firm's total costs and total revenues. A number of different relationships between durability and total cost, or between durability and total revenue, are possible, resulting in different optimal degrees of durability, and even in optimal mixes of durability. A comparison of durability under monopoly and competition, or any other form of market structure, will therefore yield different conclusions, depending on the precise forms of the relationship between durability and firms' total revenue and total cost which is assumed to exist when making the comparison.

Style Changes

A firm may attempt to influence the demand conditions associated with its product by changing the style of its product. It is possible for a firm to change the style of its product without actually increasing the level of its total costs. Thus, for example, a certain total outlay on packaging a firm's product is compatible with frequent changes in the style of packaging. Alternatively, it may be possible for style changes to be achieved by modifying items of the firm's capital equipment when it wears out and needs to be replaced. However, there is no reason why a firm should restrict itself to changing the style of its product *only* when physical obsolescence permits this without increasing costs. Style changes require inputs, which cost money. The input cost associated with a particular *rate* of change of style will, however, be a fixed cost independent of the level of output produced by the firm between style changes.

The influence of style changes on the structure of the United States automobile industry may be mentioned by way of illustration. It has been argued (Menge (34), Selander (45) and Snell (48, 49), for examples) that the use of style changes as a market weapon may have been responsible for the demise of all save the largest firms in the industry. The argument, in brief, is as follows. The dies used in automobile manufacture, which are an insert in a large metal stamping press, relate to a particular style of automobile. These dies are indivisible in the sense that the minimal durability requirements to punch even one panel result automatically in a prolonged physical life for any given die. Firms producing larger rates of output per period will use up their dies more quickly than firms producing lower rates of output. If larger firms replace their dies with dies embodying a new style, and if smaller firms follow suit and change the style of their product with the same frequency, the die cost per automobile produced will be higher for firms producing smaller rates of output. Associated with a single style change, there is a minimum cost, the cost of a new die, and the greater the number of units of output over which the cost of the die is spread, the lower the die cost per automobile produced. Given industry price, accelerated style changes involving higher style change costs per period will, it has been argued, drive small firms from the industry.

The validity of this argument rests upon a number of crucial assumptions. The basic requirement is that style-change costs are independent of the level of a firm's output, resulting in economies of scale. Another assumption is that smaller firms follow suit and change style with the same frequency as firms producing larger rates of output per period, and that there exists a fixed industry price which must be adhered to by all firms. In other words, the alternative competitive strategy of less frequent style changes and lower price must not be feasible for firms producing lower annual rates of output, presumably due to the character of demand for new automobiles. For this to be the case, annually redesigned automobiles would have to be preferred by new car buyers, for if style changes were not desired by most buyers, non-change firms would be able to survive by offering lower prices. By producing the same total volume, over a longer period, than firms with higher annual rates of output, small firms would by definition have the same die-cost per auto produced; in addition, with less frequent style changes, they would avoid the set-up costs associated with each style change and could therefore offer lower prices than firms changing style more frequently. There is some evidence to support the view that new-car buyers prefer annually restyled cars, though it should be added that this preference may be largely the result of the psychological effects of industry advertising designed to convince the consumer that annually restyled cars are more desirable. It certainly cannot be argued that the industry's advertising presents buyers with a balanced view of the alternative option of less frequent style changes at lower prices.

It must be stressed that the preceding analysis is not peculiar to style-change costs. It is merely a special case of the proposition that if there are economies of scale in an industry, whether caused by style-change costs, advertising, or some other category of costs that are independent of the scale of a firm's output, small firms will be unable to survive either price competition or, given industry price, cost competition. That is, provided there is competition in the industry, whether price or cost competition, the size of firms that are able to remain and compete in an industry will be influenced by economies of scale.

Research and Development Activities

The identifying characteristic of R&D activities is that they produce new knowledge, including knowledge of how to apply existing inventions to commercial purposes. The new knowledge resulting from a firm's R&D activities may be embodied in new products, or may result in less costly methods of producing products already marketed by the firm. See Grabowski (19), Needham (37) and Nelson (39) and, in Chapter 6, Concentration and Research and Development Activities, for more detailed analysis of the determinants of firms' R&D behavior.

A profit-maximizing firm will undertake a research project only if the total R&D cost is exceeded by the present value of the additional revenues expected to accrue to the firm as a result of the R&D outlays. These revenues will depend upon the anticipated effect of the R&D investment upon the demand or cost conditions confronting the firm. The relationship between different levels of R&D investment and a firm's cost and demand conditions could be exhibited diagrammatically in a similar manner to that employed in the second section of this chapter, substituting R&D expenditures for advertising expenditures. Since current R&D outlays yield results, and revenues, only after a considerable lapse of time, the curves in the diagram would have to relate to present values of future expected revenues (or cost reductions). This distinction should not be overemphasized, however, since advertising also usually has cumulative effects on buyer behavior, and therefore a firm's sales revenues, which persist beyond the period in which advertising expenditures occur. Also, since it is in the nature of R&D investment to change the characteristics of the firm's product, the x-axis would no longer refer, as is the case with advertising, to a physically unchanging product.

A notable feature of R&D inputs is that they are indivisible below a certain size; that is, there is a minimum size of R&D input, which can, however, vary between industries. One cannot hire half a research chemist or scientist, or conduct research without laboratory facilities which are, below a certain size, indivisible. A fixed minimum size of R&D input means that firms with limited access to investment funds may be unable to consider R&D as a competitive strategy, even though the firm might expect such a strategy to be potentially profitable. Empirical evidence (National Science Foundation (36), for example) shows that within industries which engage in R&D activities, there is indeed a minimum size of firm below which firms do not engage in R&D activities (and see M. I. Kamien and N. L. Schwartz (24) for a useful summary of empirical studies of the relationship between firm size, concentration, and R&D activities). There is, of course, nothing to prevent small firms from engaging in cooperative R&D ventures that are outside the scope of each individual firm's financial resources, or from hiring the services of independent R&D organizations. Either of these alternatives would, in effect, enable small firms to share costs of minimum-sized indivisible R&D organizations. There are, however, several reasons why this approach will not be as efficient as performing the same level of R&D activities in the research department of a single firm (see W. L. Baldwin (2) in this connection).

First, even if the firms engaging in cooperative research or utilizing the services of an independent research organization are members of the same industry, and the resulting R&D output is the same as would result if the research were carried out by the research department of a single firm, there are likely to be additional costs, which are absent in the case of a single firm, in carrying out the research. The planning, coordination, and evaluation of research by a number of independent firms is likely to require more resources than the coordination of the same amount of research undertaken by a single firm. Independent R&D organizations argue, for example, that each client needs at least one full-time trained man on its own staff in order to communicate clearly the nature of the project it wishes done, to evaluate the proposal competently, and to interpret and make effective use of the results. In one firm carrying out the same aggregate amount of research, only one such man would be needed.

Second, apart from the costs of carrying out the R&D activities provided by a minimum-sized R&D organization, the total benefits anticipated by firms sharing the cost may be smaller than in the case of a single firm. The single firm will employ the results of the R&D activity to its best advantage, whereas a number of small firms in a particular industry are potential competitors and may, for example, expect the prices received for products resulting from R&D activities to be lower as a result of competition between themselves. For this reason, a group of small firms in the same industry may be less likely to engage in R&D than a single large firm.

Third, if the firms engaging in cooperative research or employing independent R&D organizations are members of different industries, the R&D output resulting from the use of minimum-sized R&D inputs may be lower than results if the same amount of R&D input specializes in solving the problems of one industry. That is, there may be increasing returns to scale in the performance of R&D activities in particular industries. A research chemist, or scientist, who spends equal parts of his time working for two firms in different industries may produce for each industry an amount of new knowledge that is less than half the amount which would be obtained if he devoted all his time to the problem of one industry. In these circumstances, the services of independent research organizations may not be considered an effective substitute by firms unable to bear the whole cost of indivisible R&D facilities alone; such firms may prefer alternative strategies, such as advertising coupled with rapid imitation of new developments to counter the moves of large firms in the same industry possessing their own internal research facilities.

Significance of Product Differentiation in Price Theory

Conventional price theory includes in its list of market situations industries in which the products of different firms are differentiated as a result of non-price strategies pursued by individual firms. In monopolistic competition, for example, each firm's demand curve is assumed to slope down because of product differentiation and the imperfect substitutability, in buyers' minds, of the products of different firms. In equilibrium, the price of each product exceeds the marginal cost of producing the product; in addition, the assumption of easy entry into the group means that the long-run equilibrium situation of the industry group involves tangency between the anticipated demand curve for each firm's product and the curve depicting the average cost (including normal profits) of producing and distributing the product, as shown in Figure 4-4. Such an equilibrium

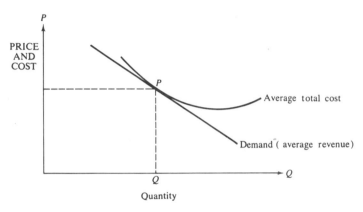

Figure 4-4. Long-run equilibrium of the firm in monopolistic competition.

situation has been contrasted unfavorably with the long-run equilibrium of a purely competitive industry on the grounds that in monopolistic competition there is excess capacity and inefficiency in the sense that if the total output of such an industry were concentrated in fewer firms, it could be produced at a lower cost in terms of money, and hence resources. In reply to this line of argument, some writers have pointed out that since average total cost (ATC) includes advertising outlays, each firm may be minimizing average production cost, as shown in Figure 4-5.

Even though firms are not minimizing average production costs, there is a more fundamental reply to the excess capacity argument. Assuming, for the moment, that the same total output would be demanded in the absence of product differentiation, concentration of total output into fewer firms necessarily results in elimination of some varieties of the product. The resulting output of the industry is, therefore, different from the output mix produced before, and it is impossible to compare the two situations from the point of view of whether the 'same' output is being produced more or less efficiently. One would require, instead, some criterion for comparing situations involving different mixes

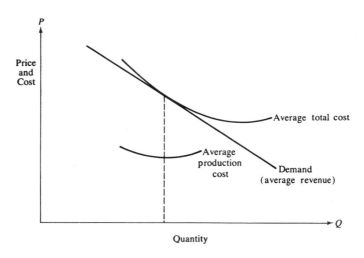

Figure 4–5. Production costs versus total costs in equilibrium.

of output. Monopolistic competition and pure competition models cannot therefore be contrasted from the point of view of 'technical efficiency', which is concerned with the efficiency with which particular output levels are produced. The output level of firms in monopolistic competition can only be compared with the output level of purely competitive firms, and with that of a monopolist, from the point of view of the resulting implications of their output levels for 'allocative efficiency' which, as indicated in more detail in Chapter 10, deals with the manner in which resources are allocated between different types of output.

Moreover, total demand for the product(s) of an industry in which the products of individual firms are differentiated is not independent of production differentiation activities. Without product differentiation, the demand and cost conditions confronting firms will differ. One must avoid the temptation to conclude that the only thing that would be changed by absence of product differentiation is the slope of the individual firm's demand curve through the existing equilibrium price. Elimination of product differentiation implies elimination of efforts to achieve differentiation, such as advertising and R&D activities.

Product differentiation activities influence resource allocation apart from making the products of different firms imperfect substitutes for each other at a point in time. The *nature* of the products available at a given point in time will be influenced by (past) R&D activities, for example. Without R&D activities, the rate of introduction of new products and processes may differ, resulting in differences in the products available at any point in time. In addition, the *knowledge* possessed by buyers concerning products available will depend upon advertising activities. Advertising may provide information which enables buyers to choose the allocation of resources they prefer best.

Conventional price theory says nothing about the determinants of the level or characteristics of product differentiation activities undertaken by a firm. In price theory, product differentiation is simply assumed to exist in certain market structures, notably monopolistic competition and oligopoly with differentiated products, and is shown to have certain implications for pricing behavior. The main implication of the existence of product differentiation is that the price of a firm's product will exceed the marginal cost of producing and distributing the product.* A particular price–cost relationship is, however, quite compatible with numerous different levels of expenditure upon product differentiation activities, and any particular level of product differentiation outlay can be spent in numerous different ways. Price theory omits consideration of these matters entirely. In the third section of this chapter, some of the factors influencing product differentiation have already been mentioned. Technological opportunity and characteristics of buyers' information in particular markets, for example, are relevant to the choice of product differentiation activity. Expectations regarding rivals' reactions, in addition, may be just as important in influencing the magnitude and character of product differentiation activities as they are in influencing pricing behavior. Although these expectations may be related to the number of firms in the market, the relationship is probably much more complex than in the case of pricing behavior, and a priori theorizing on this point is inconclusive. On the one hand, for example, larger numbers might be expected to lead to behavior which is heedless of rivals' reactions, involving a larger level of industry product differentiation activity than would be undertaken in similar circumstances if the industry were controlled by a smaller number of firms. On the other hand, larger numbers might be associated with pricing behavior leading to smaller profit margins and a smaller supply of funds to finance product differentiation activities. Another question concerns the extent to which the number of sellers in a market influences the character, as opposed to the magnitude, of product differentiation activities. Will, for example, the anticipated speed and extent of rivals' reactions be influenced by the type of product differentiation activity being contemplated by a firm? The answer to this question, and others concerning the relationship between seller concentration and product differentiation activities, can only be revealed by empirical evidence. Despite an increasing number of statistical studies, the available empirical evidence is still scanty, and, as will be indicated in more detail in Chapter 6, suggests no simple relationship between seller concentration and product differentiation. In view of the number of factors, other than concentration, which are likely to influence product differentiation, it would indeed be surprising to find a simple relationship, valid for all industries and at all times, between the number and size distribution of sellers in a market and their product differentiation activities.

For more information on the debate over the nature and welfare implications of monopolistic competition, see Barzel (3), Demsetz (9, 10, 11, 12) and Schmalensee and Demsetz (44).

Measurement of Product Differentiation

Product differentiation exists if the products of different firms in a particular industry are imperfect substitutes for each other from the point of view of buyers of those products. An industry is defined as a group of firms selling products which are close substitutes from the point of view of buyers and sellers of the products, for reasons explained in Chapter 5; product differentiation therefore refers to a degree of difference between products which is less than that which would make the firms members of different industries. However, the

---

* It must be stressed that absence of product differentiation does not guarantee equality of equilibrium industry price and marginal cost of production and distribution in firms in an industry with many firms. As demonstrated in the section of Chapter 3 entitled The Number of Firms and Pricing Behavior, equilibrium price–cost relationships involving price above marginal revenue (and hence above marginal cost, which equals marginal revenue in a profit-maximizing firm) are quite compatible with homogeneity of the industry's product; that is, with perfect substitutability of the products of different firms in the industry.

drawing of industry boundaries will greatly influence the degree of product differentiation existing within the industry so defined. The wider the boundaries are drawn, the larger will be the number of firms in a particular industry, and the greater in general will be the observed degree of product differentiation.

How can the degree of product differentiation be measured once industry boundaries have been defined? Counting the physical varieties, such as the number of differently flavored toothpastes, for example, is not always satisfactory because product differentiation refers to differentiation in the minds of buyers, and this may be achieved by advertising activities despite the existence of only minor physical differences in the products of different firms. One way to measure product differentiation would be to employ the concept of cross-elasticity of demand between the products of different firms in an industry. As indicated in Chapter 3, cross-elasticity of demand is defined as the percentage change in the quantity of one firm's product demanded due to a one per cent change in the price of another firm's product, all other things remaining unchanged. Different cross-elasticity concepts, and the difficulties involved in obtaining empirical evidence concerning their magnitude, will be discussed in more detail in Chapter 5.

Cross-elasticity measures of the degree of product differentiation do not indicate whether, in the absence of changes in the terms which different sellers offer, buyers are tightly attached to particular sellers, or whether, instead, buyers switch their purchases between sellers. High cross-elasticities of demand in a particular industry, indicating high substitutability between products and implying low product differentiation, are quite compatible with very high degrees of brand loyalty in the absence of price changes by different sellers. The cigarette industry springs to mind as an example. To deal with this second aspect of product differentiation, a number of measures have been devised which indicate the degree of brand loyalty buyers exhibit in a particular industry. For example, Professors Bernhardt and MacKenzie (4) have proposed the following measure of product differentiation indicating the extent to which buyers are attached to particular sellers in an industry:

$$\frac{S - S_b}{S}$$

S represents the degree of uncertainty as to which of a number of firms will secure the business of a buyer chosen at random, and depends on the market shares of the various sellers. S_b is the degree of uncertainty as to the identity of the seller *when the identity of a particular buyer is known*, which will depend on how buyers allocate their total purchases among different sellers. If each buyer buys all his purchases of the product from a particular seller, so that knowing the identity of the buyer removes all uncertainty as to who the seller is, then $S_b = 0$ and the above index has a value of 1. At the other extreme, if knowing the buyer is of no help in identifying the sellers, which would be the case if all buyers purchase from all of the sellers in the same proportions, then $S_b = S$ and the index has a value of 0. Just as cross-elasticity measures provide no guide to product differentiation existing in the absence of changes in prices or other terms offered by different sellers, brand-loyalty concepts of product differentiation provide no guide to the magnitude of the cross-elasticity dimension of product differentiation and the associated extent to which buyers will switch between sellers in response to changes in relative terms offered by different sellers. The reason is obvious; the brand-loyalty and cross-elasticity concepts deal with different aspects of buyer behavior, one concerned with the behavior of buyers confronted by given terms offered by different sellers, and the other with changes in buyer behavior in response to changes in the relative terms offered by different sellers. Both are, however, different aspects of product differentiation.

The degree of product differentiation, in its various dimensions, existing in a particular industry at a particular point in time, is the result of efforts by sellers to distinguish their products from those of other sellers by the use of non-price strategies. For many purposes, measuring the results of these efforts, in terms of their impact on buyers, is less important than focusing attention on firms' efforts to differentiate. This is the case, for example, if one is concerned with the determinants of the character and level of firms' efforts to differentiate their products, and with the relationship between firms' product differentiation activities and other aspects of firms' behavior. The degree of product differentiation existing in an industry need not be correlated with the level of firms' efforts to differentiate their products, for the following reasons: the degree of product differentiation resulting from a particular level of advertising or other product-differentiation activity undertaken by a firm depends on the *degree of differentiability* of the class of product which it produces. Differentiability refers to an inherent characteristic of certain kinds of goods and services, and is largely determined by characteristics of buyers, including the ability of buyers to assess and compare the qualities of competing brands, the proportion of income spent on the product and incentive to make comparisons between products, and so on. Due to differences in differentiability, some types of products and services require much larger outlays by a firm on product-differentiation activities in order to achieve a given degree of differentiation than other types of product and service.

In addition to differentiability characteristic of the class of product which it produces, the degree of product differentiation resulting from a firm's efforts in this sphere will also depend on the nature and extent of rival sellers' responses. If rivals respond by imitating a firm's product differentiation efforts, the degree of differentiation actually achieved may be quite small, despite the fact that the overall level of an industry's product differentiation efforts may be large and the resulting flow of new information or new products and services considerable. For these and related reasons, when concerned with the determinants of firms' product differentiation activities, or with the resulting flow of new information or products over time, it is appropriate to switch attention from the impact of such activities on buyers, measured by the extent to which the products of different firms are imperfect substitutes for each other at a given point in time, toward firms' efforts to differentiate their products as indicated by levels of advertising, R&D, and other inputs employed by firms, and their resulting impact on the sales, profit and other performance features of individual firms.

When viewing the various product-differentiation activities of firms, there are likely to be problems involved in attempting to allocate a particular type of expenditure, employees, or other index of input, into different categories such as advertising, R&D, and so on. Some sales promotion activities are, for example, difficult to distinguish from current production activities. The outlays invested in inputs producing free samples of a particular product are just like investment in producing the same product for sale. However, giving away such products instead of selling them is aimed at shifting the demand schedule associated with the product, and the outlays should be classified as advertising outlays. Likewise, the measurement of R&D inputs, whether measured by expenditures, R&D personnel, or some other index, may often involve problems of classifying inputs.

There are even greater difficulties associated with measuring the output of a firm's product differentiation activities than those encountered when attempting to measure inputs. For example, the following question has received much attention in recent statistical studies. Do increases in R&D inputs yield increasing returns, that is, more than proportionate increases in R&D output? The output of R&D activities is, however, a multidimensional concept; it includes increments of unpatentable new knowledge, patentable knowledge, patented knowledge, (patented) knowledge having commercial value, and so on. Unless these different concepts change in proportion to each other in response to changes in R&D input, the answer to the above question will depend upon the index of inventive output chosen. If one is interested in the flow of patentable knowledge, for example, patent applications, or patents granted, will not be a completely satisfactory index of this aspect of inventive output if the propensity to patent *patentable* knowledge varies between firms. Again, the benefits accruing from patented inventions, measured in terms of the value of sales of the invention or some other index of benefit, may vary from patent to patent, with the result that the number of patents granted will be a poor indicator of this dimension of R&D output.

Indexes of inventive output which have been employed in recent statistical studies of industrial research and development include the number of patent applications, patents granted, rankings of important inventions compiled by experts, and the value of the first two years' sales of a new product. These studies, however, frequently relate to different industries and very little attempt has been made to ascertain the extent to which different dimensions of R&D output are associated in particular industries. In the absence of this information, statements concerning the behavior of R&D output in response to changes in R&D input, or other aspects of firms' activities, must be interpreted with care.

The output of a firm's advertising activities is also difficult to define, and measure, operationally (see K. S. Palda (40) on this subject). It is clear that advertising is associated with the provision of information to buyers, and also that this may increase the sales of the firm's product. One cannot, however, measure in a very meaningful way how much information is provided to buyers by any particular level of advertising activities. This depends on information available to the buyer from all other sources, including rival sellers. There need be no correlation between the impact of a firm's advertising on the firm's sales and the amount of information provided to buyers; if competitors retaliate by increasing their own advertising efforts, for example, each firm might experience a negligible change in sales, yet buyers may be provided with more useful information than previously. From the point of view of a firm's decision-making, however, the relevant index of the output of advertising activities is the resulting effect on demand for the firm's product and its total sales revenue. In this connection it should be emphasized that the relevant impact on the firm's sales revenue is the total effect of the advertising, measured by the cumulative effects on buyer behavior and demand during successive time periods after the advertising occurs until its impact on buyer behavior is exhausted. The same is of course true for other types of expenditure on product differentiation activities. These outlays are in the nature of a capital expenditure, yielding a return in terms of the resulting effect on buyer behavior and the firm's revenues which is spread over a number of successive time periods. The problems connected with attempts to measure the magnitudes of these effects in an environment in which other factors affecting demand for a firm's product are changing continually, including repeated outlays on each type of product differentiation activity, require little elaboration.

Additional aspects of product differentiation activities, including the problems involved in attempting to define 'ideal' performance in terms of product differentiation activities, and the relationship between 'ideal' pricing behavior and these activities, are treated in Chapter 10, which deals with public policy towards industrial structure.

RECOMMENDED READINGS

1. Bain, J. S., *Barriers to New Competition* (Cambridge, Mass.: Harvard University Press, 1956), Chapter 4 and Appendix D.
2. Baldwin, W. L., Contracted research and the case for big business, *Journal of Political Economy*, June 1962.

3. Barzel, Y., Excess capacity in monopolistic competition, *Journal of Political Economy*, September 1970.
4. Bernhardt, I. and MacKenzie, K. D., Measuring seller unconcentration, segmentation, and product differentiation, *Western Economic Journal*, December 1968.
5. Brems, H., Response lags and non-price competition. In Bowman, M. J. (Ed.) *Expectations, Uncertainty, and Business Behavior* (New York: Social Science Research Council, 1958).
6. Buchanan, N. S., Advertising expenditures; a suggested treatment, *Journal of Political Economy*, August 1942. Also reprinted in Breit, W. and Hochman, H. M. (Eds.) *Readings in Microeconomics* (New York: Holt, Rinehart and Winston, Inc., 1968).
7. Coase, R. H., Durability and monopoly, *Journal of Law and Economics*, April 1972.
8. Comanor, W. S., Research and competitive differentiation in the pharmaceutical industry in the U. S., *Economica*, November 1964.
9. Demsetz, H., The nature of equilibrium in monopolistic competition, *Journal of Political Economy*, February 1959.
10. Demsetz, H., The welfare and empirical significance of monopolistic competition, *Economic Journal*, September 1964.
11. Demsetz, H., Monopolistic competition: a reply, *Economic Journal*, June 1967.
12. Demsetz, H., Do competition and monopolistic competition differ? *Journal of Political Economy*, January–February 1968.
13. Devletoglou, N. E., A dissenting view of duopoly and spatial competition, *Economica*, May 1965.
14. Devletoglou, N. E. and Demetriou, P. A., Choice and threshold: a further experiment in spatial duopoly, *Economica*, November 1967.
15. Dorfman, R. and Steiner, P. O., Optimal advertising and optimal quality, *American Economic Review*, December 1954.
16. Douglas, A. J. and Goldman, S. M., Monopolistic behaviour in a market for durable goods, *Journal of Political Economy*, January 1969.
17. Doyle, P., Economic aspects of advertising: a survey, *Economic Journal*, September 1968.
18. Doyle, P., Advertising expenditure and consumer demand, *Oxford Economic Papers*, November 1968.
19. Grabowski, H. G., The determinants of industrial research and development: a study of the chemical, drug, and petroleum industries, *Journal of Political Economy*, March–April 1968.
20. Grabowski, H. G. and Baxter, N. D., Rivalry in industrial research and development, *Journal of Industrial Economics*, July 1973.
21. Grabowski, H. G. and Mueller, D. C., Non-price competition in the cigarette industry: a comment, *Antitrust Bulletin*, Winter 1970.
22. Havrilesky, T., Reply to Grabowski and Mueller, *Antitrust Bulletin*, Winter 1970.
23. Havrilesky, T. and Barth, R., Non-price competition in the cigarette industry, *Antitrust Bulletin*, Fall 1969.
24. Kamien, M. I. and Schwartz, N. L., Market structure and innovation: a survey, *Journal of Economic Literature*, March 1975.
25. Kleiman, E. and Ophir, T., The durability of durable goods, *Review of Economic Studies*, April 1966.
26. Kormendi, R. C. and Benjamin, D. K., The interrelationship between markets for new and used durable goods, *Journal of Law and Economics*, October 1974.
27. Lambin, J. J., Optimal allocation of competitive marketing efforts: an empirical study, *Journal of Business*, October 1970.
28. Lambin, J. J., Is gasoline advertising justified? *Journal of Business*, October 1972.
29. Lambin, J. J., Naert, P. A. and Bultez, A., Optimal marketing behavior in oligopoly, *European Economic Review*, April 1975.
30. Levhari, D. and Peles, Y., Market structure, quality and durability, *Bell Journal of Economics and Management Science*, Spring 1973.
31. Levhari, D. and Srinivasan, T. N., Durability of consumption goods: competition v. monopoly, *American Economic Review*, March 1969.
32. Marcus, M., The intensity and effectiveness of advertising, *Oxford University Institute of Economics and Statistics*, November 1970.
33. Martin, D. D., Monopoly power and the durability of durable goods, *Southern Economic Journal*, January 1962.
34. Menge, J. A., Style change costs as a market weapon, *Quarterly Journal of Economics*, November 1962.
35. Mueller, Dennis, The firm's decision process: an econometric investigation, *Quarterly Journal of Economics*, February 1967.
36. National Science Foundation, *Basic Research, Applied Research and Development in Industry 1965*, NSF 67-12 (Washington, D.C.: U.S. Government Printing Office, 1967).
37. Needham, D., Market structure and firms' R&D behavior, *Journal of Industrial Economics*, June 1975.
38. Nelson, P. J., The economic consequences of advertising, *Journal of Business*, April 1975.
39. Nelson, R. R., The simple economics of basic scientific research, *Journal of Political Economy*, June 1959.

40. Palda, K. S., Measurement of cumulative advertising effects, *Journal of Business*, April 1965.
41. Parks, R. W., The demand and supply of durable goods and durability, *American Economic Review*, March 1974.
42. Schmalensee, R., Regulation and the durability of goods, *Bell Journal of Economics and Management Science*, Spring 1970.
43. Schmalensee, R., A note on monopolistic competition and excess capacity, *Journal of Political Economy*, May–June 1972.
44. Schmalensee, R., A note on monopolistic competition and excess capacity; *and* Demsetz, H., The inconsistencies in monopolistic competition: a reply, *Journal of Political Economy*, May–June 1972.
45. Selander, S. E., Is annual style change in the auto industry an unfair method of competition? A Rebuttal, *Yale Law Journal*, March 1973.
46. Sexton, D. E., A microeconomic model of the effects of advertising, *Journal of Business*, January 1972.
47. Siegfried, J. J. and Weiss, L. J., Advertising profits and corporate taxes revisited, *Review of Economics and Statistics*, May 1974.
48. Snell, B. C., Annual style change in the automobile industry as an unfair method of competition, *Yale Law Journal*, 1971.
49. Snell, B. C., A Reply, *Yale Law Journal*, March 1973.
50. Stigler, G. J., The economics of information, *Journal of Political Economy*, June 1961.
51. Stigler, G. J., Price and non-price competition, *Journal of Political Economy*, February 1968.
52. Swan, P. L., Durability of consumption goods, *American Economic Review*, December 1970.
53. Swan, P. L., The durability of goods and regulation of monopoly, *Bell Journal of Economics and Management Science*, Spring 1971.
54. Swan, P. L., Optimum durability, second-hand markets and planned obsolescence, *Journal of Political Economy*, May–June 1972.
55. Swan, P. L. and Sieper, E., Monopoly and competition in the market for durable goods, *Review of Economic Studies*, July 1973.
56. Telser, L. G., How much does it pay whom to advertise? *American Economic Review, Papers and Proceedings*, May 1961.
57. Tsurumi, H., A comparison of alternative optimal models of advertising expenditure: stock adjustment and control theoretic approaches, *Review of Economics and Statistics*, May 1973.
58. Wertz, K. L., Monopolistic pricing of durable goods, *Economic Inquiry*, 1974, pp. 169–174; *and* Comment by Hum, D.; *and* Reply by Wertz, *Economic Inquiry*, December 1975.
59. White, L. J., *The American Automobile Industry in the Post-War Period*, Ph.D. dissertation, Harvard University, 1969.

CHAPTER FIVE

THE PROBLEM OF MARKET AND INDUSTRY DELINEATION

Alternative Delineation Criteria

In the preceding four chapters dealing with determinants of various aspects of the behavior of individual firms, a firm's behavior was shown to depend on the objectives of its decision-makers and on the nature of the constraints, such as demand and cost conditions, confronting the firm. It was also emphasized that the anticipated behavior of rivals will play a crucial role in influencing the firm's behavior. The following two chapters will investigate more closely the relationship between the number and size distribution of a firm's actual and potential rivals and various aspects of the firm's behavior. First, however, a brief digression is appropriate in order to consider the problem of how firms should be grouped together into separate industries.

For some purposes, dividing the firms in an economy into industry subgroups will not be necessary. This is the case if one wishes to make international comparisons, or comparisons within a single economy at different points in time, of specific characteristics of all firms in an economy considered as a whole. Thus, for example, one might be interested in the overall level of industrial concentration in the economy, as indicated by the extent to which the total output of the economy is produced by a small number of firms. For many other purposes it is necessary to consider the characteristics of subgroups of firms in an economy.

The problem of grouping firms into industries is closely related to the problem of defining the boundaries of different markets. A 'market' is simply a group of buyers and sellers engaging in transactions or exchanges. Firms are sellers in markets for their outputs, and are buyers in markets for their inputs. All the firms which sell in a particular market, or buy if one is considering input markets, are usually termed an 'industry'. It follows that once the boundaries of a market are defined, all firms which sell in that market (or buy in the case of input markets) will automatically be defined as constituting the industry. A firm which sells in a number of different markets so defined may simultaneously be a member of different industry groups. Since the problems of defining markets and industries are virtually synonymous, we shall henceforth refer to the problem of industry definition in terms of defining the relevant market. This is appropriate because there are two sides to any market, both sellers and buyers and, as we shall see, certain characteristics of both these sides are relevant in defining a market properly from a behavioral point of view. It should be noted, however, that the boundaries of a market and the associated *domestic* industry need not be synonymous; this will be the case whenever total market sales include some imports. Also, even when there are no imports, total market sales need not always equal current production of the industry concerned; this will be the case whenever there are inventory changes in the industry or second-hand markets for the product.

One important reason for defining markets and grouping firms into industries is in order to investigate whether any relationship exists between the characteristics of markets and the terms under which transactions are conducted in those markets. As will be explained in more detail in Chapter 10, certain aspects of these terms, such as the relationship between price and marginal cost, influence the level of aggregate satisfaction in the community. Explaining what determines these terms is therefore essential in order to predict, or attempt to control, the terms of transactions in any sector of the economy. The need to define markets and to group firms into industries also arises in connection with the application of antitrust policy. For example, in the United States, Section 7 of the Clayton Act prohibits mergers which result in undue lessening of competition 'in any line of commerce in any section of the country'. In enforcing Section 7, since the courts use market share concepts in order to infer whether or not competition will be lessened by a merger, the concept of the relevant market is of obvious importance. The determination of the relevant market is the key issue in an antimerger case since the outcome hinges on which of the market definitions claimed to be appropriate by parties to the suit is ultimately accepted by the courts as the one appropriate for determining whether Section 7 has been violated by the merger. See Elzinga and Hogarty (5) and Hale and Hale (6) for more on this aspect of the problem.

Although the industry concept is part of everyday life, when one attempts to define an industry operationally, matters are not so simple. At first sight, the solution seems obvious, namely to group together all those firms that produce the same product or service. This requires a definition of what constitutes the 'same' product or service. Strictly speaking, all firms produce different products because the products of two different firms are produced at different geographical locations, but a definition yielding single-firm industries is too narrow for most purposes. At the other extreme, all products and services are the same in that they compete for buyers' purchasing power, but again a definition which yields a single economy-wide industry is too wide for most purposes. In order to regard different firms as selling in the 'same' market, and therefore constituting members of the same industry, there must be some aspect of the transactions engaged in by individual firms which is similar; this much is clear. A transaction has many characteristics, however, and there are correspondingly many possible criteria for defining market boundaries and grouping firms into industries. Some of these characteristics relate to the transaction itself, such as physical characteristics of the product exchanged or the price or other terms of the exchange (see Sissors (14) and Steiner (15) for the nature of markets in general; and Marfels (8), Pace (9), Weiss (19) and Schwartzman (13) for attempts to define the boundaries of particular markets and industries). Others relate to characteristics of the buyers, such as income class or geographical location, or to characteristics of sellers, such as location, processes or inputs used. For example, should the market for glass bottles be regarded as different from the market for tin cans, or should both be included in a single market for containers? Again, while most people could identify those firms producing automobiles, are all cars really the same? Is a Vega the same as a Cadillac, or should the market for new cars be divided into different markets reflecting different price ranges, horsepower ratings or similar differences? As a final example, should all firms producing beer be regarded as selling in the same market, or in the presence of regional differences in taste for beer should sales of beer in one geographic region of the country be regarded as a different market from beer sales in another region? These examples consider the appropriate product dimension, price range, and geographic boundaries of a market only. There are many other dimensions, and even when adoption of one of these characteristics of a transaction yields relatively unambiguous boundaries, other dimensions will often differ between different firms, leading to problems of defining industry boundaries. The drawing of market and industry boundaries is therefore complex, involving all the many dimensions of a transaction and resulting in innumerable possibilities for market classification. In general, different groupings of firms into industries are likely to result, depending on whether the 'same' product or service means physically identical, using the same process in its manufacture, using the same inputs, performing the same function, having the same price range, is sold in the same geographic location, or some combination of criteria for grouping. Occasionally, drawing industry boundaries according to different criteria may not affect the composition of the associated industry. Thus, for example, whether the automobile market is defined to encompass total sales of new cars, or is divided into markets for different classes of cars, the firms selling in those markets will be roughly the same. However, the characteristics of the markets and industry so defined will still generally differ even if the identity of the firms comprising the industry remains the same. For example, the market shares of the individual firms in markets for different classes of automobile are not the same as their shares of the car market viewed as a whole.

Substitutability Criterion

Economic theory indicates that, for a study of market behavior, it is useful to define an industry as embracing those firms producing goods or services which are regarded as *close substitutes* by buyers or sellers. The rationale of the substitutability criterion is as follows. Economic theory is largely concerned with the behavior of individual decision-making units, such as firms. The behavior of any individual firm depends, among other things, on which other firms it takes into account in its decision-making. The firm's decision-making problem is to select a set of values of the policy variables under its control, such as the price it charges, and the level of its investment in production, advertising, and R&D activities, which best achieves the firm's objective, such as profit maximization. If the profits which the firm expects to reap from a given set of policy variables are influenced by the activities of other firms, then the behavior of the firm depends also on the anticipated behavior of other firms.

All firms are likely to be affected in some degree by each other's actions. However, any particular decision-maker is likely to confine his attention only to a few firms whose behavior he considers will have a significant influence on the result of his own policies. The task, if one is interested in behavior, is to discover which firms take each other's behavior into account in deciding upon their own individual policies and to group them together accordingly, because the behavior of members of such a group will be related. Precisely *which* firms will take each other into account in their decision-making, and whose behavior is therefore related, cannot be observed directly since the required information is in the minds of the decision-makers. Even if asked, they may not be able, or willing, to articulate this information. However, the extent to which decision-makers take into account other firms' actions will be related to the degree of substitutability existing between the products of different firms, viewed from the point of view of either buyers or sellers. The reason for this is that the response of buyers and other sellers to a firm's actions will depend on the extent to which they regard other products as substitutes for the firm's own product. The nature and magnitude of this response, in turn, will influence the outcome of the firm's actions, both in terms of the consequences for the firm's own performance and for the terms of market transactions engaged in by the various sellers.

One measure of the degree of substitutability between two products or services, X and Y, is provided by the concept of cross-elasticity of demand. As already noted in connection with analysis of firms' pricing behavior in Chapter 3, cross-elasticity of demand is defined as follows:

$$CE = \frac{\text{percentage change in quantity of X demanded}}{\text{percentage change in the price of Y}}$$

where all other factors which are capable of influencing the demand for X are assumed to remain unchanged.

If the sign of this expression is positive, the two goods are termed substitutes; if the sign is negative the two goods are termed complements. Provided that the sign is positive, the greater the proportionate change in quantity of X demanded when the price of Y changes by a given amount, the greater the degree of substitutability between the two goods.

The effect of a change in the price of Y on the quantity of X demanded, all other things remaining unchanged, can be hypothetically divided into an income effect and a substitution effect. If the numerator of the above expression is the sum of these two effects, one has a measure of gross cross-elasticity of demand accompanied by corresponding definitions of gross substitutes and complements. If, on the other hand, the numerator in the expression consists only of the substitution effect of a change in the price of Y on quantity of X demanded, one has a measure of net cross-elasticity of demand, with corresponding definitions of net substitutes and complements. The choice between these two definitions of cross-elasticity of demand can affect the resulting definition of the relationship between two goods. It is possible, for example, for two goods to be simultaneously gross complements and net substitutes. This would be the case if the substitution effect of a rise in the price of Y tends to increase the quantity of X demanded, but the income effect tends to reduce the quantity of X demanded and more than offsets the substitution effect. Alternatively, it is possible for two goods to be simultaneously gross substitutes and net complements. This would be the case if the substitution effect of a rise in the price of Y tends to reduce the quantity of X demanded, but X is an inferior good so that the income effect tends to increase the quantity of X demanded and more than offsets the substitution effect.

Cross-elasticity of demand measures substitutability on the demand side, that is, from the point of view of purchasers. The grouping together of firms into separate industries should also take into account substitutability on the supply side. This means that irrespective of the extent to which consumers consider the products of the individual firms to be substitutes, firms should be grouped together if the output of one firm is considered a close substitute for the output of another firm from the producer's point of view. For example, a firm producing only left-handed golf clubs would not be grouped with firms producing only right-handed clubs if the cross-elasticity of demand measure of sub-stitutability were employed, because few buyers consider the two products to be close substitutes. The firms would be grouped together, however, using a measure of substitutability on the supply side, if one producer could easily switch his resources over to the production of the other firm's product in the event of a change in the price charged by the latter firm. Thus, one might measure substitutability on the supply side with a concept similar to cross-elasticity of demand, such as the ratio of the percentage change in the amount of X which producers of X would be willing to supply, to a percentage change in *time horizon prob.*

the price of Y, all other things remaining unchanged. Alternatively, some other measure of elasticity of technical substitution between different products might be employed.

Although the measures of cross-elasticity of demand and supply look similar, it must be emphasized that they differ; one refers to the response of potential buyers of X, and the other to the response of sellers of X, to a change in the price of Y, each response being measured in terms of the quantities of X demanded, and supplied, respectively. Neither of these measures, it should be added, necessarily reflects the change in the quantity of X *actually bought and sold*. This depends on the price of X, which is assumed to remain constant in calculating the cross-elasticity measures, and also on the possibility of non-price responses by the producers of X.

Products can be operationally defined as substitutes or complements, and measures of the degree of substitutability obtained, only after empirical information has been acquired regarding the response of quantities demanded (or supplied) to changes in the price of other goods. Moreover, as already mentioned, it is necessary to add 'all other things remaining the same' after the definition of cross-elasticities. There must be no change in the prices or in the non-price variables, such as, for example, level of advertising of other firms in response to a change in the price charged by a particular firm for its product. Reflection on this point immediately suggests the difficulties likely to be encountered in any attempt to obtain such information in practice. A problem confronting the social scientist is that he is unable to 'hold all other things constant', and instead must rely upon statistical techniques in an attempt to measure relationships such as cross-elasticities; these techniques, however sophisticated, yield estimates of a probabilistic nature.

Let us suppose, for the moment, that the required information could be obtained easily. That is, one could obtain, for any particular firm's product Y, a list of precise cross-elasticities (of demand, and also of supply if considered appropriate) linking a change in the price of Y to resulting changes in the demand for each other product in the economy. These could be ranked, commencing with large cross-elasticities indicating a closer substitute relationship between Y and another product than between Y and products yielding smaller cross-elasticity measures. A crucial problem remains. *Where* does one draw the line between successive cross-elasticity magnitudes, thereby deciding which goods are to be regarded as the 'same' and which 'different', and therefore deciding also which firms are regarded as being members of the 'same' industry?

Economic theory provides no precise answer to this problem. There is no magic value of cross-elasticity measures which divides 'close' substitutes from 'distant' substitutes. The choice of locating the dividing line is a matter of opinion. A decision to draw the line where a definite gap existed in the ranked cross-elasticity measures is just as arbitrary as drawing the line elsewhere, from the point of view of theoretical justification of such decisions.

In view of the difficulties of obtaining information about cross-elasticities, and the remaining element of arbitrariness involved in defining industry boundaries even if the required empirical evidence were obtained without cost, is it possible to conclude that the substitutability criterion is inferior, from a practical point of view, when compared with other possible criteria such as similarity of technological process, raw material, or physical characteristics? A negative answer to this question is indicated if one is interested in market behavior, which depends largely on the degree to which different alternatives confronting buyers and sellers are substitutable for each other. The use of cross-elasticity measures of substitutability is simply a method of discovering whether firms are affected by each other's pricing behavior, in order to infer which firms are likely to take each other into account in deciding upon their individual policies. It should be emphasized that one could use some other measure of substitutability instead of cross-elasticity of demand; the response of the quantity of one firm's product demanded to a change in the level of another firm's advertising outlays, prices remaining constant, could be used, for example. Another point to bear in mind is that measures of substitutability, such as cross-elasticity of demand, refer to the extent to which one firm would lose or gain sales in response to a change in another firm's price, *assuming that the first firm did nothing in response to the price change*. This, and not the *actual* change in the quantity of the first firm's product demanded, which will depend upon the response of the firm to the price change, is the relevant measure if one is attempting to measure the degree of substitutability between products.

Of course, this increases the problems associated with any attempt to obtain measures of cross-elasticity, because reactions by firms producing close substitutes for the product of a firm initiating a price change are often likely to occur in practice. However, it is important to distinguish clearly between the use of cross-elasticity measures as an indicator of substitutability, and as an indicator of the type of behavior resulting from close sub-stitutability. In the case of an industry composed of two firms selling an identical product, for example, the cross-elasticity of demand between the products of the two firms may be very large, yet the behavior of the rivals and the resulting price and production policies may take any of several forms. Again, the value of cross-elasticity of demand between the products of different firms can be interpreted as being zero under both monopoly and pure competition, yet the behavior of firms in each of these two market situations is completely different and represents two extreme limiting cases in price theory. A price change by a firm under conditions of monopoly cannot affect the sales of other firms appreciably because by definition there are no close substitutes for the monopolist's product. In pure competition, a slight increase in price by one firm will remove that firm from the market, but this does not change the market price or demand for the output of any individual firm remaining in the market. Although a price cut by one firm will tend to attract all the buyers in the market and reduce sales of other firms to zero, some economists have argued that the rising marginal cost curves of individual sellers, which are essential to the existence of pure competition, limit the ability of any single seller to supply that demand, and that realizable cross-elasticity of demand between the products of two firms in pure competition is therefore zero. Professor E. H. Chamberlin (3), on the other hand, has argued that cross-elasticity of demand can be defined in a number of different ways, and that its value in pure competition can equal zero even without taking supply conditions into account.

The degree of substitutability, as measured by cross-elasticities which do not include allowance for competitive responses, is important in determining whether there is likely to be a reaction of any kind by other firms in response to a change in the (price) strategy of one firm; it cannot indicate what type of reaction is likely, however, nor the effect of a given move on the part of one firm on the behavior of firms producing close substitutes. Despite this, the literature dealing with attempts to classify behavior according to cross-elasticities is voluminous; see Bishop (1, 2), Chamberlin (3), Heertje (7) and Pfouts and Ferguson (10, 11, 12).

Standard Industrial Classifications

Many countries, and some international organizations such as the United Nations, have their own standard industrial classifications which are used for purposes of official statistics concerning various aspects of the domestic, or world, economies. The 1968 revised edition of the United Kingdom Standard Industrial Classification (16), for example, consists of 27 Orders or major industrial groups as broad as Agriculture, Forestry, and Fishing; Mining and Quarrying; Food, Drink, and Tobacco; and so on. These in turn are divided into 181 subgroups, called Minimum List Headings. For example, within Order I, Agriculture, Forestry, and Fishing, the Minimum List Headings are as follows:

001 Agriculture and Horticulture
002 Forestry
003 Fishing

The Minimum List Headings are in turn broken down into further subdivisions. For example, within Minimum List Heading 001, Agriculture and Horticulture, there are three further subdivisions as follows:

001 1. Farming and stock rearing
001 2. Agricultural contracting
001 3. Market gardening, fruit, flower, and seed growing

Similarly, the 1967 edition of the United States Standard Industrial Classification Manual (18) lists ten alphabetical Divisions as follows:

Division A. Agriculture, forestry, and fisheries
Division B. Mining
Division C. Contract construction
Division D. Manufacturing
Division E. Transportation, communication, electric, gas, and sanitary services
Division F. Wholesale and retail trade
Division G. Finance, insurance, and real estate
Division H. Services
Division I. Government
Division J. Nonclassifiable establishments

Each Division is composed of a number of Major Groups each of which is assigned a two-digit number. For example, within Division A the Major Groups are as follows:

Major Group 01. Agricultural production
Major Group 07. Agricultural services and hunting and trapping
Major Group 08. Forestry
Major Group 09. Fisheries

Each Major Group is composed of a number of three-digit Industry Groups, each of which is further subdivided into a number of four-digit Industries. For example, Major Group 01, Agricultural production, is further subdivided as follows:

Group No.	Industry No.	
011		FIELD CROPS
	0112	Cotton
	0113	Cash grains
	0119	Field crops not elsewhere classified
012		FRUIT, TREE NUTS, AND VEGETABLES
	0122	Fruits and Tree Nuts
	0123	Vegetables
013		LIVESTOCK
	0132	Dairies
	0133	Broiler chickens
. . .	. . .	

In the United States SIC, the United States economy is divided into 99 Major Groups (designated by two-digit code numbers), subdivided into Industry Groups (three-digit code numbers) which are further divided into Industries (four-digit code numbers).

The standard industrial classifications used by individual countries differ from each other, making comparisons of data based upon domestic SICs impossible or at best hazardous. The United Nations Standard Industrial Classification (UNSIC) is the classification most frequently employed for comparisons of data relating to different countries. The 1958 revised edition of the UNSIC (17) divides the whole field of economic activity into nine Divisions, each designated by a one-digit code number, except manufacturing which receives two one-digit numbers, as follows:

Division 0   Agriculture, Forestry, Hunting, and Fishing
Division 1   Mining and Quarrying
Division 2–3 Manufacturing
Division 4   Construction
Division 5   Electricity, Gas, Water, and Sanitary Services
Division 6   Commerce
Division 7   Transport, Storage, and Communications
Division 8   Services and Activities not adequately described

Each Division has ten subdivisions, called Major Groups. Each Major Group is identified by a two-digit number, the first digit indicating the Division and the first and second digits taken together identifying the Major Group of that Division. Each Major Group, in turn, can be subdivided into ten groups, each with a three-digit number. The UNSIC provides three levels of classification only, Divisions, Major Groups, and Groups, and is therefore less detailed than the British and American SICs which have, as already mentioned, four levels of classification. In the UNSIC, the activities corresponding to the four-digit codes of the United Kingdom and United States classifications are simply listed, without separate numbers, after the three-digit code number. Apart from the difference in detail provided, however, the UNSIC, consisting of 90 Major Groups and 900 Groups, is similar in principle to the United Kingdom and United States national classifications. In each case, for example, the units classified are establishments, and the principles of assigning establishments to industries are similar.

In all of the standard industrial classifications mentioned so far, primary emphasis in defining an industry is on the supply side of the economic picture. Most of the industries are defined in terms of establishments primarily engaging in producing a product or group of products that are related by technical process or raw materials used in their manufacture. For more on this point, see M. R. Conklin and H. T. Goldstein (4). The fact that the grouping is based mainly on similarity of technical process and/or raw materials involved does not necessarily mean that the grouping is inappropriate for a study of behavior. What we have referred to as substitutability on the supply side may well be related to similarity of process or raw materials. For example, one United States SIC industry (3312 Blast Furnaces, Steel Works, and Rolling Mills) includes firms producing steel strip, tar, tubing, wire, washers, and wheels. From the point of view of users, these products could hardly be claimed to be substitutes for each other, yet producers of the products may well regard them as substitutes on the supply side. Similarly, the fact that manufacturers of scarves, suspenders, and artificial flowers are grouped together in industry code 4494 of the United Kingdom classification could conceivably be justified on the grounds that the products are regarded as substitutes by the producers of such products. The behavior of such manufacturers could therefore be related even though the products are not regarded as close substitutes by consumers.

Although substitutability on the supply side is often important, substitutability on the demand side must also be considered if one is interested in the behavior of firms, and such considerations might suggest a different grouping from that based upon similarity of process or raw material only. Different raw materials or processes may be used to produce products which consumers consider to be very close substitutes. For example, in the United Kingdom SIC, makers of cloth, leather, and fur gloves are grouped into a different industry from makers of knitted gloves, yet intuition suggests that the behavior of such firms is likely to be related because of a high degree of substitutability on the demand side. Coke produced in beehive coke ovens is probably viewed by purchasers as a close substitute for coke produced as a by-product in petroleum refining and related industries, yet establishments producing these two types of coke are classified in different industries (code 3312 and 2911 respectively) in the United States SIC. Similarly, tin cans (U.S. code 3411) and glass containers (U.S. code 3221) are close substitutes for many purposes but are found in two different Major Groups in the United States SIC (Major Groups 34 (Fabricated Metal Products) and 32 (Stone, Clay, Glass, and Concrete Products), respectively) because of the different materials, process of manufacture, or types of machinery used in their manufacture, that is, differences in supply characteristics. Again, there may well be considerable competition between manufacturing industries and non-manufacturing industries; for example, the manufacture of canned fruits and vegetables (U.S. code 2033 and 2034) is closely competitive with the sale of fresh fruits and vegetables (U.S. code 0122 and 0123).

These examples demonstrate that consideration of demand substitutability often results in wider groupings than groupings based upon supply substitutability. On the other hand, the substitutability criterion will sometimes result in narrower groupings than those groupings resulting from strict adherence to similarity of a product's physical characteristics. Output has a geographical as well as a physical characteristic. Goods and services produced at widely separated geographical locations may be very poor substitutes from the point of view of both producers and consumers if the cost of transporting the product or consumer between these locations is high. Consumers of haircuts, for example, do not regard the services of all barbers in the country, or even in the same city, as nearly perfect substitutes for each other, and because of this the behavior of any particular local barber will only be influenced by, and influence in turn, the behavior of other barbers whose services have a similar geographical characteristic.

No single industrial classification could possibly suit all purposes, and criticism of existing standard industrial classifications on the grounds that they do not suit a particular purpose amounts to little more than arid argument concerning which aspect of industry is the most important. Behavior itself has many different aspects, and different groupings may be appropriate for a study of different aspects of firms' behavior. The important requirement which a standard industrial classification must fulfill is that it should be as complete and detailed as possible, in order that the information contained can be regrouped to suit the particular purpose of anyone wishing to use the data.

The units allocated to the different industries and trades identified by the United Kingdom and United States SIC are establishments (factories, farms, shops, mines) and not firms in the sense of a productive unit operating under the direction of a unified will, which may consist of more than one establishment. From a practical point of view, it is easier to identify an establishment than a firm in the above sense of the word. More important, however, is the fact that the more detailed the unit classified, the more detailed the industrial classification that can be attempted. Despite the wealth of detail provided in many existing official industry classifications – the 1967 edition of the United States SIC Manual exceeds 600 pages, for example – it can be argued that existing classifications do not provide sufficient detail concerning some aspects of industrial structure. For example, if an establishment produces more than one product according to the British and United States official product definitions, it is usually allocated to an industry on the basis of its major activity or primary product only. That is, an establishment is classified in a particular industry if the product of that industry accounts for a greater proportion of the total value of shipments from the establishment than any other product. For this reason, the number of establishments producing any particular type of output may be understated, the total output of a particular product may be understated or overstated, and information regarding the extent of diversification within establishments cannot be extracted from data based upon the SIC.

It is impossible to overemphasize the importance of the industry definition. If different criteria for grouping firms into separate industries result in different groupings, choice of criteria must influence the structural characteristics of the industries so defined unless the characteristics of different firms' output are identical, which is unlikely. This should always be remembered in appraising the results of any particular study of industrial structure.

It has been pointed out in the first section of this chapter that the appropriate classification of products and firms is one which reflects a high degree of substitutability, either on the demand or the supply side, between the products of individual firms. Ideally, the appropriate measures of substitutability would be cross-elasticities of demand and supply between different products. Unfortunately the data required to calculate such measures are seldom available, and we are restricted to more readily available indicators of substitutability. For example, two products can be considered to be substitutes on the supply side if they are commonly produced in the same establishments by essentially the same equipment, technical processes, and labor, and the proportions in which the products are produced can vary. The existing SIC emphasis on the technical structure of production is a reflection of this criterion. On the other hand, one would consider as distinct, on the supply side, two products found in the same establishment produced by distinct technical processes, or produced in rigid proportions by the same processes. On the demand side, those goods or services serving generally similar purposes, and among which buyers are frequently observed to vary the proportions of their purchases in response to price variations, can be considered substitutes.

Even if the information required to calculate precise measures of substitutability were available, it is doubtful whether such information would be worth the effort involved in obtaining it. The relationships between commodities are not fixed but change over time with changes in consumers' tastes, productive techniques, and the introduction of new products; therefore measures of the degree of substitutability between products, such as cross-elasticities of demand, may be expected to vary with the passage of time.

Provided that the substitutability criterion is kept in mind, it should be possible to avoid major errors in classifying products and firms into industries for a study of behavior. Thus, for example, it is fairly obvious that certain SIC groupings are too narrow; beet sugar (U.S. code 2063) and cane sugar (U.S. code 2061) four-digit industries are too narrow, and the three-digit classification (206—Sugar) is more appropriate if one is interested in the selling behavior of firms producing, respectively, beet sugar and cane sugar. Other groupings will be too wide, as in the case of products produced by firms at widely separated geographical locations and having a high transportation cost.

Although a priori reasoning and observance of the substitutability criterion may assist in grouping firms appropriately for a study of behavior, empirical studies are indispensable for deciding upon proper groupings, because only such studies can reveal which groupings are most closely related to whatever aspect of behavior one is interested in. Ideally, what is required, in order to decide which groupings are useful in explaining behavior, is that statistical studies investigating the relationship between various aspects of firms' behavior be repeated for different groupings of firms. Statistical evidence often shows broadly similar results for studies using different classifications of firms into industries; of course, this does not necessarily imply that groupings are irrelevant, or that the particular groupings used were the most appropriate – they may be equally inappropriate. However, by investigating whether and how different industry classifications influence the results of statistical studies, it may be possible to improve upon existing knowledge of which groupings are significant from a behavioral point of view.

RECOMMENDED READINGS

1. Bishop, R. L., Elasticities, cross-elasticities, and market relationships, *American Economic Review*, December 1952; Comments by Fellner, W. and Chamberlin, E. H.; *and* Reply by Bishop, *American Economic Review*, December 1953, pp. 898–924; Comment by Hieser, R. *and* Reply by Bishop, *American Economic Review*, June 1955, pp. 373–386.
2. Bishop, R. L., Market classification again, *Southern Economic Journal*, July 1961.
3. Chamberlin, E. H., *Towards a More General Theory of Value* (New York: Oxford University Press, 1957), pp. 84–91.
4. Conklin, M. R. and Goldstein, H. T., Census principles of industry and product classification, manufacturing industries. In Stigler, G. J. (Ed.) *Business Concentration and Price Policy* (Princeton, N. J.: Princeton University Press, 1955).
5. Elzinga, K. G. and Hogarty, T. F., The problem of geographic market delineation in antimerger suits, *Antitrust Bulletin*, Spring 1973.
6. Hale, G. E. and Hale, R. D., Delineating the geographic market: a problem in antimerger cases, *Northwestern University Law Review*, 1966.
7. Heertje, A., Market classification systems in theory, *Southern Economic Journal*, October 1960.
8. Marfels, C., Relevant market and concentration: the case of the U.S. automobile industry, *Jahrbucher für Nationalökonomie und Statistik*, March 1973.
9. Pace, J. D., Relevant markets and the nature of competition in the electric utility industry, *Antitrust Bulletin*, Winter 1970.
10. Pfouts, R. W. and Ferguson, C. E., Market classification systems in theory and policy, *Southern Economic Journal*, October 1959.
11. Pfouts, R. W. and Ferguson, C. E., Conjectural behavior classification of oligopoly situations, *Southern Economic Journal*, October 1960.
12. Pfouts, R. W. and Ferguson, C. E., Theory, operationalism, and policy: a further note on market classification, *Southern Economic Journal*, July 1961.
13. Schwartzman, D., The cross-elasticity of demand and industry boundaries: coal, oil, gas, and uranium, *Antitrust Bulletin*, Fall 1973.
14. Sissors, J. Z., What is a market? *Journal of Marketing*, July 1966.
15. Steiner, P. O., Markets and industries, *International Encyclopedia of the Social Sciences* (New York: Macmillan & The Free Press, 1968), 9:577.
16. United Kingdom Central Statistical Office, *Standard Industrial Classification*, 3rd ed. (London: Her Majesty's Stationery Office, 1968).
17. United Nations, *International Standard Industrial Classification of all Economic Activities*, Statistical Papers, Series M, No. 4, Rev. 1 (New York: Statistical Office of the United Nations, 1958).
18. United States Bureau of the Budget, *Standard Industrial Classification Manual* (Washington, D.C.: U.S. Government Printing Office, 1967).
19. Weiss, L., The geographic size of markets in manufacturing, *Review of Economics and Statistics*, 1972.

CHAPTER SIX

SELLER CONCENTRATION

Concentration and Firms' Behavior

Seller concentration refers to the number and size distribution of firms producing a particular type of output. Seller concentration has for a long time received more attention from economists and those concerned with public policy towards industry than any other single characteristic of industrial structure. This attention is motivated by a fundamental conviction that concentration is likely to play a large part in the determination of business behavior.

As already stressed in the third section of Chapter 3, analytically the number of firms in an industry is, itself, largely irrelevant as a determinant of pricing behavior. Given the number of firms in an industry, a different pattern of industry pricing behavior will result from different assumptions about rivals' reactions. Therefore, whether numbers influence behavior depends on whether numbers themselves influence each firm's *expectations regarding the behavior of its rivals.* Unless this expectation varies as the number of firms in a given industry changes, the industry behavior pattern will not change.

In price theory, a major distinction is made between markets in which the behavior of individual sellers is heedless of rivals' reactions (pure competition, monopoly, and monopolistic competition) and those in which individual sellers take into account rivals' reactions (oligopoly). Apart from monopoly, which is defined as a single firm supplying a particular market, these market situations are not defined in terms of the precise number of sellers involved in each case. There is no magic number of sellers which is supposed to divide oligopolistic from other market situations. The theoretical distinction is in qualitative terms; behavior which takes account of rivals' reactions will exist if one seller's behavior influences noticeably other sellers in the market. The extent to which the behavior of one firm will influence other firms noticeably may well be related to the number of firms in the market. The smaller the number of sellers, for example, the larger, on average, will be the fractions of a particular market supplied by individual sellers, and any given percentage gain in sales by one seller at the expense of the others results in a more noticeable loss to each of the others and is more likely to invite retaliation. There is, however, no single number of sellers which will in all circumstances distinguish oligopoly market situations from market situations characterized by behavior which is heedless of rivals' reactions. Whether a given sales loss to a rival will be noticed and attributed to the action of that rival will depend, for example, upon the general instability of industry sales due to other causes. Thus, a certain number of sellers sufficient to produce behavior which recognizes rivals' reactions in an industry with a very stable market might not do so in one with an unstable market.

Furthermore, within market situations in which rivals are influenced considerably by, and therefore take into account, each other's behavior, different patterns of behavior, related to differences in the degree of concentration, may occur. For these reasons, although theoretical considerations suggest the relevance of concentration to a study of pricing behavior, the existence and precise nature of such a relationship can only be established by empirical evidence.

Pricing is only one aspect of a firm's behavior. The relationship between concentration and price–cost relationships cannot fully describe the character of the competitive forces at work in a sector of the economy. It is equally important to know whether there is any relationship between concentration and other aspects of firms' behavior, such as advertising or R&D activities. Such knowledge is indispensable to the formulation of public policies towards business. Will, for example, reduced concentration mean better pricing performance, measured in terms of price–cost ratios, at the expense of less investment in R&D activities? If empirical evidence suggests that the answer to this question is affirmative, the policy maker must choose, and such a choice may not be easy. Even so, knowledge that choice is involved is likely to result in better policy measures than those taken without regard to all possible effects of a particular measure.

The argument that behavior depends upon the number and size distribution of competing sellers in a market does not, of course, deny the fact that other factors influence behavior. Also relevant may be whether demand for the industry's product is growing or declining, the rate of growth of industry demand over time, the character and speed of technological change, the characteristics of information flows in particular markets, the degree to which sellers operate in other markets, and the goals of individual firms' policy. In view of the existence of differences in these other factors between industries, it would be surprising if a unique relationship between behavior and concentration were observed to exist in different industries. For this reason, studies of the relationship between seller concentration and various aspects of industry behavior should ideally take into account differences in these other factors, in order to attempt to isolate the relationship between concentration and behavior.

Later sections will describe and interpret the results of numerous studies which attempt to establish the nature of the relationship existing in practice between seller concentration and firms' behavior. First, however, it is appropriate to subject the concept of seller concentration itself to closer scrutiny, since it has many different dimensions. An understanding of the distinction between different aspects of seller concentration, and of the way in which they are related to each other, is important in interpreting properly the results of statistical studies. In addition, since the results of any particular statistical investigation will depend on the choice of concentration measure unless all dimensions of concentration are linearly related, these issues are relevant in dealing with the question of appropriate choice of concentration measure for purposes of statistical investigation.

Measurement of Concentration: Choice of Concentration Index

The degree of concentration, however it is measured for purposes of statistical study, is entirely dependent upon the industry definition used in the study (see Chapter 5 which deals with the problem of properly defining market and industry boundaries). The broader the criterion used for grouping firms into industries, the larger will be the number of firms grouped together. Once an industry has been defined, and the number of firms in the industry is therefore determined, there are many different ways of measuring the degree of concentration (see Part I of Recommended Readings: Measurement of Concentration). Several of these measures are related to the concept of the cumulative concentration curve shown in Figure 6–1. The height of the cumulative concentration curve above any point x on the horizontal axis measures the percentage of the industry's total size accounted for by the largest x firms. Size of firms, and of the industry, may be measured either in terms of sales, net output, employment, assets, or some other index of size. Choice of the appropriate size variable is discussed in this chapter in the section entitled Measurement of Concentration: Choice of Size Variable. The horizontal axis in the concentration curve diagram measures the cumulative number of firms, starting with the largest. The concentration curve rises from left to right, reaching a maximum height of 100 per cent at a point on the horizontal axis corresponding to the total number of firms in the industry. There will be one such curve for each industry in the economy, and each will refer to a specific period or point in time.

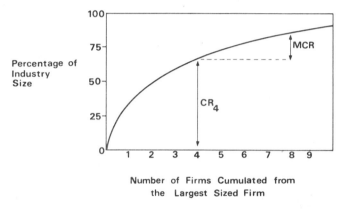

Figure 6–1. The concentration curve, concentration ratio, and marginal concentration ratio.

The index of concentration used most frequently is called the concentration ratio and indicates the percentage of an industry's size accounted for by a certain number of the largest firms in the industry. Diagrammatically, it is depicted by the height of the cumulative concentration curve above a certain point on the horizontal axis. In analyses of American data, the percentage of sales, net output, employment, or some other size variable, accounted for by the leading four firms, is frequently used; analyses of industrial concentration in Great Britain usually employ data for the three largest firms. The difference in the number of firms to which American and British ratios usually apply is the result of differences in the compilation of official statistics which have nothing to do with what is considered to be an appropriate measure of concentration.

Alternatively, instead of measuring the height of the concentration curve at a given horizontal distance from the origin, one can measure the horizontal distance to the curve at a given height. This measure of concentration yields the number of firms accounting for y per cent of industry size.

These two types of concentration index depend on only one point on the concentration curve. If the relevant concentration curves intersect, comparison of concentration in different industries, or in a particular industry at different points in time, will yield different results, depending upon the point chosen, and an ambiguity exists as to which industry has the highest degree of concentration. In Figure 6–2, for example, industry A is more concentrated than industry B if concentration is measured by the percentage of industry size accounted for by the largest four firms, but industry B is more concentrated than industry A if ratios for eight firms are used.

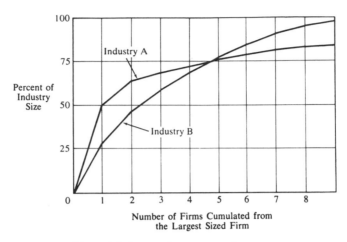

Figure 6–2. Intersecting concentration curves.

Whether concentration curves do intersect or not in any particular case can only be determined by empirical evidence. If they do not intersect, the ranking of industries by concentration at a given point in time, or the degree of concentration in a particular industry at different points in time, will not be influenced by the point on the concentration curve chosen to represent the degree of concentration. This does not, however, necessarily imply that any point is as good as any other from the point of view of measuring concentration. The best measure of concentration is the measure which is most closely related whatever aspect of industrial behavior one is interested in, and which therefore enables one to predict behavior most accurately. Agreement among ranks does not necessarily mean that the measures are good indicators of behavior; they may be equally poor indicators. On the other hand, if a concentration ratio which applies to four firms is more closely related to some aspect of industry behavior than a ratio for eight firms, the former is to be preferred to the latter, even though the ranking of concentration is independent of the number of firms used to calculate the concentration ratio.

Although the largest firms in an industry are normally used to calculate concentration ratios, in principle the concentration ratio concept can be applied to other groups of firms. For example, Professor R. A. Miller used the combined share of the fifth to eighth largest firms in a 1967 study (18), and christened this measure the 'marginal concentration ratio'. Diagrammatically, the marginal concentration ratio is depicted by the vertical height of the difference between two points on the concentration curve as shown in Figure 6–1.

The types of concentration index discussed so far, which do not take into account all firms in an industry, are usually referred to as 'discrete' measures of concentration. The value of a discrete index may be identical for two industries, yet the behavior of the industries might differ significantly as a result of a difference in the remaining number of firms which are not taken into account by the index. It is likely, for example, that the behavior of an industry in which four firms account for 80 per cent of total industry output and two firms supply the remaining 20 per cent will differ from the behavior of an industry in which the remaining 20 per cent is supplied by 20 other firms. Nor do these types of concentration index take into account the relative size of firms in the industry. This applies both to the relative size of the largest firms used in calculating the index, and to that of the remaining firms in the industry.

Measures of concentration which, in contrast to the discrete measures already mentioned, take account of all the firms in an industry are termed 'summary' concentration indexes. There are a number of different summary concentration indexes, and only the more prominent ones will be mentioned here. One such index, introduced originally by Professor Hirschman (7) and independently reformulated later by Professor Herfindahl (6), is calculated by squaring and summing the share of industry size accounted for by every firm in the industry, as follows:

$$HI = \Sigma(S_i)^2$$

The Rosenbluth summary concentration index (22) is calculated by multiplying each firm's share of industry size by the firm's rank, with firms ranked in descending order of size, as indicated by the following formula:

$$RI = \frac{1}{(2\Sigma i S_i) - 1}$$

Diagrammatically, the Rosenbluth index is equivalent to the area above the concentration curve bounded by the 100% axis of Figure 6–1.

The maximum value of both these summary concentration indexes is unity, and their lower bound is $1/n$, the reciprocal of the number of firms in the industry. The value of both indexes is unity when there is one firm in an industry. When the number of firms in an industry exceeds one, however, the value of HI falls below unity and approaches $1/n$ the more equal are firm sizes, reaching $1/n$ when all firms in the industry are of equal size; in contrast, RI is unity when firms are of equal size, and approaches $1/n$ the more unequal are firm sizes.

Another concentration index, consisting of a mixture of discrete and summary components and termed the 'comprehensive concentration index', was proposed by Professor J. Horvath in 1970 (9). This index is calculated by adding the market share of the largest firm in the industry to a summary index covering the remaining firms in the industry, as follows:

$$CCI = S_i + \Sigma S_j^2(2 - S_j)$$

The summary component of CCI is similar to HI, the only difference being that each of the squared firm sizes in CCI is weighted by the term $(2 - S_j)$; since this expression will exceed unity the CCI assigns greater weight to all the non-largest firms in the industry than would the HI. Likewise, since the proportionate market share of the largest firm is not squared, the weight assigned by the CCI to the largest firm is also greater than in HI. The upper bound of the CCI is unity, and occurs when there is one firm in the industry; it can be shown that the minimum value of the CCI always exceeds $1/n$, the lower bound for the HI and RI, due to the weighting scheme just mentioned.

The basic difference between the various summary concentration indexes lies in the weights which are assigned to the market shares of firms in calculating the respective indexes. Indeed, this is also true of the discrete concentration indexes, which assign weights of unity to the shares of the largest firms, or to the shares of the fifth to eighth largest firms in the case of the marginal concentration ratio, and zero weights to the shares of other firms. The Herfindahl index assigns weights of unity to each firm's market share, and the squaring of firm shares means that the smaller firms contribute less than proportionately to the overall value of the index. The Rosenbluth index uses the ranks of firms as weights, with smaller firms receiving a higher ranking, so that smaller firms in an industry receive greater weight than in the HI and influence the overall concentration index more. As already explained, the CCI assigns every firm in an industry a greater weight than does the HI. Since the weight of the largest firm is doubled, compared to the HI, the influence of the largest firm on the CCI is greater than on the HI. However, considering the remaining firms, the influence of smaller firms is greater in the CCI than in the HI due to the weighting scheme employed by the CCI. The weights assigned to smaller firms by the CCI are still smaller than the weights assigned by the RI, however, so that the influence of small firms on the RI is greater than that on either of the other two indexes. Because of the different weighting schemes of the various indexes, a particular size distribution of firms in an industry will be evaluated differently by each index, and a change in size distribution of firms will produce changes of different relative magnitudes in the various indexes. For example, the HI will be relatively insensitive to a change in the share of small firms, the CCI will react more strongly, and the RI very strongly, due to the different weights assigned to small firms by each index.

Before proceeding to consider which concentration index is most appropriate, it is necessary to mention yet another class of measures, usually termed 'relative' concentration measures in contrast to the previously discussed indexes which are usually referred to as 'absolute' concentration measures. Measures of relative concentration focus attention on the degree of inequality of firm sizes in an industry, and can be depicted diagrammatically in terms of the Lorenz curve concept, shown in Figure 6–3, which measures the cumulative percentage of industry size accounted for by the various percentages of the number of firms in the industry. Apart from measuring cumulative percentage rather than cumulative number of firms on the horizontal axis, the only difference between the Lorenz curve and the concentration curve is that the former starts with the smallest firms in the industry, while the concentration curve starts with the largest firms.

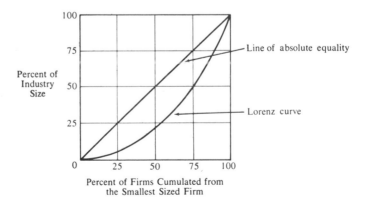

Figure 6–3. The Lorenze curve.

The diagonal line which the Lorenz curve would follow if all firms in an industry were of equal size is referred to as the diagonal of equal distribution or line of absolute equality. The extent to which the Lorenz curve deviates from this line is an indicator of relative concentration and the area between the Lorenz curve and the diagonal of equal distribution is usually termed the area of concentration. Gini's concentration ratio is the ratio of the area of concentration to the total area below the diagonal of equal distribution and bounded by the axes of the diagram. If all firms in a particular industry were of equal size, the Gini coefficient would equal zero; the Lorenz curve would coincide with the diagonal of equal distribution, and there would be no area of concentration. At the other extreme, where one firm accounts for total industry size, the area of concentration coincides with the area under the diagonal of equal distribution and the Gini coefficient is equal to unity.

There are numerous other measures of relative concentration, either based on intercepts of the Lorenz curve or summarizing the whole size distribution. For example, the relative mean deviation intercept is found by drawing a positively sloped line parallel to the diagonal of equal distribution and tangent to a line showing the percentage of firms cumulated from the largest-sized firms. The point of intersection of this line with the vertical axis of the Lorenz curve diagram marks the relative mean deviation intercept, which is equal to one half the value of the relative mean deviation of firm sizes in the industry. The relative mean deviation equals the mean deviation of firm sizes in the industry divided by the mean firm size and is an index of inequality of firm size. Alternatively, another index of inequality, termed the Pietra ratio, is the ratio of the maximum triangle which can be inscribed in the area of concentration to the area under the diagonal of equal distribution and bounded by the axes of the Lorenz curve diagram. The Pietra ratio, it can be shown, is equal to the relative mean deviation intercept.

The basic difference between absolute and relative concentration measures, again, lies in their weighting schemes. Measures of absolute concentration are weighted *sums* of the firms' shares, and measures of relative concentration are weighted *averages* of firms' shares. Although different, absolute and relative concentration measures are related. For example, it can be shown that the Herfindahl index is equal to $(c^2 + 1)/n$, where c is the coefficient of variation of firm sizes and n is the number of firms in the industry. The coefficient of variation equals the standard deviation of firm sizes – a measure of size inequality – divided by the mean firm size in the industry. The above formulation of the index enables the limiting values of HI to be easily interpreted. When all firms in an industry are of equal size, the standard deviation of firm sizes equals zero, and the HI equals $1/n$, its lower bound; at the other extreme, if there is only one firm in the industry the coefficient of variation is zero and the index reaches its maximum value of unity.

Absolute concentration measures can often be converted into relative concentration measures, and vice versa, provided that the measures have certain specific properties. For example, absolute concentration measures with upper and lower bounds of 1 and $1/n$ respectively, and relative concentration measures with upper and lower bounds of $1 - 1/n$ and 0 respectively, are related in a manner indicated by the following formulas:

$$C_r = 1 - (1/nC_a) \text{ and } C_a = 1/n(1 - C_r)$$

These relationships reveal that size inequality (C_r) increases with absolute concentration (C_a) with a given number of firms, and vice versa. With a variable number of firms, and with C_a being a function of n, size inequality decreases with absolute concentration, and vice versa. A corresponding measure of size inequality can therefore be established for absolute concentration measures having the above mentioned properties. All pure summary measures of concentration qualify in this respect, and the Rosenbluth index offers a prominent example, since it yields Gini's index of concentration as its counterpart inequality measure. The possibility of converting summary measures should be intuitively apparent from the fact that the concentration curve, and measures based on it, can be transformed into a Lorenz curve simply by transforming absolute numbers of firms into percentages, and cumulating from smallest to largest firms instead of from largest to smallest. The above formulas correspond to the geometric device of transforming a concentration measure based on the concentration curve into a measure based on the Lorenz curve. Conversion of the CCI into a corresponding inequality measure by means of the above formula is not possible, however, due to the fact that its lower bound exceeds $1/n$.

Although absolute and relative concentrations are related, one of these concepts may change without any change in the other, and they are capable of changing in opposite directions. For these reasons, it is important to specify whether one is referring to absolute or relative concentration when speaking of degrees of, and changes in, concentration. Some writers use the term concentration as synonymous with disparity of firm sizes within an industry, so that the greater the disparity between the sizes of the largest and smallest firms, the greater the degree of concentration. According to this approach, an industry with size equally distributed among member firms is not concentrated at all, even though the industry may consist of very few firms and possesses a high degree of absolute concentration. An industry which consists of five firms each with 20 per cent of total industry sales, for example, has a high degree of absolute concentration since the top four firms account for 80 per cent of sales, but relative concentration is nil since each firm is equal in size as measured by their respective sales. Similarly, it is possible for relative concentration to decrease simultaneously with an increase in absolute concentration. A merger which leaves the remaining firms in an industry closer in size will reduce relative concentration or inequality, even though the degree of absolute concentration may be increased by the reduction in the number of firms in the industry.

Which of the various alternative concentration measures is most appropriate? Despite a recent spate of articles clarifying the relationship between different concentration measures, little progress has been made in answering this question. On the contrary, a step backward may have been taken, due to the shift of emphasis in the literature towards consideration of the mathematical properties of concentration measures, which implies that the choice between alternative concentration measures depends on their mathematical properties. This view is erroneous. Which measure of concentration is optimal depends on the intended use of the measure. If one is concerned with the relationship between seller concentration and industrial behavior, the crucial issue is whether some aspect of the number and size distribution of firms in an industry influences the behavior of firms in the industry. In other words, from a behavioral point of view, what is important is the weight accorded to the number and size distribution of rival firms by decision-makers in an industry in their decision-making.

As already explained, the difference between alternative concentration indexes lies in the weights which they assign to the market shares of firms in an industry. Accordingly, it follows that arguments for a particular concentration measure reflect little more than the proponent's belief that the weighting system inherent in that index reflects the weighting system which is operative in the minds of decision-makers in industry in practice. Thus, for example, the Rosenbluth index will be advocated by persons who feel that small firms contribute significantly to the pattern of behavior in an industry. In contrast, those who feel that the role of small firms is relatively insignificant will advocate the Herfindahl index, or perhaps concentration ratios, as being superior. Alternatively, persons who believe that the largest firm in an industry will exert a dominant influence on the industry's behavior will favor Horvath's comprehensive concentration index over other indexes. It is not difficult to construct plausible examples to support the use of one absolute concentration index rather than another. For example, as an argument against summary measures, it might be argued that it is unrealistic to assume that decision-makers in an industry take all rival firms into account in their decision-making; and even if they do, they may not give weight to rival firms in relation to their current market shares as the Herfindahl index does.

For example, a subsidiary of a giant conglomerate with a small market share may get considerable attention in rival decision-makers' minds due to the threat which its parent represents. Or, against the CCI, it may be argued that the largest firm in an industry may not influence the behavior of the next three largest firms if the latter are vying for second place since they may confine their attention mainly to the likely reactions of each other.

A priori arguments in favor of and against the use of absolute rather than relative concentration measures are likewise commonplace. In support of absolute concentration measures, some economists have argued that the latter type of measure is more directly relevant than the former as an influence upon industry behavior. In support of this argument it has been pointed out, for example, that two firms each producing 50 per cent of an industry's output yield the same value of the Gini coefficient (zero) as 100 firms each supplying one per cent of industry output, yet industry behavior will probably differ in the two cases. This may be true, but the argument advanced by some economists, that the number of sellers alone is important and that inequality of size has no economic significance, must be rejected. It can be argued just as plausibly on a priori grounds that inequality, not numbers, is more important in influencing industry behavior in certain situations, and differences in the disparity of firm sizes which have important implications for industry behavior may not be reflected by absolute concentration measures. The creation of a large firm through merger of smaller firms may challenge the market power of existing large firms and change behavior in the industry even though absolute concentration, measured by the share of the market supplied by the former leading firms, does not change, for example. Even when an absolute concentration measure can be transformed into a corresponding measure of relative concentration, or inequality, this does not mean that they are equally important in influencing behavior in an industry. As already explained, these two types of concentration measure differ in their weighting schemes, and one weighting system rather than the other may be more closely related to the weights present in decision-makers' minds.

One can go on constructing a priori arguments for or against various concentration measures ad infinitum. Unfortunately, however, the question of which concentration index is best cannot be decided by resort to a priori arguments alone, but requires empirical investigation of the relationship between aspects of firm, or industry, behavior and various concentration indexes. If concentration measures are to be used to indicate differences in behavior, the best index will be the one which is most closely related to whatever aspect of behavior one is interested in. Different indexes may be appropriate for different aspects of behavior. Ideally, it would be useful to use different concentration measures when undertaking any particular study, in order to discover whether the results of the study are influenced by the measures used. There are, however, only a very limited number of statistical studies of the relationship between concentration and industrial behavior which employ either summary or relative concentration measures. The main reason is the lack of published data on individual firm shares, information which is necessary to calculate these indexes. To preserve anonymity concerning individual firms, officially published data generally refer to the combined share of a number of firms, and firms themselves are naturally reluctant to provide information to researchers which might prove detrimental to them in the hands of rival firms. The argument is sometimes heard that summary and relative concentration measures are more difficult to obtain because the number of firms in an industry is not usually known with any precision. If valid, this argument would also rule out the calculation of absolute concentration measures. After all, measures which indicate the percentage of total industry size accounted for by a specific number of firms can only be calculated if information regarding the total industry size is available, and this requires information regarding the total number of firms in the industry, and their size. Conversely, if this information is available, it can be used for measures of summary and relative concentration. The problem of industry delineation, discussed in Chapter 5 is of crucial importance, however, since the manner in which this problem is solved will automatically influence the number and size distribution of firms in an industry, and therefore the results of all concentration measures.

Although few statistical studies of industrial behavior use summary or relative concentration measures, several articles have compared the effect of using different concentration measures on the results of individual studies. Even though the various concentration measures will differ in magnitude, due to their different weighting schemes, there is general agreement that the ranking of concentration in different industries will be the same whichever index of concentration is used. This means that if a relationship is observed between some aspect of industry behavior and seller concentration as measured by one of the concentration indexes, a relationship with the same sign, positive or negative, would also be observed even if a different concentration index were used instead. The precise *form* of the relationship between behavior and different seller concentration measures would differ, however, due to the different weighting systems employed by different indexes.

In the light of this evidence, it is frequently concluded that choice of concentration measure will not influence materially the results of any particular study of the relationship between concentration and behavior. Several comments are appropriate in interpreting this evidence. Similar rankings of concentration in different industries when using different concentration measures does not mean that all the concentration measures are equally important in influencing behavior. Since the weighting schemes of different concentration measures differ, decision-makers' own weighting schemes *cannot possibly* simultaneously correspond to those of all concentration measures, and one measure may be more closely related to behavior than another. In this writer's view, however, the evidence reinforces the thesis, which is supported by theory and the results of a number of empirical studies to date (M. Gort and R. Singamsetti (5), for example), that seller concentration plays an insignificant independent role in influencing industrial behavior. The analysis in Chapters 4 and 5 indicates that the optimal levels of a firm's decision-variables depend on the magnitude of the firm's own market share, independently of any influence of the firm's expectations regarding its rivals' reactions. Therefore, since all concentration indexes are calculated using firms' market shares, each concentration measure will *automatically* be correlated with firms' behavior even in the absence of any independent influence of seller concentration on a firm's expectations regarding its rivals' behavior. The precise nature of this automatic relationship between concentration and behavior will vary for different indexes, due to their different weighting systems. The real issue is whether seller concentration exerts an independent influence on firms' behavior by influencing decision-makers' expectations regarding their rivals' reactions. To answer this question it is necessary to determine whether any observed relationship between seller concentration and behavior remains not only after eliminating the independent influence of other factors such as market elasticity of demand and a firm's own market shares on behavior, *but also allowing for the automatic overlapping of market shares and any particular concentration measure used.* Although arguments concerning which concentration measure, if any, is most closely related to industrial behavior cannot be settled by a priori argument alone, as already noted, theory can determine the extent to which any particular concentration measure will be automatically correlated with behavior due to overlapping of concentration measures and market shares. Although there are scattered signs of some beginnings in this direction, little progress has been made to date. For this reason, despite a preponderance of empirical studies indicating that concentration ratios and industry profit rates are positively related, to be discussed in more detail after the next section, whether seller concentration exerts an independent influence on industrial behavior remains an unsettled issue. Even when statistical regressions include the market share of a firm as an independent explanatory variable, the positive correlation between concentration and behavior may merely reflect the influence of market shares inherent in the concentration index itself.

Measurement of Concentration: Choice of Size Variable

Apart from the question of which index of concentration is appropriate, there remains the question of whether to employ sales, net output, employment, assets, or some other size variable, as an index of firm, and industry, size. Although economic theory cannot offer much help in choosing between alternative indexes of concentration, theoretical considerations may help in choosing the most suitable quantity in terms of which to measure concentration.

If concentration measured in terms of different size variables were the same, choice of size variable would be irrelevant. Theoretical considerations suggest that this is unlikely, and empirical evidence supports the view that choice of size variable will influence measured concentration in many, if not most, industries. In many industries, absolute concentration measured by fixed capital assets is higher than concentration measured by sales, reflecting the fact that firms with larger sales have a larger ratio of assets to sales than firms with smaller sales. Large firms may use more capital and less labor per unit of final output than small firms, either because the relative price of capital equipment is lower for large firms than small, or because the optimal capital–labor ratio per unit of output increases with scale of output despite constant relative input prices. The higher degree of asset than sales concentration may, in other words, simply reflect a difference in the optimal capital–labor combination at higher levels of output. If this were the only factor underlying the observed relationship, however, one would expect employment concentration to be less than sales concentration. In some industries this is the case, but in others the relationship is reversed and both asset and employment concentrations exceed sales concentration. In the latter industries, another influence, apart from the capital–labor ratio, is presumably at work, namely, vertical integration.

Even when the ratio of capital to labor is the same in firms with different levels of sales of a particular product, the ratio of assets (and employment) to sales will be higher in firms that are more vertically integrated than others, that is, in firms which themselves perform a greater number of preceding stages involved in the production of the final product. The use of assets, employment, or value added (sales minus purchases of inputs from other firms) as an index of firm size will mean that the resulting concentration measure reflects both horizontal and vertical aspects of firm size. The level of a firm's sales at a particular stage in the productive process refers to one dimension of firm size, and vertical integration to another, the number of successive stages involved in the production of the final product performed by the firm. Even when the capital–labor ratio per unit of output is the same in all firms, asset, employment, and value-added concentration will differ from sales concentration unless all firms in the industry in question are equally vertically integrated, and will reflect vertical aspects of firms' size in addition to horizontal aspects. Vertical integration may of course influence behavior just as much as horizontal size. However, horizontal size and vertical size, as well as their measurement, should be kept separate.

Finally, if the drawing of industry boundaries results in a situation in which a firm is a member of other industries in addition to the one studied, calculation of the proportion of the firm's total employment, or assets, actually 'in' one of the industries involves an allocation of unspecialized inputs between different outputs, and therefore industries. This introduces an element of arbitrariness into the calculation of asset or employment concentration in any single industry, which can be avoided by using sales or value added as a measure of size.

Although asset, employment, sales, and net output concentration often differ within a given industry, the ranking of industries by concentration is often much the same no matter which standard of size is used. This will be the case if, for example, asset concentration tends to exceed sales concentration, which tends to exceed employment concentration, in all industries which are being studied. In these circumstances, analytical results which depend only upon rankings of concentration in different industries will not be greatly affected by the index of size used.

The Concentration–Profitability Relationship

The price–marginal-cost relationship in a firm, or industry, has important implications for the efficiency with which resources in an economy are allocated, as will be explained in detail in Chapter 10. The influence of seller concentration on this aspect of firms' behavior has therefore been of prime interest to economists concerned with industrial performance, and there have been many statistical studies aimed at discovering the nature of this influence. Because data on marginal cost is rarely available, instead of using data on $P - MC$ the majority of statistical studies have used data either on $P - AC$ or, more usually, profit rates. Before considering the results of these studies, therefore, it is appropriate to explain the relationship between these alternative concepts. Marginal and average cost are related as follows: $MC = kAC$, where k, which expresses the ratio of MC to AC at any particular output level, will depend on the rate of change of the firm's total cost with respect to changes in its output level. When total cost increases in proportion to output level changes, $MC = AC$ and $k = 1$; when total costs increase less than proportionately with increases in output, a situation usually described as one involving 'economies of scale', MC is less than AC and k will therefore be less than unity; when total costs increase more than proportionately with increases in output, a situation involving 'diseconomies of scale', MC will exceed AC and k will exceed unity. Thus any particular equilibrium $P - MC$ relationship implies a corresponding relationship $P - kAC$, and the corresponding $P - AC$ relationship will be determined by the magnitude of k, which will depend on the firm's cost conditions and the scale of the firm's output. Conversely, a particular $P - AC$ relationship will imply a relationship between P and MC given by $P - kAC$. Although some statistical studies use $P - AC$ instead of $P - MC$ data, the majority of studies employ profit-rate data. The two major profit-rate variants which have been used are the profit return on equity and the profit return on total assets of the firm. The former expresses the firm's after-tax profits in relation to the owner's equity, while the latter expresses after-tax profits plus interest paid to persons who lend to the firm in relation to the total assets, or capital, of the firm. Thus, the equity profit rate is given by the following expression:

$$\frac{R - C - I - T - D}{E}$$

and the asset profit rate by the following expression:

$$\frac{R - C - T - D}{A}$$

where R represents the firm's revenues, C its currently incurred costs, I interest payments on capital loaned to the firm, D depreciation charges, T taxes, E owners' equity, and A total assets.

These profit-rate concepts are related to $P - AC$. Thus, for example, if i represents the cost of capital, it is possible to express the equity profit rate in terms of the $P - AC$ relation as follows:

$$\frac{R - C - I - T - D}{E} = i + \frac{R}{E}\frac{(P-AC)}{P} \qquad \textit{incorrect}$$

where $AC = C + I + T + D + iE$, and iE expresses the opportunity cost represented by the return on owners' capital which is forgone by using their capital in the firm instead of lending it elsewhere. The asset profit rate can similarly be expressed in terms of the $P - AC$ relationship. The above relationship indicates that, given the ratio of R to E (or R to A), larger profit rates on equity (or assets) indicate larger excesses of price over average cost. The constancy of R/E is an important condition, however; two firms with equal profit rates on equity will not have the same $P - AC$ if their R/E ratios differ.

Although there is no problem, conceptually, in using profit-rate data instead of $P - MC$ or $P - AC$ to investigate the relationship between seller concentration and firms' pricing behavior, a number of problems are raised when accounting data are used to estimate profit rates. Profits are defined in economics as the excess of total revenue over the opportunity cost of the resources used in generating those revenues. As already explained in Chapter 1, accounting costs often differ from opportunity costs, for a number of reasons. Accounting costs do not include the opportunity cost of labor or capital invested by owners, measured in terms of the best return to these resources which individuals could earn elsewhere. Accounting measures of depreciation charges are not generally adjusted for price level changes, so that in a period of rising prices the depreciation charges will understate replacement costs. For these reasons, accounting profit measures will tend to overstate true economic profit measures. Another reason why accounting profit rates may differ from the true economic profit rates is that some types of expenditure, such as advertising or R&D outlays, are really investment outlays which create intangible capital assets such as buyer goodwill. These capital assets depreciate over time and if such expenditures were treated as investment outlays, only a portion of the total expenditure would be treated as current expenses in each period of the life of the asset created while the assets which they create would be added to the firm's total assets. In practice, however, advertising and similar expenditures are treated as current expenses. This tends to lower current pre-tax profits and current taxes; it also tends to understate the firm's total assets. The net result is that accounting profit rates may considerably overstate the true economic profit rates. The implications of the preceding examples for accounting measures of AC used in statistical studies of the relationship between $P - AC$ and seller concentration are similar; that is, the empirical accounting data may under- or overstate the true AC involved, and the degree of distortion may vary for different industries. For these reasons, care must be taken in interpreting observed relationships between concentration and either price–cost margins or profit rates.

In order to place statistical studies of the concentration–profitability relationship in perspective, and to assist in interpreting their results, it is useful to consider the manner in which seller concentration might influence firms' pricing behavior and profitability. A useful starting point, in this connection, is the analysis contained in the second section of Chapter 3, where it was demonstrated that the following relationship will be established by a profit-maximizing firm:

$$\frac{P-\mathrm{MC}}{P} = \frac{1}{E_d} = \frac{S_f}{E_m + E_s\, S_r}$$

This relationship indicates that, for profit-maximizing firms, the optimal $P - \mathrm{MC}$ relationship, and the associated profit implied by the relationship $\mathrm{MC} = k\mathrm{AC}$, depend on the firm's market share (S_f), the price-elasticity of market demand (E_m), and the anticipated reaction of the firm's rivals to a change in the level of the firm's product price (E_s). Seller concentration, which refers to the number and size distribution of rival sellers accounting for the remainder of the market share (S_r), itself appears nowhere in the preceding expression. This reflects the fact that, analytically at least, any particular number or size distribution of rival sellers is compatible with a particular 'anticipated reaction of rivals' and resulting value of E_s. In practice, however, seller concentration may influence the nature of the reaction which a firm anticipates from its rivals in response to changes in its own policies, thereby influencing E_s in the above expression, and the firm's pricing behavior and profits. The primary objective of statistical studies of the concentration–profitability relationship is to determine whether such an influence exists in practice, and its nature and magnitude. Such studies usually use data on seller concentration and price–cost margins or profit rates existing in different industries in an attempt to infer the nature of any underlying concentration–profitability relationship. Since the price–cost margin and associated profit rate depend on the firm's market share and price-elasticity of market demand, it is obviously desirable that the influence of these other factors on the profitability of firms and industries be taken into account in order to determine whether any relationship between seller concentration and profitability exists after their influence has been removed. This is particularly necessary in view of the fact that some dimensions of seller concentration will automatically be correlated with some of the other factors which influence the profitability of firms and groups of firms, even when seller concentration itself plays no causal role in influencing pricing and profitability.

For example, the concentration ratio, which is defined as the share of industry size accounted for by the largest x firms (four in most statistical studies) will obviously be mechanically correlated with the market shares of the firms included in the measure, since it is simply the sum of the market shares of those firms. Even if seller concentration, measured by the concentration ratio, has no influence on rivals' reactions anticipated by individual firms in the industry, and therefore does not influence pricing behavior by influencing E_s in the above expression, the optimal $P - \mathrm{MC}$ will be higher for each of the leading firms, the higher its market share (S_f), and the concentration ratio will automatically be larger, the larger these market shares of the leading firms. In these circumstances, the observed relationship between seller concentration and profitability is spurious from a causal point of view. Concentration only plays an independent causal role in influencing profitability to the extent that it influences the expectations of individual firms in the industry regarding their rivals' reactions (E_s in the preceding expression). The influence of firms' market shares on profitability must obviously be taken into account in attempting to infer the nature of the concentration–profitability relationship.

There is an additional factor underlying firm and industry profitability which is not apparent from the above relationship, namely the *absolute size* of the firm and market. A proportionate change in these two will not change S_f, or the optimal $P - \mathrm{MC}$ relationship; it may, however, change the profit rate of the firm if cost conditions relating to the product exhibit economies or diseconomies of scale. As was previously indicated, $P - \mathrm{MC}$ is equal to $P - k\mathrm{AC}$, and when economies and diseconomies of scale exist, the absolute scale of a firm's output will influence the magnitude of k and $P - \mathrm{AC}$, which determines the firm's profit rate. As Figure 6–4 indicates, if there are economies of scale up to a certain scale of

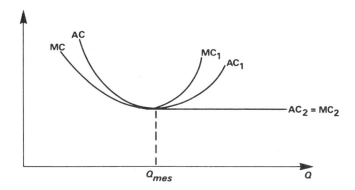

Figure 6–4. Alternative cost conditions with a given minimum efficient scale of output.

output, Q_{mes}, usually termed the 'minimum efficient scale' of output, k will be less than unity and will approach unity as scale of output increases to Q_{mes}. Given the optimal $P - MC$, the $P - AC$ margin and profit rate will therefore increase as the absolute size of the firm increases up to Q_{mes}. If there are diseconomies of scale beyond this output level, as indicated by AC_1 and MC_1 in the diagram, k will exceed unity and will increase with the scale of output. Given $P - MC$, the firm's profit rate will therefore decrease with increases in the absolute size of the firm beyond Q_{mes}. Alternatively, if there are no diseconomies of scale, and cost conditions are depicted by $AC_2 = MC_2$ in the diagram, k will equal unity beyond Q_{mes}, and at a given $P - MC$ the firm's profit rate will be proportional to increases in the absolute size of the firm. To summarize: absolute firm size can influence a firm's profit rate in two distinct ways. First, the larger the absolute firm size in relation to the market, the larger will be S_f, which implies a lower price-elasticity of demand for the firm (given E_m and E_s) and a higher optimal $P - MC$. Second, if cost conditions exhibit economies and diseconomies of scale, an increase in absolute firm size will increase or reduce the firm's profit rate resulting from a given $P - MC$ depending on whether the firm's scale output is below or above the minimum efficient scale.

The existence of economies and diseconomies of scale will also lead to a mechanical relationship between some dimensions of seller concentration and absolute market size. Given the magnitude of the minimum efficient scale of output, absolute market size determines the maximum number of firms which can produce at that scale of output, N*. If there are diseconomies of scale beyond that output scale, N* also represents the minimum number of firms which can produce efficiently. Industry profitability at a given optimal $P - MC$ (or set of optimal $P - MCs$ if the products of different firms are differentiated) will depend on the efficiency with which the industry's total output is produced, and in the presence of economies and diseconomies of scale this will depend on the number of firms in the industry. Increases in the number of firms above N* will imply firms producing output scales in the range of increasing returns and will imply lower industry profit at a given optimal $P - MC$. Reductions in the number of firms below N* will also imply lower industry profit at a given optimal $P - MC$ if there are diseconomies of scale. In the presence of economies or diseconomies of scale, the number of firms in the industry and industry profit at a given $P - MC$ will be related in non-linear fashion, even in the absence of any causal influence between seller concentration in the industry and pricing behavior.

There are also some ways in which absolute firm size and scale economies can influence optimal $P - MC$ relationships in an industry, by affecting entry barriers and the behavior of potential entrants to the industry which is anticipated by established firms. Discussion of the actual and empirical relationship between entry barriers and industry pricing will however be postponed until the next chapter.

Turning now to the results of statistical studies of the concentration–profitability relationship, discussion of each of the many studies which have been made is precluded by space limitations, and the interested reader may consult the references listed under Part II of Recommended Readings at the end of this chapter. Several features of these studies are particularly noteworthy, however. First, although the conclusions of different studies concerning the precise nature of the concentration–profitability relationship differ considerably, almost all the studies suggest a positive, though often weak, association between concentration and profitability. In view of the wide differences between the data base, sample size, industry definitions, other explanatory variables included, profitability concepts, and precise statistical methodology utilized in individual studies, this general consensus is itself rather remarkable. In part, this is due to another notable feature of most studies, the use of the concentration ratio as a measure of seller concentration. To some extent, the consensus may merely reflect failure of some studies to correct for the automatic positive correlation between the concentration ratio and profitability which is attributable to the relationship between either a firm's market share or its absolute size, and which exists independently of any influence of seller concentration on the anticipated reaction of rivals (E_s) and pricing behavior, as explained earlier in the section dealing with choice of concentration index. Despite this, the more careful studies which attempt to take into account the overlapping between concentration ratios and the market shares or absolute size of the group of leading firms to which they refer still generally show a weak independent positive relationship between concentration and profitability. However, the result of these studies also lends support to the view that statistical studies of the concentration–profitability relationship which omit market shares and absolute firm size as independent explanatory variables underlying firm and industry profitability will overstate the magnitude of the positive relationship between concentration and profitability. The evidence suggests that a firm's market share and profitability are strongly positively associated, independently of other influences, while absolute firm size also appears to exert a significant positive impact on profitability.

Price-elasticity of market demand has not generally been included as an explanatory variable in statistical studies of the concentration–profitability relationship, despite its analytical significance in influencing optimal $P - MC$ relationships. This will not influence the results of a statistical study provided that for all industries in the study the price-elasticity of industry demand is the same. The implicit assumption that this is always the case is questionable, however, and could affect the results of the study considerably. For example, if the elasticity of demand were lower in industries with higher concentration, a positive relationship between industry profits and concentration could be attributable to differences in elasticity rather than to concentration itself. The opposite relationship between elasticity and concentration would lead to understatement of the positive impact of concentration on profitability.

Another feature of most statistical studies is the use of linear regression and correlation analysis, which implicitly assumes that the concentration–profitability relationship is linear in the sense that the relationship is the same at all concentration levels. If it is not, as would be the case, for example, if there is some threshold degree of concentration before concentration influences behavior, the use of linear regression analysis will result in biased estimates of the true relationship, and the relationship obtained will also depend crucially on the choice of sample for reasons which will be explained in the next section. Although a few attempts have been made to investigate the possibility of a non-linear relationship between concentration and profitability, the evidence thus far is conflicting and inconclusive. This is not too surprising, since even if the relationship is non-linear, the threshold level of concentration necessary before behavior is affected will vary between industries, depending on other factors such as the degree of buyer turnover, and the instability of total industry demand.

Although it appears from the numerous statistical studies that absolute firm size, market share, and economies of scale have a much stronger influence on the profitability of firms and industries than seller concentration, measured by the concentration ratio, these results must be interpreted with care. Since the concentration ratio masks wide differences in the distribution of firm sizes within the leading group of firms to which it applies, differences which may lead to differences in the anticipated reaction of rival firms (E_s) and pricing behavior, it is not too surprising that no strong concentration–profitability relationship emerges from the statistical studies. Indeed, it could be reasonably argued that despite the vast volume of literature on the subject, the hypothesis that *some* aspect of seller concentration influences firms' behavior *has not really been tested yet*. All we know is that there appears to be a weak positive relationship between concentration ratios and industry profit rates; whether a stronger relationship between other dimensions of seller concentration and behavior exists remains an unanswered question. Moreover, as was emphasized earlier, in interpreting the generally weak positive correlation between concentration ratios and industry profit rates which most statistical studies reveal, the real question at issue is whether the observed relationship is different *from the one which would still exist even if seller concentration had no independent influence on firms' expectations regarding their rivals' reactions*. If not, the widespread agreement between different statistical studies may merely reflect the automatic positive correlation which exists between concentration ratios and group profits when E_s is independent of seller concentration.

The implications of a positive relationship between seller concentration, however measured, and industry profitability have been the subject of much recent debate. Professor Y. Brozen (5) has argued that such a relationship is *disequilibrium* phenomenon, and has presented statistical evidence to support his contention that the positive relationship will disappear with the passage of time due to competitive pressures which tend to eliminate profit-rate differences in different industries over time. There is some debate concerning the extent to which empirical data actually support this contention. Moreover, even if valid, it still remains true that disequilibrium behavior in different industries is important in influencing the path of prices, quantities and resource allocation in an economy through time, and that public policies designed to influence disequilibrium behavior by affecting concentration might still be appropriate methods of improving that path of resource allocation through time. It should be added, however, that in the light of the statistical studies previously discussed, policies designed to influence market shares directly might have more significant effects on industrial behavior.

Concentration, Advertising and Profitability

The long-standing interest of economists in the concentration–profitability relationship has in recent years been closely rivalled by their interest in the relationship between advertising, concentration and profitability. Much effort has been directed to testing the hypothesis that advertising will influence an industry's pricing behavior and profitability. Two distinct causal chains linking advertising and profitability have been hypothesized by different writers. In one, associated initially with Professor N. Kaldor (12), advertising is assumed to increase seller concentration due to the existence of economies or increasing returns to scale of advertising. In the other, advertising is assumed to lead to entry barriers, which influence the profitability of an industry independently of the degree of concentration existing among established firms in the industry. Both hypotheses lead to the expectation of a positive relationship between advertising and profitability, but only the first to a definite positive association between advertising and concentration. In both cases, the implicit chain of causation runs from advertising to profitability. The second hypothesis, linking advertising to entry barriers, will be dealt with in the next chapter; in this section we shall focus primarily upon the relationship between advertising and concentration. See Part III of Recommended Readings for prominent theoretical and empirical contributions to the debate over the concentration–advertising relationship.

The hypothesis that advertising and concentration will be positively related due to economies of scale in advertising has not gone unchallenged. A contrary viewpoint put forward by some economists is that advertising may be a means by which new entrants enter an industry, leading to a negative relationship between concentration and advertising. To resolve these conflicting hypotheses, the need for empirical investigation of the nature of the relationship existing in practice between these two variables is obvious. A number of statistical investigations of the concentration–advertising relationship has been undertaken in recent years, involving the correlation and regression of advertising intensity (the ratio of advertising expenditures to sales) and concentration ratios for a sample of industries. The most notable feature of these studies is their conflicting results; some studies suggest that a positive relationship exists between advertising and concentration, while others reveal no significant relationship. Different authors arrive at different conclusions even when the data used are the same. There are several reasons underlying the apparently conflicting conclusions. Perhaps most important, the implicit causal chain linking advertising and concentration in these studies is unnecessarily restrictive, for it omits consideration of the factors which determine advertising, and the possibility that concentration may play a part in determining the level of industry advertising. This is reflected by the omission in the statistical regressions of other relevant variables which might help to determine advertising.

Although a number of economists have stressed the possible role played by concentration in the determination of firms' advertising expenditures, there are again several conflicting hypotheses concerning the form of the relationship one would expect to find between the two variables. According to one line of reasoning, increasing concentration among a group of sellers will lead to increased recognition of interdependence between their activities, resulting in the elimination of 'neutralizing' competitive advertising and a reduction in the industry's advertising. The logic underlying this argument is analogous to that underlying the reduction of industry output which results from a change from competition to monopoly. A different conclusion is reached, however, by economists who argue that as concentration increases, sellers in an industry will substitute competition by means of advertising for price competition, so that concentration and industry advertising will be positively related. In order to gain perspective over these various hypotheses, and to assist in understanding the reasons for the apparently conflicting results of statistical studies undertaken to date, it is useful to relate the various hypotheses concerning the concentration–advertising relationship to the analytical framework dealing with advertising decisions which was developed in Chapter 4. It was demonstrated there that, for profit-maximizing firms, the following relationship must be established in order for a firm's advertising to be at an optimal level:

$$\frac{\text{Advertising Outlay}}{\text{Sales}} = \frac{P - \text{MC}}{P} \cdot E_a = \frac{P - \text{MC}}{P}(E_A + E_{\text{conj.}} \cdot E_{A_r})$$

The argument, that as concentration rises industry advertising will fall due to increased recognition by firms in the industry of the interdependence existing between their activities, can be interpreted in terms of the preceding expression. The implicit hypothesis is that as concentration rises, $E_{conj.}$, which measures the anticipated advertising reactions of a firm's rivals to changes in the level of the firm's own advertising, will change in value, leading to a reduction in the level of individual firms' advertising sales ratios. This will occur if $E_{conj.}$ is positive, indicating that rivals are expected to increase their advertising in response to an increase in the firm's own advertising, and increases in magnitude as concentration rises. Alternatively, it will also occur if $E_{conj.}$ changes from positive to negative as concentration rises, indicating that rivals are expected to increase their advertising at low levels of concentration, but are expected to respond by reducing their advertising at high concentration levels. The last case could occur if there is some threshold level of concentration above which sellers are aware of the industry-wide optimal advertising level, and react to a change in one seller's advertising by undertaking a compensating change in their advertising levels. The situation would then be analogous to that involving the output level of a group of firms acting in a manner necessary to maximize group profits. Presumably, some degree of collusion would be necessary for this to occur with advertising, as with output changes, because changes in distribution of a given total industry-wide advertising level between different firms would also probably change the allocation of buyers, and industry profits, between firms.

The argument that advertising competition will be substituted for price competition as seller concentration increases can also be interpreted in terms of the optimal advertising–sales condition, by substituting the firm's price-elasticity of demand (E_d) for $P - MC/P$ in the above expression, which results in the following relationship (which, as indicated in Chapter 4, is termed the 'Dorfman–Steiner condition'):

$$\frac{\text{Adv.}}{\text{Sales}} = \frac{E_a}{E_d} = \frac{(E_A + E_{conj.} \cdot E_{A_r})}{\dfrac{E_m}{S_f}\left(\dfrac{E_s \cdot S_r}{S_f}\right)}$$

The preceding relationship indicates that the lower the price-elasticity of demand for a firm's product (E_d), all other things remaining the same, the larger will be the firm's optimal advertising intensity (A/S). The possibility that seller concentration may influence E_s, which measures the anticipated output reactions of rival firms in response to a change in the level of the firm's product price, has already been extensively discussed in the preceding section. If E_s is negative and increases in magnitude as seller concentration increases, all other things remaining unchanged, this will imply a decrease in E_d and an increase in the firm's optimal advertising–sales ratio, as is envisaged by those economists who argue that advertising competition will be substituted for price competition as seller concentration increases. It must be emphasized that the preceding conclusion assumes that E_a remains unchanged as concentration varies. Moreover, testing this hypothesis is likely to be complicated by the fact that some dimensions of seller concentration, including concentration ratios, may be automatically correlated with optimal $(P - MC)/P$ and E_d levels even in the absence of any causal influence of concentration on pricing, for reasons already explained in the preceding section. As a result, a positive statistical relationship between concentration ratios and advertising could exist even if the preceding hypothesis is invalid, and part of the positive concentration–advertising relation found by some of the statistical studies may be due to differences in average firm size between industries in the sample, rather than to differences in concentration.

The implicit assumption that E_a remains unchanged as seller concentration changes is of course inconsistent with the argument outlined earlier supporting a negative association between advertising and concentration. Intuition suggests that E_d and E_a may both vary in practice with changes in the level of seller concentration. If E_a and E_d varied proportionately in the same direction with changes in concentration, for example, there would be no net effect on the firm's optimal advertising–sales ratio, and advertising. This is, however, only one of numerous possibilities, and even if the relationships between concentration and E_a, and between concentration and E_d were linear, the net outcome in terms of the observed relationship between concentration and advertising could be positive or negative depending on the signs and relative strengths of each of the relationships. Moreover, if either of the relationships were non-linear, so that the strength of the relationship between concentration and E_a, or E_d, varied over different ranges of concentration, the association between advertising and concentration could also be non-linear, and could be positive over some ranges of concentration and negative over others. Finally, it must not be forgotten that E_a and E_d themselves depend on other factors in addition to any influence seller concentration might have on the reactions of a firm's rivals. The advertising-elasticity of a firm's demand (E_a), for example, depends also on E_A, which measures the effect of a change in advertising on buyers independently of any reactions by other sellers. The argument that there are economies of scale in advertising, to be discussed in more detail below, is a hypothesis that the magnitude of E_A will increase as the absolute level of a firm's advertising increases. Changes in E_A may reinforce, or offset, any influence of concentration on $E_{conj.}$ and therefore need to be separated from the influence of concentration, if any, on E_a.

As the preceding discussion indicates, the relationship between advertising and concentration is the net outcome of a number of relationships. The various hypotheses concerning the expected form of this relationship outlined earlier focus on individual factors which underlie a firm's advertising behavior. In practice, the existence of a number of simultaneous relationships between concentration and the various factors influencing firms' advertising cannot be discounted a priori. As already explained, the form and strength of each of these relationships will determine the net outcome in terms of the relationship between advertising and concentration which is observed in practice. If one or more of the underlying relationships is non-linear, the advertising–concentration relationship will also very likely to be non-linear. In view of the numerous possible forms and permutations of the relevant underlying relationships, and the resulting advertising–concentration relationship, it is not really surprising that statistical investigations of the form of this relationship have so far produced contradictory results. Apart from a failure to include all the relevant relationships in the investigation, the majority of studies implicitly assume, by their use of linear regression techniques, that the relationship is linear. If it is not linear, as is very likely in view of the preceding discussion, the results of any particular study will be greatly influenced by the choice of sample, and the studies will produce biased estimates of the true relationship.

This may be explained with the aid of Figure 6–5. If the true relationship between concentration and advertising is shown by the solid line ABC, a sample of concentration–advertising observations obtained only from segment AB will suggest that the two variables are unrelated. On the other hand, a sample of observations obtained from the BC segment will indicate that a positive relationship exists between the two variables. Alternatively, a sample containing observations from both segments will yield an estimate of the true relationship such as the dotted line in Figure 6–5 if linear regression techniques are used; in this case the estimated relationship is positive, but biased. It is possible that differences in the composition of the samples which form the basis of different statistical investigations of the concentration–advertising relationship explain in part the

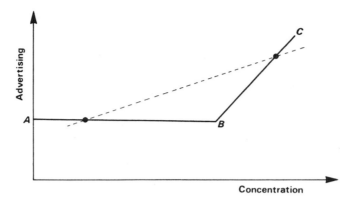

Figure 6–5. A non-linear advertising-concentration relationship,

apparently contradictory results which have been obtained in different studies. That is, studies in which observations with low concentration make up the bulk of the sample may accurately estimate a true zero relationship between advertising and concentration such as AB in Figure 6–5, while studies where observations with high concentration form a bulk of the sample may be accurately estimating a positive relationship over higher ranges of concentration, such as BC.

Apart from the concentration–profitability relationship itself, the hypothesis that there are economies of scale in advertising has also received considerable attention from economists. As argued initially by Professor Kaldor, if economies of scale exist in advertising, firms with larger absolute levels of advertising (even if their advertising–sales *ratios* are the same) will gain market share at the expense of smaller advertisers, eventually driving the latter out of business and increasing the degree of concentration. As explained earlier in this section, the economies-of-scale-in-advertising hypothesis can be interpreted to mean that E_A increases with the absolute level of a firm's advertising expenditures. All other things remaining the same, increases in E_A will lead to larger optimal advertising–sales (A/S) ratios for firms with larger absolute levels of advertising. Some economists have suggested that the existence of economies of scale in advertising can therefore be determined by reference to the A/S ratios of different sized firms existing in practice, and have concluded that since size of firms and A/S appear to be positively related, economies of scale exist in practice. The flaw in this line of reasoning is the omission of other factors which underlie the optimal A/S choice of a firm. Optimal A/S could increase with the size of firm for reasons other than economies of scale, such as reductions in a firm's price-elasticity of demand (E_d) as firm size increases. It was explained in the preceding section that statistical studies reveal a positive relationship between firm size and price–cost margins, suggesting that E_d declines with increases in firm size; for this reason the optimal A/S will tend to increase with increases in the size of the firm even if E_a were unchanged. In addition, the firm's advertising elasticity of demand (E_a) depends on the anticipated advertising reactions of rivals $(E_{\text{coni.}})$ which may vary with firm size independently of any relationship between the firm's size and E_A. For these reasons, evidence of rising A/S with firm size cannot be taken as conclusive evidence of the existence of economies of scale in advertising.

After carefully reviewing the empirical evidence accumulated to date concerning economies of scale in advertising, Professor J. Simon concluded in 1965 (25) that the evidence appears inconsistent with the existence of generalized economies of scale in advertising when considering a firm advertising an individual product. Conclusive evidence is difficult to obtain, for what is relevant in this connection is the total effect of a given advertising expenditure, over the entire time period that it is operative, and holding all other factors which influence buyer behavior unchanged. Sophisticated statistical analyses incorporating many relevant variables are clearly necessary in order to obtain estimates of advertising effects, and the majority of studies undertaken to date lack the necessary degree of sophistication. Another point worth emphasizing is that although there may be no economies of scale in advertising individual products, economies of scale may result from joint advertising of several products, joint use of a common brand name for several products, and from obtaining discounts on multi-product purchases of advertising media.

Even if there are no economies of scale in advertising, this merely eliminates one possible source of a relationship between advertising and concentration; the other relationships linking advertising and concentration discussed within this section remain to be investigated empirically in order to yield an understanding of the causal chains underlying any observed relationship between these two variables. Only if the form of the individual underlying relationships is known will it be possible to formulate appropriate public policy measures designed to change the form of the advertising–concentration relationship, should such changes be deemed desirable in the interests of securing improved industrial performance.

Concentration and Research and Development Activities*

In recent years there has been much theoretical discussion and empirical investigation of the factors underlying firms' expenditures on R&D activities (for articles dealing with this subject see Part IV of Recommended Readings). The relationship between seller concentration and an industry's R&D activities in particular continues to be the subject of intense theoretical debate. In a seminal article, Professor K. Arrow (1) examined the incentives for cost-reducing invention provided, respectively, by a monopoly and a competitive industry facing the same demand conditions. He concluded that the incentive to innovate, measured in terms of the increase in industry profit resulting from a cost-reducing invention, will be greater in a competitive industry than under monopoly. This is because although the profit attributable to the invention is the same at the same post-invention output level in each type of industry, the pre-invention profits of the monopoly must be subtracted from this post-invention profit to arrive at the net increase in profit resulting from the invention. In a later article, Professor H. Demsetz (6) criticized Arrow for assuming that the post-invention output level of the two industries is equal and showed that if the industries were producing the same output level prior to the invention, the increase in profit resulting from a cost-reducing invention is greater in the case of monopoly, the opposite conclusion to that reached by Arrow. In order for the pre-invention output levels of monopolistic and competitive industries to be the same, however, it is necessary to assume that the demand conditions confronting the two industries are different, and that demand is twice as great at any price under monopoly than under competition. As Professor Ng showed in a subsequent article (23), this assumption implies that the post-invention output level is twice as great under monopoly

* This section is based on Needham, D., Market structure and firms' R&D behavior, *Journal of Industrial Economics*, June 1975, and we are grateful to the publishers and editor of that journal for permission to reprint most of the article here.

than under competition, and this is the basic reason why Demsetz is able to show that the incentive to invent is greater under monopoly. Professor Ng demonstrates that when both the pre-invention *and* post-invention output levels in the two industries are equal, which occurs when demand conditions facing both industries are identical and cost-reductions are proportionate (though differing in absolute magnitude), Arrow's conclusion that the incentive to invent is smaller under monopoly remains valid.

In another article, Professor Hu (11) notes that in all the discussions previously cited, the incentive to invent is measured in terms of the *total* returns from invention accruing to an industry. He points out that although an industry receiving the higher total return from invention will benefit more from R&D efforts, this does not necessarily mean that it will devote more resources to R&D activities, because what determines the optimal amount of R&D effort is not the total return associated with this type of activity, but the *marginal* return. It is possible for an industry with a lower total return from invention to have a higher marginal return at any given level of R&D activity, resulting in a larger level of resources devoted to R&D efforts. Hu shows that in the Arrow model where the competitive and monopolistic industry each face the same demand curve, the competitive industry has greater marginal returns from an invention resulting in a relatively small cost reduction, while both industries have the same marginal returns from inventions resulting in relatively large cost reductions. However, in the Demsetz model, where the demand curve for the competitive industry coincides with the marginal revenue curve of the monopolist, the marginal returns are higher for all types of cost-reducing inventions under monopoly than under competition, due to the larger post-invention output level under monopoly in that model. Although the ranking of marginal and total returns to invention is therefore the same in the Demsetz model, Hu argues that the difference between the total returns from invention under monopoly and competition is less than the difference between the respective marginal returns, thereby tending to understate the difference between the monopolistic and competitive incentives to invent in that model.

Several unsatisfactory features of the preceding controversy require emphasis, for they serve to reduce considerably the practical relevance of the conclusions reached by the respective contributors. In comparing the incentive to innovate under monopoly and competition, whereas the monopolist itself can invent, in the case of the competitive industry it is assumed that an inventor sells his invention to the industry by setting a royalty rate per unit of output for the use of the invention. In other words, the competitive industry itself does not invent, and collectively pays a total amount to the inventor which is assumed to equal the maximum possible increase in industry profit resulting from the use of the invention. Since the inventor could be one of the firms in a competitive industry, the analysis also applies to the incentive to invent facing individual firms in the industry *provided that invention itself is monopolized*. This last proviso is crucial, however, for the following reasons: the amount of profit from an invention depends on the output level of the industry using the invention. By controlling the royalty rate charged for use of the invention, which is part of the cost of producing output with the invention, a single owner of an invention in effect controls the output level of a competitive industry. Thus, an individual firm in such an industry which invents and has complete control over the invention also in effect controls the output reactions of its rivals and can select the royalty rate which results in the industry output level which maximizes the profit from the invention. In contrast, if control over an invention is not monopolized, maximizing the return from an invention requires collusion between individual firms using the invention in determining the industry's output level. If successful, this will result in exactly the same situation as occurs with a single owner of the invention. This is, however, only one limiting possibility. 'Competitive' output level decisions by individual firms which result in larger total industry output levels will reduce the total profits from the invention below the maximum level, and in the limiting case of 'purely competitive' output decisions by individual firms the total return to the invention will be zero since industry output will be at a level where price equals production cost, leaving no return to the invention itself.

Moreover, even if control over a *single* invention can be monopolized, by means of patent protection or some such device, *invention in general* cannot be monopolized. For this reason, the profit from any particular invention, and therefore the incentive to invent, will depend not only on the output levels of individual firms in an industry, but also on their R&D behavior. The return which a firm anticipates from its own R&D activities will depend, in part, not only on the degree to which it can expect to control the use of the resulting inventions, but also on the anticipated R&D reactions of rival firms. The greater the response of rivals in initiating or expanding their own R&D activities, the greater in general will be the likelihood of competing inventions appearing, reducing the return to the first firm's inventive efforts.

In addition to ignoring the possibility of competitive output reactions and R&D reactions by individual firms in the competitive industry, both of which affect the return to an invention, the participants in the controversy over the incentive to innovate under monopoly and competition outlined earlier also make arbitrary assumptions concerning demand conditions in the industries being compared. Arrow and Ng assume that demand conditions facing the monopolist and competitive industries are identical, while Demsetz assumes that demand at any price is twice as large under monopoly than under competition. All participants in the debate fail to take into account the *interdependence* which exists between output levels and other decision variables under either type of market organization. The assumption that demand conditions facing a monopolistic and a competitive industry are identical implies that the level of all other decision variables which influence industry demand, such as advertising, for example, are identical under either type of market organization. It is somewhat inconsistent to assume that price and output levels are the only decision variables which differ when comparing monopoly and competitive industries. On the other hand, Demsetz's assumption that industry demand is greater under monopoly than under competition is also inconsistent with generally accepted notions concerning the relative levels of decision variables under monopoly and competition. Greater demand under monopoly implies larger levels of other non-price decision variables than under competition, but 'competitive' levels of non-price variables are generally assumed to be larger than is necessary to maximize industry profits, not smaller as Demsetz's argument implicitly assumes. The nature of the interdependence between a firm's R&D decisions and levels of its other decision variables will be examined further below.

The debate over which form of market organization is most conducive to invention and innovation is not confined to consideration of monopoly and competition. Some economists argue that the incentive to invent will be greatest under oligopoly, rather than under monopoly or competition. In support of this contention, larger profits to finance R&D investment under oligopoly than under competition, and a greater competitive spur to use those funds for R&D under oligopoly than under monopoly are cited with varying degrees of emphasis. The main point in reply to this line of argument is that 'oligopoly' is merely a general class of behavior encompassing all types of behavior which explicitly takes account of rivals' reactions. The term itself says nothing, however, about *what kinds of reactions* firms anticipate from their rivals, and firms' behavior will differ depending on the exact nature of these anticipated reactions. Indeed, as was explained in Chapter 3, there will be no difference between the behavior of a group of oligopolists and a monopolist, or between an oligopolist and purely competitive industry, if firms' anticipations regarding their rivals' reactions exhibit certain characteristics. Monopoly behavior is compatible with any number of firms in an industry, provided that each firm in the group assumes that its rivals will imitate its price and output policies. In these circumstances each firm will expect its own actions to be magnified by n, the number of firms in the group, and this will lead each firm to behave in a manner which maximizes the group's profit–monopoly behavior. In contrast, if each firm in the group expects 'accommodating' reactions by its rivals, in the sense that other firms in the industry are expected to vary their output level in an opposite direction by an equivalent amount in response to a change in the firm's own output level, it was explained in Chapter 3 that this results in group behavior which corresponds to that of a purely competitive industry.

Although there are innumerable other possible types of anticipated reaction, resulting in behavior which differs from the two limiting cases of monopoly and pure competition, the two preceding examples illustrate an important point. From them emerges the somewhat paradoxical conclusion that 'imitation', which many people would intuitively regard as a relatively competitive reaction, leads to monopoly behavior by a group of firms, while 'accommodating' behavior in the sense described above, which many people would view as a less competitive reaction, leads to group behavior which corresponds to that of a 'purely competitive' industry. The paradox is repeated when other types of reactions are considered. Thus, for example, if firms expect their rivals to less than fully imitate their actions, in the sense of changing output in the same direction but by a smaller amount, this will lead to group behavior involving larger levels of industry output than if the industry were monopolized – behavior which is closer to 'competitive' as that term is used in economics. On the other hand, if firms expect rivals to more than imitate their actions, in the sense of changing output in the same direction but by a larger amount than the firm, this will lead to group behavior involving smaller levels of industry output than if the industry were monopolized, and behavior which is further removed from 'purely competitive' industry output levels. These examples emphasize that the term 'pure competition' in economics has a very special meaning and refers to one limiting case of the many possible forms of group behavior. The type of anticipated reactions which result in this type of group behavior, such as totally ignoring rival firms and assuming that demand for a firm's product is infinite at the ruling price, or expecting rivals to act in an 'accommodating' manner as described above, are not what most people would regard as 'competitive' at all.

Many of the contradictory theoretical conclusions, and most of the resulting confusion connected with the issue of firms' inventive activities under alternative market structures, are attributable to lack of a comprehensive analytical framework which includes the interdependence between optimal levels of a firm's different decision variables. This in turn contributes toward failure to recognize that 'expectations regarding rivals' reactions', which are relevant in determining the extent of a firm's inventive efforts is a multidimensional concept which includes anticipated reactions regarding a number of different decision variables. In order to gain perspective over some of the issues, and in order to interpret empirical evidence relating to the influence of various factors on firms' R&D activities, it is useful to consider the determinants of optimal levels of a firm's R&D investment in terms of the same analytical framework already utilized in Chapter 4 in connection with advertising decisions. In order for the level of a firm's R&D investment to be at a profit-maximizing level, the effect of a change in the level of R&D investment on the firm's total revenue and total cost must be equal. As in the case of expenditure on advertising, this condition may be written in any of the following forms:

$$\frac{\text{R\&D Outlay}}{\text{Sales}} = \frac{P - MC}{P} \cdot E_{rd} = \frac{E_{rd}}{E_d} = \frac{E_R + E_{\text{conj.}} E_{Rr}}{\dfrac{E_m}{S_f} + \dfrac{E_s S_r}{S_f}}$$

where, as before, E_d = price-elasticity of demand for the firm's product

E_m = market price-elasticity of demand

S_f = the firm's share of industry output

S_r = rivals' share of industry output $(1 - S_f)$

E_s = expected reaction of rivals' output level

and where

E_{rd} = $\dfrac{\text{proportionate change in quantity of the firm's product demanded}*}{\text{proportionate change in the firm's R\&D outlays}}$

E_R = $\dfrac{\text{proportionate change in demand for the firm's product}}{\text{proportionate change in the firm's R\&D}}$

when rivals' R&D levels remain unchanged

$E_{\text{conj.}}$ = $\dfrac{\text{proportionate change in rivals' R\&D investment}}{\text{proportionate change in the firm's own R\&D}}$

E_{Rr} = $\dfrac{\text{proportionate change in demand for the firm's product}}{\text{proportionate change in rivals' R\&D investment}}$

The above condition indicates that the optimal ratio of a firm's R&D investment to sales, or R&D intensity as the ratio will henceforth be termed, will be larger the smaller the price-elasticity of demand for the firm's product (E_d), given the research elasticity of demand for the firm's product (E_{rd}). The price-elasticity of demand for the firm's product depends on the price-elasticity of market demand (E_m), the firm's share of industry output (S_f), and the firm's expectations regarding its rivals' output-level reactions (E_s). Whatever the form of industry organization, E_d will be larger, and the optimal R&D intensity will therefore be smaller, the larger is E_m. This conclusion conflicts with that reached by M. Kamien and N. L. Schwartz, who concluded (13) that the incentive to invent in an industry *increases* with the elasticity of market demand regardless of market structure. As in the Arrow–Demsetz controversy they define the incentive to invent as the maximum increase in industry profit resulting from a cost-reducing invention, and it is easy to show that this maximum increase in industry profit will indeed be larger the more price-elastic is industry demand. However, as was previously indicated, their analysis in effect assumes that the competitive industry acts as a monopolist in setting its total output level to maximize industry profit from the invention. In contrast, since our analysis does not assume collusion in output determination between firms under competitive market structure, the influence of E_m is different.

The influence of alternative forms of market organization on the optimal R&D intensity of individual firms, and level of industry R&D activities, can also be explained in terms of the above optimal condition. Given E_m, E_d reaches its minimum value under monopoly since $S_f = 1$, while under pure competition, since E_d is assumed to equal infinity in

---

* In the present formulation, R&D investment is viewed as a demand-increasing strategy rather than a cost-reducing strategy. However, since any cost reduction can be transformed into an equivalent 'demand increase' by adding the unit cost reduction at each rate of output to the firm's demand curve, the formulation is also compatible with cost-reducing results of R&D investment.

magnitude, individual firms in the industry will not undertake R&D investment at all. This conclusion can also be reconciled with the Arrow–Demsetz controversy since the 'competitive' industry which they compare with monopoly acts as a monopolist in setting its output level to maximize the return from an invention, as already explained. They are therefore comparing the incentive to invent facing the competitive industry as a whole, rather than that facing individual firms. In terms of the above optimal condition, this is equivalent to assuming that the denominator of the optimal condition is the same in both cases (given E_m).

Under both monopoly and purely competitive forms of market organization, rivals' reactions are ignored by individual firms, so that $E_s = 0$ in both cases. It must be emphasized again, however, that the monopolistic and purely competitive forms of industry output behavior are *also* compatible with particular types of anticipated output-level reaction by a firm's rivals. The expectation of price and output imitation by each of a firm's rivals, which as explained earlier results in monopolistic group behavior with respect to industry output level, is a situation where the denominator of the above optimal condition varies proportionately with the number of firms in an industry, while leaving the output level of the group of firms as a whole unchanged at the monopoly level. The expectation of 'accommodating' output reactions by a firm's rivals, which as explained earlier results in a purely competitive industry output level irrespective of the number of firms in the group, is also a situation where the denominator of the above optimal condition varies proportionately with the number of firms in the industry. The difference between the output level of individual firms, and the industry, in these two cases is accounted for by different expectations regarding rivals' output reactions, and therefore values of E_s in the above expression.

So far we have considered only the influence of price-elasticity of demand on the optimal R&D intensity of a firm or group of firms; the R&D elasticity of demand for the firm's product, E_{rd}, must also be considered. This depends on E_R, the effect of a change in the firm's R&D investment on demand for its product in the absence of R&D reactions by rivals, on the nature of the firm's expectations about its rivals' R&D behavior ($E_{conj.}$), and on the anticipated effect of that behavior on the return to its own R&D efforts (E_{Rr}). The magnitude of E_R will depend on a number of factors, including the extent of 'technological opportunity' in the industry, which refers to the extent to which a firm's R&D efforts are likely to result in commercially exploitable inventions. This will be related to the extent to which the broad advance of science and technology provides a supply of new technical possibilities which are exploitable in the industry in question. Another factor influencing E_R will be the extent to which a firm has control over any inventions resulting from its R&D efforts, by means of patent protection or secrecy over processes or ingredients utilized. Although E_R will tend to be higher the greater the control which the firm has over its inventions, it should be noted that this does not necessarily imply that E_{rd} will also be higher, for the existence of patent protection may lead rival firms to increase their own R&D efforts rather than pay royalties to the firm for its invention, and the net effect of these responses may be to lower the anticipated marginal return to the first firm's R&D investment.

Next we turn to the influence of a firm's expectations regarding its rivals' R&D reactions, and the relationship between alternative forms of market organization and firms' and industry's R&D behavior. Under monopoly, $E_{conj.}$ is zero and $E_{rd} = E_R$. A level of industry R&D equal to the monopoly level will also result if each of a group of firms expects imitative R&D behavior by its rivals. If, instead, firms expect their rivals to do less than fully imitate their R&D policies, their individual R&D levels will be larger than if imitative behavior is expected, and industry R&D will exceed the monopoly level. In the limiting case where firms expect 'accommodating' R&D reactions from their rivals, in the sense of equal and opposite changes in rivals' R&D levels, there will exist a situation analogous to the purely competitive output level of a group of firms, and industry R&D will be carried to a level where the group's profits from R&D investment are zero. It was pointed out earlier that in a purely competitive industry there will be no R&D investment by individual firms because E_d equals infinity. A direct comparison between the magnitude of E_{rd} under monopoly and pure competition is not possible, therefore. However, it is important to recognize that expectations regarding rivals' output reactions (which influence E_d) and expectations regarding rivals' R&D reactions (which influence E_{rd}) are *both* relevant in determining a firm's optimal R&D intensity. Even if the output reactions which firms in two industries anticipate from their rivals are the same, the R&D behavior of firms in the two industries will differ if anticipated R&D reactions are different in the two industries. Thus, for example, even in the Arrow–Demsetz model, where firms in a competitive industry are assumed to act like a monopolist in setting the industry output level, the R&D level of such an industry will not be the same as that of a monopoly industry unless individual firms in the competitive industry anticipate imitative R&D behavior by their rivals.

'Monopoly' and 'pure competition' are two limiting forms of industry behavior which result from certain types of rivals' reactions anticipated by individual firms in the industry. These forms of industry behavior are not, in theory, associated directly with any particular number or size distribution of firms in an industry. Rather, in considering the influence of seller concentration on industrial R&D behavior, the fundamental question at issue is whether a firm's expectations regarding its rivals' reactions are related to the number and/or size distribution of rival firms. Again, it is extremely important to recognize that more than one dimension of rivals' reactions is relevant in determining a firm's R&D behavior. The relationship between seller concentration and a firm's expectations regarding its rivals' output reactions *and* their R&D reactions must be considered. For example, even if E_d facing individual firms in an industry falls with increases in seller concentration, if E_{rd} also falls proportionately the firm's optimal R&D intensity will remain unchanged on balance. It must be emphasized, however, that it is equally possible that the number and size distribution of firms in an industry may affect expectations regarding the different dimensions of rivals' reactions in different ways. For example, there is no reason why a degree of seller concentration which results in the expectation of imitative price and output behavior by a firm's rivals should also simultaneously result in the expectation of imitative R&D behavior. On the contrary, as the discussion of the concentration–advertising relationship in the preceding section indicated, it is possible to envisage numerous different plausible a priori relationships between seller concentration and a particular dimension of a firm's behavior. To repeat but two of the possibilities mentioned in that discussion, rising seller concentration could lead either to R&D competition replacing price competition, or to increased recognition of interdependence and the elimination of competitive R&D behavior. Moreover, some of these forces may operate simultaneously, with varying strength, over different ranges of seller concentration, so that the relationship between industry and R&D behavior and seller concentration observed in practice is the net result of several simultaneous interacting relationships between concentration and R&D behavior.

It is appropriate, before reviewing the results of empirical studies of firms' R&D behavior, to consider briefly the influence of firm size on optimal R&D intensity. Absolute firm size may influence optimal R&D intensity via two different routes. First, as the optimal R&D condition indicates, the larger a firm's share of industry output (S_f), all other things remaining the same, the lower is E_d and the larger will be the firm's optimal

R&D–sales ratio. Secondly, if there are increasing or decreasing returns to scale of R&D investment, the absolute level of a firm's R&D investment will affect the magnitude of E_R and therefore the optimal R&D intensity. The explanation is analogous to the case of returns to scale of advertising, and will not therefore be repeated here. These remarks are sufficient to indicate that no clear relationship between absolute firm size and R&D behavior is predicted by theoretical considerations. Also, it must be added that if there are increasing or decreasing returns to scale of R&D investment, it is important to recognize that the relationship between firm size and R&D input will automatically differ from the relationship between firm size and R&D output. These two dimensions of a firm's R&D activities must therefore be kept distinct in thinking about the relationship between firms' R&D behavior and its determinants, and in interpreting the results of various statistical studies of R&D relationships. In addition, as already discussed in the section of Chapter 4 dealing with measurement of product differentiation, the output of R&D activities itself is a multidimensional concept, so that R&D output behavior will generally depend on which facet of inventive output is chosen for investigation.

Since a priori theorizing concerning the nature of the relationship existing between a firm's R&D activities and various factors such as firm size or seller concentration is inconclusive, for reasons already noted in the preceding paragraphs, empirical investigation of these relationships is clearly warranted. A number of statistical studies of the relationship between firm size and inventive input or output have been undertaken in recent years. They indicate that most industrial R&D is performed by larger firms, measured in terms of absolute size, a fact which is partly explained by the indivisibilities of expensive R&D inputs already discussed in Chapter 4 in the section entitled Research and Development Activities. However, when attention is focused only on firms which do some research, the empirical evidence suggests that beyond a certain size level, which varies from industry to industry, the ratio of R&D inputs or outputs to some index of firm size does not generally increase as firm size increases, and sometimes even declines. In a 1965 study, for example, F. M. Scherer (26) concluded that inventive output, measured by patents issued, increases less than proportionately with firm sales. Similarly, in a 1967 study of the relationship between firm size and R&D input, W. S. Comanor (4) concluded that while there are few instances where the larger firms in an industry account for a larger proportion of industry R&D input than their share of industry size, in many cases the R&D–sales ratios of smaller firms in an industry are larger than those of larger firms. As a final example, a 1971 study using Swedish data by B. Johannisson and C. Lindstrom (12) indicated that inventive output in a firm, measured by the number of patent applications, varies almost proportionately with firm size, measured in terms of the number of employees, when their data are viewed as a whole. When firms are grouped into industries there are some exceptions to this general tendency, however; for example, the number of patent applications rises more than proportionately with increasing firm size in the chemical sector, and less than proportionately in the engineering, metal manufactures, and rubber industries.

Large absolute firm size is not, of course, the same thing as large relative size, or market share. However, given the size of an industry or market, larger absolute size implies larger market share for a firm, and the findings of Comanor and Johannisson and of Lindstrom both indicate that a firm's R&D intensity does not increase with increasing market share. As the authors of the last-mentioned article themselves acknowledge, it is possible that the market definitions used in the study, since they are confined to sales in Sweden only, are too narrow and are not the markets which are significant from a behavioral point of view in the minds of decision-makers in the firms analyzed. Despite this possibility, it is appropriate to reconcile evidence of absence of a relationship between a firm's market share and its R&D intensity with the optimal R&D intensity condition depicted earlier in this section. This condition indicates that as market share increases E_d falls and, all other things remaining the same, optimal R&D intensity increases. Two different types of explanation may account for the observed failure of a firm's R&D intensity to increase with the firm's market share. One is that all other things influencing the firm's R&D intensity may not remain unchanged as the firm's market share increases. For example, falling E_d may be accompanied by falling E_{rd} as a firm's market share rises. The fall in E_{rd} may be due to a fall in E_R, resulting, for example, from the existence of decreasing returns to scale of R&D investment, and/or expectations of more aggressive R&D reactions by the firm's rivals, as the firm's market share increases. An alternative explanation is that firms may lack the information which is necessary to ensure that the optimal R&D intensity condition is satisfied, and may instead adopt simple rules-of-thumb which make the firm's R&D investment depend on the absolute level of sales or some other index of absolute firm size.

Turning next to the relationship between R&D activities and seller concentration, the empirical evidence available to date is still rather inconclusive. Although industrial research is largely centered in industries which have moderate to high levels of concentration, these industries are also the industries in which technological opportunity is greater, and the fact that the advance of science opens up more exploitable inventions could conceivably account for higher levels of R&D in these industries, rather than higher concentration. The important question, therefore, is whether in industries with similar technological opportunity, R&D activities are related to the degree of seller concentration. In the 1965 study referred to earlier in connection with R&D and firm size, F. M. Scherer found that the relationship between the number of patents of the four largest firms in an industry and the four-firm concentration ratio was positive but statistically insignificant. In a subsequent study in 1967 (27), however, Scherer found that when interindustry differences in technological opportunity are taken into account, there appears to be a modest but statistically significant positive relationship between industry R&D input, measured by the employment of scientific and technical personnel, and the four-firm concentration ratio at low levels of concentration. This tendency appears to be absent at high levels of concentration; Scherer found that when the four-firm concentration ratio exceeds 50 or 55 per cent additional concentration is not associated with increases, and may even be associated with decreases, in industry R&D input.

In interpreting Scherer's findings, it is necessary to remind ourselves of an important point made in the second section of this chapter: any measure of seller concentration, since it involves the use of firms' market shares in its calculation, will be automatically correlated with the market shares of firms in the industry, and market shares themselves affect firms' behavior independently of any influence of seller concentration on firms' expectations regarding rivals' behavior, which in turn also affect firms' behavior. In other words, it is necessary to eliminate the influence of firm size and implied market share on R&D behavior in order to investigate whether any relationship between R&D behavior and seller concentration remains, which might signify an independent role for concentration in influencing behavior. In his 1967 study, W. S. Comanor (4) attempted to correct for the influence of differences in average firm size between industries before investigating the remaining relationship between seller concentration and industry R&D behavior. Using an eight-firm concentration ratio, he concluded that there is some evidence that, for given levels of firm size, higher concentration is associated with greater research in those industries where the prospects for achieving product differentiation are limited, and where as a result research is *not* a major element of industry behavior. In contrast, where prospects for product differentiation are high and where, as a result, competition in research is likely to be important, there is no evidence that increased concentration is associated with increased research in firms of a given size. Interpreting these findings in terms of our optimal R&D intensity condition, Comanor appears to be saying that where E_R is small and rising seller concentration is not associated with expectations of more aggressive R&D behavior on the part of a firm's rivals, higher seller concentration may raise optimal R&D–sales ratios by lowering E_d while leaving E_{rd} unchanged at any given size of firm. In contrast, where E_R is large higher seller concentration may lead to expectations of more aggressive R&D reactions by a firm's rivals, resulting in lower E_{rd} as well as lower E_d, and leaving optimal R&D intensity unchanged at any given size of firm.

Although these and a number of other statistical studies dealing with firms' R&D behavior are useful and illuminating, much work remains to be done to develop an adequate and generally accepted theoretical framework underlying R&D decisions, and to refine empirical studies which attempt to test hypotheses based on such a framework. Many of the more important areas requiring further investigation and refinement in this connection have already been noted and discussed in earlier sections of this chapter, and will be mentioned only briefly again here. Thus, for example, theoretical treatment of R&D decisions to date generally fails to consider adequately the interdependence between R&D and other aspects of a firm's behavior, or to recognize the multidimensional nature of a firm's expectations regarding its rivals' reactions which are relevant in determining R&D behavior. Partly as a result of this, many empirical studies of R&D behavior omit possibly significant explanatory variables in their statistical regressions, and fail to consider the possibility that seller concentration may influence R&D decisions via a number of different channels. Similarly, the possibility that the empirically observed concentration–R&D relationship is the net outcome of interactions between a number of simultaneous concentration–R&D relationships operating causally in both directions has not been sufficiently explored. Another weakness of statistical R&D studies to date is the excessive use of concentration ratios as the relevant concentration concept; it is necessary to investigate whether other dimensions of seller concentration are significant in influencing behavior even if concentration ratios are not. Also, most statistical studies do not properly take account of the problem of overlapping between firm size, market share, and concentration concepts. Finally, most statistical studies employ linear regression techniques; the possibility that some of the relevant relationships are non-linear also needs further investigation.

Determinants of Concentration

In the preceding three sections, attention has been focused upon the role of concentration as a possible determinant of firms' behavior. Concentration must be regarded not only as one of the factors which possibly influence *current* behavior of firms, but also as one of the results of *previous* behavior, since the present degree of concentration is a *state* reached in a *process* of competition. For this reason, even though concentration and various aspects of firms' behavior are observed to be closely related, correct interpretation of these relationships may be difficult. Possible cause and effect may be very difficult to disentangle because, as already indicated earlier in this chapter, the number and size distribution of firms in an industry may be closely related to the extent of economies of scale in relation to the size of the market. As an example of the causality problem, high advertising or R&D expenditures may, by raising entry barriers, be a cause rather than a result of high concentration. The degree of concentration existing in a particular industry at any point in time will be influenced by a number of factors. Firms' objectives, other structural features, and assumptions about rival firms' behavior, whether established firms or potential entrants, will all be relevant in determining the degree of concentration. This section outlines the major forces which play a part in this process, and the empirical evidence relating to their relative strength in determining concentration in practice.

Given a drive on the part of firms in an industry to exploit economies of scale and produce output levels which minimize the average cost of producing and distributing the industry's product, an upper limit to the number of firms in the industry will be determined by the size of the market in relation to the scale of output at which economies of scale become exhausted. Similarly, if there are diseconomies of scale beyond a certain scale of output, this will place a lower limit upon the number of firms supplying a given total market demand, provided always that the firms attempt to minimize unit costs. The upper and lower limits to the number of firms in the industry will only coincide if the long-run average cost curve of the industry in question were U shaped so that there were only one scale of output which minimized unit cost. In these circumstances the number of firms in an industry, and hence the degree of seller concentration in the industry, would be determined by scale economies and the size of the market. In practice, in many industries, there is a wide range of scales of output which minimize the unit cost of the industry's product, so that a number of different degrees of seller concentration are quite consistent with attempts to minimize unit costs in individual firms. Moreover, there is no reason why firms should necessarily attempt to produce a scale of output which minimizes unit cost; if a firm's objective is profit maximization, then, since profits are influenced by things in addition to unit cost, such as the price at which the firm can sell its output, for example, this objective may be achieved at scales of output which do not minimize unit cost. One reason, for example, why firms may not seek to expand output to levels which minimize average cost is that the anticipated reaction of other firms established in the industry is relevant to the price at which the firm expects to be able to sell its output. Firms producing scales of output lower than the scale which minimizes unit cost of the industry's product may feel no inclination to expand the level of their output by, say, cutting price, for fear of retaliation resulting in lower price and lower profits at a larger scale of output. Some industries tend to be less concentrated than scale economies alone would suggest (see the evidence presented by Weiss (31), for example). On the other hand, firms may produce scales of output larger than those which minimize unit cost. The ability of firms in an industry to produce scales of output which do not minimize unit cost, and to sell at prices which cover these costs, depends to a large extent upon the existence of entry barriers into the industry concerned. If entry is easy, firms may be compelled to operate within the range of scales of output which minimize unit costs; this compulsion will be reduced as the height of entry barriers increases. Of course, even with high entry barriers, the behavior of established firms may compel operations at scales of output which minimize unit costs. Thus, if the established firms compete on a price basis, or on the basis of product differentiation activities which raise costs, firms producing scales of output which result in higher than minimum unit costs will be driven from the industry. The drive for profits may, however, lead to merger or collusion between independent firms in an industry rather than competition. The anticipated profits of a firm depend upon the firm's anticipations regarding its rivals' reactions. These can be eliminated by reducing the number of rivals, either by merger or collusion between independent firms. Opposing the concentration-increasing forces which result from entry barriers and a desire to eliminate competition within an industry, legal factors may in some countries operate to limit concentration. The antitrust laws of the United States are a prominent example in this connection. Similarly, market growth will influence concentration, because more rapid market growth normally implies lower barriers to entry and concentration in an industry will fall unless the established firms expand at the same rate as the market.

The empirical evidence gathered to date on the relative strength in practice of the preceding forces influencing concentration suggests that economies of scale relative to market size explain most of the variation in concentration between industries. If the growth rate of the market is used as a proxy for the ease of entry into an industry, a weak negative relationship between this proxy and concentration appears to exist. However, for reasons to be explained in more detail in Chapter 7, satisfactory tests of the relationship between concentration and entry barriers are not possible in the current state of knowledge, due to the fact that many of the variables underlying concentration and entry barriers are identical.

Debate about whether existing degrees of seller concentration reflect monopolistic or competitive forces continues at a lively pace among economists. A drive for efficiency which, in the presence of economies of scale, leads to higher concentration can also lead to more monopolistic pricing behavior, in the sense of prices being higher in relation to costs than under competition. If this is the case, the relevant question from the point of view of the aggregate satisfaction of the community is the magnitude of the efficiency gains in production relative to the magnitude of the monopolistic resource-allocation distortions. This issue is dealt with in the section of Chapter 10 entitled Measurement of the Welfare Loss Attributable to Monopoly. In the present context, it is sufficient to note that the existence of a positive relationship between seller concentration and industry profit rates is compatible with either, or both, of the preceding tendencies; that is, it may reflect higher concentration leading to greater efficiency and lower costs, and/or to higher prices in relation to costs. As was indicated earlier in the section on the concentration–profitability relationship, absolute firm size of the leading group of firms in an industry will automatically be correlated with industry concentration ratios, and absolute firm size itself will influence the profitability of firms, by influencing a firm's price-elasticity of demand and, where economies of scale are present, the firm's efficiency. For these reasons, profit rates will tend to be higher in industries with higher concentration ratios even if concentration itself does not affect pricing behavior by influencing firms' expectations about their rivals' behavior. To eliminate the influence of differences in firm sizes between industries, and to focus on any remaining relationship between concentration and industry profit rates, a number of economists have pointed out that it is appropriate to focus attention on the observed relationship between profit rates of firms *in particular size classes* in industries with different degrees of concentration. In a recent article, for example, Professor H. Demsetz (7) has argued that if higher concentration leads to more collusion and monopolistic pricing, there should be a positive correlation between rates of return earned by firms in any particular size class and concentration, because firms in an industry with higher concentration should experience higher rates of return, compared to firms of similar size in less concentrated industries. Demsetz argues that empirical data on profit rates of firms in different size classes in different industries do not seem to support the notion that concentration and collusion are closely related. His interpretation of the data is questionable, however. The data he presents indicate that the rate of return earned by firms in any asset size class does not increase uniformly with concentration, and frequently falls with increases in concentration within the 10 to 50 per cent range of concentration. However, in industries with concentration ratios of 50 to 60 per cent, the rate of return to firms in every size class is higher than in industries with concentration ratios of 40 to 50 per cent, and the rate of return to firms in every size class except the smallest is even higher in industries with concentration ratios exceeding 60 per cent. This evidence is quite consistent with the hypothesis that higher concentration leads to higher profit rates once a certain 'threshold' level of concentration is reached.

Demsetz also argues that if higher concentration is the result of competitive striving for efficiency by firms in the industry, the difference between the rates of return to large and small firms in an industry should be greater, the more concentrated the industry. He shows that the difference between rates of return to larger and smaller firms in any two size classes generally increases with the degree of industry concentration, and claims that this evidence supports his view that higher concentration reflects competitive superiority rather than monopolistic behavior. Several comments are appropriate in reply to this argument. First, larger profit-rate differences between large and small firms in an industry as concentration increases are also quite compatible with a positive relationship between concentration and price–cost margins attributable to the influence of concentration on the level of industry price. Whatever the level of price in an industry, the difference between profit rates of large and small firms depends on the form of the industry's cost function. For example, given the minimum efficient scale of output in the industry, the more steeply the average cost curve declines with increases in output up to this output scale, the greater will be the difference between the average cost, and therefore the profit rate, of large and small firms in the industry. If industries with higher concentration also have more steeply sloping average-cost curves, this will account for larger differences in the profit rates of large and small firms in any two size categories, irrespective of the level of industry price. If increased concentration affects the level of industry price in relation to costs, this will merely affect the level of profit rates of firms in all size classes, not the difference in profit rates between size classes. The existence of a positive relationship between profit-rate differences between size classes of firms in an industry and concentration cannot therefore be taken as supporting the competitive role of concentration. Moreover, as was previously indicated, profit rates in any size class do seem to rise with increases in concentration at high concentration levels, which is consistent with a positive relationship between concentration and price–cost margins attributable to more monopolistic pricing. However, it would be premature to conclude that the higher profit rates of firms in any particular size class as concentration rises above 40 per cent reflect more monopolistic pricing. The reason is that the profit rate of firms in any particular absolute size class depends on other factors in addition to economies of scale and any influence which concentration might have on firms' anticipations of their rivals' reactions. The absolute size of the market will determine the share of the market, S_f, which a particular absolute size of firm implies and, as already explained in Chapter 4, a firm's profit rate will be positively related to the firm's share of the market, all other things remaining the same. What is required, therefore, instead of expressing firm size classes in absolute terms, is to express them in relation to industry size, in order to eliminate any influence of differences in market shares implied by different absolute firm sizes on the observed concentration–profitability relationship in each size class. If a positive relationship between concentration and profit rates in any size class remains after eliminating the influence of market share differences and differences in the magnitude of scale economies in different industries, it would be reasonable to infer that concentration exerts an independent influence on firms' expectations and pricing behavior. In the current state of knowledge, however, whether the positive relationship between concentration and profit rates which appears to exist in any particular size of class of firms at high concentration levels reflects differences in market shares or the shape of the cost function in different industries, rather than the influence of concentration on firms' expectations regarding rivals' reactions and consequent pricing behavior, remains an unanswered question.

RECOMMENDED READINGS

I: Measurement of Concentration

1. Adelman, M. A., The measurement of industrial concentration, *Review of Economics and Statistics*, November 1951. Reprinted in Heflebower, R. B. and Stocking, G. W. (Eds.) *Readings in Industrial Organization and Public Policy* (Homewood, Ill.: Richard D. Irwin, Inc., 1958). Published under the sponsorship of the American Economic Association. Also in Levin, H. J. (Ed.) *Business Organization and Public Policy* (New York: Holt, Rinehart and Winston, Inc., 1963).
2. Bailey, D. and Boyle, S. E., The optimal measure of concentration, *Journal of the American Statistical Association*, December 1971.
3. Boyle, S. E., The average concentration ratio: an inappropriate measure of industry structure, *Journal of Political Economy*, Part 1, March–April 1973.
4. Boyle, S. E. and Sorensen, R. L., Concentration and mobility: alternative measures of industry structure, *Journal of Industrial Economics*, April 1971.
5. Gort, M. and Singamsetti, R., Concentration and profit rates: new evidence on an old issue, *Explorations in Economic Research*, Vol. 3, No. 1, Winter 1976, pp. 1–20.
6. Herfindahl, O. C., *Concentration in the Steel Industry* (Ph.D. dissertation, Columbia University, 1950).
7. Hirschman, A. O., The paternity of an index, *American Economic Review*, September 1964.
8. Horowitz, A. R., Suggestion for a comprehensive measure of concentration: comment; *and* Reply by Horvath, J., *Southern Economic Journal*, April 1972.
9. Horvath, J., Suggestion for a comprehensive measure of concentration, *Southern Economic Journal*, April 1970.
10. Horvath, J., Absolute and relative concentration measures reconsidered: comment; *and* Reply by Marfels, C., *Kyklos*, Vol. 25, No. 4, 1972.
11. Horvath, J., Measuring conglomerate concentration: a proposal, *Antitrust Bulletin*, Fall 1972.
12. Kilpatrick, R. W., The choice among alternative measures of industrial concentration, *Review of Economics and Statistics*, May 1967.
13. Marfels, C., A guide to the literature on the measurement of industrial concentration in the postwar period, *Zeitschrift für Nationalökonomie*, Vol. 31, 1971.
14. Marfels, C., Absolute and relative measures of concentration reconsidered, *Kyklos*, Vol. 24, No. 4, 1971.
15. Marfels, C., The consistency of concentration measures: a mathematical evaluation, *Zeitschrift für Nationalökonomie*, June 1972.
16. Marfels, C., On testing concentration measures, *Zeitschrift für Nationalökonomie*, Vol. 32, 1972.
17. Marfels, C., Relevant market and concentration: the case of the U.S. automobile industry, *Jahrbucher für Nationalökonomie und Statistik*, March 1973.
18. Miller, R. A., Marginal concentration ratios and industrial profit rates: some empirical results of oligopoly behavior, *Southern Economic Journal*, October 1967.
19. Mueller, W. F. and Hamm, L. G., Trends in industrial concentration 1947–70, *Review of Economics and Statistics*, November 1974.
20. Pashigian, P., Market concentration in the U.S. and Great Britain, *Journal of Law and Economics*, October 1968.
21. Rosenbluth, G., Measures of concentration. In Stigler, G. J. (Ed.) *Business Concentration and Price Policy* (Princeton, N. J.: Princeton University Press, 1955).
22. Rosenbluth, G. *Concentration in Canadian Manufacturing Industries* (Princeton, N. J.: Princeton University Press, 1959).
23. Singer, E., The structure of concentration indexes, *Antitrust Bulletin*, January–April 1965.
24. Utton, M. A., *Industrial Concentration* (Harmondsworth, England: Penguin Books, 1970).
25. Utton, M. A., Aggregate versus market concentration: a note, *Economic Journal*, March 1974.

II: The Concentration–Profitability Relationship

1. Asch, P., Industry structure and performance: some empirical evidence, *Review of Social Economy*, September 1967.
2. Bain, J. S., Relation of profit rate to industry concentration: American manufacturing 1936–40, *Quarterly Journal of Economics*, August 1951.
3. Brozen, Y., Significance of profit data for antitrust policy, *Antitrust Bulletin*, Spring 1969.
4. Brozen, Y., The antitrust task force deconcentration recommendation, *Journal of Law and Economics*, October 1970.

5. Brozen, Y., Concentration and structural and market disequilibria, *Antitrust Bulletin*, Summer 1971.
6. Brozen, Y., Wenders, J. T., McKie, J. M., Preston, L. E. and McAvoy, P. W., *Journal of Law and Economics*, October 1971, pp. 351–370 and 485–512.
7. Collins, N. R. and Preston, L. E., Concentration and price–cost margins in food manufacturing industries, *Journal of Industrial Economics*, July 1966.
8. Collins, N. R. and Preston, L. E., Price–cost margins and industry structure, *Review of Economics and Statistics*, August 1969.
9. Demsetz, H., Industry structure, market rivalry, and public policy, *Journal of Law and Economics*, April 1973.
10. Fuchs, B. R., Integration, concentration and profits in manufacturing industries, *Quarterly Journal of Economics*, May 1961.
11. Gale, B. T., Market share and rate of return, *Review of Economics and Statistics*, November 1972.
12. George, K. D., Concentration and specialization in industry, *Journal of Industrial Economics*, April 1972.
13. Gort, M., Analysis of stability and change in market shares, *Journal of Political Economy*, February 1963.
14. Gort, M. and Singamsetti, R., Concentration and profit rates: new evidence on an old issue, *Explorations in Economic Research*, Vol. 3, No. 1, Winter 1976.
15. Jacoby, N. H., The relative stability of market shares: theory and evidence, *Journal of Industrial Economics*, March 1964.
16. MacAvoy, P. W., McKie, J. W. and Preston, Lee E., High and stable concentration levels, profitability, and public policy: a response, *Journal of Law and Economics*, April 1971.
17. Mann, H. M., Seller concentration, barriers to entry, and rates of return in thirty industries, 1950–1960, *Review of Economics and Statistics*, August 1966.
18. Miller, R. A., Marginal concentration ratios and industrial profit rates: some empirical results of oligopoly behavior, *Southern Economic Journal*, October 1967.
19. Miller, R. A., Market structure and performance: relation of profit rates to concentration, advertising intensity, and diversity, *Journal of Industrial Economics*, April 1969.
20. Pashigian, P., The effect of market size on concentration, *International Economic Review*, October 1969.
21. Qualls, D., Stability and persistence of economic profit margins in highly concentrated industries, *Southern Economic Journal*, April 1974.
22. Rhoades, S. A., The concentration–profitability relationship: policy implications and some empirical evidence, *Antitrust Bulletin*, Summer 1973.
23. Rhoades, S. A. and Cleaver, J. M., The nature of the concentration price–cost margin relationship for 352 manufacturing industries, 1967, *Southern Economic Journal*, July 1973.
24. Shepherd, W. G., A comparison of industrial concentration in the United States and Britain, *Review of Economics and Statistics*, February 1961.
25. Shepherd, W. G., Trends in concentration in American manufacturing industries, 1947–58, *Review of Economics and Statistics*, May 1964.
26. Shepherd, W. G., Changes in British industrial concentration, 1951–1958, *Oxford Economic Papers*, March 1966.
27. Weiss, L. W., Average concentration ratios and industrial performance, *Journal of Industrial Economics*, July 1963.
28. Wenders, J. T., Profits and antitrust policy: the question of disequilibrium, *Antitrust Bulletin*, Summer 1971.
29. Winn, D. N. and Leabo, D. A., Rates of return, concentration, and growth questions of disequilibrium, *Journal of Law and Economics*, April 1974.

III: Concentration, Advertising and Profitability

1. Asch, P. and Marcus, M., Returns to scale in advertising, *Antitrust Bulletin*, Spring 1970.
2. Bloch, H., Advertising and profitability: a reappraisal, *Journal of Political Economy*, March–April 1974.
3. Butters, G. R., A survey of advertising and market structure, *American Economic Review, Papers and Proceedings*, May 1976.
4. Doyle, P., Advertising expenditure and consumer demand, *Oxford Economic Papers*, November 1968.
5. Ekelund, R. B. Jr and Gramm, W. P., Advertising and concentration: some new evidence, *Antitrust Bulletin*, Summer 1970.
6. Ekelund, R. B. Jr and Gramm, W. P., Advertising and concentration: more on tests of the Kaldor hypothesis, *Antitrust Bulletin*, Spring 1971.
7. Ekelund, R. B. Jr and Maurice, C., An empirical investigation of advertising and concentration: comment, *Journal of Industrial Economics*, November 1969.
8. Goldschmidt, H. J., Mann, H. M. and Weston, J. F. (Eds.) *Industrial Concentration: The New Learning* (Boston: Little, Brown & Co., 1974), Chapters 3, 4 and 5.

9. Greer, D. F., Advertising and market concentration, *Southern Economic Journal*, July 1971.
10. Guth, L. A., Advertising and market share revisited, *Journal of Industrial Economics*, April 1971.
11. Henning, J. A. and Meehan, J. W., Advertising and market concentration: comment; *and* Reply by Greer, D. F., *Southern Economic Journal*, January 1973.
12. Kaldor, N., The economic aspects of advertising, *Review of Economic Studies*, Vol. 18, 1949–1950.
13. Lambin, Jean-Jacques, Advertising and competitive behavior: a case study, *Applied Economics*, Vol. 2, 1970.
14. Mann, H. M. and Meehan, J. W., Advertising and concentration: new data and an old problem, *Antitrust Bulletin*, Spring 1971.
15. Mann, H. M., Henning, J. A. and Meehan, J. W., Advertising and concentration: an empirical investigation, *Journal of Industrial Economics*, November 1967.
16. Mann, H. M., Henning, J. A. and Meehan, J. W., Testing hypotheses in industrial economics, *Journal of Industrial Economics*, November 1969.
17. Marcus, M., Advertising and changes in concentration, *Southern Economic Journal*, October 1969.
18. Marcus, M., The intensity and effectiveness of advertising, *Oxford University Institute of Economics and Statistics*, November 1970.
19. Miller, R. A., Profit rates, concentration, advertising and diversity, *Journal of Industrial Economics*, April 1967.
20. Miller, R. A., Advertising and competition: some neglected aspects, *Antitrust Bulletin*, Summer 1972.
21. Reekie, W. D., Advertising and market structure: another approach, *Economic Journal*, March 1975.
22. Rees, R. D., Advertising, concentration and competition: a comment and further results, *Economic Journal*, March 1975.
23. Schnabel, M., A note on advertising and industrial concentration, *Journal of Political Economy*, September–October 1970.
24. Siegfried, J. J. and Weiss, L. W., Advertising, profits and corporate taxes revisited, *Review of Economics and Statistics*, May 1974.
25. Simon, J. L., Are there economies of scale in advertising? *Journal of Advertising Research*, June 1965.
26. Simon, J. L., The effect of the competitive structure on advertising expenditures, *Quarterly Journal of Economics*, November 1967.
27. Simon, J. L. and Crain, G. H., The advertising ratio and economies of scale, *Journal of Advertising Research*, September 1966.
28. Telser, L. G., Advertising and competition, *Journal of Political Economy*, December 1964.
29. Telser, L. G., Another look at advertising and concentration, *Journal of Industrial Economics*, November 1969.
30. Vernon, J. M., Concentration, promotion and market share stability in the pharmaceutical industry, *Journal of Industrial Economics*, July 1971.
31. Weiss, L. W., Advertising, profits, and corporation taxes, *Review of Economics and Statistics*, July 1963.

IV: Concentration and Research and Development Activities

1. Arrow, K. J., Economic welfare and the allocation of resources for invention. In *The Rate and Direction of Inventive Activity* (Princeton, N. J.: Princeton University Press, 1962).
2. Comanor, W. S., Research and competitive product differentiation in the pharmaceutical industry in the U.S., *Economica*, November 1964.
3. Comanor, W. S., Research and technical change in the pharmaceutical industry, *Review of Economics and Statistics*, May 1965.
4. Comanor, W. S., Market structure, product differentiation and industrial research, *Quarterly Journal of Economics*, November 1967.
5. Comanor, W. S. and Scherer, F. M., Patent statistics as a measure of technical change, *Journal of Industrial Economics*, November 1966.
6. Demsetz, H., Information and efficiency: another viewpoint, *Journal of Law and Economics*, April 1969.
7. Demsetz, H., Industry structure, market rivalry, and public policy, *Journal of Law and Economics*, April 1973.
8. Griliches, Z. and Smookler, J., Inventing and maximizing, *American Economic Review*, September 1963.
9. Hirschleifer, J., The private and social value of information and the reward to inventive activity, *American Economic Review*, September 1971.
10. Horowitz, I., Firm size and research activity, *Southern Economic Journal*, January 1962.
11. Hu, S. C., On the inventive to invent: a clarificatory note, *Journal of Law and Economics*, April 1973.
12. Johannisson, B. and Lindstrom, C., Firm size and inventive activity, *Swedish Journal of Economics*, December 1971.

13. Kamien, M. I. and Schwartz, N. L., Market structure, elasticity of demand and incentive to invent, *Journal of Law and Economics*, April 1970.
14. Kamien, M. I. and Schwartz, N. L., Timing of innovation under rivalry, *Econometrica*, January 1972.
15. Kamien, M. I. and Schwartz, N. L., Market structure, rivals' response, and the firm's rate of product innovation, *Journal of Industrial Economics*, April 1972.
16. Kamien, M. I. and Schwartz, N. L., On the degree of rivalry for maximum innovative activity, *Discussion Paper 64*, Northwestern University, Center for Mathematical Studies in Economics and Management Science, January 1974.
17. Kamien, M. I. and Schwartz, N. L., Patent life and R&D rivalry, *American Economic Review*, March 1974.
18. Kamien, M. I. and Schwartz, N. L., Market structure and innovation: a survey, *Journal of Economic Literature*, March 1975.
19. Leibenstein, H., Organizational and frictional equilibria, X-efficiency, and the rate of innovation, *Quarterly Journal of Economics*, November 1969.
20. Markham, J. W., Market structure, business conduct and innovation, *American Economic Review*, May 1965.
21. Mueller, D. C., Patents, R&D, and the measurement of incentive activity, *Journal of Industrial Economics*, November 1966.
22. Needham, Douglas, Market structure and firms' R&D behavior, *Journal of Industrial Economics*, June 1975.
23. Ng, Y. K., Competition, monopoly and the incentive to invent, *Australian Economic Papers*, June 1971.
24. Phillips, A., Patents, potential competition and technical progress, *American Economic Review*, May 1966.
25. Scherer, F. M., Corporate invention, output, profits and growth, *Journal of Political Economy*, June 1965.
26. Scherer, F. M., Firm size, market structure, opportunity, and the output of patented inventions, *American Economic Review*, December 1965.
27. Scherer, F. M., Market structure and the employment of scientists and engineers, *American Economic Review*, June 1967.
28. Steele, H., Monopoly and competition in the ethical drug market, *Journal of Law and Economics*, October 1962.
29. Swan, P. L., Market structure and technical progress: the influence of monopoly on product innovation, *Quarterly Journal of Economics*, November 1970.
30. Villard, H. H., Competition, oligopoly and research, *Journal of Political Economy*, December 1958.
31. Weiss, L. W., The survival technique and the extent of sub-optimal capacity, *Journal of Political Economy*, June 1964.
32. White, L. J., A note on the influence of monopoly on product innovation, *Quarterly Journal of Economics*, May 1972.
33. Williamson, O. E., Innovation and market structure, *Journal of Political Economy*, February 1965.

CHAPTER SEVEN

BARRIERS TO ENTRY

The term entry barriers refers to obstacles preventing new firms from engaging in the production of a particular category of output. Conventional price theory concludes that the price charged for the product of an industry characterized by perfectly easy entry cannot, in the long run, exceed average cost of production. Perfect ease of entry is said to exist if there are no barriers to entry into the industry concerned. If any entry barriers exist, price cannot in the long run exceed cost by more than the 'height' of such barriers, it is argued. More recently, some economists have argued that the threat of potential entry may affect the price charged by firms already established in an industry and preserve the aforementioned relationship even in the short run, and despite the absence of actual entry. If valid, this line of reasoning elevates entry barriers, and in particular their height, to a position of great importance in determining price and output patterns in the economy as a whole.

We turn now to examine the role of entry barriers as a regulator of price, focusing particular attention upon the behavioral assumptions required to validate the above propositions.

Alternative Reactions to Entry

Entry into an industry shall be defined as the production, by a firm new to the industry, of a product that is a perfect substitute, in the minds of buyers, for the product of firms already established in the industry. This definition is quite consistent with variety in the physical and other characteristics of the products of different firms in a given industry. It must also be emphasized that entry as defined is not accomplished if a firm previously outside an industry simply acquires the plant of an already established firm and operates it; that is, the mere change of ownership of existing plant capacity does not constitute entry. On the other hand, entry by a firm new to the industry need not necessarily involve the creation of a new firm; a firm already established in a particular industry may enter another industry if it builds capacity and adds an additional product to its product line. See H. Hines (19) and F. J. Kottke (26) on the importance of entry by already established firms.

Whether a decision-maker will enter a particular industry or not depends upon the anticipated profitability of such a course of action. The profits anticipated by a potential entrant as a result of producing the product in question depend upon his cost conditions and upon the post-entry demand conditions anticipated by the firm for its product. These demand conditions, and therefore the profits anticipated by a potential entrant, depend upon the anticipated reaction of existing producers in the industry to entry. The greater the post-entry quantity of output produced by established firms, for example, the lower the price obtainable for any given quantity of the entrant's output. The many alternative reactions that are possible can each be viewed as a quantity of output which the existing firms can elect to produce after entry while reducing the price, or accepting reductions, to the extent required to enforce such an output policy. Diagrammatically, the potential entrant will then be confronted by a sloping demand curve which is the segment of the industry demand curve to the right of the *post-entry* quantity which the potential entrant expects existing firms to select, as shown in Figure 7–1.

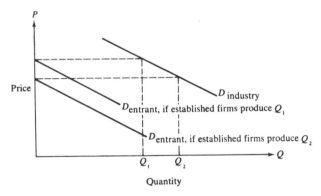

Figure 7–1. The demand curve facing a potential entrant.

Sylos Postulate

Much of the existing theory of entry is based upon the implicit or explicit assumption that potential entrants behave as though they expected existing producers in an industry to maintain their output at the pre-entry level in the face of entry, and that established firms do in fact behave in this manner if entry occurs. This assumption is sometimes referred to as the Sylos postulate, following the publication of a book by P. Sylos-Labini (51), and is analogous to the Cournot assumption of traditional price theory, which assumes that individual firms established in an industry expect rivals to maintain their output at an unchanged level.

Given the Sylos postulate, the potential entrant is confronted by a sloping demand curve which is the segment of the industry demand curve to the right of the *pre-entry* quantity produced by existing firms. The potential entrant will decide whether or not to enter the industry by comparing this demand curve with his own cost conditions. The entrant's costs must include the opportunity cost of the profit which can be earned in other industries; only if a firm can earn more profits in the industry being considered than can be earned elsewhere will the firm enter that industry.

Three main types of barrier to entry are customarily distinguished. First, preferences of buyers for the products of established firms as compared to those of new entrants. Such preferences can, however, always be overcome if the new entrant invests sufficiently in sales promotion activities, and the essence of preferences as a barrier to entry is that to secure comparably favorable price for any given quantity of output, the entrant would have to incur sales promotion costs per unit of output which are greater than those of established firms. In view of the definition of entry given earlier, preference barriers, if they exist, will emerge as a difference in the unit costs of established and potential entrant firms respectively. For this reason, preference barriers will be grouped for purposes of this analysis with the second major category of entry barrier, absolute cost advantages. Absolute cost advantages exist if the costs of established firms, at any comparable scale of output, are lower than those of potential entrants. Such advantages may result from the need of new entrants to overcome accumulated buyer preference for the product of established firms, or from other factors such as lower prices paid by established firms for inputs or investment funds. The third major type of entry barrier is economies of scale, resulting in a declining long-run average cost curve for the product in question. Some economists list legal barriers as a fourth type of entry barrier, while others would not distinguish them as a separate type of barrier, preferring instead to include the various types of legal barrier under the three main categories of barrier already listed. For example, patents giving established firms exclusive rights over strategic productive techniques or product designs may place potential entrants at a disadvantage in cost if they must use more costly techniques or must pay royalties for use of the patented technique or product. Such legal barriers may therefore be included with absolute cost barriers. Other legal barriers, however, such as laws prohibiting entry absolutely, or requiring operators to obtain government granted licenses, may not be reflected in costs, and must be listed as a separate category of entry barrier. The succeeding analysis confines itself to the three main categories of barrier already listed.

The presence of absolute cost differences, or scale economies, is not by itself sufficient to guarantee a barrier to entry – entry will occur despite such factors, provided that the entrant's anticipated demand conditions result in a situation in which the entrant expects to be able to make a profit. This is the case, for example, in both situations shown in Figure 7–2. The curves labeled 'ATC entrant' and 'ATC established' depict, respectively, the average cost curves of a potential entrant and an established firm.

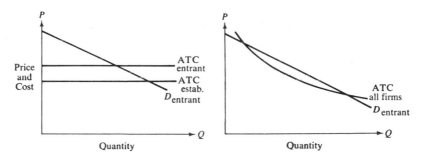

Figure 7–2. Entry despite absolute cost differences and scale economies.

Given the Sylos postulate, the position of the demand curve confronting a potential entrant is determined by the pre-entry price and output of established firms. Where absolute cost differences exist, if the pre-entry price exceeds the average cost in established firms by more than the difference in average cost between potential entrant and established firms, the entrant's demand curve will be above his cost curve (in view of the assumed constancy of established firms' output at the pre-entry level) and entry will occur since the entrant expects to make a profit. Entry will lower market price if established firms do in fact behave in the expected manner and attempt to maintain output at the pre-entry level.

Entry will not occur if the pre-entry price exceeds cost in established firms by less than the difference in average cost between potential entrant and established firms, for in such circumstances, given the Sylos postulate, the entrant's anticipated demand curve will be below his cost curve. The greater the difference in absolute costs of established firms and potential entrant the greater the amount by which industry price can exceed cost of established firms without inducing entry. If the extent to which industry price can exceed average cost in established firms is used as a measure of the height of entry barriers, the height of absolute cost entry barriers, given the Sylos postulate, is measured by the distance xy in Figure 7-3(a). The distance equals precisely the absolute cost difference between established firms and potential entrants.

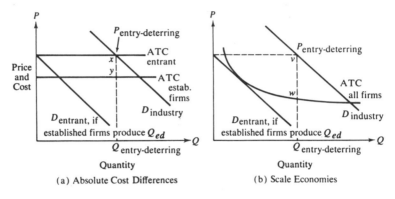

Figure 7-3. Maximum price–cost differences under the Sylos postulate.

If scale economies exist, the maximum amount by which price can exceed average cost without inducing entry, given the Sylos postulate, is determined by the size of the market, the elasticity of market demand at any price, the scale at which economies of scale are exhausted and the rate at which average cost declines. The height of the scale economies barrier to entry is measured by the distance vw in Figure 7-3(b).

If both types of entry barrier exist, the maximum amount by which price can exceed average cost without inducing entry, given the Sylos postulate, will be determined by the height of the larger of the two barriers.

The following propositions are valid if firms behave in accordance with the Sylos postulate:

1. Entry will occur if price exceeds average cost of the marginal, or least efficient, established firm by more than an amount that is directly related to the magnitude of scale economies and absolute cost differences between established firms and new entrant, and price cannot exceed cost by more than this amount in the long run, though it may do so in the short run, that is, until entry has occurred.
2. If existing producers in an industry try to deter potential entrants, this relationship between price and cost will be preserved even in the short run. That is, in order to deter entry, existing producers must charge a price which does not exceed average cost by more than the height of scale economy or absolute cost difference entry barriers. Only if such a price is set, and the resulting market demand at that price is produced by established producers, will entry seem unprofitable to potential entrants, provided that they expect existing firms to maintain an unchanged output level in the face of entry.

Although it is always *possible* for established firms to deter entry under the Sylos postulate, because potential entrants are assumed to believe that established firms' output will remain unchanged, entry-deterring behavior need not be *optimal*, in the sense of achieving the highest possible level of profits for established firms. D. K. Osborne (40) has analyzed the circumstances in which entry-deterring behavior will be optimal for established firms if potential entrants behave in accordance with the Sylos postulate. For a selection of other useful articles dealing with the theory of entry under the Sylos postulate, and limit pricing, see Baron (5, 6), Bhagwati (7), Cohen (11), Gaskins (15), Pashigian (41) and Wenders (55, 56, 57). Osborne's analysis clearly demonstrates that the relevant choice for established firms is *not* that between the entry-deterring profit level and a profit stream equal to that obtained by ignoring entry and setting price at the monopoly level until entry occurs. The reason is that, under the Sylos postulate, the optimal level of a potential entrant's output, and therefore the scale of entry, is directly related to the pre-entry price and output policy of established firms. Given the potential entrant's cost conditions, the higher the excess of the pre-entry price over the entry-deterring price level, the larger will be the scale of entry. Established firms will therefore take into account the entrant's alternative possible reactions and will select a pre-entry price and output level which maximizes established firms' profits in the light of these reactions. Only if the resulting optimal price and output policy of established firms involves an output level equal to or exceeding the entry-deterring level will it be optimal for established firms to attempt to deter entry even under the Sylos postulate.

Osborne's conclusions, and an interesting and important implication of his analysis which in our view was not sufficiently emphasized, can readily be demonstrated using an alternative and more conventional diagrammatic framework to that employed by Osborne. In Figure 7–4 D_m depicts the total market demand curve for the product in question, and the cost curves of established firms and potential entrant reflect absence of scale economies merely for expositional convenience. Given the Sylos postulate, the anticipated profits of an entrant will be zero and entry will not occur if established firms set price and quantity at P_{ed} and Q_{ed}, respectively. At higher prices the output level of established firms will imply profits for entrants. Moreover, since the anticipated post-entry demand for the entrant's output will be larger at any given price the lower the established

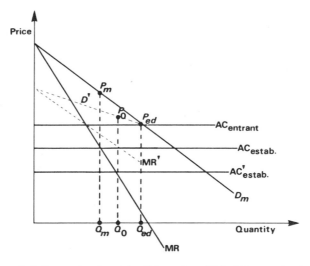

Figure 7–4. Demand and cost conditions of established firms under the Sylos postulate.

firms' output level, the optimal scale of entry will be larger the higher the pre-entry price charged by established firms, given the cost conditions of the entrant. The output level of the entrant corresponding to different pre-entry price levels may be subtracted from the market demand curve to yield the dotted demand curve D' and associated marginal revenue schedule MR'. These schedules, together with those portions of the original market demand and associated marginal revenue curves at output levels above Q_{ed}, represent the demand for the product of established firms *taking into account the reactions of potential entrants*. It is these schedules which determine the optimal policies of established firms and whether entry-deterring behavior will be optimal for established firms. For example, if established firms' costs are represented by the curve labeled AC in Figure 7–4, the profit-maximizing price and output level for established firms are P_0 and Q_0 and it will not be optimal to deter entry. In contrast, if established firms' costs are represented by the curve labeled AC', entry-deterring behavior will be optimal. When scale economies are introduced into the analysis, they will also influence the scale of entry at prices above the entry-deterring level, and will therefore also play a part in determining the elasticity of the dotted demand curve and whether entry-deterring behavior will be optimal.

The important implication of Osborne's analysis which we referred to earlier is also apparent from Figure 7–4. It is that even if established firms do not attempt to deter entry, their optimal prices will still always be lower than the monopoly level provided that they take into account potential entrants' reactions. The optimal price will lie on the dotted demand curve at an output level somewhere to the right of the monopoly output level for the following reasons: since both MR and MR' bisect the horizontal distance between the price axis and the point on the market demand curve corresponding to the entry-deterring price P_{ed}, MR' must lie above MR and will therefore intersect MC above the monopoly output level. Although these conclusions elevate the mere existence of potential entrants to a position of considerable importance in influencing established firms' pricing behavior even in the absence of attempts to deter entry, it must be emphasized that the conclusions are critically dependent on the validity of the Sylos postulate as a description of potential entrants' behavior, or more precisely as a description of how established firms *think* potential entrants behave. As noted in the following section, the ability of established firms to deter entry depends on their ability to influence entrants' expectations regarding the *post-entry* behavior of established firms, and there is no more reason to believe that potential entrants in general expect established firms to leave their output policies unchanged if entry occurs than to believe otherwise. Potential entrants' anticipations regarding the post-entry behavior of established firms may be entirely outside the control of established firms; for example potential entrants into a particular market may expect antitrust policies to prevent entry-deterring reactions by established firms. Alternatively, potential entrants may expect either entry-deterring or accommodating reactions to occur if seller concentration exceeds a certain level. In either case, entry will be unrelated to the pre-entry policies of the established firms, and attempts by established firms to deter entry will be ineffective and non-optimal. Conversely, the threat of potential entry will not act as a constraint on the behavior of established firms in these circumstances, though actual entry, if it occurs, may affect their behavior. Established firms *cannot* influence potential entrants' behavior by selecting appropriate current policies unless it can be shown that there is some systematic link between the pre-entry and post-entry policies of established firms in the minds of potential entrants. No body of economic reasoning has yet demonstrated convincingly why such a relationship should exist in general, though there are a few specific pre-entry policies which suggest the likely occurrence of entry-deterring behavior, such as established firms building capacity in advance of demand.

Consequences of Alternative Reactions

The propositions in the preceding section cease to be valid if potential entrants do not assume that established firms will maintain their output at the pre-entry level. It is the *post-entry* output of existing firms anticipated by potential entrants that determines the anticipated price at which the entrant can sell any given output level. *Pre-entry* price and quantity sold are themselves generally irrelevant as far as the potential entrant is concerned, and only become relevant to the entry decision in special cases in which entrants assume that the post-entry quantity supplied by established firms will equal the pre-entry quantity. It is not true, as is often stated in elementary price theory texts, that the relevant question for a new entrant is whether existing firms are charging prices at which the new entrant can make above normal profits. Rather, it is whether the reaction of established firms to entry will result in a *post-entry* price which permits the entrant to make above normal profits.

The post-entry quantity supplied by existing firms which will deter entrants (since it will imply a post-entry market price which will not enable the entrant to cover costs at any level of output), and the entry-deterring price, are uniquely determined by long-run demand and cost functions of the industry, as explained in the previous section. However, entry will not necessarily occur if pre-entry price exceeds the entry-deterring price so determined. If, for example, the potential entrant expects established firms to produce a post-entry quantity which will not permit the entrant to cover his costs, entry will not occur irrespective of the pre-entry price that is being charged by established firms. The size of absolute cost differences and scale economies relative to the size of total market demand no longer place a limit on the amount by which price can permanently exceed unit cost in the established firms, even in the long run. Conversely, if potential entrants expect established firms to reduce output in response to entry, entry may occur even though price exceeds cost in established firms by no more than the absolute cost difference between established firms and potential entrants. In short, entry barriers cannot be measured solely by absolute cost differences and scale economy factors, because the profits anticipated by an entrant will depend on, and vary with, the precise nature of the reactions of established firms.

Moreover, if the pre-entry price charged by established firms has no influence on the entrant's decision, it follows that charging a price lower than the industry profit-maximizing price, in order to deter entry, cannot possibly be an optimal strategy from the point of view of established firms with profit-maximizing objectives. This conclusion is obvious in the example quoted in the preceding paragraph in which entry does not take place, for in this event the established firms are forgoing profits if they charge a price other than the price which maximizes industry profit. It is perhaps less obvious, but equally true, even if potential entrants decide to enter the industry because they expect the reaction of existing producers to entry will be such as to permit the entrant to earn a profit. If entry is independent of pre-entry price charged by existing firms, the post-entry profits of existing firms will be the same whether or not those firms charged a pre-entry price that maximizes industry profits in the pre-entry period; therefore, pricing to deter entry and earning pre-entry profits below the maximum possible level must lower the total profits of firms practicing such a policy relative to the profits that can be earned if potential entry is ignored. Limit pricing will not be the most profitable course of action for existing producers unless they believe that potential entrants expect established firms to attempt to maintain their output at the pre-entry level in the face of entry.

The question remains, what grounds are there for assuming that potential entrants expect established firms to attempt to maintain output at the pre-entry level, or that established firms expect them to behave in this way? Some economists have suggested that this is the policy that is most unfavorable to new entrants. In the absence of some constraint which prevents established firms from increasing the level of their output in response to entry, however, this conclusion is not warranted. (Such a constraint could be provided, for example, by an antitrust policy which would regard increases in output by established firms in response to entry as a restrictive practice.) If existing firms increase their output after entry has occurred, the price which the entrant can obtain for any given quantity of output is lower than if existing firms maintained their output at the pre-entry level. Thus, by increasing output after entry has occurred, established firms can force losses upon the entrant firm. There is no such thing as the most unfavorable policy for entrants, short of driving price down to zero. From the point of view of potential entrants, the most unfavorable policy which established firms are likely to consider adopting is surely the policy of trying to deter entrant firms by supplying a post-entry quantity which drives market price down below the entrant firm's costs. There is, however, no more reason why potential entrants should expect established firms to react in this way in all circumstances than there is reason to believe that they will attempt to maintain output constant in all circumstances, as the Sylos postulate assumes. In atomistic market structures, to be sure, the behavior of potential entrants will very likely correspond to the Sylos postulate. Under pure competition or monopolistic competition, for example, no individual established seller will take account of entry, any more than it will take account of the behavior of its existing rivals. By definition, in such markets the actions of any individual seller, whether established firm or new entrant, will have no noticeable effect upon other sellers, and will not, therefore, provoke any reaction. Therefore, the Sylos postulate is a valid description of the behavior of potential entrants considering entering an atomistic industry. The situation is different in oligopolistic industries. In such industries, individual established firms are by definition affected by and aware of the actions of other firms, whether established firms or new entrants, and may be expected to react by potential entrants. The exact nature of the reaction, however, cannot be determined by a priori reasoning. It is sometimes argued that entry-deterring reactions are more likely to occur in highly concentrated industries where established firms can more easily detect and respond collectively to entry. It could just as reasonably be argued, however, that accommodating reactions are more likely in such industries due to established firms' fear of the antitrust repercussions stemming from entry-deterring behavior. In the final analysis, how potential entrants actually behave, or how established firms believe them to behave, is a matter for empirical investigation.

Before we leave the subject of the determinants of potential entrants' behavior, it is necessary to mention briefly one other possible barrier to entry. Thus far it has been pointed out that if the entrant's anticipated demand and cost conditions indicate that a profit can be made, entry will occur. In order to enter, however, the firm must, in addition, have sufficient money capital to purchase the inputs required to produce the level of output which it expects to be able to sell at a profit. If the cost of investment funds is higher for a potential entrant than for established firms, this will be reflected as an absolute cost difference and will therefore be covered by the analysis of absolute cost barriers. If, however, a potential entrant is unable to obtain funds at any price, the capital requirements barrier will not be reflected in the entrant's cost curves and must therefore be treated as a separate category of entry barrier. The belief is widely held that the requirement of a large amount of liquid funds for investment by an entrant firm constitutes some sort of barrier to its entry. While the argument that potential entrants simply cannot raise enough money (presumably at any price) to finance entry, or that established firms can raise money more easily and cheaply than potential entrants, is plausible if the new entrant is a new firm setting up business for the first time, it is less so if one considers the possible entry of a large going business concern into a new industry.

Actual Entry and the Level of Industry Price and Output

Although the height of entry barriers will not place a limit on the amount by which price can exceed average cost, even in the long run, if potential entrants expect entry-deterring behavior by established firms after entry has occurred, entry will occur whenever potential entrants expect the reaction of established firms will permit entrants to make profits. The question remains, will *actual* entry itself lower market price and place a limit on the amount by which price can exceed average cost in the long run?

The answer to this question depends on how established firms and new entrants behave after entry has taken place. If established firms attempt to maintain their output at the pre-entry level, entry will drive down the market price, but the resulting market price may continue to exceed average cost by more than the height of absolute cost and scale economy entry barriers, as Figure 7–5 demonstrates.

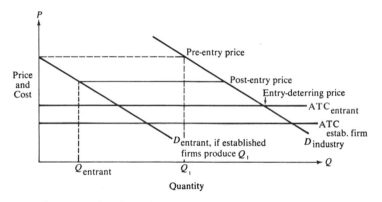

Figure 7–5. The effects of actual entry on industry price and output.

Only if additional entry occurs will market price be driven down further, and this depends on whether new potential entrants expect the established firms to continue to react to entry by attempting to maintain output at the pre-entry level.

If, contrary to the expectations of new entrants, established firms try to deter entry by increasing output, market price will be driven down at least until it exceeds cost by no more than the height of entry barriers until the entrant has been eliminated, but can then be raised again unless and until entry occurs again. It can hardly be argued that further entry will prevent price being raised again, unless entrants ignore the previous behavior of established firms in response to entry.

The third possibility is that existing firms may reduce their output in the face of entry, and that industry price continues to exceed cost by more than the height of entry barriers, perhaps even remaining unchanged despite the occurrence of entry and despite the absence of any collusion between firms in the industry. This possibility can be illustrated by the following example employing the extreme assumption that there are no scale economy or absolute cost barriers to entry into a particular industry. If each firm in an industry assumes that any price it charges will be matched by all other firms in the industry, each firm's demand curve will be a fraction of the industry demand curve, the size of the fraction determined by the anticipated share of market demand accruing to the firm if all firms charge the same price for the same product. Figure 7–6 illustrates this proposition in the case of a linear market demand curve.

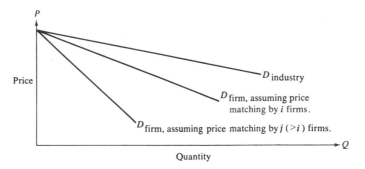

Figure 7–6. Entry with price matching.

Increases in the number of firms in the industry will cause the subjective demand curve assuming price matching of each established firm to pivot down without changing the intercept of that curve. Since, by definition, there are no economies of scale and no absolute cost differences, the cost curves of established and newly entered firms will be identical, and marginal cost of production and distribution will be constant.

With linear cost and demand functions, the price which maximizes a firm's profits depends only on the intercept of the demand curve and on marginal cost of production and distribution. For example,

with the demand function $p = a - bq$
and the total cost function $C = cq + K$
Profit $= aq - bq^2 - cq - k$

For maximum profit, $\dfrac{dP}{dq} = 0$

Therefore, $a - 2bq - c = 0$, or $q = \dfrac{a - c}{2b}$

Substituting the profit-maximizing quantity into the demand function we obtain the profit-maximizing price as a function of its determinants, as follows:

$$p = a - b\frac{(a - c)}{2b} = \frac{2a - a + c}{2} = \frac{a + c}{2}$$

Thus, the profit-maximizing price depends solely on c, the marginal cost of production, and a, the y intercept of the demand curve.

In the absence of scale economies, marginal cost is by definition constant; further, the entry of an additional firm leaves the intercept of an established firm's demand curve assuming price matching unchanged. Therefore, if the industry demand curve is linear (and firms expect rivals to behave as postulated), it follows that entry will leave the profit-maximizing price of each established firm unchanged. Finally, since the new entrant's cost conditions are identical with those of established firms, and its demand curve is linear with the same intercept as the demand curve of established firms, the profit-maximizing new entrant will charge the same price as established firms. In these circumstances, entry does not change industry price and output, but merely changes the number of firms producing that output – an output which maximizes industry profits.

The preceding example emphasizes that the relationship between industry price and unit cost depends upon the behavior of individual firms established in the industry, and that this behavior can take a number of different forms. Even in the absence of entry barriers, actual entry into the industry will not necessarily drive price down to equality with unit cost unless firms in the industry ignore each other's behavior in deciding upon their individual policies. The example also shows that the number of firms in an industry is only relevant to explaining industry behavior insofar as it influences expectations about rivals' behavior.

If entry barriers exist, it is still possible for industry price to remain unchanged despite the entry of additional firms into the industry. For example, with absolute cost barriers added to the previous example, although the price which maximizes profits, given the assumption of price matching by all firms, remains unchanged for established firms, this price will be higher for new entrants. However, the entrant may passively accept the price which maximizes established firms' profits, given entry, believing that established firms are unlikely to match a higher price set by the entrant, although believing that established firms will very likely match any attempt to undercut them. Given this expectation, passive acceptance of the price set by established firms may be the most profitable course of action for an entrant.

Theory of Entry as an Extension of Oligopoly Theory

Two main points emerge from the preceding discussion. First, whether entry into an industry will occur depends upon the *post-entry* behavior of established firms anticipated by potential entrants. This anticipated behavior can take various alternative forms, each of which implies a different level of profits accruing to the entrant, and need not necessarily correspond to the pre-entry behavior of established firms. Second, the effect of entry on industry price and output depends upon the actual post-entry behavior of firms in the industry including any new entrants, and varies with the exact nature of firms' assumptions regarding rivals' reactions after entry has occurred.

In each case, the analogy between the theory of entry and the analysis of oligopoly in conventional price theory should be apparent to the reader. Oligopoly theory deals with firms' behavior, taking into account the firms' expectations regarding the behavior of other firms *already producing the product*. Although conventional oligopoly theory deals with the behavior of firms already established in an industry, the same principles are obviously applicable in analyzing the determinants of potential entrants' behavior. As for the influence of potential entrants on the behavior of firms established in an industry, entry theory merely extends the number of firms which established firms may consider in formulating their policies to include other *firms not currently producing the product* in question who may react to the established firms' policies by entering the industry and producing the product.

The discussion contained in previous sections of this chapter, and the relationship between entry-barrier theory and conventional oligopoly theory, may be clarified by reference to the optimal pricing conditions developed in Chapter 3. The price–cost relationship which maximizes a firm's profits was shown to be $(P - \mathrm{MC})/P = 1/E_d$, where E_d is the price-elasticity of demand for the firm's product. It was also shown that E_d itself depends on the price-elasticity of market demand for the product (E_m), the firm's share of market demand (S_f), and the anticipated output-level reactions of the firm's rivals to the firm's pricing policies (E_s), and when these factors are taken into account the preceding profit-maximizing price–cost relationship can be expressed alternatively as follows:

$$\frac{P - MC}{P} = \frac{1}{E_d} = \frac{S_f}{E_m + E_s \cdot (1 - S_f)}$$

The influence of entry barriers on the pricing behavior of established firms in an industry can easily be incorporated within this analytical framework. The expression E_s, which refers to the anticipated output reaction of a firm's rivals to changes in the firm's pricing policy, can be divided into two components. One component (E_{se}) refers to the output reactions of firms already selling the product in question, and the other component (E_{spe}) refers to the output reactions of potential entrants who are expected to respond to established firm's pricing policies by entering the market. If a firm does not take into account the reactions of any firms except those firms already established in its market, E_{spe} is zero and potential entrant behavior will only exert an influence on market pricing behavior if entry actually occurs. On the other hand, if E_{spe} is not zero, potential entrants will influence market pricing behavior of established firms even in the absence of actual entry. For example, if E_s equals E_m in absolute magnitude, which corresponds to the case explained in more detail in Chapter 3 where each established firm expects its established rivals to imitate its price and output policies, established firms will behave collectively like a monopolist if potential entrants are ignored. When potential entrants' behavior is also taken into account, however, the optimal market price for established firms will be below the monopoly level as long as E_{spe} is not zero.

Whether E_{spe} will be non-zero depends on whether potential entrants expect entry to be profitable which in turn depends on a potential entrant firm's own cost conditions and on the demand conditions which the entrant anticipates will face him if he enters the market. As was previously explained, these demand conditions are determined by the reactions and *post-entry* behavior of established firms which the entrant anticipates. The factors determining a potential entrant's behavior can also be explained by reference to the optimal pricing condition outlined above, for entry will occur provided that the optimal price–marginal cost relationship for the potential entrant implies positive profits for the entrant firm. The conclusions reached in the earlier analysis of entry under the Sylos postulate can be demonstrated within this alternative generalized algebraic framework as follows: under the Sylos postulate, the E_{se} term is assumed to be zero, so that an entrant's optimal pricing condition reduces to the following expression:

$$\frac{P - MC}{P} = \frac{S_f}{E_m}$$

Since $S_f = 1 - S_r$, where S_r refers to the share of total market demand supplied by established firms, a sufficiently large level of S_r can always result in zero profits for the entrant. If there are no scale economies or absolute cost disadvantages for entrants, however, the S_r level which results in zero profits for the entrant will *also* result in zero profits for established firms, whose optimal pricing condition will then be identical to that of an entrant. Although entry-deterring behavior by established firms is unlikely to occur in these circumstances, entry will ensure that market price does not exceed average cost in the industry in the long run. If there are absolute cost differences between established firms and entrants, but scale economies are absent so that $MC = AC$, the level of S_r which makes $(P - AC) = 0$ for the entrant will imply positive profits for established firms whose AC is by assumption lower. Thus, given the Sylos postulate, entry will be profitable whenever price exceeds average cost in established firms by more than the difference between average cost in entrant and established firms, and market price cannot exceed average cost in established firms by more than this amount in the long run. Finally, if there are no absolute cost differences, but economies of scale exist in the production of the product, $MC = kAC$ where k is less than unity, indicating that MC is below AC, up to the minimum efficient scale of output of the product in question. It follows that a positive optimal $P - MC$ for an entrant does not necessarily imply positive profits for the entrant unless $P - AC$ is positive, which depends on the magnitude of k. Given k, a large enough S_r can reduce an entrant's optimal $P - MC$ below the level which is necessary for the entrant to earn positive profits. The level of S_r, and hence $P - MC$ in established firms, which achieves this result depends, in addition to k, on the magnitude of E_m; as explained in connection with the diagrammatic analysis of the Sylos postulate earlier in this chapter, the entry-deterring S_r will be larger, and the implied $P - MC$ difference in established firms will be lower, the larger is E_m.

Summarizing the preceding paragraph, when $E_{se} = 0$ as assumed by the Sylos postulate, entry will be profitable and will occur whenever price exceeds average cost in established firms by more than any absolute cost differences, or an amount related to scale economies and market price-elasticity, whichever is larger, and market price cannot exceed average cost in established firms by more than this amount in the long run, whether established firms attempt to deter entry or not. Under the Sylos postulate, it is always *possible* for established firms to deter entry by setting price and quantity at the entry-deterring level, because entrants are assumed to believe that established firms' post-entry output level will be the same as their pre-entry output level. The reader is reminded that entry-deterring behavior need not be *optimal*, however, in the sense of achieving the highest profit level for established firms, as the analysis in the section entitled Sylos Postulate demonstrated.

In general, the ability of established firms to deter entry depends on their ability to influence entrants' expectations regarding the *post-entry* behavior of established firms. The assumption that entrants believe that $E_{se} = 0$, so that the pre-entry and post-entry behavior of established firms is identical, is responsible for making it possible for established firms to deter entry under the Sylos postulate. As previously noted, however, there is no more reason to believe that in practice potential entrants expect established firms to leave current output policies unchanged if entry occurs than to believe otherwise. Entry will not occur, irrespective of the pre-entry behavior of established firms, if entrants expect entry-deterring reactions so that E_{se} in the entrant's optimal pricing condition is sufficiently high to make entry unprofitable. Conversely, entry can occur even if existing prices do not exceed costs in established firms by more than any absolute cost differences or scale economy factors, if a potential entrant anticipates output reductions by established firms in response to entry. The key issue, therefore, concerns the determinants of E_{se} in an entrant's optimal pricing condition, and in particular whether established firms can influence its magnitude by their pre-entry behavior.

It is possible that E_{se} may be entirely outside the control of established firms. For example, potential entrants may expect antitrust policies to prevent entry-deterring reactions by established firms. Alternatively, entrants may either expect entry-deterring reactions, or perhaps even accommodating reactions, to occur if seller concentration among established firms is above a certain level. In any of these cases, entry may or may not occur, but is unrelated to the pre-entry policies of the established firms, and attempts by established firms to deter entry in these circumstances will be ineffective, and non-optimal, whether entry occurs or not. Conversely, the threat of potential entry will not act as a constraint on the behavior of established firms in these circumstances, though actual entry, if it occurs, may affect the behavior of established firms. It should be noted that $E_{spe} = 0$ in established firms' optimal pricing condition is perfectly compatible with the occurrence of entry in these circumstances; the point is that such entry is by definition not occurring in response to established firms' pre-entry policies.

Much has been made in economic theory, and current antitrust policies, of the threat of potential entry as a constraint on the behavior of established firms in a particular market. In the light of the preceding analysis two points need to be emphasized: first, established firms *cannot* influence entry by selecting appropriate current policies unless it can be shown that there is some systematic link between pre-entry and post-entry policies of established firms in the minds of entrants. As already indicated, this amounts to establishing a systematic relationship between pre-entry policies of established firms and E_{se}, the expected reaction of established firms to entry. No body of economic reasoning has yet demonstrated why such a systematic relationship should exist in general, though there are a few specific pre-entry policies which suggest the likely occurrence of entry-deterring behavior, such as established firms building capacity in advance of demand. The second important point is that even if it is *possible* for established firms to deter entry by selecting appropriate levels of policy variables, such a course of action need not be *optimal*, in the sense of maximizing the present value of the established firms' profits.

Before concluding this section, one other factor influencing the behavior of a potential entrant and thus far omitted should be mentioned. Established firms are not the only rivals who may react to the entry of a particular potential entrant; other potential entrants may exist and may also enter the industry. Therefore, another term, E_{spe}, referring to reactions of other potential entrants should in principle also be added to the optimal pricing condition of an entrant. As R. Sherman and T. D. Willett have pointed out (49), the existence of other potential entrants may result in expected output reactions which make entry seem unprofitable from the point of view of an individual potential entrant, so that it is not necessarily true that more potential entrants into a particular market imply lower entry barriers. See V. Goldberg and S. Moirao (17) for more on this aspect of entry theory.

Entry Barriers and Industry Profitability: Empirical Evidence and Measurement Problems

Theoretical analysis indicates that the behavior of potential entrants depends on the entrant's cost conditions and anticipations regarding the post-entry behavior of established firms, represented by E_{se} in the entrant's optimal pricing condition. Theory is inconclusive, however, regarding the determinants of E_{se} and, in particular, the relationship between the pre-entry behavior of established firms and E_{se}. The impossibility of establishing a unique a priori relationship between entrants' expectations and the degree of seller concentration existing among established firms is exactly analogous to the situation encountered in connection with discussions of the relationship between seller concentration and expectations in established firms, since it is simply the same problem viewed from the point of view of an entrant rather than from the point of view of an established firm. It is necessary, therefore, to resort to empirical evidence in an effort to determine whether, and if so how, entry barriers affect market pricing behavior in practice.

Ideally, the influence of other factors which underlie the observed pricing behavior and profitability of established firms in various industries should be taken into account and eliminated in attempting to infer the nature of the relationship which exists in practice between entry barriers and pricing behavior. For example, seller concentration may affect the pricing behavior and profitability of established firms by influencing their expectations regarding established firms' reactions (E_{se} in the optimal pricing condition relating to established firms), independently of entry-barrier considerations affecting the reactions of potential entrants and therefore the magnitude of E_{spe}. In order to isolate the impact of entry barriers on pricing and profitability in practice, empirical studies by J. Bain (4), H. M. Mann (28) and more recently by D. Qualls (43) have therefore classified industries with similar concentration levels into 'very high', 'substantial' and 'moderate-to-low' entry-barrier classes on the basis of the estimated height of entry barriers in the individual industries studied. (Other empirical studies dealing with the entry barrier–concentration–profitability relationship which the reader may find useful are those by George (16), Gupta (18), Kamerschen (22), Mann (29, 30, 31, 32) and Rhoades (46).) In industries with high concentration, the 'very high' entry-barrier group of industries was found to have a considerably higher profit rate than the 'substantial' entry-barrier group, and this difference was statistically significant. No statistically significant difference was observed between the average profit rate of the highly concentrated industries with 'substantial' and 'moderate-to-low' entry barriers, however. One possible explanation for failure to find a distinct difference between the profit rate of industries with 'substantial' and 'moderate-to-low' entry barriers may be that the 'substantial' barrier group may be practicing 'limit pricing' and charging an entry-deterring price whereas firms in industries with 'moderate-to-low' entry barriers may be charging prices above the entry-deterring level, temporarily earning profits above the long-run equilibrium level.

The preceding evidence regarding the influence of entry barriers on pricing behavior must be interpreted with some care, however, since the results are heavily dependent on the entry-barrier classification scheme used to assign individual industries to the three different entry-barrier classes. For example, the study by D. Qualls (43) indicated that by reassigning only one industry from the 'very high' to the 'substantial' barrier class, the latter has a statistically significant higher average profit rate than the 'moderate-to-low' entry-barrier class. Moreover, it is unlikely that the relative height of entry barriers in individual industries was correctly measured in these or any other studies of entry barriers which have been undertaken to date, for two major reasons: the first reason is the emphasis on cost-related factors such as scale economies and absolute cost differences in measuring the height of entry barriers. The height of entry barriers into an industry will be reflected by the extent to which price can exceed average cost in established firms without inducing entry. Earlier in this chapter it has been demonstrated that, given the Sylos postulate, price cannot in the long run exceed average cost in established firms by more than an amount which is directly related to scale economies and absolute cost differences between established firms and potential entrants. In these circumstances, information concerning the magnitude of scale economies and absolute cost differences alone *would* enable one to rank industries in terms of the height of entry barriers. If potential entrants' behavior does not correspond to the Sylos postulate, however, the amount by which price can exceed cost in established firms without inducing entry *need not be related to scale economies and absolute cost differences*. If potential entrants anticipate entry-deterring behavior by established firms, for example, price may exceed average cost in established firms by much more than absolute cost differences or scale economies alone would warrant, without inducing entry. One cannot in these circumstances measure the height of entry barriers only by reference to scale economies and absolute cost differences, because the anticipated reaction of established firms to entry is also relevant in determining the profitability of entry and therefore the behavior of potential entrants. Because the height of entry barriers into an industry depends also on the conjectures of potential entrants concerning the reactions of established firms to their entry, some kind of index is required which would indicate the nature of these anticipated reactions in various industries. If potential entrants into different industries anticipate different kinds of reaction from firms established in those industries, the height of entry barriers and hence the influence of entry barriers on pricing in those industries will not be systematically related to differences in cost-related factors including scale economies and absolute cost differences.

Of course, since the reaction of established firms anticipated by potential entrants is a subjective phenomenon, it cannot be directly observed. Despite this, certain observable characteristics of the structure or behavior of established firms may be influential in determining the nature of these anticipated reactions, and hence the height of entry barriers into particular industries. For example, entry may be more likely to occur if total market demand is increasing over time, for a potential entrant may then be able to enter the market without encroaching upon the sales of established firms and perhaps without necessitating a decline in the profitability of the pre-entry levels of output produced by established firms. As usual, theoretical analysis alone is not conclusive, however; if established firms build capacity in advance of demand this may deter entry even in fast-growing industries, for example (see J. T. Wenders (56, 57) and M. I. Kamien and N. L. Schwartz (25) whose articles deal with excess capacity and entry). Rapidly expanding technology, likewise, may or may not make entry easier and more likely, depending on whether control over technology is in the hands of established firms or potential entrants. Empirical studies are necessary in order to determine the factors which underlie potential entrants' anticipations regarding their actions of established firms before one can estimate the height of entry barriers properly; the current practice of simply *assuming* that the height of entry barriers is systematically related to cost-related factors is inadequate.

The second reason for questioning the accuracy of the entry barrier classifications employed in various empirical studies of entry barriers is connected with their use of industry advertising-intensity variables to measure the magnitude of 'product differentiation' entry barriers into an industry. The analysis of optimal levels of advertising intensity in Chapter 4 indicates that profit rates and advertising intensity in individual firms may be positively related even in the absence of any influence of advertising on entry barriers. In order for advertising to create entry barriers, it must result in a situation in which entrants must spend more than established firms in order to achieve the same level of sales at any particular price level; otherwise the resulting profits of entrants will be no lower than those of established firms. As R. Schmalensee has recently demonstrated (47), the fact that advertising creates brand loyalty does not necessarily mean that advertising creates an entry barrier, if similar levels of advertising by an entrant can result in the same degree of brand loyalty and sales over the life of the advertising's effectiveness. Entry-barrier classifications based on advertising intensity differences between industries may not, therefore, correctly reflect the height of entry barriers into the industries in question. The relationship between non-price aspects of firms' behavior and entry-barrier theory will be examined in more detail in the following section.

Apart from the problem of entry-barrier definition and empirical measurement, another relevant but unsettled issue is the possible existence of simultaneity in the concentration–entry-barrier–profitability relationship. Seller concentration may influence the pricing behavior of established firms directly by influencing their anticipations regarding established firms' reactions (E_{se} in the optimal pricing condition of established firms), without playing any role in influencing potential entrants' anticipations concerning established firms' reactions and therefore without influencing E_{spe}. Another possibility, however, is that seller concentration may not only influence established firms' pricing behavior directly via its influence on E_{se}, but may also influence it indirectly via its impact on potential entrants' behavior and E_{spe}. In these circumstances, the influence of seller concentration and entry barriers on pricing will not be independent as is sometimes inferred. A reasonable degree of agnosticism concerning the precise nature of the concentration–entry-barrier–profitability relationship existing in practice would seem prudent, therefore, until we have more refined empirical measures of entry barriers and statistical techniques which are adequate to determine the nature of the interacting relationships underlying observed relationships between these factors.

Non-Price Aspects of Entry-Barrier Theory*

The conventional theory of entry barriers outlined in the preceding sections of this chapter focuses upon the price and output policies of established firms as a determinant of potential entrants' behavior. According to this body of analysis, advertising or similar non-production activities can affect entry barriers by influencing firms' cost conditions, either causing scale economies or, if entrants must advertise more than established firms in order to achieve any given level of sales, by creating absolute cost differences between established firms and entrants. See D. Mueller and J. E. Tilton (34) and O. E. Williamson (58) whose articles deal with barriers to entry created by R&D and with advertising expenditures, respectively. This approach to the influence of advertising and similar activities on entry barriers is incomplete, however, for several related reasons. Although a situation in which entrants must advertise more than established firms can legitimately be treated in terms of an absolute cost disadvantage for entrant firms, conventional entry-barrier theory does not explain what *determines* the optimal advertising level of established firms and entrants, and the circumstances under which entrants will have higher advertising costs per unit of sales than established firms. A particular level of advertising for entrants and established firms is *implicit* in conventional entry-barrier analysis, since both the market demand curve and demand curve for an entrant's product will depend on the level of advertising undertaken by these firms. Moreover, it is usually simply *assumed* that advertising outlays per unit of sales will be higher for entrants than established firms; as will be demonstrated below this conclusion does not necessarily follow even when established firms' advertising is more effective than that of entrants. The determinants of firms' advertising policies must be explicitly integrated into entry theory, since optimal price and advertising policies of any firm are interrelated. Accordingly, in what follows we shall first consider the implications of advertising expenditures for a potential entrant's behavior, then examine the issue of the circumstances in which it is *possible* for established firms to deter entry by their advertising behavior, and whether it will be *optimal* for them to do so. Although we shall deal with the implications of advertising for entry-barrier theory, the analysis and conclusions apply equally to any type of non-production activities which affect the demand conditions for a firm's product.

The appropriate starting point for analysis of how advertising affects potential entrants' behavior is the profit-maximizing condition which requires that the marginal revenue and marginal cost of any activity such as advertising be equal. In Chapter 4 it was shown that this condition may be written as follows:

$$\frac{A}{S} = \left(\frac{P - MC}{P} \right) E_a$$

where A/S is the firm's optimal ratio of advertising to sales, P is the price of the firm's product, MC the marginal production cost of the firm's product, and E_a is the advertising-elasticity of demand for the firm's product.

Even if $(P - MC)$ is positive, this does not necessarily mean that the firm is making

---

* This section is based on Needham, D., Entry barriers and non-price aspects of firms' behavior, *Journal of Industrial Economics*, September 1976. We are grateful to the publishers and editor of that journal for permission to reprint most of that article here.

profits. One reason is that MC may be below average production cost (AC) due to the existence of economies of scale in production, and if AC is above P the firm will make losses. Assuming, purely for expositional convenience, that production costs are constant at different scales of output so that MC = AC, there is an additional reason why the firm need not be making profits even though $(P - AC)$ is positive. $(P - AC)$, the margin between price and production cost per unit of output, includes expenditures on activities other than production, such as advertising, in addition to any profit. That is

$$\frac{(P - AC)}{P} = \frac{(n + a)}{P}$$

where 'n' and 'a' are the firm's profit and advertising cost per unit of output. Multiplying the numerator and denominator of the expression on the right-hand side of the equality sign by the optimal level of the firm's output, Q^*, yields

$$\frac{(P - AC)}{P} = \frac{(n + a)}{P\,Q^*}Q^* = \frac{\pi}{S} + \frac{A}{S}$$

where π/S is the ratio of the firm's total profits to total sales and A/S is the ratio of the firm's total advertising expenditures to sales. It is clear from the preceding expression that when the optimal advertising–sales ratio for a firm equals $(P - AC)/P$ in magnitude, the firm's profits are zero or negative, respectively. Given the price-elasticity of demand for a firm's product (E_d), which as explained in Chapter 3 determines the firm's profit-maximizing level of $(P - MC)/P$, whether the firm's profits will be positive or not therefore depends on the optimal level of the firm's advertising–sales ratio (A/S), which depends on E_a.

Applying the preceding analysis to a potential entrant, given the expected *output reactions* of established firms and hence the E_d and optimal $(P - MC)/P$ of the potential entrant, whether entry will occur depends on the optimal level of A/S for the entrant. The conventional analysis of entry barrier theory outlined in earlier sections demonstrated that, given the advertising levels of established firms and entrants, whether an entrant's profits are positive, and therefore whether entry will occur, depends on the optimal level of $(P - MC)/P$ for the entrant. It was shown that at any particular level of advertising by the entrant, there is an output reaction by established firms which will deter entry by reducing the level of E_d for the entrant, thereby raising the optimal level of $(P - MC)/P$ for the entrant, to a level which exceeds the $(P - MC)/P$ of established firms. However, in order to determine whether entry will occur it is *also* necessary to indicate what determines the optimal level of A/S for the entrant. The reason for this is that if advertising by an entrant increases demand for the entrant's product, this will increase the entrant's profits if the resulting increase in total revenue exceeds the increase in total costs of the firm.

Given a potential entrant's optimal $(P - MC)/P$, which as previously explained depends on E_d, inspection of the optimal advertising–sales condition reveals that the entrant's optimal A/S depends on E_a, which indicates the response of demand for the entrant's product to the entrant's advertising. When E_a is unity or less at the entrant's optimal advertising level, the entrant's optimal A/S will equal or exceed $(P - MC)/P$, which implies zero profit for the entrant as previously explained and entry will not occur. Since, given E_d and hence $(P - MC)/P$, E_a is the main factor determining the optimal level of the potential entrant's A/S and the profitability of entry, the key question is what determines the magnitude of E_a? As the analysis contained in Chapter 4 demonstrated, E_a depends on the response of buyers to changes in a firm's advertising when other firms' advertising remains unchanged (E_A), and on advertising reactions by rival sellers, in the following manner:

$$E_a = E_A + E_{\text{conj.}} \cdot R_{A_r}$$

where $E_{conj.}$ represents the elasticity of rivals' advertising in response to a change in the firm's advertising, and E_{A_r} represents the elasticity of demand for the firm's product in response to changes in rival firms' advertising.

If a potential entrant expects established firms to react to its advertising by increasing their advertising, $E_{conj.}$ will be a positive number, and since E_{A_r} is generally negative, this will reduce the size of E_a for the potential entrant's product. Clearly, at any given level of $(P - MC)/P$, a sufficiently large anticipated increase in advertising by established firms can always reduce E_a for a potential entrant's product to unity or less, thereby rendering the prospect of entry unprofitable despite advertising by the entrant. In this respect, price- and resulting output-level reactions at a given advertising level, and advertising reactions at a given price level, are substitutes for one another from the point of view of established firms who wish to deter entry. However, just as entry-deterring output reactions by established firms are unlikely to occur unless established firms can deter entry whilst simultaneously making profits themselves, the same is true of entry-deterring advertising reactions. Specifically, the entry-deterring level of A/S for established firms must be lower than the optimal level of A/S for entrants. Otherwise, entry-deterring advertising behavior by established firms would imply zero profits for established firms as well as for entrants at a given level of $(P - MC)/P$.

Since the entry-deterring level of A/S for established firms must be lower than the optimal A/S of entrants in order for established firms to be able to deter entry whilst simultaneously earning profits themselves, it follows that this can occur only if there is some asymmetry in the response of buyer demand to advertising by established firms and by entrants, respectively, which makes it possible for established firms to obtain higher sales per unit of advertising outlay than entrants. The assumption that advertising cost per unit of output sold is higher for entrants than for established firms is often automatically included in discussions of advertising and entry barriers without the support of any rigorous analysis. As already noted, Richard Schmalensee has demonstrated recently (47) that even if advertising creates brand loyalty which extends over several time periods, this does not automatically mean that previous advertising by established firms creates an entry barrier. This is true even if an entrant must incur penetration costs in order to overcome unexpired buyer preference created by previous advertising by established firms. The reason is as follows: the buyer goodwill which is created by a firm's advertising is a depreciating asset, and if the advertising expenditures are properly expensed over the life of the advertising's effectiveness, corresponding to any unexpired portion of this goodwill which an entrant must attempt to overcome there will be a corresponding 'advertising expense' in the accounts of the established firm when properly viewed from an economic point of view. As a result, the advertising cost per unit of sales in any given period will in reality be just as high for established firms as they are for an entrant, in the absence of some asymmetry in demand.

The next point which requires emphasis is that even if the sales associated with any given level of advertising are greater for established firms than for an entrant, this does not necessarily imply that the optimal level of A/S will be lower for established firms than for entrants. This proposition may be demonstrated by reference to Figure 7-7 below, which indicates the total sales revenue associated with different levels of advertising by a potential entrant firm and an established firm, assuming that the price charged by both firms is the same. As indicated, the diagram reflects the assumption that any given level of advertising by an established firm results in more demand and greater sales than the same level of advertising undertaken by an entrant. The *optimal* or profit-maximizing level of a firm's advertising depends on the marginal revenue and marginal cost associated with advertising, which are depicted diagrammatically by the slope of the total revenue and

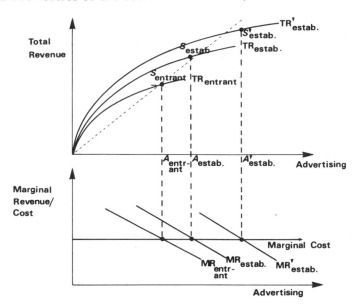

Figure 7–7. Optimal advertising levels of entrant and established firms.

total cost of the firm's activities at different advertising levels. Purely for expositional convenience the firms' total costs are not depicted in Figure 7–7; instead, they are simply assumed to change at a constant rate when advertising changes, so that the marginal cost of advertising is constant as shown in the lower half of the diagram. The optimal level of advertising for the entrant firm is $A_{entrant}$, and the optimal level of advertising for the established firm is either $A_{estab.}$ or $A'_{estab.}$, depending on whether the total revenue curve is $TR_{estab.}$ or $TR'_{estab.}$. Since the marginal cost of advertising is assumed to be the same for all firms, it follows that the advertising's marginal revenue is the same at the optimal advertising level in each firm, reflected diagrammatically by the fact that the slope of each firm's total revenue curve is the same at the optimal advertising level. However, whether the optimal level of A/S is higher for entrants than established firms depends on which total revenue curve is applicable for established firms. The slope of the dotted line from the origin through the point $S_{entrant}$ indicates the optimal S/A ratio for the entrant. $S_{estab.}$ lies above this line, indicating that the optimal S/A for established firms will be higher, and their optimal level of A/S will be lower than that of entrants, if $TR_{estab.}$ is the relevant total revenue curve for established firms. In contrast, if $TR'_{estab.}$ were the relevant curve for established firms, the level of total revenue $S'_{estab.}$ at the optimal advertising level implies a higher optimal level of A/S for established firms than for entrants. Clearly, even when the advertising of established firms is more effective than that of entrants, no generalizations are possible regarding whether the optimal level of A/S will be higher for entrants or established firms.

Thus far this section has explained the circumstances under which it is possible for established firms to adopt advertising policies which prevent an entrant from earning any profits whilst simultaneously earning profits themselves. Entry will not occur if potential entrants anticipate established firms to adopt such entry-deterring behavior, but in order for established firms to be able to deter entry prior to its occurrence it must somehow be possible for them to influence potential entrants' expectations regarding the post-entry behavior of established firms. The situation is exactly analogous to that encountered in the discussion of entry-deterring output reactions in earlier sections. If potential entrants expected established firms to maintain their advertising unchanged in response to entry, as occurs if the Sylos postulate also applies to advertising behavior, established firms would be able to deter entry by adopting entry-deterring advertising levels. Again, however, there is no more reason to suppose that potential entrants in general expect established firms to maintain advertising policies unchanged in response to entry than to anticipate competitive increases or accommodating reductions in advertising in response to entry. The factors which determine potential entrants' anticipations regarding the post-entry behavior of established firms are crucial in determining the validity of theories purporting to show that established firms' behavior will be influenced by potential entrants, since such theories stand or fall on the question of whether the post-entry behavior of established firms anticipated by potential entrants is systematically related to the pre-entry behavior of established firms. If potential entrants' anticipations regarding the post-entry behavior of established firms are determined by factors which are unrelated to the current behavior of established firms and which are largely outside the control of established firms, such as existing levels of seller concentration, anticipated antitrust reactions, or past behavior of established firms, for example, it follows that attempts by established firms to deter entry by adopting certain pre-entry policies will be ineffective. Despite its obvious importance, however, the issue of what factors actually determine potential entrants' expectations regarding the post-entry behavior of established firms has received virtually no theoretical or empirical attention in the literature to date. As a result, the fundamentally important question of whether it is *possible* for established firms to deter entry, even if asymmetry in the response of demand to advertising by entrants and established firms is present, remains unanswered.

There is another similarity between the earlier discussion of entry-deterring output reactions and the present discussion of entry-deterring advertising reactions. If there is asymmetry in the response of demand to advertising by entrants and established firms, and if, in addition, established firms are able to influence potential entrants' expectations regarding the post-entry behavior of established firms, entry-deterring advertising behavior by established firms will be possible, and profitable. However, whether it will be *optimal*, in the sense of maximizing established firms' profits, is also relevant in determining whether established firms will actually adopt entry-deterring advertising strategies or will instead adopt other strategies and allow entry to occur. As in the case of entry-deterring price and output policies, discussed earlier in this chapter, even if potential entrants' behavior is related to the pre-entry advertising behavior of established firms, the *exact form* of this reaction function will be relevant in determining whether or not entry-deterring behavior will be optimal from the viewpoint of established firms. The reaction function can take many different forms, each with different consequences in terms of the profits of established firms and entrants, and no generalizations regarding the optimality of entry-deterring advertising behavior are therefore possible.

Before concluding this section, it is appropriate to indicate and comment upon some of the results of empirical studies of the relationship between advertising and entry barriers which have been undertaken to date. A conclusion which is reached consistently in these studies is that a positive and statistically significant relationship between profit rates and advertising intensity in firms and industries remains after eliminating the effects of other explanatory variables which underlie profitability (see W. S. Comanor and T. A. Wilson (12), for example). Two major issues still remain to be resolved, however. The first is whether the observed positive correlation between advertising intensity and profit rates is attributable to the fact that profit rates have been incorrectly measured due to inappropriate accounting treatment of advertising expenditures. The profit rate measures which are used in empirical studies generally equal the ratio of reported profits to reported assets or net worth of the firms studied. For accounting purposes firms treat advertising expenditures as a current expense, which is inappropriate if advertising has effects on buyer behavior and sales which extend over a number of periods. If advertising has such long-lived effects, it is like an investment expenditure since it creates an asset, buyer goodwill, which depreciates over time. The proper accounting treatment is then to allocate to the firm's costs in any period only a portion of the advertising outlay corresponding to the current depreciation of the total stock of buyer goodwill created by the advertising outlay in question.

Because the reported assets on the balance sheets of firms exclude the value of the undepreciated stock of buyer goodwill created by advertising in earlier periods, the reported *net worth of firms is understated.* However, whether this means that measured profit rates will be above true profit rates, defined as the profit rates which would prevail if advertising expenditures were treated as an investment and depreciated over their full economic lives, depends in addition on the effect of treating advertising as a current expense on the *reported profits* of firms. If an advertising outlay with long-lived effects is treated as a current expense, the reported profits of the firm in a given period will *exceed* their true level if current advertising outlays are less than an amount corresponding to the depreciation of buyer goodwill resulting from advertising in earlier periods. In this case, the expensing of advertising will clearly lead to overstatement of true profit rates. In contrast, if current advertising exceeds the depreciation associated with advertising in earlier periods, which corresponds to a situation where a firm's net investment in advertising is positive in the current period, reported profits of the firm will be less than true profits. In this case, therefore, although reported net worth understates true net worth, whether ratios of reported profit and net worth over- or understate true profit rates depends on the degree to which reported profits understate true profits. This depends on factors such as the rate of growth of firms' advertising expenditures and the rate of depreciation of the buyer goodwill created by advertising, which can vary between firms and industries. Empirical evidence concerning these factors is therefore needed in order to determine whether reported profit rates will over- or understate true profit rates in practice. In a study published in 1969 (54), L. W. Weiss attempted to adjust the profit rates of a sample of industries to correct for the influence of expensing of advertising, and concluded that the necessary adjustments did not significantly change the strong positive relationship between industry profit rates and industry advertising intensity. In a recent article, however, Harry Bloch (8) has questioned the accuracy of Weiss's profit rate adjustments, on the grounds that the use of industry data involves aggregation problems. Bloch found that when corrections for the expensing of advertising are made to the reported profit rates of a sample of firms instead of industries, no positive relationship between firms' profit rates and advertising intensity remains.

As the preceding discussion indicates, there is as yet no consensus as to whether correctly measured profit rates of firms and industries are positively correlated with advertising intensity. Even if advertising intensity and profit rates were found to be positively related when profit rates are correctly measured, a second major issue would remain to be resolved; namely, whether the positive relationship is attributable to the influence of advertising on entry barriers and the resulting behavior of potential entrants or whether it can instead be explained wholly in terms of the influence of advertising on the behavior of established firms. In approaching this second issue, a problem immediately presents itself. While there exists a well-defined theoretical framework showing the circumstances in which the reported profit rates of firms will over- or understate true profit rates, no generally accepted theoretical framework exists to date for dealing with the relationship between advertising and entry barriers. Although it is often simply assumed that advertising by established firms creates entry barriers, the analysis earlier in this section clearly demonstrates that advertising may or may not create entry barriers depending on a number of relevant factors. The key considerations were shown to be (i) the nature of the post-entry behavior of established firms anticipated by potential entrants, and (ii) whether these anticipations are related to the pre-entry behavior of established firms.

In order to provide perspective over the issue of whether a positive relationship between profit rates and advertising intensity reflects entry barriers related to advertising, it is useful to start by considering again the following profit-maximizing advertising-intensity condition for an individual firm:

$$\frac{A}{S} = \frac{(P - MC)}{P} \cdot E_a, \text{ or } \frac{A}{S} = \frac{E_a}{E_d}$$

where the symbols have exactly the same meaning as in earlier discussions. Some economists (J. M. Vernon and R. E. M. Nourse (53), for example) have attempted to explain why one would expect to find a positive correlation between advertising intensity and profit rates for reasons other than entry barriers by reference to the above condition as follows: if the only difference between firms in two different industries is that $\frac{P - MC}{P}$ in industry A is higher than in industry B, it follows that the optimal advertising–sales ratio will also be higher in A than in B, and if $\frac{P - MC}{P}$ is positively correlated with profit rates, advertising intensity and profit rates will be positively correlated also. When MC = AC, profit rates and $(P - MC)/P$ will be positively correlated, for the following reasons: Since $(P - AC)/P = (\pi/S + A/S)$, it follows that, when MC = AC, a lower level of E_d will imply a proportionate increase in the optimal level of $(P - AC)/P$, A/S, and π/S. However, it must be remembered that although optimal advertising intensity and $(P - MC)/P$ are positively associated when E_a is given, a higher level of $(P - MC)/P$ could itself still be attributable to entry barriers related to advertising. The price-elasticity of demand for a firm's product, E_d, depends on a number of factors including the firm's anticipations regarding the reactions of its rivals, either established firms or potential entrants, to price changes initiated by the firm. By influencing the anticipated reactions of potential entrants, advertising policies of established firms could influence E_d for the products of established firms and therefore the optimal level of $(P - MC)/P$. In order for this to occur, established firms' current advertising policies must influence the potential entrants' expectations regarding the post-entry behavior of established firms, as was emphasized earlier in this section.

It is illuminating to determine precisely what conditions are necessary in order to produce a positive relationship between optimal levels of firms' A/S and profit–sales ratios or profit rates by reference to the optimal advertising condition. As explained in the preceding paragraph, when MC = AC a reduction in E_d and consequent increase in the optimal level of $(P - MC)/P$ will be associated with a proportionate increase in the optimal level of A/S and a proportionate increase in the profit–sales ratio (π/S) if E_a is unchanged. The optimal advertising condition also indicates that an increase in the magnitude of E_a at any level of advertising will increase the optimal level of A/S at any given level of $(P - MC)/P$ and the associated level of $(P - AC)/P$. Because $(P - AC)/P = (\pi/S + A/S)$, it follows that an increase in E_a will reduce π/S, however. These relationships imply that firms with higher optimal levels of A/S and profit–sales ratios must have lower levels of E_d, and levels of E_a which may be the same, or higher or lower, than in firms with lower advertising intensity and profit–sales ratios. If E_a levels are similar in different firms, profit rates and optimal levels of A/S will increase proportionately if MC = AC as already explained. Alternatively, profit rates will increase (i) less than proportionately with A/S if E_a is higher in firms with larger optimal levels of A/S, and (ii) more than proportionately with A/S if E_a is lower in firms with larger optimal levels of A/S. In the last case, since $A/S = E_a/E_d$, the reduction in E_a at higher levels of A/S must obviously be less than proportionate to the reduction in E_d. The form of the positive relationship between A/S and profit rates in different firms and industries observed in practice will reveal which of these situations occurs in practice. The main point, however, is that in order to determine whether an observed positive correlation between profit rates and advertising intensity is attributable to advertising entry barriers, it is necessary to determine *why* E_d and E_a levels are different in firms and industries with higher advertising intensity and profit rates. The reader is reminded that E_d and E_a each depend on several factors, including anticipated buyer reactions to a firm's price and advertising policies (E_m and E_A), anticipated reactions of established rival sellers (E_{se} and $E_{conj.e}$), and anticipated reactions of potential entrants (E_{sp} and $E_{conj.p}$). The relationships between these factors, already discussed earlier in this section, are reproduced below for convenience, with the symbols e and p representing established rival firms and potential entrants respectively:

$$E_d = \frac{E_m + (E_{se} + E_{sp})(1 - S_f)}{S_f}$$

$$E_a = E_A + (E_{conj.e} + E_{conj.p}) . E_{Ar}$$

With these relationships in mind, it is clear that three different types of explanation may account for firms and industries with larger optimal levels of A/S and profit–sales rates: (i) Differences in *buyer reactions* between industries may explain why E_d and E_a differ between industries, in other words, E_m and E_A, the price and advertising elasticities of market demand, may differ between products and industries. (iii) Differences in the anticipated *reactions of established rivals* may account for differences in E_d and E_a between firms and industries. Larger anticipated increases in established rivals' output levels in response to price reductions by a firm reduce E_d, and larger anticipated increases in advertising by established rivals in response to an increase in advertising by the firm reduce E_a, for example. However, it needs to be emphasized that the reactions which a firm anticipates from its established rivals need not necessarily be the result of their current advertising policies; they may instead be related to other characteristics of established rivals which happen to be positively associated with their current advertising levels. Whether the degree of seller concentration is a plausible explanatory factor in this connection remains an open question since different studies have obtained conflicting results regarding the existence of a statistically significant positive correlation between concentration and industry advertising intensity. (iii) Differences in the anticipated *reactions of potential entrants* may account for differences in E_d and E_a resulting in higher optimal advertising intensity and profit rates. Again, however, these differences may or may not be related to the *current* advertising policies of established firms, since it is the anticipated post-entry behavior of established firms which determines potential entrants' behavior. In order for potential entrants' behavior to be affected by the current advertising policies of established firms, there must be some systematic link between this behavior and the post-entry behavior of established firms anticipated by potential entrants. Moreover, even if this link exists so that established firms could deter entry by adopting suitable pre-entry advertising strategies, whether they actually do so depends on whether such strategies are optimal from the point of view of established firms.

As the preceding paragraph indicates, an observed positive relationship between advertising intensity and profit rates may be the result of factors underlying E_d and E_a other than entry barriers influencing the behavior of potential entrants created by established firms' advertising. Therefore, until we can explain why E_d and E_a are different for firms and industries with higher optimal advertising intensity and profit rates, and until we are able to reject other plausible explanations, it is premature to attribute this relationship to the influence of established firms' advertising policies on potential entrants' behavior.

In a recent empirical study J. M. Vernon and R. E. M. Nourse (53) found that the positive correlation between industry advertising intensity and industry profit rates was stronger than that between the advertising intensity and profit rates of individual firms. The authors concluded that this finding supports the hypothesis that the relationship is attributable to advertising entry barriers rather than alternative explanatory hypotheses, claiming that the reverse finding would be true if the advertising–profitability relationship were attributable to other factors. This conclusion is invalid, however, since it is not difficult to see why a positive association between advertising intensity and profit rates *should* be stronger when firms are grouped into industries than when they are not, whether or not advertising entry barriers are present. Firms which operate in the same industry are likely to have similar E_d and E_a levels, and therefore similar relationships between profit rate and A/S levels, because E_m, E_A, and the anticipated reactions of established firms and potential entrants into the industry will be similar for individual firms in that industry. In contrast, firms operating in different industries are more likely to have different levels of E_d and E_a, due to differences in E_m, E_A, or the anticipated reactions of established and potential rivals between industries, resulting in a weaker relationship between profit rate and A/S levels when the firms are not grouped into industries. For these reasons, one would therefore expect to find a closer correlation between the advertising intensity and profit rates of industries (i.e., groups of firms selling in the same markets) than between the advertising intensity and profit rates of individual firms in different industries, whatever the underlying causes of differences in E_d and E_a between firms in different industries. The issue of whether a positive relationship between advertising intensity and profit rates is attributable to entry barriers associated with advertising by established firms remains unresolved, therefore.

RECOMMENDED READINGS

 1. Alemson, M. A. and Burley, H. T., Demand and entry into an oligopolistic market: a case study, *Journal of Industrial Economics*, December 1974.
 2. Bain, J. S., A note on pricing in monopoly and oligopoly, *American Economic Review*, March 1949.
 3. Bain, J. S., Conditions of entry and the emergence of monopoly. In Chamberlin, E. H. (Ed.) *Monopoly and Competition and their Regulation* (London: Macmillan & Co., 1954), pp. 215–241.
 4. Bain, J. S., *Barriers to New Competition* (Cambridge, Mass.: Harvard University Press, 1956).
 5. Baron, D. P., Limit pricing and models of potential entry, *Western Economic Journal*, September 1972.
 6. Baron, D. P., Limit pricing, potential entry, and barriers to entry, *American Economic Review*, September 1973.
 7. Bhagwati, J., Oligopoly theory, entry-prevention, and growth, *Oxford Economic Papers*, November 1970.
 8. Bloch, H., Advertising and profitability: a reappraisal, *Journal of Political Economy*, March–April 1974.
 9. Brozen, Y., Barriers facilitate entry, *Antitrust Bulletin*, Winter 1969.
10. Brunner, E., A note on potential competition, *Journal of Industrial Economics*, July 1961.
11. Cohen, H. A., Effects of demand and cost changes on the 'limit price', *Mississippi Valley Journal of Business and Economics*, Winter 1971–1972.

12. Comanor, W. S. and Wilson, T. A., Advertising, market structure and performance, *Review of Economics and Statistics*, November 1967.
13. Deutsch, L. L., Structure performance, and the net rate of entry into manufacturing industries, *Southern Economic Journal*, January 1975.
14. Frank, C. R. Jr, Entry in a Cournot market, *Review of Economic Studies*, July 1965.
15. Gaskins, D. W., Dynamic limit pricing: optimal pricing under threat of entry, *Journal of Economic Theory*, September 1971.
16. George, D. W., Concentration, barriers to entry and rates of return, *Review of Economics and Statistics*, May 1968.
17. Goldberg, V. and Moirao, S., Limit pricing and potential competition, *Journal of Political Economy*, November–December 1973.
18. Gupta, V. K., Cost functions, concentration, and entry barriers in 29 manufacturing industries of India, *Journal of Industrial Economics*, November 1968.
19. Hines, H., Effectiveness of 'entry' by already established firms, *Quarterly Journal of Economics*, February 1957.
20. Imel, B. and Helmberger, P., Estimation of structure–profit relationships with application to the food processing sector, *American Economic Review*, September 1971.
21. Johns, B. L., Barriers to entry in a dynamic setting, *Journal of Industrial Economics*, November 1962.
22. Kamerschen, D. R., An empirical test of oligopoly theories, *Journal of Political Economy*, July–August 1968.
23. Kamerschen, D. R., The determination of profit rates in 'oligopolistic industries', *Journal of Business*, July 1969.
24. Kamien, M. I. and Schwartz, N. L., Limit pricing and uncertain entry, *Econometrica*, May 1971.
25. Kamien, M. I. and Schwartz, N. L., Uncertain entry and excess capacity, *American Economic Review*, December 1972.
26. Kottke, F. J., Market entry and the character of competition, *Western Economic Journal*, December 1966.
27. Lee, W. Y., Oligopoly and entry, *Journal of Economic Theory*, August 1975.
28. Mann, H. M., Seller concentration, barriers to entry, and rates of return in thirty industries, 1950–1960, *Review of Economics and Statistics*, August 1966.
29. Mann, H. M., A note on barriers to entry and long-run profitability, *Antitrust Bulletin*, Winter 1969.
30. Mann, H. M., Asymmetry, entry barriers and rates of return in 26 concentrated industries 1948–57, *Western Economic Journal*, March 1970.
31. Mann, H. M., The interaction of barriers and concentration: a reply, *Journal of Industrial Economics*, July 1971.
32. Mann, H. M., Concentration, barriers to entry and rates of return revisited: a reply, *Journal of Industrial Economics*, April 1973.
33. Modigliani, F., New developments on the oligopoly front, *Journal of Political Economy*, June 1958.
34. Mueller, D. C. and Tilton, J. E., R&D costs as a barrier to entry, *Canadian Journal of Economics*, November 1969.
35. Myers, M. and Weintraub, E. R., A dynamic model of firm entry, *Review of Economic Studies*, Vol. 38, 1971.
36. Needham, D., Entry barriers and non-price aspects of firms' behavior, *Journal of Industrial Economics*, September 1976.
37. Orr, D., The determinants of entry: a study of Canadian manufacturing industries, *Review of Economics and Statistics*, February 1974.
38. Orr, D., An index of entry barriers and its application to the market structure performance relationship, *Journal of Industrial Economics*, September 1974.
39. Osborne, D. K., The role of entry in oligopoly theory, *Journal of Political Economy*, August 1964.
40. Osborne, D. K., On the rationality of limit pricing, *Journal of Industrial Economics*, September 1973, pp. 71–80.
41. Pashigian, P., Limit price and the market share of the leading firm, *Journal of Industrial Economics*, July 1968.
42. Pyatt, F. G., Profit maximization and the threat of new entry, *Economic Journal*, June 1971.
43. Qualls, D., Concentration, barriers to entry, and long-run economic profit margins, *Journal of Industrial Economics*, April 1972.
44. Qualls, D., Stability and persistence of economic profit margins in highly concentrated industries, *Southern Economic Journal*, April 1974.
45. Quandt, R. E. and Howrey, P., The dynamics of the number of firms in an industry, *Review of Economic Studies*, Vol. 35, July 1968.
46. Rhoades, S. A., Concentration, barriers, and rates of return: a note, *Journal of Industrial Economics*, November 1970.
47. Schmalensee, R., Brand loyalty and barriers to entry, *Southern Economic Journal*, April 1974, pp. 579–588.
48. Schmalensee, R., Advertising and profitability: further implications of the null hypothesis, *Journal of*

Industrial Economics, September 1976.
49. Sherman, R. and Willett, T. D., Potential entrants discourage entry, *Journal of Political Economy*, August 1967.
50. Siegfried, J. J. and Weiss, L. W., Advertising, profits, and corporate taxes revisited, *Review of Economics and Statistics*, May 1974.
51. Sylos-Labini, P., *Oligopoly and Technical Progress* (Cambridge, Mass.: Harvard University Press, 1962).
52. Vernon, J. M. and McElroy, M. B., Estimation of structure–profit relationships: comment, *American Economic Review*, September 1973.
53. Vernon, J. M. and Nourse, R. E. M., Profit rates and market structure of advertising intensive firms, *Journal of Industrial Economics*, September 1973, pp. 1–19.
54. Weiss, L. W., Advertising, profits, and corporate taxes, *Review of Economics and Statistics*, November 1969.
55. Wenders, J. T., Entry and Monopoly Pricing, *Journal of Political Economy*, October 1967.
56. Wenders, J. T., Collusion and entry, *Journal of Political Economy*, November–December 1971.
57. Wenders, J. T., Excess capacity as a barrier to entry, *Journal of Industrial Economics*, November 1971.
58. Williamson, O. E., Selling expenses as a barrier to entry, *Quarterly Journal of Economics*, February 1963.

CHAPTER EIGHT

VERTICAL INTEGRATION

The degree of vertical integration refers to a state of industrial organization; it refers to the extent to which successive stages involved in the production of a particular product or service are performed by different firms, or the converse, the extent to which a firm performs different successive stages in the production of a particular product. Vertical integration is also used to describe the action of a firm in acquiring or constructing facilities for carrying out productive stages which formerly either preceded or succeeded its original productive activities. Backward and forward vertical integration refer to the acquisition of preceding or succeeding stages respectively. Where two existing firms merge, and the decision is a joint one, whether the situation is one of backward or forward vertical integration depends upon the point of view. One can also distinguish partial from complete vertical integration, considering any two successive stages. In the former case, a firm may still use the market for acquiring part of its supplies, or for the disposal of part of its output, producing only part of its total requirements of a particular input, or processing further only part of its output at an earlier stage.

If one defines the output of different stages as different products, vertical integration is an aspect of diversification. However, the considerations motivating firms to diversify in the sense of vertical integration, and the results, differ in a number of respects from the considerations motivating diversification in the sense of producing vertically unrelated outputs. In this book, the term diversification refers only to activities that are not vertically related.

Determinants of Vertical Integration

In discussing the determinants of vertical integration we shall first consider the motives prompting backward integration.

Consider a firm purchasing inputs and combining these to produce a particular final product. Some of the inputs purchased may themselves be the final product or service of firms at an earlier stage of the productive process. Backward integration by the firm at the later stage may reduce the cost of producing the firm's final product, for one or both of the following reasons. First, even though the cost of performing each successive stage remains unchanged, or increases, profits included in the price formerly paid to firms selling the product of earlier stages can be avoided, and on balance the cost of obtaining the output of the earlier stage may be reduced. Second, and perhaps more important, vertical integration may mean that certain costs of using the market are avoided, thereby reducing the cost of performing the successive stages when these are combined under a single managerial supervision. Costs of using the market may fall on one or both of two separate firms performing vertically related productive processes, and can take many different forms. For example, a firm at an earlier stage may engage in advertising or other sales promotion activities aimed at securing the custom of firms at the later stage. The second stage of a vertically integrated firm provides, on the other hand, a certain market for the output of the firm's first stage. Alternatively, an unintegrated firm performing a later stage may keep a greater level of stocks of the product of the earlier stage than if it controls the earlier stage itself and can therefore coordinate the flow of output between different stages. As a final example, if each successive stage in the production of a particular final product requires that the output of the previous stage be heated, the cost of the final product may be reduced by performing the successive operations before cooling of intermediate outputs takes place.

There are many other examples of the way in which costs of using the market can be avoided by vertical integration. However, vertical integration may result in additional costs which would not be present in the unintegrated firms. Coordinating two successive stages may, for example, require administrative inputs over and above those required to run the two separate stages, resulting in additional administrative costs per unit of final output. Any such costs of vertical integration must be compared with the saving in costs of using the market plus intermediate profit payments avoided, in order to determine whether backward vertical integration will reduce costs of the final product.

By reducing the cost of producing the integrating firm's final product, backward vertical integration may contribute to a number of different objectives. A firm with profit-maximizing objectives will integrate backwards if this reduces the total cost of producing any given level of its final product for, given the demand conditions for its final product, a reduction in cost at any level of output represents an increase in profit at that level of output.

It must be stressed that a profit-maximizing firm may not produce the same level of final output after integration. As explained in this chapter in the section entitled Vertical Integration and Level of Output, the scale of the firm's final output will remain unchanged if the cost saving attributable to vertical integration is the same at all levels of output. In this case the slope of the firm's total cost curve, and therefore marginal cost of final output, remains unchanged, as does marginal revenue if demand conditions at the final stage are constant. If the cost saving decreases with scale of final output, the profit-maximizing level of final output will decrease as a result of vertical integration; the reverse is true if the cost saving increases with scale of final output.

A firm with sales-revenue-maximizing objectives will also integrate backwards provided that the cost of the final product is thereby reduced. The act of backward vertical integration itself does not increase sales revenue. However, it was pointed out in Chapter 1 that a sales-revenue maximizer is constrained by the need to make some profits, either to finance current dividend payments or growth of output and sales revenue in the next period. If the unintegrated sales-revenue maximizer is producing a level of final output which satisfies this constraint, a reduction in the cost of that output and consequent increase in profits will permit sales revenues to be increased. In contrast to the profit maximizer, backward vertical integration by a sales-revenue maximizer will always lead to an increase in the scale of final output because, given demand conditions for the final product, increases in sales revenue can only be obtained by increasing the scale of output, assuming of course that price elasticity of demand for the final product exceeds unity so that marginal revenue is positive.

Finally, consider a firm which desires to maximize the growth rate of some aspect of the firm's operations. In Chapter 1 it was pointed out that growth depends upon profits, because profits are required either to finance growth internally, or to obtain additional external finance. If backward vertical integration increases profits, it will increase the maximum attainable growth rate of the firm; therefore, a growth rate maximizer will also integrate if this reduces the cost of producing its final product.

We have been discussing the considerations motivating a firm to integrate backwards, pointing out that, given the demand conditions for its final product, any move that reduced the cost of a given output level must increase the profits associated with that output level. The reduction in cost may be the result of eliminating an intermediate profit, or may also include a reduction in the actual costs of performing successive productive stages when these are combined under a single managerial supervision.

Forward vertical integration may take place for reasons similar to those motivating backward vertical integration. If the cost of performing successive stages is not affected, the integrating firm will be able to add to the profits from performing its original stage the profits associated with performing the later stage, which depend upon the cost and demand conditions associated with the later stage. Integration may, in addition, reduce the cost of performing the combined stages by eliminating costs of using the market; any such reduction will represent an additional increase in profits over and above the profit that can be earned by unintegrated firms performing the later stage. Against these two sources of increased profit must be set any costs of vertical integration, in order to determine whether forward vertical integration is on balance profitable.

A firm may integrate forward partially in order to separate the market for the product of its original stage and increase the firm's profits by enabling it to discriminate on a price basis. In the absence of vertical integration, the possibility of resale between different sectors of the market for the unintegrated firm's product may prevent price discrimination even though it would be profitable. Consider, for example, a firm selling to buyers located in two different geographical areas. For simplicity, assume that transportation costs between seller and each area are the same. If the elasticity of demand for the product at any particular price differs in the two areas, the firm could earn more profit if it charges a different price for its product in each area than by charging the same price in each area. Any attempt to charge a different mill price to buyers in the different areas will, however, tend to be thwarted by resale from low-price to high-price buyers. In order to separate the markets and prevent such resale, the firm could integrate forward and perform also the transportation stage. In these circumstances, the prices charged in the two areas can differ by any amount up to the cost of transporting the product direct between the two areas before resale from low-price to high-price area becomes profitable. As indicated in Chapter 3 in the section entitled Price Discrimination, the seller need not necessarily perform the transportation function himself in order to separate the market; an alternative method of separating the market would be to charge delivered prices while hiring the services of some independent firm to transport the product from seller to buyers.

The fact that a firm expects vertical integration to increase its profits is not, by itself, sufficient to result in integration. Performing productive processes that are linked to each other vertically requires the investment of capital in the productive activities carried out at each stage. Differences in vertical integration between firms may reflect differences in the supply of capital available to the firms rather than differences in the expected profitability of vertical integration. Finally, even though a firm has sufficient capital to meet the requirements of vertical integration, the firm will not integrate unless the profit per unit of capital invested in performing an additional stage exceeds the return that could be earned if the capital were invested elsewhere, including additional investment in diversification or horizontal growth in existing markets. Only if vertical growth achieves the firm's objectives better than these other forms of expansion will the firm select this form of investment. Thus, for example, even though a firm can perform a stage of production preceding or succeeding its current operations just as efficiently as firms currently performing the stage, and can therefore cut out the middleman's profit by integrating, there will be no incentive to do so if the firms currently performing that stage are earning only normal profits.

Vertical Integration and Level of Output

In this section we shall consider the effect of vertical integration, that is, the combining under one decision-making unit of two or more formerly independent successive stages involved in the production of a particular product, on the price and output of the final product. It will be assumed, for the present, that conditions of demand for the final product remain unchanged, and that firms wish to maximize profits.

If vertical integration leaves the cost conditions associated with each stage in the productive process unchanged, then vertical integration will not change the price and level of output of the final product in each of the three following cases:

1. Vertical integration between two firms at successive purely competitive stages.
2. Vertical integration between a monopoly at one stage and a single firm at another purely competitive stage.
3. Vertical integration between a monopoly at one stage and all of the firms at a purely competitive stage.

In cases 1 and 2, combined firm profits will not, for example, be increased if the first stage of the combined firm sells its output to the second stage at a lower price than before integration. Since demand conditions facing stage two, and cost conditions facing stage one are unchanged, this merely transfers profits from the first to the second stage, leaving profits of the combined firm the same as before vertical integration. Likewise, combined profits will not be increased if the second stage of the combined firm pays more to the first stage for inputs; this merely transfers profits from the second to the first stage.

In case 3, if the monopoly is at the second stage, formerly buying inputs from a purely competitive earlier stage, it is easy to understand why vertical integration between the two stages will not affect the price and output of the final product. Before integration, the supply curve of the purely competitive stage was part of the average cost curve of the monopolist; after vertical integration this is still the case, the only difference being that the portion of average cost formerly comprising the monopolist's purchases from other firms is now part of the value added of the integrated firm.

It is less obvious, but equally true, that vertical integration between a monopolist at stage one and a purely competitive industry at stage two will leave the level of final output unchanged (given constant final demand conditions and cost conditions at each stage of production). It is less obvious because, after all, elementary economic theory concludes that, all other things remaining equal, monopolization of a purely competitive industry will raise price and reduce output in that industry. However, this proposition concerning monopoly and the level of output is valid as long as there is a monopoly at *any one* of a number of separate successive stages in the productive process, and mere combination of successive stages will not change the level of output because the already existing monopoly at one stage will have *taken into account* the effect of its output level on the price of the final product. Figure 8–1 may help to clarify this point.

In order to simplify the diagrammatic exposition, it is assumed that one unit of the output of Stage 2 requires one unit of the output of Stage 1; that is, it is assumed that the

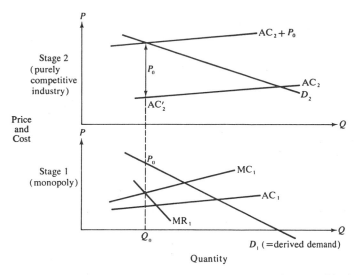

Figure 8–1. Vertical integration between a monopolist and a purely competitive industry.

inputs are combined in fixed proportions to yield a unit of the final product. This means that revenues and costs associated with levels of output of one stage can be expressed as a function of levels of output of the other stage also. Before integration, the demand curve confronting the monopolist at Stage 1 is a derived demand curve obtained by subtracting, from the demand price associated with any given quantity of the final product, the average cost (AC_2) of transforming a unit of the monopolist's product into a unit of the final product. The profit-maximizing monopolist will sell Q_0 units of output at P_0 per unit, and the total supply price of final output will be $(AC_2' + P_0)$.

In order to examine the effect of vertical integration on the level of output, let us concentrate on the diagram depicting equilibrium at Stage 1. When the two firms combine, the monopolist's demand curve shifts upward and becomes the final demand curve; also, the monopolist's average cost curve shifts upward, because the average cost of performing Stage 2 is now added to that of Stage 1 in order to obtain the average cost of performing both stages in the integrated firm. What effect will this have on the optimal (profit-maximizing) level of output? The answer is none, for although the monopolist's marginal revenue and marginal cost curves both change as the result of vertical integration, they each change by the same amount at any given level of output.*

---

*Since, for any given quantity of output,

final demand price = derived demand price + Stage 2 AC
and
combined AC = Stage 1 AC + Stage 2 AC

it follows that the demand price and average cost associated with any given level of the monopolist's output are each increased by the same amount as a result of vertical integration. Hence TC and TR are each increased by the same amount at any given level of output. Selecting any two levels of output, and using subscripts to refer to these two levels of output,

change in TR_2 − change in TR_1 = change in slope of TR
and
change in TC_2 − change in TC_1 = change in slope of TC

Since the change in TR_2 is equal to the change in TC_2, and since the change in TR_1 equals the change in TC_1, the slope of the TR curve is changed by the same amount as the slope of the TC curve; that is, marginal revenue and marginal cost are changed by the same amount at any level of output.

What can be said of the effect of vertical integration on the optimal level of final output if vertical integration changes the cost conditions at one or more stages of the combined firm? By using the above analysis, we can explain the condition that must be satisfied in order that vertical integration *will not* change the optimal level of final output.

If, for example, vertical integration reduces the average cost of producing the final output, it is as though, in the previous diagram, after vertical integration has occurred, the combined average cost curve now shifts down. At any output level, this will reduce the total cost associated with the two stages of the productive process. However, the optimal level of output will not be changed if the slope of the total cost curve remains unchanged at every level of output. For this to happen, total cost must be reduced by the same absolute amount at any level of output, that is, the cost saving must be independent of the level of output produced.

It is apparent that, even apart from the case of price discrimination or that of bilateral monopoly, both of which are discussed below, one must qualify the statement that vertical integration will leave the optimal level of output of the final product unchanged. For this to be the case, either vertical integration must not change cost conditions at any stage of the productive process or, if it does so, any change in total cost must be independent of the level of output produced.

There are two cases in which vertical integration may change the output level and price of the final product, even though demand conditions for the final product, and cost conditions at each stage of the productive process, remain unchanged. The first is associated with price discrimination, the second with bilateral monopoly, which is a situation in which a single seller, or monopolist, deals with a single buyer, or monopsonist.

Forward vertical integration by a monopolist may permit a policy of price discrimination, formerly impossible because of the possibility of resale between different sectors of the monopolist's market, to be practiced. For reasons explained in Chapter 3, the ability to discriminate on a price basis may either increase or decrease the optimal level of the monopolist's output, and hence the output of the final product.

Finally, still assuming constant demand conditions for the final product and unchanged cost conditions at each stage, vertical integration between a monopolist and a monopsonist at successive stages of the productive process can, in certain circumstances, lower the price and increase output of the final product. This can be illustrated with the aid of Figure 8-2.

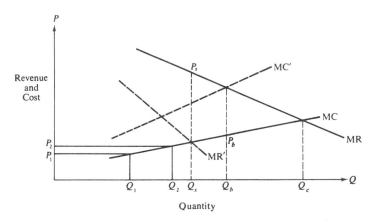

Figure 8-2. Vertical integration and bilateral monopoly.

The curve labeled MC is the marginal cost curve of S, the monopolist, and MR is the marginal revenue product curve of B, the monopsonist. Curve MR indicates the marginal revenue obtained by B from employing different quantities of the monopolist's output. At a fixed price, such as P_1, S would be willing to supply Q_1 units of output (an amount which equates the monopolist's marginal revenue and marginal cost), at P_2, S would be willing to supply Q_2, and so on. That is, the average cost curve of the product to the buyer, B, is MC, and the curve marginal to MC, labeled MC' in Figure 8–2, is the marginal cost of the product to B. The monopsonist would maximize profits if price were P_b and quantity supplied Q_b, for at this combination B's marginal cost (MC') equals his marginal revenue product (MR). The monopolist, S, however, desires a different price–quantity combination. MR indicates the quantities that B would be willing to buy at alternative fixed prices of the monopolist's product, and is therefore the average revenue curve of the monopolist. The curve marginal to MR, labeled MR', is therefore the marginal revenue to S, and the monopolist would maximize profits if price were P_s and quantity demanded Q_s.

The price agreed, and quantity of the monopolist's product traded, will depend upon bargaining between the parties, and there are numerous possibilities. If bargaining takes place in terms of price only, the agreed price will lie between P_s and P_b because, at a price above P_s both parties would agree to lower price, while at a price below P_b both parties would agree to raise price. The output traded at the agreed price may, however, be less than Q_c, the output level which maximizes the joint profits of the two firms. If the two firms integrate, the output decision will be determined with regard to the original MR and MC curves, and the level of output of the intermediate product may be increased relative to the output resulting under bilateral monopoly. Given the assumption of fixed production coefficients between the output of the monopolist and the final product sold by the monopsonist, levels of intermediate output indicate also quantities of the final product.

Variable Input Proportions and Vertical Integration

A crucial assumption underlies the analysis contained in the preceding section, namely, that the inputs used to produce a unit of final output are combined in fixed proportions whether two successive stages of production are vertically integrated or not. The consequences of removing this assumption are fundamental, and will be dealt with in this section. The major implication of variable input proportions is to change the conclusion that vertical integration between a monopolist at one stage of production and a competitive industry at another stage will not change the price and output level of the final product. It will be demonstrated that, with variable input proportions, vertical integration between a monopolist at one stage and a competitive industry at a succeeding stage of production will result in a higher price and reduced output level of the final product. This conclusion was first articulated by M. L. Burstein in 1960 (5) but received little or no recognition in the field of industrial organization. More recently, R. L. Moomaw (12) has elaborated upon the implications of vertical integration in the variable input proportions case, and the present section is very similar to his analysis.

The appropriate starting point for our analysis of the impact of variable input proportions is the analysis of vertical integration between a monopoly producer at Stage 1 and a purely competitive industry at Stage 2 contained in the preceding section. In Figure 8–3(a), the curve D_f represents the demand conditions for the monopolist's output (hereafter termed Input-A) when input proportions are fixed as before; in contrast to Figure 8–1, however, the monopolist's output is in the present context assumed, merely for expositional convenience, to be produced under constant cost conditions. Q_c represents

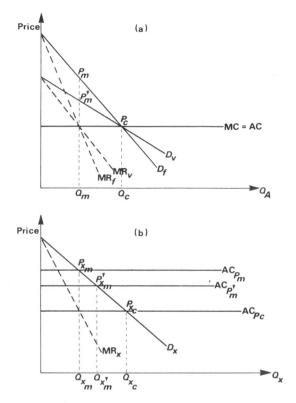

Figure 8–3. Vertical integration with variable input proportions.

the quantity of A that would be demanded by Stage 2 producers if the output of Stage 1 were priced at marginal cost. At higher prices of A, the quantity of A demanded by Stage 2 producers is reduced, by an amount which depends on (i) the extent to which demand for the final product is reduced when its price rises and also on (ii) the extent to which the price of other inputs which are combined with A at Stage 2 is reduced as the quantity of those other inputs demanded is also reduced. The relationship between these two factors and D_f is easy to comprehend diagrammatically since, when input proportions are fixed, D_f is derived quite simply by subtracting the cost of the (fixed) quantity of the other input (B) which is combined with A at Stage 2 to produce a unit of final output, from the demand price associated with any given quantity of the final product. Diagrammatically, this corresponds to subtracting AC_2 from D_2 at each quantity of the final product in Figure 8–1. The profit-maximizing price and quantity of A associated with D_f are P_m and Q_m respectively. Figure 8–3(b) indicates the implications of the price of the monopolist's product for the second stage of production, which is also assumed to operate under constant cost conditions purely for ease of diagrammatic exposition. The curve labeled AC_{P_c} represents cost conditions at Stage 2 if A were priced at its marginal cost, and AC_{P_m} represents cost conditions at Stage 2 when the monopolist's product is priced at P_m. As Figure 8–3(b) demonstrates, when input proportions are fixed, choice of the monopolist's output level in effect determines the output level of the final product and the monopolist at Stage 1 is able to extract all of the monopoly profit obtainable from sales of the final product at Stage 2.

Matters are different, however, when the proportions in which A and B are combined to produce a unit of final output can be varied. In this case, an increase in the price of A above its marginal cost will lead to a *larger* reduction in quantity demanded, since Stage 2 producers will *substitute* some input B for input A in producing any given output level of the final product. The demand curve for A when input proportions are variable will therefore be D_v, and the associated marginal revenue curve is MR_v. It is also appropriate to note that in these circumstances D_v can no longer be derived by simply subtracting AC_2 from D_2. The reason is that AC_2, which represents the cost of other inputs combined with A at Stage 2 per unit of final output, now depends on the quantity of B used per unit of final output, which in turn depends on the price of A. There will therefore be a different AC_2 curve corresponding to each different price of A. Moreover, the quantity demanded of the final product will no longer indicate the quantity of A demanded, since the quantity of A per unit of final product will also vary with the price of A. Despite these complications, it is easy to see that the profit-maximizing price of A which corresponds to D_v is lower than when input proportions are fixed, and corresponds to P'_m in Figure 8–3(a). This, in turn, implies that the height of the cost curve at Stage 2 will be lower at each level of output of the final product, as indicated by the curve labeled $AC_{P'_m}$ in Figure 8–3(b). The cost of any given output level of the final product will be lower not only because the price of A is lower, but also because less A will be used to produce any given output level than when the price of A is P_m. With cost conditions at Stage 2 represented by $AC_{P'_m}$ the price of the final product will equal P'_{xm}, since Stage 2 is assumed to be purely competitive. This price of the final product is lower, and the output level higher, than in the case of fixed input proportions; in other words, when input proportions are variable, an unintegrated monopolist at Stage 1 *will not be able to extract all of the monopoly profits obtainable from sales of the final product.* Unexhausted monopoly profits will exist at Stage 2, and can only be reaped by the monopolist at Stage 1 if he can prevent substitution of B for A. By integrating vertically, the monopoly supplier of A can therefore increase his profits for two reasons: first, by changing the input mix and using a larger amount of the monopolized input to produce any given level of final output, it is possible to lower the cost of final output because input mixes will be based on the marginal cost of A rather than on the price of A. Second, profits can be further increased by reducing the level of output of the final product to the profit-maximizing level Q_{xm} in Figure 8–3(b).

The preceding diagrammatic argument demonstrating that an unintegrated monopolist at Stage 1 cannot extract the maximum monopoly-profit potential inherent in the market for the final product when input proportions are variable can also be explained in an alternative manner as follows: it was explained in Chapter 3 that the profit-maximizing price–marginal cost relationship for a firm selling any particular product is represented by the following expression:

$$\frac{P - MC}{P} = \frac{1}{E_d}$$

where E_d is the price-elasticity of demand for the firm's product. If, as in the present context, the firm's product is not a final product, but instead is an input which is combined together with other inputs to produce a final product, the price-elasticity of demand for this input (E_{di}) depends on the price-elasticity of demand for the final product (E_{df}), the elasticity of supply of the other inputs, the elasticity of substitution between the input and other inputs (s), and the proportion of the total cost of the final product represented by outlays on the input in question (k). For an illuminating discussion on the factors underlying the elasticity of demand for an input, see the articles by M. Bronfenbrenner and J. R. Hicks in reference (4) of Recommended Readings. When the elasticity of supply of other inputs is infinity, which occurs when the price at which other inputs can be purchased is independent of the quantity purchased, the relationship between the preceding factors is as follows:

$$E_{di} = kE_{df} + (1 - k)s$$

When s is zero, which occurs when input proportions are fixed, this expression reduces to $E_{di} = kE_{df}$; that is, E_{di} depends only on the price-elasticity of demand for the final product, and the proportion of total expenditures on the input in question. When s is positive, as occurs when input proportions are variable, E_{di} is clearly increased, all other things remaining unchanged. This implies that the profit-maximizing price–marginal cost relationship for the monopoly seller of the input is reduced, which in turn implies a lower total and average cost of any particular quantity of the final product. When unintegrated, the monopolist at Stage 1 *is* maximizing profits from the sale of his product *given the elasticity of substitution* between his product and other inputs used at Stage 2. However, when the elasticity of substitution is positive, the price-elasticity of demand for the monopolist's product is greater, and his profits at any given level of output of the final product are lower. The intuitive explanation for the lower profit of the monopolist, at any given level of output of the final product, is that a larger part of the price of the final product is spent on other inputs, more of which are being used per unit of output when substitution is possible than would be used if substitution were not possible.

One possibly important constraint on the ability of a monopolist at Stage 1 to extract the full monopoly profit from sales of the final product by integrating forward to Stage 2 needs to be mentioned. If, without using any A, other producers can produce the final product at a cost which is below the monopoly price, the monopolist will not be able to charge the monopoly price for the final product. Whether it will be possible to produce the final product at a cost below the monopoly price without using A will depend mainly on the elasticity of substitution between inputs; given the prices of the inputs, this determines the number of units of other inputs which must be substituted for A in order to produce the final product in question.

The policy implications of vertical integration in the variable input proportions case are clearly very different from those of the fixed proportions case. The analysis contained in the preceding section indicated that vertical integration could either leave the output level and price of the final product unchanged or, alternatively, could lead to price reductions and increases in output of the final product due to cost savings attributable to vertical integration, price discrimination, or the elimination of non-optimal bilateral monopoly solutions. Since no undesirable allocative efficiency effects in the form of price increases and reductions in output of the final product were associated with vertical integration in this case, public policy could justifiably regard the practice favorably, or neutrally at worst, in terms of its implications for aggregate satisfaction in the community. When input proportions are variable, however, a monopolist producing an intermediate product which is purchased by a competitive industry can increase monopoly profits by integrating forward and restricting the output level of the final product. As explained in more detail in Chapter 10, this output restriction has adverse effects on the efficiency with which resources in the economy are allocated between different markets if markets for other final products are competitive. Whether input proportions are variable in practice, and therefore whether vertical integration can have adverse effects on allocative efficiency, is largely an empirical question. However, even if variable input proportions do exist in the majority of industrial processes in practice, this does *not* automatically reverse the appropriate policy stance even in the case of vertical integration between a monopoly producer of an intermediate product and a competitive industry at a succeeding stage of production. The reason is that even if adverse effects on allocative efficiency are present in this case, one cannot ignore the favorable effects on technical efficiency which are also inherently associated with vertical integration in this case. Technical efficiency refers to the efficiency with which inputs are combined in producing any particular output level. Apart from restricting the output level of the final product, the monopoly producer of an intermediate product also increases its profits by changing the input mix which is used to produce the final product, using more of the monopolized input per unit of output than was used by independent producers at Stage 2. Because the monopolist's input-mix decision will be based on the marginal cost of the monopolized input, instead of on its price as occurred when production was unintegrated, the total cost of producing any particular level of output of the final product will be reduced. As explained in more detail in Chapter 10, the use of input mixes which minimize the total money cost of producing output will maximize technical efficiency in the economy when the marginal cost of any input is the same for all firms in the economy, because it implies that the resulting economy-wide output mix cannot be produced with fewer resources by changing the input mixes used in individual firms and industries. These gains in technical efficiency resulting from vertical integration due to input-mix changes, plus any other technical efficiency gains due to avoiding costs of using the market referred to in the first section of this chapter, must be compared with any adverse effects on allocative efficiency due to output level restrictions, in a manner described in detail in the section of Chapter 10 dealing with measurement of welfare losses attributable to monopoly, in order to determine whether vertical integration on balance increases or reduces aggregate satisfaction in the community.

Another relevant consideration which should be mentioned is that the allocative efficiency implications of output restriction in a particular market themselves depend on price–marginal cost relationships existing in other markets; as explained in the section of Chapter 10 dealing with the 'theory of second-best', reductions in output in one market will reduce allocative efficiency in the economy only if, initially, the amount of resources allocated to other sectors of the economy is 'just right', as indicated by price–marginal cost relationships in other markets. If, instead, other sectors have too few resources, output restriction in one market can increase, rather than diminish, allocative efficiency in the economy as a whole. For these reasons, no general conclusions regarding the desirability of vertical integration are possible, even when input proportions are variable and vertical integration results in output restrictions.

Before concluding this section, it is appropriate to say something about the mechanism by which a monopoly producer of an intermediate product may integrate forward. As Moomaw (12) has stressed, predatory vertical price squeezes by the monopolist at Stage 1 are an effective and rational means for extending the monopoly to Stage 2. By raising the price of the monopolized input above the profit-maximizing level when production is not integrated (P'_m in Figure 8–3(a)), the monopolist at Stage 1 can increase the cost of production at Stage 2. This will cause short-run losses for producers at Stage 2, who by assumption are earning only normal profits, and this in turn will enable the monopolist to purchase such firms at or below their competitive market value. In effect, the monopolist at Stage 1 can be viewed as attempting to replace the demand curve D_v in Figure 8–3(a) by the demand curve D_f by driving out independent producers at Stage 2 and leaving the monopoly as the sole source of supply for buyers of the output of Stage 2. Moreover, there is a difference between the vertical price squeeze and price squeezes which are aimed at rival firms at the same stage of production. In the case of horizontal price squeezes, once other rivals have been driven out it is necessary for the predatory price cutter to raise the price of the product to earn monopoly profits. In contrast, in the case of the vertical price squeeze it is not necessary to lower the price of the monopolized input after rival firms at Stage 2 have been driven out in order for the monopolist to increase his profits; rather, the high price of monopolized input is a means of preventing independent producers from producing the final product at and competing with the monopolist at Stage 2. There is, however, one qualification, already noted, on the ability of the monopolist at Stage 1 to succeed in reaping the maximum monopoly profit obtainable at Stage 2; it must be impossible for independent producers at Stage 2 to produce the final product at a cost below the monopoly price without using the monopolized input. This, as indicated earlier, depends on the elasticity of substitution between the monopolized input and other inputs used to produce the final product.

Vertical Integration and Entry Barriers

The previous section considered how vertical integration affects the pricing behavior of established firms in an industry, given the demand conditions for the final product facing the industry group. The question considered in this section is whether, and if so how, vertical integration affects the behavior of potential entrants. In this context the relevant question to be answered is the following. Does vertical integration by established firms affect either the potential entrant's cost or demand conditions? For, as explained in Chapter 7, it is these two sets of conditions that determine whether a potential entrant will enter an industry.

The relationship between vertical integration and entry barriers is a matter about which there is still a certain amount of controversy, even among economists. All that can be done in a book of this nature is to point out the nature of arguments linking vertical integration to entry barriers.

One must compare the situation in which a potential entrant at some stage (Stage 2) in the process of production and distribution is confronted by established firms performing only that stage, with a situation in which the established firms performing that stage also perform earlier (Stage 1), or later (Stage 3), stages.

Let us assume for the moment that vertical integration has no effect upon cost conditions at any stage of production. The potential entrant may face increased entry barriers for either of the two following reasons. First, backward vertical integration by established firms at Stage 2 may enable the latter to acquire control of scarce raw materials required by a Stage 2 entrant and hence deter entry at Stage 2 by simply refusing to supply inputs to a new entrant. In these circumstances, the entry restrictions on Stage 2 are founded upon entry restrictions at Stage 1, and the returns earned at Stage 1 by vertically integrated firms will consist primarily of the rents associated with a scarce resource. Nonetheless, by deterring entry at Stage 2, control of Stage 1 may enable the integrated firms to earn higher returns at Stage 2 than they would have earned in the absence of integration. Although, in the absence of integration, entry at Stage 1 is still effectively barred, the independent Stage 1 firms may supply new entrants and established firms at Stage 2 alike; the new entrant at Stage 2 can compete for inputs with established firms at Stage 2, in contrast to the situation in which established firms at Stage 2 also control Stage 1. Forward vertical integration by established firms at Stage 2 may increase barriers to entry for similar reasons, if it confers upon established firms a monopoly over limited distributive outlets at Stage 3. Such outlets may be limited in number for legal reasons such as licensing requirements or zoning laws. In the absence of control of Stage 3 by established firms, demand for the product of an entrant at Stage 2 depends upon the entrant's anticipations regarding the post-entry price and/or output policies of established firms at Stage 2. If established firms control Stage 3, and refuse to buy from the entrant, entry will be unprofitable irrespective of established firms' Stage 2 behavior.

Second, even though established integrated firms do not have complete control over limited inputs required at Stage 2, or of limited distributive outlets at Stage 3, a refusal by established firms to supply, or purchase from, an unintegrated entrant at Stage 2 may mean that the new entrant is compelled to begin operations at both stages. This will increase the amount of capital required for entry, compared to single-stage entry. Increased capital requirements may increase barriers to entry if there is a constraint on capital funds facing the potential entrant. This last point is important, for unless the potential entrant is unable to obtain the required amount of capital, or must pay more than established integrated firms for capital, increased capital requirements themselves do not increase barriers to entry. Since potential entrants may be large firms established in other industries, rather than newly created firms, there is no a priori reason why potential entrants should have less access to internally generated, or external, funds in amounts and at terms which are similar to those applying in the case of established firms.

If vertical integration lowers cost, single-stage entry by a new entrant will mean that the entrant's costs are higher, relative to the costs of established firms at that stage, than if established firms were unintegrated. However, any cost reduction occasioned by vertical integration is not, itself, an increased barrier to entry. The entrant can achieve the same cost savings by entering as a vertically integrated unit, and only if there is a constraint on the entrant's capital funds will this be impossible. Given such a constraint, vertical integration by established firms which makes it necessary for the entrant to enter more than one stage in order to be just as efficient as established firms will make entry more difficult. However, if vertical integration lowers costs, it is desirable on grounds of efficiency that entrants should be forced to integrate.

Measuring the Degree of Vertical Integration

Hypotheses regarding the relationship between vertical integration and other characteristics of industrial structure must be tested with respect to their factual relevance. This requires a quantifiable measure of the degree of vertical integration. Several different methods of measuring the degree of vertical integration, in the sense of the number of vertically related stages performed by a firm operating in a particular industry, have been discussed in the literature dealing with industrial structure.

One possible index employs the ratio of value added (that is, sales less expenditures for raw materials, fuel, and power) by a firm to the firm's sales revenues. The rationale underlying the use of such a measure is that the more successive stages in the productive process that are performed by a firm, the greater will be the magnitude of this ratio. Such a measure has, however, several defects as an index of the degree of vertical integration.

Differences in the rate of change over time of input and output prices respectively will change the index even though the physical processes performed by a firm remain unchanged. As a result, the reliability of the index as an indicator of changes in the degree of vertical integration over time may be impaired.

Value added includes profits and, comparing two firms performing identical productive operations, the firm with greater profits will show a higher index of integration. Hence the index is not a reliable measure of vertical integration even with respect to firms operating at the same stage in the same industry.

If one attempts to use the index to compare the degree of vertical integration in different firms, whether in the same or in different industries, even greater limitations reveal themselves. Suppose that each of the successive stages involved in the production of a particular final product is performed by a separate firm, and that each firm contributes an equal amount to the total value of the final product. The degree of vertical integration, measured by the ratio of value added to sales, will decline progressively as one considers firms closer to the final stage, despite the fact that all firms are by definition equally integrated. Since the index reflects the stage in the productive process which is being measured, rather than the degree of vertical integration, the index is of little use even when comparing different firms in the same industry unless they are at the same stage in the productive process. When making comparisons between firms in different industries, the index will yield even more ambiguous results.

Another defect of the index, closely related to the last, arises when using the index to indicate changes in vertical integration. The index will reflect differences in the direction of vertical integration, yielding different values for the same increase in value added, depending upon whether the additional stages previously preceded or succeeded the firm's original operations. Thus, if two firms, originally located at the same stage in the same industry, integrate in opposite directions, each firm taking over one additional stage which contributes an equal amount to the value of the final product, the index will show a greater degree of vertical integration for the firm integrating backward than for the firm integrating forward. Similarly, forward integration by a raw material producer yields no change in the index – it remains unchanged at a value of unity.

The ratio of the value of inventory to sales has been suggested as an alternative measure of the degree of vertical integration. The notion that increases in this index indicate a larger number of successive stages performed by the firm rests upon the implicit assumption that the greater the number of stages performed, the greater will be the level of the firm's total inventory. Vertical integration which enables a firm to economize on stocks will invalidate this line of reasoning and result in a smaller value of the index the larger the number of stages performed. Like the ratio of value added to sales, the ratio of inventory to sales will be affected by differential rates of change in inventory and final product prices respectively. Such changes will change the index even though the number of stages, and physical characteristics of the firm's operations, remain unchanged.

The ratio of value added to sales and the ratio of inventory to sales both attempt to measure the degree of vertical integration in the sense of the number of successive stages performed by a firm selling in a particular market. A slightly different kind of index of vertical integration shows the degree to which a firm performing any particular stage of production or distribution is dependent upon markets for obtaining the inputs of that stage, or for the disposal of the output of that stage. This requires separate measures of the degree of backward and forward integration for each stage of production or distribution performed by a firm. For example, total interfirm purchases, or transfers, of inputs required at a particular stage, expressed as a proportion of the total amount of the input used by the firm, yield a measure of backward vertical integration at that stage. This measure indicates the extent to which the firm relies upon the market to supply it with inputs at any particular stage of the productive process. Similarly, total interfirm transfers of the output of a particular stage, expressed as a proportion of the total output of that stage, measure the degree of forward vertical integration at that stage and indicate the extent to which the firm performing that stage is dependent upon the market for disposition of its product.

An advantage of this type of measure is that either value or quantity data may be employed and the ratios are invariant to price-level changes since both numerator and denominator of the value ratios involve use of the same price. Most of the problems arising out of the use of such measures are likely to revolve around the definition of a stage in the productive process. Much of industry involves two or more successive stages in production which might theoretically be split among two or more producers. However, attention is generally focused upon those situations in which successive stages of production controlled by a single managerial supervision are also, or were previously, performed by separate firms.

RECOMMENDED READINGS

1. Adelman, M. A., Concept and statistical measurement of vertical integration. In Stigler, G. J. (Ed.) *Business Concentration and Price Policy* (Princeton, N. J.: Princeton University Press, 1955).
2. Bork, R., Vertical integration and the Sherman Act: the legal history of an economic misconception, *University of Chicago Law Review*, Autumn 1954, pp. 194–201.
3. Bork, R., Bowman, W. S., Blake, H. M. and Jones, W. K., The goals of antitrust: a dialogue on policy, *Columbia Law Review*, March 1965, pp. 363–466, especially pp. 389–394, 403–412, 417–422, 440–458, 463–466.
4. Bronfenbrenner, M., Notes on the elasticity of derived demand, *Oxford Economic Papers*, October 1961; *and* Hicks, J. R., Marshall's third rule: a further comment. (Same journal, pp. 254–265.)
5. Burstein, M. L., A theory of full-line forcing, *Northwestern University Law Review*, March–April 1960.
6. Coase, R. H., The nature of the firm, *Economica*, November 1937; reprinted in Heflebower, R. B. and Stocking, G. W. (Eds.) *Readings in Price Theory* (Homewood, Ill.: Richard D. Irwin, Inc., 1952). Published under the sponsorship of the American Economic Association.
7. Comanor, W. S., Vertical mergers, market powers, and the antitrust laws, *American Economic Review, Papers and Proceedings*, May 1967, pp. 254–265; *and* Comment by McGee, J. S., pp. 269–270.
8. Crandall, R., Vertical integration and the market for repair parts in the U.S. automobile industry, *Journal of Industrial Economics*, July 1968.
9. Greenhut, M. L. and Ohta, H., Related market conditions and interindustrial mergers, *American Economic Review*, June 1976.
10. Hay, G. A., An economic analysis of vertical integration, *Industrial Organization Review*, Vol. 1, 1973.
11. Machlup, F. and Taber, M., Bilateral monopoly, successive monopoly, and vertical integration, *Economica*, May 1960.
12. Moomaw, R. L., Vertical integration and monopoly: a resolution of the controversy, *Rivista Internazionale di Scienze Economiche e Commerciali*, January 1974.
13. Schmalensee, R., A note on the theory of vertical integration, *Journal of Political Economy*, March–April 1973.
14. Sichel, W., Vertical integration as a dynamic industry concept, *Antitrust Bulletin*, Fall 1973.
15. Vernon, J. M. and Graham, D. A., Profitability of monopolization by vertical integration, *Journal of Political Economy*, July–August 1971.
16. Warren-Boulton, F. R., Vertical control with variable proportions, *Journal of Political Economy*, July–August 1974.
17. Williamson, O. E., The vertical integration of production: market failure considerations, *American Economic Review, Papers and Proceedings*, May 1971, pp. 112–123.

CHAPTER NINE

DIVERSIFICATION AND CONGLOMERATE FORMS OF ENTERPRISE

Meaning and Measurement of Diversification

A diversified firm is a firm which, instead of specializing in the production of a single product or service, produces a number of different products or services. The term conglomerate has recently become synonymous with diversified firms. In subsequent sections of this chapter we shall investigate the motives and reasons for diversification, and the relationship between diversification and competition. First, however, it is necessary to mention some problems of defining and measuring which are encountered in every study of diversification.

The first major point which requires emphasis is that the degree of diversification existing at any point in time in firms, industries, or the economy as a whole, depends critically on the definition of what constitutes a 'different' product or service. For example, strictly speaking, vertical integration is an aspect of diversification, since the activities engaged in at different levels of the production process are different from each other. Conventionally, however, vertical integration is treated as a characteristic that is separate from diversification in firms' activities. Thus, for example, the Federal Trade Commission divides mergers into three categories: *horizontal* mergers between firms producing the same product, *vertical* mergers between firms at different levels of the production process, and *conglomerate* mergers. The Federal Trade Commission distinguishes between three types of conglomerate merger: product extension, market extension, and all other mergers. In product-extension mergers, the firms involved produce products which do not compete directly with one another but are still related in production and/or distribution. The term concentric is sometimes used to describe diversification into a product either sold to the current customers of a firm (marketing concentricity) or produced by a similar technology (technological concentricity). In market-extension mergers the firms involved produce the same products but they are sold in different geographic markets. The last category of conglomerate mergers includes all mergers between firms where none of the above relationships can be found to hold.

Unfortunately, the preceding categories do little more than encourage misplaced concreteness, since which category a particular merger falls into still depends on the way in which different products are defined. As explained in Chapter 5, there are innumerable ways in which the boundaries between products and markets may be drawn, reflecting the multidimensional characteristics of buyers, sellers, and products themselves. There are, correspondingly, innumerable possible definitions of diversification, and the degree of diversification which is observed to exist in particular firms, or industries, will depend on which solution to the market-boundary problem is adopted. Which one of the many market-boundary solutions and corresponding diversification concepts is appropriate depends on the purpose of those using the concepts. If one is interested in the determinants of diversification, for example, then the appropriate concept of diversification is the one which is *behaviorally* significant, in the sense of the concept which decision-makers themselves consider in their decision-making. In Chapter 5 it was pointed out that the degree of substitutability between products, either from the point of view of buyers or from the point of view of sellers, influences the behavior of buyers and sellers. However, it was also stressed that substitutability is a matter of degree, rather than of clear-cut differences. The implications of this point for the appropriate concept of diversification may be illustrated with an example: a firm's decision-makers may produce different varieties of what they regard as the 'same' product in order to separate the total market for the product for purposes of price-discrimination. To an outside observer, this may appear to be 'diversification', while to the firm's decision-makers it may simply be 'differentiation' of the same product. Similarly, the outside observer would then regard a merger between such a firm and another firm producing yet another variety of the product as a 'conglomerate' merger, while the firm would regard this as a 'horizontal' merger. The opposite conclusions would hold if the firm views its activities in terms of 'diversification' and the outside observer views them in terms of 'differentiation'.

Whatever criteria are used in defining product and market boundaries, a second point which must always be borne in mind is that the resulting degree of diversification can be measured in a number of different ways. For example, it could be measured in terms of the ratio of the firm's non-primary activities to its total activity. This measure corresponds to the primary product specialization ratio used by the U.S. Census of Manufactures. One limitation of such a measure is illustrated by comparing two firms, each with an identical ratio of non-primary to total output but with the non-primary output of one firm divided among a number of different products while the other firm's non-primary output is concentrated in a single product. No difference in diversification would be revealed by the diversification index, though for most purposes the first firm may be considered to be more diversified. Another way to measure the degree of diversification is to count the number of different products a firm produces. Such an index of diversification may, however, give disproportionate weight to many activities which, in the aggregate, account for only a small proportion of a firm's total operations. Such an index would indicate that a firm with fewer products than another firm, but with larger absolute levels of output of each product, is less diversified, even if less than one per cent of the first firm's total activities is diversified.

The two preceding examples indicate that diversification can be measured either in terms of the number of industries in which a firm operates, or in terms of the distribution of the firm's productive activities among those industries. Composite measures of diversification, which attempt to measure both of these aspects of diversification, also exist. One such index is obtained by multiplying the ratio of non-primary to total output of the firm (or industry) by the number of industries that account for a specified percentage of the total output of the firm. Another alternative is to count the number of industries that account for a specified percentage of the total output or employment of the firm. As another example, Professor C. Berry (4) recently used an index of diversification which applies the Herfindahl Index of Industrial Concentration to the distribution of a *firm's* industrial activity instead of to the distribution of an *industry's* sales among firms. The resulting index of diversification, which equals unity minus the sum of the squared proportions of the firm's activity in different markets, takes the value 0 when a firm is active in a single industry, and approaches unity when the firm in question produces equally in a large number of different industries.

The analogy between the problem of measuring industrial concentration, defined as the number and size distribution of firms in a particular industry, and that of measuring the degree of diversification in a firm, defined as the number and size distribution of the firm's activities among different industries, may be further extended. Since the two problems are analytically equivalent, it follows that all the different methods of measuring industrial concentration which were discussed in the second section of Chapter 6 could also in principle be applied to the measurement of a firm's diversification. Thus, one could distinguish between absolute and relative diversification measures, as well as between the varieties of different measures associated with each of these two categories. Since most of the discussion in Chapter 6 on the problem of measuring industrial concentration applies equally to the problem of measuring industrial diversification, it will not be repeated here. One point is worth emphasizing again, however: the great danger of using composite indices of diversification is that they may conceal more information than they reveal. For example, if the ratio of non-primary to total output in one firm is 1 to 2, and the firm operates in five other industries in addition to the primary industry, the first composite index mentioned yields $6/2 = 3$, which would also result in the case of a firm operating in 12 industries, with a ratio of non-primary to total output of 1 to 4. Clearly, no *single* index can indicate what are essentially differences in two or more dimensions of firm size. Another point to bear in mind, already discussed in Chapter 6 also, is that any measure of diversification which employs size variables such as employment, assets, or net output, may reflect aspects of firm size other than diversification. The use of employment or assets as a size variable involves problems of allocating non-specific inputs between different products, a more or less arbitrary procedure in some firms. In addition, all three size variables will reflect vertical aspects of firm size in addition to diversification. If, for example, two firms are identical in all respects except that one firm is more vertically integrated than another in producing one of its final products, employment, assets, or net output weights will assign a greater degree of diversification to that firm. The resulting index will reflect vertical diversification in addition to diversification proper. For these reasons, sales might be a more appropriate size variable with which to measure diversification. Of course, even a simple count of industries in which a firm operates will reflect vertical integration unless industries that are vertically related are counted only once.

As is usual in such matters, a priori reasoning alone cannot provide a complete answer to the question of which concept or measure of diversification is the most appropriate. Empirical investigation of which measure of diversification is closely related to those aspects of firms' behavior one is interested in may provide a guide to the best measure, in the sense of the measure with the most predictive value. The existence of a close relationship between diversification and some aspect of firms' behavior does not necessarily imply cause and effect, however, for reasons explained in more detail at the end of the next section.

Whatever the concept and measure of diversification which one considers appropriate, the degree of diversification within firms cannot generally be ascertained either from official published statistics or from the published accounts of firms. The relevant data available at the Bureau of the Census cannot be published except in aggregated form without violating the requirement that there be no disclosure of information pertaining to individual firms. Moreover, even if one is interested only in the degree of diversification in industries viewed as a whole, in census of production and similar data the output or employment of establishments producing more than one product as defined by the official product classification is generally classified under the heading of the principal product of the establishment. For these reasons, precise calculation of firm and industry diversification from official statistics is impossible, even if one accepts the official classification of products as appropriate. Firms themselves do not generally publish adequate breakdowns of either their sales or profits by product lines, and even if they did, published figures for profits and fixed assets in different firms are often not comparable with one another because of differences in accounting procedures. The lists of products produced by *Fortune* and by investment brokers have provided a valuable additional source of data on diversification for researchers interested in this characteristic of industrial structure.

Determinants of Diversification

Like other features of firms' behavior, diversification is the outcome of firms' attempts to achieve certain objectives subject to a number of constraints. A wide variety of explanations has been offered for diversified forms of enterprise, some stressing the nature of firms' objectives themselves and others focusing on some of the constraints involved. This section outlines the essential features of these alternative explanations, and reconciles the divergent views regarding the determinants of diversification.

A firm's profits depend on the cost and demand conditions associated with its productive activities. One type of explanation for diversification frequently advanced stresses the operating economies obtainable from spreading the cost of indivisible inputs over a greater variety of products, thereby resulting in a lower operating cost per unit of individual products. Several comments are appropriate in reply to this line of reasoning: first, the argument confuses economies of absolute size of firms with economies of diversification, and is an argument for increased absolute scale of a firm's overall operations, not for diversification per se, since the same argument applies to expansion of a specialized firm, or to vertical expansion of the firm. Second, the argument only applies to diversified expansion if the activities performed by the indivisible inputs in question are 'non-specific' in the sense that they are required whether the firm produces a specialized or diversified output mix; otherwise the expanded level of activities which is necessary to utilize the inputs fully would have to be the same as the original output mix. Although managerial, financial, and marketing inputs are usually cited in this connection, it is by no means obvious that the nature of the activities of inputs performing such functions are likely to be the same irrespective of a firm's output mix. Finally, even if the functions are similar, irrespective of whether the firm is specialized or diversified, this does not lead to a preference for expansion by diversification; for this to occur, the activities performed by the indivisible inputs in question must be such that diversified expansion and not specialized expansion are required to utilize them fully. The circumstances in which these conditions are likely to be fulfilled are clearly very limited. On the other hand, when attention is switched from expansion of the overall level of a firm's operations to the appropriate comparison of specialization to diversification *at a given size* of a firm's overall operations, there are reasons why the unit costs of individual products are generally likely to be higher the more diversified a firm's operations: if economies of scale exist in the production of individual products, attributable to indivisible inputs which are specific to the production of those products, lower output levels of individual products associated with more diversified operation at a given overall size of firm will imply higher unit costs. Of course, whether the profitability of diversification is lower than that of specialization at small firm sizes depends not only on cost conditions but also on demand conditions, which are dealt with below. First, however, it is appropriate to mention another reason why total costs in a diversified firm are sometimes alleged to be lower than in an otherwise identical group of specialized firms, which is connected with the supply of investment funds available to the firm.

The cost of investment funds is also a component of the total cost of a firm's operations in addition to the cost of the inputs involved in productive activities. It is sometimes alleged that the cost of investment funds will be lower for a diversified firm than for a group of otherwise identical specialized firms because there is less risk attached to the diversified firm's operations. In this connection risk is defined as the variance of the anticipated earnings associated with the investment of a given sum of money in productive activities. As was indicated in Chapter 1, in the presence of uncertainty the revenues anticipated take the form of a range of possible outcomes, each associated with a probability assigned by the decision-maker himself.

Part of the uncertainty underlying the anticipated earnings from producing a single product is due to the possibility that buyers may spend their incomes on other products. If a firm also produces other products, the variance of the distribution of alternative possible earnings outcomes will be reduced, because the probability of an extreme occurrence such as losses on all products is less than the probability of loss on any single product. Even though the mean probable expected sales revenue from producing a single product or a mix of products is the same, the variance of the anticipated earnings will be smaller in the case of diversification than in the case of specialization, thereby making diversified operations less risky.

There is no question that the variance of the combined anticipated earnings stream associated with a number of dissimilar productive activities is reduced compared to the variance of the earnings associated with the individual activities. However, this does not give a diversified firm an advantage over a group of specialized firms producing the same mix of products, *from the point of view of lenders*, because a lender can effectively achieve the same degree of diversification and risk reduction by allocating his lending and share portfolio among the specialized firms. For the lender who lends only a very small amount, and cannot thereby acquire a fully diversified share portfolio himself, there is always the mutual fund. The findings of a study by K. V. Smith and J. C. Schreiner (41) which compared the efficiency of portfolio selection by diversified firms with that of investment companies indicated superior portfolio performance for investment companies. As a number of economists have pointed out, risk reduction in the above sense can be used to defend the diversified lending portfolio, not the diversified firm, from the point of view of lenders. However, it should also be noted that although a diversified firm offers no advantages, in terms of reduced variance per dollar of gross expected return, compared to portfolio diversification, diversification of productive activities may still offer advantages to management. If management is concerned with the survival and continued existence of the firm it manages, corporate diversification will be superior to specialized operations, given the same mean expected earnings, since portfolio diversification by the firm itself is not a feasible alternative method of reducing earnings variance whilst simultaneously achieving the firm's survival as an industrial enterprise.

There are two sources of external finance available to a firm: debt finance in exchange for which the firm incurs legally-enforceable fixed-interest obligations to lenders; and equity finance provided by shareholders. The cost of these sources of finance equals the ratio between the interest or profit return to lenders and the price they are willing to pay for a firm's debt instruments. For reasons indicated in the preceding paragraph, the debt instruments of a diversified firm are no more attractive to lenders from the point of view of reducing the variance per dollar of expected return than portfolio diversification among a group of otherwise identical separate firms each specializing in a single activity. As far as this particular aspect of lending risk is concerned, therefore, lenders will not be willing to pay more for the debt instruments of the diversified firm than for those of the separate firms, so that the cost of finance will not be lower for the diversified firm. Instead of focusing on the variance of the gross earnings stream associated with a collection of productive activities, several economists have recently demonstrated that the risk of default on the fixed-interest obligations of a diversified firm will be lower than the default risk in a group of otherwise identical separate specialized firms. The reason is quite simple: a fixed-interest lender faces a loss if one of the separate firms cannot meet its fixed-interest obligations; in contrast, if he lends to a diversified firm the poor performance of one of the firm's activities alone merely means that the lender can place his claim against the earnings of other parts of the firm. This reduction in default risk makes fixed-interest lending to diversified firms more attractive than fixed-interest lending to a group of otherwise identical separate firms, so that the diversified firm can obtain a given amount of debt finance at a lower interest rate, or what is the same thing, a larger amount of debt finance at a given interest rate (see W. G. Lewellen (21), for example).

Although the preceding argument is valid, it deals only with the gain, in terms of reduced default risk, to fixed-interest lenders, and ignores the effect of this reduction in default risk on shareholders. Shareholders who lend to a separate group of firms need not draw on their earnings from other firms to pay debtors if one of the firms defaults on its debts. In contrast, in a diversified firm it is the shareholders whose residual income stream would be reduced to meet fixed-interest obligations if one of the firm's activities failed. In other words, whatever the expected gain to debt lenders in terms of reduced default risk, the same amount becomes an expected loss for the shareholders of a diversified firm, and the burden of default risk is merely *shifted* from debt lenders to shareholders in a diversified firm. Viewing a diversified firm's supply of funds as a whole, therefore, the increased supply of debt finance at any given rate of return will tend to be matched by a reduction in the supply of equity finance, so that on balance there would seem to be no reason why the total supply of funds to a diversified firm should be greater or, what is the same thing, why the cost of a given amount of investment funds should be lower, than for a collection of otherwise identical specialized firms. The only difference would be that a larger proportion of the diversified firm's funds will take the form of debt finance rather than equity finance.

As Roger Sherman (40) and several other writers have demonstrated, once taxes are introduced into the picture, however, there are additional reasons why the shares of diversified firms may seem relatively attractive, compared to the shares of a group of otherwise identical specialized firms, resulting in a willingness on the part of shareholders to pay more for a given expected gross earnings stream than if the same gross earnings stream is associated with separate firms. The basic reason is that diversified operations reduce the amount of taxes paid on a given gross earnings stream, and thereby raise the after-tax earnings stream, compared to independent operations. There are several ways in which taxes achieve this result. Because interest payments are considered a deductible expense for tax purposes, greater use of debt as opposed to equity finance by a firm will lower the total taxable profits of a firm. Moreover, by transforming the gross profit on a share into interest on debt the total tax liability of the firm falls, leaving the resulting tax-saving to be allocated between the remaining shares, and the after-tax return per share will be higher. Since the proportion of debt which can be used to finance a given level of operations is higher in a diversified firm than in an otherwise identical group of independent firms, for reasons already explained in the preceding paragraph, diversification can increase the after-tax return per share to the firm's shareholders. Apart from the tax advantages associated with greater use of debt finance, diversified operations also yield tax advantages to shareholders due to the differential taxation of capital gains and dividend income. As long as the tax rate on dividend income exceeds the tax rate on capital gains for an individual, as under current tax schedules, stockholders can enjoy more after-tax income if their increases in wealth take the form of capital gains associated with profit retention and resulting share-price appreciation rather than dividend income. A specialized firm can also retain profits rather than distributing them in the form of dividends. However, the diversified firm can yield *more* capital gains to shareholders, because it can shift investment funds internally from activities with low marginal returns to those with higher marginal returns. In contrast, the shareholder in a specialized firm, even if the firm retained its profits to maximize share-price gains, would have to liquidate his share holdings, thereby becoming subject to capital gains taxation, in order to transfer financial resources to another specialized firm yielding higher returns.

One other rather obvious tax advantage of diversification is the ability of the firm to offset losses in one activity against profits in another. If a specialized firm experiences losses, it simply pays no corporate income tax, but the corporate income tax of other profitable specialized firms is not thereby reduced. In contrast, when losses can be combined in the same firm with profits from other activities, the losses will serve to reduce income tax owed as a result of the profitable activities. Of course, the coexistence of losses and profits in a single firm reflects a disequilibrium situation, and such tax advantages are not therefore a feature of diversified firms' equilibrium behavior. The same is true of another argument which is sometimes offered to explain why diversified firms might have a lower cost of investment funds, namely, the alleged loss of information available to shareholders or debt lenders regarding the performance of individual activities in a diversified firm, and the consequent possibility that they may overestimate the returns attainable from lending to such firms, compared to a group of otherwise identical separate firms. This argument is sometimes reinforced by the argument that the complicated nature of some of the debt instruments issued by diversified firms, sometimes referred to as 'funny money', tends to deceive lenders regarding the true value of the debt instruments. In reply to these arguments, it can be pointed out that while temporary valuation errors may result, it is unlikely that they will be large-scale, or persistent. Moreover, as Lorie and Halpern have pointed out (23), the empirical evidence concerning the performance of diversified firms' share values and the return to holders of their debt instruments during periods following the issue of 'funny money' suggests that shareholders holding such shares have not been exploited.

To this point, the preceding analysis of the advantages of diversification has considered the possible lowering of the total production cost, finance costs, or tax liabilities, associated with a collection of dissimilar productive activities combined in a single firm, compared to an otherwise identical group of independent specialized firms. Another possible effect of diversification is the raising of total revenues associated with any particular overall level of a firm's operations, compared to specialized operation at that level. The aspect of demand conditions which is most frequently cited as a factor responsible for diversification is limited demand for individual products. Also, discussions of diversification in this context are often within the framework of expansion in the overall level of a firm's productive activities; this is because interest in diversification was originally stimulated largely by the conglomerate merger phenomenon. Diversification and growth are not synonymous, however, and many diversified firms have been diversified from the start. Focusing upon the issue of diversification versus specialization at a given overall size of a firm helps to underline the essential nature of the diversification decision and its possible advantages in terms of effects on the firm's total costs and total revenues.

Emphasis on limited demand for individual products tends to obscure what may in practice be one of the major reasons for diversification, which is connected with the analysis of price discrimination and product differentiation contained in Chapter 3. There it was pointed out that a firm can increase the total revenue from sales of a particular product by discriminating in price between different groups of buyers whose price-elasticity of demand is different. It was also emphasized that in order to discriminate in price the firm must separate the total market for its product into segments, and that differentiation of different varieties of the firm's product may be an effective method of achieving this result. As already noted in the first section of this chapter, the distinction between diversification and differentiation is a matter of degree only, and what to an outside observer may appear to be diversification may merely reflect differentiation aimed at segmenting the total market for a firm's product for optimal pricing purposes. This view is supported by some of the empirical evidence relating to diversification. In a study published in 1971, for example, Charles H. Berry (3) concluded that diversification in the United States between 1960 and 1965 has generally been into markets related to firms' original activities, and is only one small step removed from horizontal expansion.

Neglect of the preceding revenue-increasing aspect of diversification is reflected in analyses of conglomerate merger, which generally assume that the demand conditions facing the combined firms involved remain unchanged, and that none of the revenue-increasing possibilities associated with horizontal merger and increased market power are present in the case of a merger between firms performing dissimilar productive activities. It should be noted here that the assumption that demand conditions facing the merged firms remain unchanged in a case of conglomerate merger may be invalid, because these demand conditions depend on the behavior of rival sellers, whose behavior may differ depending on whether a set of dissimilar productive activities is undertaken by a group of separate firms or a single diversified firm. This aspect of diversification will be considered in more detail in the next section. Even if the demand conditions facing separate firms are not changed by combination of the activities within a single firm, there are reasons connected with the revenue-increasing aspect of diversification noted in the preceding paragraph why a single decision-making unit may be able to earn higher total revenues, on the basis of those demand conditions, than a group of separate firms. Speaking in terms of 'unrelated' activities in connection with diversification tends to obscure the fact that demand for all products which compete for buyers' incomes is related, and the demand for each individual product depends on the prices of other products. One reason why a group of independent firms producing different products may be able to earn less total revenue than a single diversified firm is the possibility of competitive behavior by separate firms, in the sense of behavior which does not maximize the joint total revenue possible from the combined group of activities. Group-maximizing behavior not only requires that each firm take into account the behavior of firms producing different products, but also will only result from certain kinds of assumptions about how those firms will react. Even with perfect certainty about rivals' reactions, and an intent to 'collude' in order to maximize total revenue and profits from a group of dissimilar activities, the ability to do so depends on the availability of information regarding the way in which the demand for individual products is affected by changes in the prices of each of the other products. Obtaining this kind of information, or communicating it between different divisions of a diversified firm may be easier and/or less costly than in a group of independent firms performing the same activities. The conclusion that conglomerate merger has no revenue-raising possibilities ignores these considerations and implicitly assumes that the merging firms were independently maximizing joint revenues prior to the merger. Also, where such revenue-increasing possibilities have been perceived, and attributed to 'increased recognition of interdependence', they have usually been condemned as an adverse effect of diversification from the point of view of society. As indicated in more detail in the next section, however, this charge may be premature. Finally, even where the revenue-increasing possibilities of diversification have been recognized and viewed favorably, they have usually been viewed in the context of a dynamic disequilibrium adjustment process. Thus, for example, D. E. Logue and P. A. Naert (22) emphasize the greater flexibility in the operation of a diversified firm and the importance of being able to shift resources when conditions confronting the firm change. Similarly, in explaining why an economy organized along diversified lines might enjoy advantages over a specialized firm economy, O. E. Williamson (48) stresses delayed responses to market signals under the latter form of organization. While these dynamic advantages of diversification exist, and may be important, it needs to be emphasized that the revenue-increasing possibility of diversification outlined earlier exists *also* in equilibrium, and that such static gains have been overlooked or underemphasized in the literature dealing with motives for diversification.

Focusing on the information-flow requirements for maximizing total revenue from a group of dissimilar activities, and on the possible differences between a diversified firm and a group of independent firms performing the same activities, leads to yet another factor influencing diversification, apart from cost and demand conditions: several writers have emphasized the importance of the form of a firm's internal organization for diversification. O. E. Williamson (48, 49) has demonstrated the superiority of the internal-control properties of the multidivision form of corporate organization compared to a unitary form, for example. C. J. Sutton (42) has also argued that the degree and direction of diversification in a firm will depend on the authority structure within the firm. He points out that since marketing and research staff are more likely than production staff to perceive diversification opportunities and may have stronger incentives to press for their acceptance, more diversification is likely to occur where marketing or research staff, rather than production staff, carry more authority in a firm's decision-making processes.

Several other factors which may influence a firm's diversification may be noted briefly: if public policy penalizes market power in individual markets, extending operations beyond a certain scale in a single market, or in vertically related activities, may not be feasible for a firm. In these circumstances, diversification may be the only feasible alternative for firms above a certain overall size. Apart from the nature of constraints such as cost and demand conditions relating to investment finance, tax laws, and antitrust laws, the precise nature of the objectives pursued by a firm's decision-makers may themselves affect the degree of diversification undertaken by a firm. Dennis Mueller (27), for example, has offered an explanation for conglomerate mergers based on the pursuit of growth maximization rather than shareholder-welfare maximization by a firm's managers. To a firm's managers interested in maximizing the growth rate of the firm, the opportunity cost of funds invested in the firm will equal the return on marginal projects within the firm, rather than the return on the highest-yielding investment projects in other firms, which is the opportunity cost of funds invested in the firm by shareholders. Thus, the managers' discount rate will be lower than that of shareholders, resulting in higher levels of investment in productive activities than if managers pursue shareholder-welfare maximization. This will raise the optimal levels of the firm's investment in horizontal, vertical, and diversified activities; if public policy constraints prevent horizontal and vertical expansion, this will increase further the optimal level of the firm's investment in diversified activities.

In assessing the importance in practice of the various reasons for diversification outlined in this section, the following point needs to be borne in mind: since the optimal levels of all aspects of a firm's behavior, including diversification, depend on the objectives and all the constraints confronting the firm's decision-makers, a number of factors responsible for diversification may be operating simultaneously to produce any given observed degree of diversification. Rarely will there be a single explanation for diversification, therefore, even in the context of a particular firm in a given set of circumstances at a particular point in time. Furthermore, when considering the relationship between diversification and other aspects of a firm's behavior, it must be remembered that optimal levels of all aspects of the firm's behavior are interdependent and simultaneously determined by the objectives and all constraints facing the firm's decision-makers. There are, accordingly, many possible relationships between diversification and other aspects of a firm's operations, corresponding to differences in objectives and constraints, so that theorizing alone will not suffice. It is also necessary to investigate the nature of these relationships existing in practice, in an effort to reject some of the many hypotheses which have been advanced to explain diversification, and to determine the major factors operating in practice. The results of some of the empirical studies relating to diversification will be reviewed presently. First, however, it is appropriate to consider the relationship between diversification and competition.

Diversification and Competition

Since the term 'competition' is used in many different senses and means different things to different people, it is appropriate to state in what sense the term will be used in this section. Competition will be used to refer to the price and other characteristics of output offered by firms; in other words, competition and the behavior of firms are synonymous terms. In considering the relationship between diversification and competition it is useful to distinguish between the behavior of a diversified firm itself, the behavior of rival sellers operating in the various markets in which the firm sells, and the behavior of potential entrants into those markets. As explained in Chapter 7, potential entrants include firms operating in other markets whose behavior is taken into account by firms established in a particular market, and whose behavior therefore influences the policies of the established firms. Another useful distinction is that between the pricing behavior and the non-price behavior of these three classes of firm. Such distinctions are helpful in clarifying the relationship between diversification and competition, since some fairly complex interactions are involved.

The influence of diversification on the behavior of a diversified firm itself has already been considered in the preceding section. Among other things, it was pointed out that even if the demand conditions for individual products produced by a diversified firm are unchanged, diversification may enable the firm to separate the total market for its product and earn higher total revenues by discriminating in price between different classes of buyers. It was also noted that the demand conditions facing the diversified firm depend in part on the behavior of rival sellers, including those already selling in the same markets as the firm, and potential entrants into those markets. Before we turn to analyze the effect of diversification on the behavior of established rivals and potential entrants, however, it is appropriate to note several types of behavior associated with diversified firms themselves, including tie-in sales, cross-subsidization, and reciprocal and exclusive dealing arrangements. Treatment of these types of behavior has been postponed until this section since they are usually considered to have adverse consequences for competition, a supposition which will now be examined.

Tie-in sales, also sometimes referred to as full-line forcing, is the practice of requiring that the purchaser of product A (the tying good) purchase his 'requirements' of one or more other products, B, C, etc. (the tied goods) from the seller of A. One possible reason for tie-in sales may be to enable a firm to practice price discrimination. Thus, suppose a producer of A wishes to charge different prices to different buyers of A in accordance with differences in their price-elasticity of demand. He may tie in a product B which is used with A in order to meter the intensity of use by buyers of A and thereby effectively charge higher prices to those buyers who use A more intensively. Tying inputs used with a machine, such as punch cards to computers or mimeograph supplies to mimeograph machines, is an obvious example of this practice. As M. L. Burstein demonstrated in two lucid articles published in 1960 (5, 6), there is another reason for tie-in sales, however, which applies independently of price discrimination. Even if the price-elasticity of demand of different buyers of a firm's product were identical so that price discrimination would not be profitable, or even if a firm is already practicing price discrimination, tie-in sales can further increase the firm's total profits. Burstein's argument, in brief, is as follows: Figure 9–1 depicts the demand conditions for product A associated with a single buyer of the product. At the profit-maximizing price charged by the seller, OC, the buyer purchases OA units of the product, paying the firm $OABC$ dollars. The triangle CBD, termed consumer's surplus, represents the sum of the difference between what the buyer is willing to pay for each unit of A purchased and the amount he actually pays. The consumer's surplus may be viewed as the dollar sum which the buyer would be willing to pay for the right to buy A at OC dollars per unit rather than go without A at all. The firm could extract this sum from the buyer by charging a different price for each of the OA units of A, corresponding to the maximum price the buyer is willing to pay for each unit. However, this will not generally be possible, due to the necessary information requirements or legal prohibitions. If, instead, the firm succeeds in stipulating that the buyer also obtain all his 'requirements' of some other product B from the firm, at a price above the cost of B to the firm, the firm will make profits from selling B. If the buyer's demand for A and B is independent, so that demand conditions associated with A are not changed despite any rise in the price of B compared to the price charged by other producers of B, the firm's profits from the tying good will be unchanged, and the firm's total profits will be increased. Burstein demonstrates that even when A and B are complements or substitutes, so that a buyer's demand for A is affected by a change in the price of B, the same conclusion follows: tie in sales are a means of achieving profits above and beyond those attainable simply by manipulation of the price of the tying good.

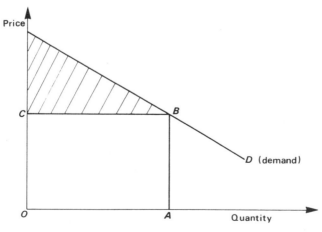

Figure 9–1. Consumers' surplus associated with uniform pricing to an individual buyer.

Whether the firm will be successful in inducing buyers of A to accept the tie-in stipulation, and therefore the profitability of any particular tie-in arrangement, will depend on several factors. A rise in the price of B, compared to the price at which B could be obtained from other sellers, will reduce the consumer's surplus associated with purchases of B. If this reduction in the consumer's surplus exceeds the consumer's surplus associated with purchases of A, a buyer will prefer to purchase B elsewhere and to forgo A entirely, since acceptance of the tying arrangement would reduce his total satisfaction. Given the rise in price of B, the relative magnitude of the consumer's two surpluses depends on buyer preference patterns, and any given tying arrangement can be expected to result in loss of some of the firm's customers and acceptance by others due to differences in these preferences. Secondly, the reduction in the consumer's surplus of B will tend to be larger for any buyer, the larger the price of B sold by the tying firm relative to the price charged by other sellers of B. The behavior of rival sellers of B is therefore an important determinant of the profitability of any particular tie-in arrangement. Finally, the profitability of a tie-in arrangement will also depend on whether the tying firm is the sole producer of A; if not, a buyer may reject the tie-in arrangement in favor of purchases of A from other producers. However, the terms offered by other producers of A are also obviously relevant in this connection; if, for example, all other producers of A also stipulated similar tie-in arrangements, a buyer in effect has no alternative source of A, and once again must either accept the tie-in or forgo consumption of A completely.

As Burstein emphasizes, tie-in sales are consistent with rather straightforward principles of profit maximization. He rejects the view that the purpose of a tie in is primarily to extend monopoly power from one product to another; rather, it is a method of enabling a firm to extract all the profit potential from the market for the tying good. Moreover, the effect of a tie in will very often be to lower the profit-maximizing price of the tying good. Burstein points out that this will occur when demand for the tying and tied goods is independent and also when the goods are complements. The basic reason is that the price-elasticity of demand for the tying good will tend to increase at any price as some buyers of A reject the tying arrangement. On the other hand, if a substitute good is tied, the price of the tying good may increase, depending on the relative strength of demand-reducing rejections of the tying arrangement by some of the firm's customers and the demand-increasing influence of a rise in the price of the substitute product B. In view of these considerations, it is apparent that tie-in sales will affect the structure of price–cost relationships for different products in the economy in a manner which cannot be predicted a priori. The consequent implications for resource allocation and allocative efficiency in the economy depend, moreover, not only on the effect of tie-in sales on price–cost relationships, but also on the nature of optimal welfare-maximizing price–cost relationships. As will be explained in Chapter 10, these optimal welfare-maximizing price–cost relationships themselves depend on the precise nature of the constraints present in any particular situation. No general conclusions are possible, therefore, regarding either the effect of tie-in sales on firms' pricing behavior, or on the consequences of any particular effect on pricing behavior for allocative efficiency and aggregate satisfaction in the community.

The practice of exclusive dealing is analogous to tie-in sales, since it involves the stipulation by a firm producing product A that buyers of product A also buy products B, C, etc. solely from the firm instead of from other sellers of B and C. As in the case of tie-in sales, if the producer of product A is unable to reduce consumers' surplus associated with product A to zero by setting the terms of sale for A, exclusive dealing represents a potential alternative method for reducing consumers' surplus and raising the firm's profits. The arguments are the same as those already outlined in connection with tie-in sales, and therefore need not be repeated.

Turning next to the practice of cross-subsidization, the idea is deeply ingrained in many persons' thinking about diversified firms that such firms can use the profits from the sale of one product to permit sales of another product below cost, thereby driving other firms producing the subsidized product out of business. Several comments are appropriate in reply to this line of reasoning. First, this practice cannot succeed in driving rival producers out of business unless there are entry barriers preventing them from also producing the product sold in the profitable market. Second, even if entry barriers to the profitable market exist, so that pricing below cost could drive rival firms out of business without simultaneously impoverishing the diversified firm, there will be no long-run gain to the firm in remaining in the industry unless there are entry barriers to this industry also, which permit monopoly power to be exercised. In the absence of entry barriers to the subsidized market, any attempt by the remaining firm to raise price above cost will be met by competition from new entrants. Third, even if entry barriers do exist which would permit the exercise of monopoly power after other firms have been driven from the industry, Lester Telser, John McGee and a number of other economists have clearly pointed out that there are methods of achieving monopoly power in the industry which are much less costly than temporarily pricing below cost, such as collusive pricing behavior or merger and acquisition of rival firms.

The final practice with allegedly harmful effects on competition which a diversified firm may engage in is reciprocal dealing, which occurs when two or more firms agree, either tacitly or explicitly, to buy from each other instead of from other available sources of supply. By itself, the fact that two firms deal with each other over a long period of time is not sufficient to prove the existence of reciprocity; they may simply be purchasing inputs on the most favorable terms. The key issue is whether each party is free to turn to alternative sources of supply. In certain circumstances, reciprocity may simply reflect a desire by the firms in question to avoid certain costs of using the market associated with locating customers and persuading them to buy from one's own firm rather than from competitors. This efficiency-increasing aspect of reciprocity is very similar to the economies associated with the vertical integration argument in Chapter 8. In other circumstances, however, the practice of reciprocity may be based on considerations very similar to those outlined earlier in this section in connection with tie-in sales. For example, if a firm selling product A is unable to extract all the consumers' surplus associated with sales of A by discriminating perfectly in price between different units of A sold to each buyer, the firm may try indirectly to reduce consumers' surplus by requiring a purchaser of A to *sell* another product, B, to the firm producing A at prices below those ruling in the market for B. If successful, this will clearly raise the profits of the producer of A, and as in the case of tie-in sales, the success and profitability of the reciprocal dealing arrangement will depend on the behavior of other sellers of A and on the behavior of other buyers and sellers of B which influence the market terms for B. If the producer of A is a monopolist, or if all sellers of A require similar reciprocal dealing arrangements, reciprocal dealing is more likely to occur since the buyer then has no alternative other than to accept the arrangement of obtaining no A.

Instead of monopoly in the production of a particular product, monopsony in the purchase of a product may also result in reciprocal dealing arrangements. Thus, suppose that a firm buying product C cannot extract all the producers' surplus, which is defined as the excess of selling price over the price at which the seller is willing to sell each unit of C. The Robinson–Patman Act, which prevents the seller of C from granting any more favorable terms to one buyer than another, may be responsible for this state of affairs. The buyer of C may be able to require the seller to buy some other product, D, from it on terms less favorable than the market terms for D. If successful, this will reduce the producers' surplus on sales of C and raise the profits of the firm buying C. Again, the profitability of a reciprocal dealing arrangement and likelihood of its occurrence will depend on the behavior of other sellers and buyers in the market for D, and on the behavior of other buyers of C, if any. The consensus of opinion among economists regarding the practice of reciprocity is that it is a means of exerting monopoly power which already exists, rather than a method of extending monopoly power to other products, and that the practice is in general unlikely to harm competition.

Some economists have attempted to determine the effects of diversification on competition in the individual markets in which a diversified firm operates by reference to the effect of diversification on market shares of firms in those markets. In this connection it is appropriate to distinguish between diversification accomplished by acquisition and/or merger between the diversifying firm and a firm already operating in another industry, and that achieved by internal expansion. The first method of diversification does not increase the number of sellers operating in the market in question, while the second method represents entry by an additional seller. Of course, diversification which occurs through acquisition and merger need not leave the pattern of behavior in the market unchanged. Lawrence Goldberg (14) examined the effect of diversification achieved by merger on the market share of the acquired firm; although some of the acquired firms in his study increased their market share, others did not, and overall Goldberg found no statistically significant tendency for diversification via merger to increase the market share of the acquired firm. Moreover, those acquired firms whose market shares did increase showed no tendency to be associated with merger by large firms rather than small; the pre-merger growth rate of the acquired firms seemed to be the most important factor underlying their post-merger market shares. Goldberg concluded on the basis of this evidence that diversification via merger does not have harmful effects on competition.

Unfortunately, however, the effect of diversification via merger on acquired firms' market shares does not indicate the effect on competition, in the sense of the behavior of firms serving the market, for two related reasons: first, a firm's market share depends in part on the response of rival sellers to its actions, and their behavior must also therefore be analyzed in assessing the implications of diversification for competition. Second, to the extent that market shares indicate anything about competition in a market, most economists would agree that the market share of the leading firms is the relevant focus of attention, rather than the market share of the acquired firm. An increase, a decrease, or no change in the market share of an acquired firm are each compatible either with an increase, a decrease, or no change in the market share of the leading firms serving the market in question. In a 1974 study, Charles H. Berry (4) examined the extent to which diversification by 461 large firms in the United States between 1960 and 1965 tended to increase the market share of leading firms in markets into which diversification occurred. He found that the market shares of leading firms were in fact reduced, and that this tendency was stronger the more highly concentrated the industry into which diversification occurred. Therefore, to the extent that the market share of leading firms in an industry is inversely correlated with competition in the industry, this evidence supports the hypothesis that diversification aids rather than hinders competition. It should be added that the concentration-reducing impact of diversification applied to diversification by large firms; Berry also found that diversification by small firms has a concentration-reducing effect which diminishes and approaches zero when concentration in the markets entered is high.

The assumption that market shares themselves indicate anything about competition in a market is highly questionable, however, and even where they do, they cannot indicate the multidimensional characteristics of firms' behavior. As already noted, it is necessary to examine the behavior of other sellers in response to diversification into a market, whether via merger or internal expansion. In both cases, whether and how the behavior of other sellers will be affected depends on how their expectations regarding the policies of the diversifying firm, and each other, are affected. In the case of diversification via merger, for example, one possibility is that the behavior of other sellers will not be affected if they expect the post-merger behavior of the firm to be the same as its pre-merger behavior. If, on the other hand, they expect the reactions of the acquired firm to their own policies to be different from those anticipated prior to the merger, their behavior will change. Just how it will change depends on precisely how they expect the acquired firm to react to their policies, however, and there are innumerable possible consequences for the resulting behavior of the group of sellers serving the market ranging anywhere between the two extremes of 'monopoly' and 'purely competitive' forms of group behavior. In this connection, the reader is reminded that expectations regarding non-price aspects of a firm's behavior are also relevant expectations in determining the behavior of rival sellers. Even if the pricing behavior of established rival sellers is not changed, their non-price behavior might change, resulting in a change in group behavior. Exactly the same arguments apply to diversification achieved via internal expansion. The fact that this involves an increase in the number of sellers in the entered market does not, itself, imply any specific effect on the group's behavior. Chapters 3 and 6 have amply demonstrated that any particular number and size distribution of rival sellers in a market is compatible with a variety of alternative behavior patterns. The key element, again, is the effect of diversification on established firms' expectations regarding rivals' reactions to their policies. No generalizations are possible regarding the influence of diversification on these expectations and on the consequences for group behavior; accordingly, no generalizations are possible regarding the relationship between diversification and that aspect of competition which relates to the behavior of a diversified firm's established rivals.

The last aspect of the relationship between diversification and competition to be considered concerns the effect of diversification on potential entrants' behavior. As explained in Chapter 7, potential entrants are firms not currently operating in a particular market who may enter the market in response to profit opportunities they perceive to exist there. The behavior of such firms may be taken into account by the firms already selling in the market, and may in certain circumstances influence the policies adopted by the established sellers even in the absence of actual entry.

Three separate arguments relating to the effect of diversification on potential competitors may be distinguished for expositional convenience. See D. Berger and M. Peterson (2) for a similar distinction and analysis. Two of these arguments are concerned with diversification which removes a potential entrant into the diversifying firm's original market. One of these arguments, which is often used against conglomerate mergers, is that elimination of a recognized potential entrant will reduce competition. In order for removal of a recognized potential entrant to affect competition adversely, however, several conditions must be fulfilled: first, in order for this to change the behavior of established sellers in the market in question, the potential entrant must be exerting an influence over their behavior. For this to occur, established sellers must believe that their current behavior influences the potential entrant's behavior. However, as was explained in Chapter 7, the behavior of potential entrants themselves depends on their cost conditions and the *post-entry* behavior of established firms which the potential entrant anticipates. The fact that established sellers currently set prices above the entry-deterring level, perhaps thereby drawing the attention of potential entrants to the existence of high current profit levels in the market, does not mean that entry will be encouraged; what matters to entrants is the *post-entry* level of prices and profits in the market. In other words, the *current* behavior of established sellers will only influence the potential entrants' decision on whether or not to enter the market if it somehow determines the post-entry behavior of established firms anticipated by entrants. As was also explained in Chapter 7, this would be the case if potential entrants expected established firms to attempt to keep their output levels unchanged if entry occurred. This is only one of innumerable possible reactions, however, and there are reasons outlined in Chapter 7 why other types of reactions are more likely to be anticipated. For these reasons, even if current prices exceed what would be an entry-deterring level, entry will not occur if entry-deterring reactions are anticipated in response to entry; conversely, entry could occur even if the current price is at or below what would be an entry-deterring level, if an entrant anticipates 'accommodating' reactions by established sellers. Accordingly, only if established sellers believe that their *current* behavior influences the post-entry behavior anticipated by potential entrants will that current behavior itself be influenced by the behavior of potential entrants. It follows that unless this condition is satisfied, removal of potential entrants will not change the behavior of established sellers in a market.

Even if the current behavior of established firms does affect, and therefore itself is influenced by, the behavior of potential entrants, a second condition must also be met before removal of a single recognized potential entrant will affect established firms' behavior: namely, that potential entrant must be recognized by firms already operating in the market as a uniquely qualified potential entrant in the sense that barriers to entry by other potential entrants are significantly higher. If this condition is met, removal of the potential entrant in effect raises barriers to entry, possibly enabling the established firms to raise prices relative to costs without inducing entry. On the other hand, if this second condition is not met, so that a potential entrant remains whose responses to the behavior of established firms are likely to be similar to those of the potential entrant removed, there is in effect no change in the anticipated behavior of potential entrants to the industry, and accordingly no change in the behavior of established sellers will occur. Both of the preceding conditions must be met simultaneously in order for the removal of a recognized potential entrant to reduce potential competition and affect the behavior of established sellers in a market. This rather stringent requirement will not often be met in practice.

The second argument involving diversification which removes a potential competitor occurs in the case of mergers which remove a firm which would *actually have entered* the original market of the diversifying firm by internal expansion. Whereas the preceding argument envisages removal of a potential entrant who exerted an influence over the behavior of established sellers, this second argument is not concerned with the pre-merger influence of the potential entrant, and there need be no such influence. Rather, the argument is that the merger prevented future entry into the original market of the diversifying firm. Once again, however, in order for competition to be adversely affected several conditions must be fulfilled: first, it must be established that the potential entrant would have definitely entered the market in absence of the merger; second, it must be established that the potential entrant would have behaved differently from the diversified firm. It has been repeatedly emphasized throughout this book that the number of firms selling in a market and competition are not synonymous. The entry of another firm into a market can leave industry output and price unchanged if established firms act in an accommodating manner, for example. Conversely, even if entry of the potential entrant had increased industry output and lowered the market price, this can also occur if the diversified firm expands its output level in its original market following the merger with the potential entrant firm. Such an output expansion could be associated with the revenue-increasing potential of diversification itself. Moreover, even if the two preceding conditions are met, there is a third which must also be satisfied in order for removal of the potential competitor to affect competition adversely: there must be no other potential entrants with cost conditions and anticipations similar to those of the potential entrant which is removed; otherwise these other firms can be expected to respond to the same stimulus which would have motivated the moved firm to enter the market. Unlike the recognized potential entrant case, however, the uniquely qualified potential entrant which is removed by merger does not have to be recognized as such by the established sellers in the market. Once again, these three simultaneously required conditions are sufficiently stringent to limit the practical relevance of the argument that removal of a potential entrant will adversely affect competition.

The third type of argument relating diversification and potential competition does not involve removal of a potential entrant. Rather, it focuses on the question of whether the behavior of potential entrants to a market will differ depending on whether the established sellers serving that market are specialized or also produce and sell in other markets. This, in turn, depends on whether the reactions of established firms anticipated by potential entrants are different when the established firms are specialized from those anticipated when they are diversified. It is possible to list plausible reasons why there may be a difference in these anticipated reactions when a potential entrant is confronted by diversified firms serving a particular market compared to when those firms are specialized. For example, if established firms are diversified, a potential entrant may expect them to react with cross-subsidization and pricing even below cost in established firms in the entered market, which would not be possible if the established firms were specialized. Entry-deterring behavior in these circumstances can involve losses only for the entrant, even if the entrant firm has no cost disadvantage compared to established firms, a possibility which is ruled out when established firms are specialized. However, the reader is reminded of several points already made in discussing cross-subsidization earlier in this section: the practice is not possible unless entry barriers prevent entrants from also entering the profitable markets served by the diversified established firms; it is not profitable unless entry barriers also exist to the entered market which enable established firms to price above cost once an entrant has been driven out; finally, even if the two previous conditions are met, predatory pricing to drive out competition is a more costly method of establishing monopoly than other methods such as merger or collusion. Despite these points, potential entrants may nonetheless expect established diversified firms to react in the above manner, so that diversification by established sellers in a market raises entry barriers compared to specialized operations, permitting higher profit rates for established sellers.

Empirical evidence on this issue is still very scarce. In 1973, however, Stephen A. Rhoades (36) presented empirical evidence in support of the hypothesis that diversification raises entry barriers. His study indicates that price–cost margins are higher in markets where the sellers are more diversified, where diversification is measured by the ratio between the sellers' total employment and the employment engaged in serving only those markets. According to Rhoades, the two entry barriers most likely to be associated with diversification are the potential for predatory pricing, noted above, and the information-loss on profits in individual markets which, if available, might otherwise induce entry.

It is possible to think of other ways in which diversification could also raise entry barriers, compared to specialized operations. The important point in the present context, however, is that the higher profits observed to exist in more diversified industries could also reflect the greater ability of diversified sellers to maximize total revenue from given demand conditions, for reasons already explained in the first section of this chapter, which apply even if diversification has no influence on the behavior of potential entrants into individual markets served by the sellers. That is, the profit potential of a group of markets depends on buyer behavior, on established seller behavior and on potential entrant behavior. Even if the behavior of potential entrants were not affected, diversified operations by firms established in each of these markets may raise the equilibrium level of total revenue and profits from serving those markets, compared to specialized firms serving the same markets. To this may be added dynamic reasons for higher profits, such as the superior ability of diversified firms to reallocate resources in response to changes in demand or cost conditions in individual markets, compared to specialized firms serving the same markets. For these reasons, Rhoades' finding, that industry profits are higher the more diversified the firms operating in individual markets, is also quite consistent with the hypothesis that diversification does *not* raise entry barriers into individual markets.

In addition to the relationship between diversification and competition in general, that between diversification and R&D competition in particular has attracted a considerable amount of attention from economists. One hypothesis that has been advanced is that diversification stimulates invention. The argument, in brief, is that research yields inventions and discoveries in unexpected areas. A diversified firm, it is argued, will generally be able to produce and market a higher proportion of these unexpected inventions than a firm whose product line is narrow. Therefore, it is argued, the expected profitability of research is greater for highly diversified firms, and such firms will accordingly undertake more research and development than less diversified firms.

This argument implies that new knowledge is worth more to firms which use the knowledge themselves rather than license or sell the knowledge to other firms. Why should the expected profitability of an invention which is patented by a firm and leased or sold to other firms for commercial exploitation be less than the expected profitability of the same invention assuming that the firm uses the invention itself? One possible explanation might be that the market for ideas is imperfect and that the firm will receive less by selling the invention than it can earn by exploiting the invention itself because other firms are imperfectly informed of the existence or potential applications of the invention when it is offered for sale.

Empirical evidence obtained by Gort (16) and others (see F. M. Scherer (38), for example) shows that diversification and R&D are indeed closely related. Diversification, measured by the number of industries in which a firm operates, is strongly correlated in a positive manner with R&D inputs, measured by R&D expenditures, scientific manpower, and the ratio of technical to other personnel, and also with R&D output, measured by patents issued. At first sight, the evidence seems consistent with the hypothesis that diversification increases invention. On further inspection, however, it can be argued that the relationship is largely spurious (Scherer (38)). Little relationship between R&D input, or output, remains after allowing for the influence of technological opportunities upon the observed relationship. That is, technological opportunity is generally greater in those industries into which firms diversify than in the original industry of the firm. After diversification, a larger proportion of the firm's operations takes place in industries in which the ratio of R&D input to other inputs is high relative to the ratio in a firm's original industry. Accordingly, higher degrees of diversification and a larger ratio of R&D to other inputs go hand in hand, considering the firm's total operations. The influence of technological opportunity upon the observed relationship between diversification and R&D can be eliminated by comparing more diversified and less diversified firms operating in industries which individually have roughly similar ratios of R&D input to total input. If more diversified firms tended to do more R&D in these circumstances, the evidence would be more consistent with the hypothesis that diversification per se increases invention. As yet, however, there is little evidence in support of this contention, while some evidence tends to reject the hypothesis. For example, evidence relating to the pharmaceutical industry in the United States (8) showed that innovation (measured by the value of two years' sales of new products) was inversely related to the extent of diversification within the pharmaceutical industry. That is, measuring diversification by the division of output among various pharmaceutical product submarkets, the statistical evidence suggests that for a given level of R&D input, higher rates of technical change will be achieved if a firm's product line is narrow rather than broad.

In our discussion up to this point, the effects of diversification on 'competition' have been viewed as synonymous with effects on the behavior of the diversified firm itself, its established rivals, or the behavior of potential rivals in the markets served by diversified firms. There is another, narrower sense in which the term 'competition' is used in economic analysis, namely, in the sense of forms of seller behavior which are optimal from the point of view of maximizing the aggregate level of satisfaction in a community. The nature of these optimal forms of behavior will be explained in some detail in Chapter 10. In the present context, it is necessary to emphasize that any particular effect of diversification on firms' behavior cannot be judged to be adverse, or favorable, for competition without such optimal standards of behavior. Moreover, for reasons which will be explained in Chapter 10, the precise nature of these optimal forms of seller behavior can themselves vary with certain circumstances existing in the community to which they apply.

In assessing the implications of diversification for competition in the sense of optimal forms of seller behavior, emphasis has traditionally been almost exclusively confined to the adverse effects of diversification for competition. Usually, these adverse effects involve alleged effects on the behavior of the diversified firm, its established rivals, or of potential entrants, which result in more monopolistic pricing behavior in individual markets of the economy. As the discussion earlier in this section indicates, such adverse effects usually require the existence of a number of other conditions in addition to diversification itself, and their practical relevance is probably greatly exaggerated.

The traditional assumption that diversification can have no favorable consequences for competition, in the sense of welfare-maximizing forms of market behavior by sellers, is also unwarranted. Neglect of the total-revenue-raising possibilities inherent in diversification due to its potential for market separation and price discrimination, or misinterpretation of the consequences of price discrimination for the level of aggregate satisfaction in the economy, are to a large extent at the root of the traditional view that diversification cannot have favorable effects on allocative efficiency in the economy. The fact that a firm practicing price discrimination has higher total revenue and profits does not necessarily mean that the aggregate level of satisfaction in the community is thereby reduced. Profit-maximizing price discrimination generally implies a different relationship between price and cost in different segments of a firm's overall market, compared to uniform pricing. The consequences of these price changes for the pattern of resource allocation between different markets are what matter as far as the level of satisfaction in the community is concerned. For profit maximization, assuming zero cross-elasticities of demand and supply purely for expositional convenience, price–marginal cost differences in individual markets served by the firm will be set in relation to price-elasticities of demand in those markets. As will be explained in Chapter 10, maximization of the aggregate level of satisfaction in a community requires that price equal marginal cost in every market of the economy. If, as usually occurs in practice, constraints exist which prevent price from equalling marginal cost in every market of the economy simultaneously, setting price equal to marginal cost will not be required for maximizing the satisfaction of the community. Instead, as will be explained in the section dealing with the theory of second-best, welfare-maximizing pricing rules will often require that price–marginal cost differences be set in relation to price-elasticities of demand in different markets. In these circumstances, the only difference between this prescription and the profit-maximizing pricing rule lies in the absolute magnitude of the price–marginal cost difference, which will be higher for profit maximization than for welfare maximization. In other words, *relative* prices in different markets will be the same for profit and welfare maximization, but the absolute level of price will be higher in every market under profit maximization than is required for welfare maximization.

The implications for resource allocation of these two pricing systems are as follows: a given total amount of resources will be allocated between different markets in the same way under both pricing systems, but the total amount of resources allocated is less under profit maximization than under welfare maximization, so that output in each market is lower under profit maximization than under welfare maximization.

The implications of the preceding discussion for diversification are these: if diversification and multi-product operations by firms permit price–marginal cost differences to correspond more closely to price-elasticities of demand in different markets of the economy than would be the case if production occurred only in specialized firms in the economy, the resulting pattern of resource allocation between different markets could be superior from the point of view of maximizing the level of aggregate satisfaction in the community. Specialized firms could, in principle, set the same price–marginal cost relationships as diversified firms if they are aware of the price- and cross-elasticities of demand in individual markets; the information-flow and internal control properties of diversified firms may, however, enable this to be achieved more easily or at less cost.

The preceding argument is concerned with the possible existence of improved resource allocation between different markets associated with the equilibrium behavior of diversified firms. To these static resource-allocation gains must be added any dynamic gains in resource allocation attributable to diversification, in the form of more rapid adjustments in resource allocation in response to changes in demand or cost conditions than would occur if production took place in specialized firms. In a specialized firm economy, if firms do not distribute all their earnings, this may delay the transfer of capital funds and physical resources between different sectors in response to changes in demand or cost conditions, thereby prolonging the time period required for the economy to move from one welfare-maximizing pattern of resource allocation to another. In contrast, in a diversified firm, funds and resources will be reallocated in response to changes in prospective yields in different activities. The possibility that an economy consisting of diversified firms may perform the resource allocation function more rapidly and effectively, by acting as a miniature capital market, than an economy of specialized firms, has been emphasized by several economists, including O. E. Williamson (48, 49). Moreover, it should be noted that any dynamic advantages of diversification apply irrespective of, and do not depend on, the precise nature of seller behavior which is optimal from the point of view of achieving allocative efficiency and maximum aggregate satisfaction in the economy.

The existence and magnitude of either adverse or beneficial effects of diversification, from the point of view of maximizing the level of aggregate satisfaction in a community, cannot be determined without resort to empirical evidence. Proposals for the control of diversification should recognize the likelihood of both kinds of effects existing in practice. The appropriate form of control should involve policies to eliminate any adverse consequences of diversification existing in practice, rather than policies to eliminate diversification itself. This prescription applies even if it were found that diversification results in few beneficial effects. The reason lies in the difficulty of defining market boundaries, discussed in Chapter 5, and the virtual impossibility of objectively distinguishing between diversification and horizontal differentiation of products. In view of these problems, any attempt to limit diversification itself is likely to result in arbitrary decisions, anomalies, and worsened rather than improved resource allocation. If control of some aspects of the behavior of diversified firms is warranted, moreover, it is illogical to confine such control only to firms which have recently diversified. As L. G. Goldberg has pointed out (14), many older firms, such as R.C.A., General Motors and General Electric, have as diverse a product mix as the so-called conglomerates of recent vintage. In fact, G.E. and Westinghouse produce the greatest number of products, as defined by the Census of Manufacturers, of any U.S. firm.

Even the issue of which method of diversification, merger or internal expansion, is most desirable from the point of view of maximizing the aggregate level of satisfaction in the community has no clear-cut answer. The traditional presumption that internal expansion is preferable to merger on these grounds can be challenged on several grounds. As Kurt Retwisch pointed out in 1969 (35), it is possible for diversification by merger to result in lower per unit costs of output over all future time periods, or more rapid reduction in unit costs to the minimum feasible level, than diversification via internal expansion. Unit costs will be lower over all time periods if a merger can avoid certain costs, such as the costs involved in recruiting and setting up a new organization, compared to internal expansion. More rapid reductions in unit costs to the minimum feasible level will result if temporary adjustment costs involved in diversification are lower in the case of merger than in the case of internal expansion.

In addition to the implications of merger and internal expansion for costs and technical efficiency in the economy, the implications for the level of industry price and resource allocation in the economy must also be compared. In this connection, it is incorrect to assume that the increase in the number of sellers in a market which is involved in diversification via internal expansion will result in lower price than if diversification occurs via merger. A point repeatedly emphasized in this book is that the behavior of a group of sellers is not so much a function of their number as of the sellers' expectations regarding each other's reactions. Entry into a market by internal expansion can result in accommodating reactions by established sellers which leave market price unchanged, for example. Conversely, entry via merger may change established sellers' expectations regarding the post-merger behavior of the merged firm, compared to their pre-merger expectations, and this can result in more competitive group behavior and lower market price.

For these reasons, the view that diversification via internal expansion necessarily results in improved resource allocation compared to merger must be rejected. Moreover, it does not automatically follow that entry by internal expansion will occur if entry via merger is prohibited. Potential entrants may view the profitability of entry by these two means differently, and reject entry by internal expansion. In these circumstances, the effect of banning entry by merger would be to raise entry barriers into the markets in question, possibly resulting in changes in the behavior of established sellers which would worsen resource allocation in the economy.

Empirical Studies of Diversification

This section will indicate briefly the results of empirical studies of diversification. The first part will deal with evidence concerning characteristics of diversified firms themselves, including size, profitability, growth rates, debt–equity ratios, and method of diversification, merger or internal expansion. The second part will review empirical evidence concerning characteristics of the markets from which and into which firms diversify, including profitability, concentration, rate of growth of market demand, and technological change.

A seminal study of diversification by M. Gort (16) indicated that the degree of diversification, measured by the ratio of primary product to total output, does not increase with firm size, but that diversification measured in terms of the number of industries in which a firm operates does increase with firm size. To some extent, this may reflect the existence of economies of scale in the production of individual products. As explained in the second section of this chapter, the existence of economies of scale in the production of individual products will imply that a firm will have to produce a certain minimum rate of output in order to compete effectively with firms producing larger rates of output of those products. This may limit the degree of diversification which is profitable at small firm sizes. Greater diversification as firm size increases could however also reflect the fact that further expansion in a firm's original markets is expected to be less profitable than diversification.

Gort found no clear relationships between any measure of diversification and either profit rates or growth. In contrast, in a more recent study, S. R. Reid (32) classified firms into categories of internal growth (which included horizontal and vertical as well as diversified growth) and horizontal, vertical, concentric, and conglomerate mergers, and found that the conglomerate merging firms were growing significantly faster than all other categories in terms of sales, assets, and employees. Comparing growth of earnings per share, however, conglomerate firms performed half as well as internal-growth firms, and twice as well as horizontal, vertical and concentric merging firms. The same ranking was also obtained when growth of share prices was compared, though the relative gap between internal-growth and conglomerate merging firms was found to decrease.

In a subsequent article (47), J. F. Weston and S. K. Mansinghka tested the hypothesis that Reid's finding – of lower growth in the earnings per share or in the share price of conglomerate merging firms – was due to the relatively early terminal dates employed by Reid. They calculated growth rates for total assets, sales, net income, earnings per share, and market price of shares, for 63 conglomerate merging firms and two control samples of other firms. Although they found that the growth rates for conglomerate firms were higher on all items, they attached no great importance to this fact, recognizing that such differences reflected the greater extent of recent merger activity among the conglomerate firms than firms in the control sample, a point which will be amplified below. Profitability measures were calculated for the 63 conglomerates and two control groups of firms in 1958 and 1968. In both years, the price–earnings ratios of conglomerate firms were on average not significantly different from the price–earnings ratios of other firms. Moreover, by using higher ratios of debt to equity finance, conglomerate firms were able to raise the ratio of net income to net worth slightly above that of other firms, though the difference is not statistically significant. Weston and Mansinghka place greatest emphasis on the ratio between a firm's total earnings, profits and interest, and its total assets, as a measure of profitability. For the year 1958, the profitability of the conglomerate firms in this sense was significantly lower than that of the other groups of firms; by 1968, however, there were no significant differences between conglomerates and other firms in respect of this measure of profitability. The interpretation placed by Weston and Mansinghka on these findings was that the improvement in profitability of conglomerates between 1958 and 1968 reflected successful defensive diversification by these firms, defined as diversification to avoid adverse effects on profitability from developments taking place in the firms' traditional markets.

In yet another study, P. A. Prosper and J. E. Smith Jr (31) attempted to determine whether the means of various ratios between conglomerate firms and non-conglomerate firms were significantly different. A group of manufacturing firms was selected from the 1968 *Fortune* list of 500 corporations and data concerning their characteristics were obtained from *Moody's* (New York). The results indicated that conglomerates carry more debt than non-conglomerates, a feature already noted in the second section of this chapter.

The price–earnings ratios of conglomerates and non-conglomerates were identical, as Weston and Mansinghka also found, but the ratio of operating profits to assets was lower for conglomerates.

The sometimes conflicting results of different statistical studies often reflect differences in the time period studied, and the data base, industry-classification criteria and diversification measures utilized. The length of the time period studied is particularly important in comparing the growth and profitability of firms which diversify via merger with those which diversify or grow horizontally or vertically by means of internal expansion. If two firms, A and B, diversify at the same point in time into a given market, by means of internal expansion and merger respectively, B will generally have grown more in size than A if a relatively short period of time is adopted for purposes of comparing their growth rates. Over a longer period of time, if similar objectives and external conditions apply to both firms, there would seem to be no clear reason why their growth rates should differ appreciably. The same problem occurs in connection with comparisons of the profitability of the two firms: if a relatively short period of time is adopted for the purpose of making a comparison, firm A may not yet have expanded its output to the profit-maximizing level, while what will have happened to B's profitability will depend on the previous profitability of the acquired firm, on the extent of the premium that B had to pay to acquire the assets of the acquired firm, and upon any changes that have occurred in the profitability of either of the merged firms as a result of the merger. Over a longer period of time, there may be no difference between the profitability of the two firms.

In interpreting the failure of empirical studies of diversification to reveal any systematic relationship between diversification and profitability, it must be remembered that a number of underlying reciprocal influences are at work. One might expect high profits and diversification to be related either because profits are a source of investment funds which can be used to finance diversification or because diversification increases profits. Firms may, however, use their investment funds to expand in a horizontal or vertical direction. Gort's study, noted earlier, indicates that diversification and vertical integration are inversely related, suggesting that a substitute relationship exists in managers' minds between these two alternative forms of expansion. Therefore, the absence of a systematic relationship between profits and diversification does not necessarily imply that diversification fails to increase profits; it may merely reflect the fact that, for some firms, the anticipated profits from growing in other ways may be greater. Also, where a firm diversifies for defensive reasons, the firm's profits may even decline on balance; they may, however, have declined more in the absence of diversification.

Turning next to characteristics of the markets from which and into which firms diversify, a number of studies, including that by C. H. Berry referred to in the first section of this chapter, and another by Adrian Wood (50) indicate a marked preference by managers for diversification into markets which are closely related to each other in terms of demand- or supply-side characteristics. The rationale of such narrow-spectrum diversification, which is different from horizontal 'differentiation' only in degree, has been discussed in the second section of this chapter.

Whether a firm will expand horizontally or diversify will depend in part on the relative profitability of these alternative methods of expansion from the point of view of the firm. Factors which are likely to influence the profitability of expansion in existing markets will include the industry profit rate, degree of seller concentration, and rate of growth of demand, in those markets. Gort found the extent of diversification in 1954, measured by the ratio of non-primary employment to total employment of firms in the industry, to be significantly positively related to the industry's degree of seller concentration and ratio of technical personnel to total employment, but negatively related to the rate of growth of industry demand. The finding with regard to seller concentration is not surprising. One would expect it to be more difficult, other things being equal, for firms to expand profitably in original markets in which sellers are few in number, since efforts to obtain a larger share of the market are more likely to be noticed and countered by other sellers in the market. Gort's finding that the rate of growth of demand in a firm's original market is positively related to diversification by the firm is perhaps more unexpected. A possible explanation is that faster growth in original markets generates more funds to finance expansion. The positive influence of the technical personnel ratio in original markets may be explained by C. J. Sutton's argument (42), noted in an earlier section, that technical personnel are more likely to perceive opportunities for diversification, and are likely to be successful in pressing for their adoption when occupying a position of authority in firms' decision processes. The results of another statistical study of diversification, by A. Wood (50), also indicate that diversification is positively related to research expenditure in the industry of origin, but differ from Gort's results in finding diversification unrelated to the rate of growth of demand, concentration ratio, or profit rate in the firm's original market.

As regards the characteristics of markets into which firms diversify, Gort's study indicates a strong positive relationship between diversification and both the rate of growth of demand in the markets entered and rapid technological changes as measured by the proportion of technical personnel and the rate of increase in labor productivity in those markets. Diversification and concentration in the markets entered were unrelated, however, and many cases of diversification involved entry into highly concentrated industries. Moreover, in a substantial proportion of the markets entered, the entrant rose to be one of the top eight firms, though this occurred less often the greater the rate of growth of demand in the entered market. Technical change and high growth rates of demand in receiving markets both indicate relatively low entry barriers. Rapid growth of market demand makes it easier for a firm to enter without encroaching upon the markets of established sellers serving those markets, and therefore reduces entry barriers to such markets. Given the reaction of established sellers anticipated by potential entrants, the expected profitability of entering such industries will be greater than the profitability of entry if total market demand were stable. Moreover, when technology is changing, new entrants may even have a cost advantage over sellers already established in the entered markets. A. Wood's findings were similar to those of Gort in that diversification was strongly positively related to research expenditures and growth of demand in markets entered, and was unrelated to concentration. An additional finding by Wood was the existence of a very strong negative relationship between diversification and average industry profit rate. This finding may cast some doubt on the profitability of diversification; on the other hand it may merely reflect a short period studied in which temporary costs associated with diversification are still being incurred by diversifying firms, or may reflect defensive diversification in response to low profitability in original markets. In view of the wide differences in time periods studied, and in the samples, the variables included in regression equations relating diversification and other factors, industry boundary classifications, and measures of diversification utilized in different statistical studies of diversification, it is rather surprising that there is as much agreement among the results of these studies as appears to exist.

Other empirical studies already referred to in earlier sections of this chapter and listed in Recommended Readings are those by Berry (3, 4), Goldberg (14), Lorie and Halpern (23), Monroe (26) and Rhoades (36).

RECOMMENDED READINGS

1. Amey, L. R., Diversified manufacturing businesses, *Journal of the Royal Statistical Society*, Series A, Vol. 127, Part 2, 1964.
2. Berger, D. and Peterson, M., Conglomerate mergers and criteria for defining potential entrants, *Antitrust Bulletin*, Winter 1969.
3. Berry, C. H., Corporate growth and diversification, *Journal of Law and Economics*, October 1971.
4. Berry, C. H., Corporate diversification and market structure, *Bell Journal of Economics and Management Science*, Spring 1974.
5. Burstein, M. L., The economics of tie-in sales, *Review of Economics and Statistics*, Vol. 42, February 1960.
6. Burstein, M. L., A theory of full-line forcing, *Northwestern University Law Review*, Vol. 55, March–April 1960.
7. Burstein, M. L., Conglomerate merger: an economic primer, *Intermountain Economic Review*, Spring 1971.
8. Comanor, W. S., Research and technical change in the pharmaceutical industry, *Review of Economics and Statistics*, May 1965, p. 184.
9. Conn, R. L., Performance of conglomerate firms: comment; *and* Reply by Weston, J. F. and Mansinghka, S. K., *Journal of Finance*, June 1973.
10. Federal Trade Commission, Staff Report, *Conglomerate Merger Performance: an Empirical Analysis of Nine Corporations* (Washington, D.C.: U.S. Government Printing Office, 1972).
11. Felton, J. R., Conglomerate mergers, concentration and competition, *American Journal of Economics and Sociology*, July 1971.
12. Ferguson, J. M., Tying arrangements and reciprocity: an economic analysis, *Law and Contemporary Problems*, Vol. 30, No. 3, Summer 1965.
13. George, K. D., Concentration and socialization in industry, *Journal of Industrial Economics*, April 1972.
14. Goldberg, L. G., The effect of conglomerate mergers on competition, *Journal of Law and Economics*, April 1973.
15. Goldberg, L. G., Conglomerate mergers and concentration ratios, *Review of Economics and Statistics*, August 1974.
16. Gort, M., *Diversification and Integration in American Industry* (Princeton, N.J.: Princeton University Press, 1962).
17. Kamerschen, D. R., A theory of conglomerate mergers: comment; *and* Logue, D. E. and Naert, P. A., A theory of conglomerate mergers: comment and extension (Comments on Mueller); *and* Reply by Mueller, D. C., A theory of conglomerate mergers: reply, *Quarterly Journal of Economics*, November 1970.
18. Keyes, L. S., Proposals for control of conglomerate mergers, *Southern Economic Journal*, July 1967.
19. Kitching, J., Why do mergers miscarry? *Harvard Business Review*, November–December 1967.
20. Lev, B. and Mandelker, G., The microeconomic consequences of corporate mergers, *Journal of Business*, January 1972.
21. Lewellen, W. G., A pure financial rationale for the conglomerate merger, *Journal of Finance*, August 1971.
22. Logue, D. E. and Naert, P. A., A theory of conglomerate mergers: comment and extension, *Quarterly Journal of Economics*, November 1970.
23. Lorie, J. H. and Halpern, P., Conglomerates; the rhetoric and the evidence, *Journal of Law and Economics*, April 1970.
24. Maass, R. O. and Hutchins, R. C., Measurement of multicompany diversification, *Journal of Economics and Business*, Fall 1973.
25. McGee, J. S., Predatory price cutting: the Standard Oil (N.J.) case, *Journal of Law and Economics*, October 1958.
26. Monroe, R. J., Comment: financial characteristics of merged firms: a multivariate analysis, *Journal of Financial and Quantitative Analysis*, March 1973.
27. Mueller, D. C., A theory of conglomerate mergers, *Quarterly Journal of Economics*, November 1969.
28. Mueller, W. F., Conglomerate mergers: a crisis in public policy, *Nebraska Journal of Economics and Business*, Autumn 1970.
29. Nicolaou, C. A. and Spence, B. J., Product diversification and the multiproduct firm, *Southern Economic Journal*, July 1975.
30. Peterson, R. D., Service diversification and market control among small advertising agencies, *Mississippi Valley Journal of Business and Economics*, Vol. 3, Spring 1968.
31. Prosper, P. A. and Smith, J. E. Jr, Conglomerate mergers and public policy, *Journal of Economic Issues*, June 1971.
32. Reid, S. R., The conglomerate merger: a special case, *Antitrust Law and Economics Review*, Fall 1968.
33. Reid, S. R., A reply to the Weston/Mansinghka criticisms dealing with conglomerate mergers, *Journal of Finance*, September 1971.
34. Reid, S. R., Conglomerate performance measurement: reply, *Journal of Finance*, June 1974.

35. Retwisch, K., A note on the presumed desirability of internal over external growth, *Antitrust Bulletin*, Winter 1969.
36. Rhoades, S. A., The effect of diversification on industry profit performance in 241 manufacturing industries: 1963, *Review of Economics and Statistics*, May 1973.
37. Rhoades, S. A., A further evaluation of the effect of diversification on industry profit performance, *Review of Economics and Statistics*, November 1974.
38. Scherer, F. M., Firm size, market structure, opportunity, and the output of patented inventions, *American Economic Review*, December 1965, especially pp. 1114–1116.
39. Shepherd, W. G., Conglomerate mergers in perspective; *and* Comment by Weston, J. F., *Antitrust Law and Economics Review*, Fall 1968.
40. Sherman, R., How tax policy induces conglomerate mergers, *National Tax Journal*, December 1972.
41. Smith, K. V. and Schreiner, J. C., A portfolio analysis of conglomerate diversification, *Journal of Finance*, June 1969.
42. Sutton, C. J., Management behavior and a theory of diversification, *Scottish Journal of Political Economy*, February 1973.
43. Telser, L., Cut throat competition and the long purse, *Journal of Law and Economics*, October 1966.
44. Turner, D. F., Conglomerate mergers and S.7 of the Clayton Act, *Harvard Law Review*, May 1965.
45. U.S. Department of Justice, *Merger Guidelines*, May 1968.
46. Weston, J. F., Conglomerate firms in perspective, *Intermountain Economic Review*, Spring 1973.
47. Weston, J. F. and Mansinghka, S. K., Tests of the efficiency and performance of conglomerate firms, *Journal of Finance*, September 1971.
48. Williamson, O. E., *Corporate Control and Business Behavior* (Englewood Cliffs, N. J.: Prentice-Hall, 1970), pp. 142–145.
49. Williamson, O. E., Managerial discretion, organization form, and the multi-division hypothesis. In Marrus, R. and Woods, A., *The Corporate Economy: Growth, Competition and Innovation Potential* (Macmillan: New York, 1971).
50. Wood, A., Diversification, merger, and research expenditures: a review of empirical studies. Appendix C in Marris, R. and Wood, A., *The Corporate Economy: Growth, Competition and Innovation Potential* (Macmillan: New York, 1971).

CHAPTER TEN

PUBLIC POLICY
TOWARD INDUSTRIAL BEHAVIOR

Public Policy Objectives

If public policy toward industry is to amount to more than the whim of politicians or bureaucrats, laws against price agreements, horizontal and vertical mergers, or any other interference with the unregulated pattern of industrial structure must be shown to contribute towards some generally accepted objective or objectives. Which structure of industry is desirable depends upon the nature of the objectives being pursued. Some objectives may have little to do with economics; a number of commentators on the United States antitrust laws are of the opinion, for example, that these laws have been more concerned with preserving small firms on the grounds of protecting democratic institutions, securing equality of opportunity, improving business ethics, and discouraging behavior which offends notions of fair play than with securing good economic performance. The pursuit of some objectives may even conflict with the achievement of economic objectives; one might, for example, favor an industrial structure involving small individual proprietorships, despite the fact that economic efficiency in some sense is thereby impaired, if one believes that such a structure is desirable on the grounds of securing equality of opportunity, or preserving democratic institutions, or on other social grounds. The economist has no special competence for choosing what the objectives of public policy shall be. Nonetheless, it may still be important to know the cost, in terms of the alternative economic benefits forgone, of achieving non-economic objectives.

This chapter deals solely with possible economic objectives underlying public policy towards industrial structure, and with the measures designed to achieve these objectives. One objective which has long occupied a central place in economic theory, and which is sometimes claimed to be the basis of much existing public policy towards business, is that of maximizing the welfare derived by the community from the use of its scarce productive resources. The welfare of the community is said to depend upon the level of subjective satisfaction experienced by each of its individual members, and this in turn will be influenced by three aspects of economic performance, namely, how the community's resources are allocated between different kinds of output, what methods are used to produce the output, and how the output is allocated among members of the community.

The productive resources of the community, consisting of human skills, the stock of fixed capital equipment, and natural resources, are capable of producing many different alternative combinations of output. One aspect of economic performance, which we shall refer to as allocative efficiency, is the extent to which the existing combination of outputs corresponds to the combination which will maximize the aggregate welfare of individual members of the community. Another question is whether resources producing any particular output combination are allocated in such a manner that the output in question is being produced efficiently. We shall refer to this aspect of economic performance as technical efficiency. Finally, irrespective of what is produced or how efficiently it is produced, there is the question of how any particular aggregate output should be allocated among members of the community in order to maximize welfare. We shall refer to this aspect of economic performance as distributive efficiency.

The welfare of the community cannot be said to be maximized if it is possible, by changing the existing resource allocation or distribution of output among members of the community, to increase the satisfaction of some members without reducing the satisfaction of any other members. A situation in which all possible improvements of this variety have been made is referred to as a Pareto optimum, after the economist Vilfredo Pareto who originally formulated the criterion. Although distributive, technical, and allocative efficiency are related, we shall in the remainder of this section consider them separately in turn. In each case, certain conditions are outlined which must be fulfilled in order that the welfare of the community be maximized according to the Pareto criterion. In addition, the manner in which the welfare of the community can be improved by a change in resource allocation or output distribution if these conditions are violated is explained. See the articles by F. M. Bator (4) and P. B. Kenen (40) which also deal with the necessary conditions for welfare maximization in a diagrammatic framework.

Consider, first, the characteristics of an optimal distribution of products among consumers. In order that a particular aggregate output of products be distributed optimally among members of the community, it must be impossible, by reallocating the output among consumers, to make someone better off without making someone else worse off. This requires that the ratio of the marginal utilities of any two products be the same for all consumers. Marginal utility refers to the change in satisfaction experienced by an individual consumer as the result of increasing or reducing by one unit the quantity of a particular commodity consumed. Marginal utility itself is subjective and cannot be measured; however, a ratio of marginal utilities − termed a marginal rate of substitution (hereafter referred to as MRS) expresses an individual consumer's relative evaluation of one additional unit of one good in terms of another good, and can be measured. Symbolically, the condition for an optimal allocation of output among consumers can be written as

$$\frac{MU_x^1}{MU_y^1} = \frac{MU_x^2}{MU_y^2} = \frac{MU_x^3}{MU_y^3} = \cdots$$

where the subscripts x and y refer to two different products and the superscripts 1, 2, 3 . . . refer to different individuals. Hereafter this condition, that the MRS between any two goods shall be the same for all consumers, is referred to as rule one. This is the rule of distributive efficiency.

As the reader can easily verify for himself, if the condition were violated so that an additional unit of good X were not worth the same number of units of good Y to two different consumers, both consumers can increase the total satisfaction they derive from consumption by exchanging some of the goods which they possess. If, for example, given the combination of apples and bananas which consumer A possesses, he values an extra apple at one banana (that is, the marginal utility of an apple, and that of a banana, are the same for A) and consumer B values an extra banana at two apples (that is, the marginal utility of a banana is twice the marginal utility of an apple for B) both can experience an increase in total satisfaction by exchanging goods, B giving A anything between one and two apples in exchange for one banana. The possibility of mutually advantageous exchange will continue to exist until the ratio of marginal utilities associated with apples and bananas is the same for both A and B.

Next we turn to the problem of technical efficiency in producing a given combination of products. In order that a given combination of products be produced as efficiently as possible, it must be impossible to produce the same combination of products by using fewer productive resources, or inputs. This requires that the ratio of marginal physical products of any two inputs be the same in the production of all different commodities produced. The marginal physical product of an input refers to the change in total output of a product when the amount of the input in question is increased or decreased by one unit. Symbolically, the condition for efficient allocation of inputs between the production of different outputs can be stated as follows:

$$\frac{MPP_x^i}{MPP_x^j} = \frac{MPP_y^i}{MPP_y^j} = \frac{MPP_z^i}{MPP_z^j} = \cdots$$

where the superscripts i and j are inputs and the subscripts $x, y, z \ldots$ refer to different products. This condition will hereafter be referred to as rule two, and is the rule of technical efficiency.

The reader can verify for himself, by substituting numbers into the ratios, that if the ratios differ, it is possible to produce the same total output while using fewer resources. Suppose, for example, that the relevant numbers are:

$$\frac{MPP_x^{labor}}{MPP_x^{capital}} = \frac{4}{10} \quad \text{and} \quad \frac{MPP_y^{labor}}{MPP_y^{capital}} = \frac{4}{6}$$

By transfering one unit of capital input from the production of Y (which tends to reduce total output of Y by 6 units) into production of X (which tends to increase output of X by 10 units), and substituting one and a half units of labor input from X into Y production in order to leave the total output of Y unchanged, the effect is to increase output of X by 10 minus 6 equals 4 units. By implication, this demonstrates that the existing level of total output of X and Y, whatever its magnitude, can be produced with fewer resources. Efficiency in production is not optimal.

After considering the problem of efficiency in the production of any particular combination of products, we turn finally to the problem of securing an optimal allocation of resources between different alternative combinations of products, the problem of allocative efficiency. Given any particular combination of outputs which is being produced, the rate at which one good, say X, can be transformed into another good, say Y, by shifting resources from X production into Y production is called the marginal rate of transformation (MRT). If rule one is satisfied, the combination of outputs will be distributed among members of the community in such a manner that the rate at which any consumer is willing to exchange X for Y (the marginal rate of substitution) is the same for all consumers. Unless, given the existing combination of products being produced, the rate at which every member of the community would be willing to exchange one good for the other (given by the MRS) is equal to the rate at which that good can be transformed into the other by reallocating resources between the products (given by the MRT), it would be possible to make some members of the community better off and no one worse off by reallocating resources and producing more of one good and less of the other. Suppose, for example, that it is possible to obtain two X by diverting resources and reducing Y output by one unit, while the (equalized) MRS between X and Y is one, indicating that consumers would be willing to exchange one Y for one X. In these circumstances, by shifting resources and producing two more X and one less Y, and giving one additional X to people who have suffered a reduction in Y consumption, everyone would by definition be as well off as before; since we are then still left with one extra unit of X, which can be distributed among some or all members of the community, the satisfaction of some or all members of the community can be increased without reducing that of any other members.

The rule of optimal resource allocation dealing with allocative efficiency, hereafter referred to as rule three, is therefore that for any pair of commodities produced and consumed:

$$MRS_1 = MRS_2 = MRS_3 \ldots = MRT$$

where the subscripts denote different individuals and MRS, as already explained, is the ratio of the marginal utilities of the two commodities for the individual consumer to which the subscript refers. Unless this rule is satisfied, the allocation of resources between different kinds of output will not be optimal, for by shifting resources from the production of one good into the production of another good, it is possible to make some members of the community better off without making others worse off. We shall return to examine rule three in more detail after considering the way in which purely competitive pricing behavior satisfies the necessary conditions for economic efficiency discussed in this section.

Pure Competition and Resource Allocation

The properties of a purely competitive general equilibrium are alleged to result in an optimal allocation of resources among different kinds of output, an optimal manner of production of the output, and an optimal distribution of output among members of the community according to the Pareto criterion.

The requirements of rule one are satisfied for the following reasons. In order to maximize satisfaction, any individual must allocate his income between different goods in such a manner that the marginal utility of every good consumed is proportional to the price of the good; unless marginal utility is proportional to price, it follows that the individual can increase the total satisfaction which he derives from his income by reallocating his income and buying a different combination of goods. Each consumer, if he behaves optimally, will therefore buy commodities in such amounts that for him the ratio of marginal utilities of any pair of goods is equal to the price ratio of those goods. Since in pure competition the price of any good is the same for all consumers, and individual consumers cannot influence price, the ratio of marginal utilities of any pair of goods will be the same for all consumers. This will be so despite differences in tastes or incomes, which may result in different amounts of the goods purchased, comparing different consumers. Hence the requirements of rule one, the condition necessary for an optimal distribution of goods among consumers, will be satisfied.

The requirements of rule two are satisfied for the following reasons. Profit-maximizing producers will choose that combination of inputs which minimizes the total money cost of producing any given level of output they produce. For such a combination the ratio of the marginal physical productivities of any pair of inputs employed must be equal to the price ratio of the inputs; any input combination which does not satisfy this requirement will be inefficient in the sense that the same output can be produced at a lower money cost by using a different combination of inputs. Because, in pure competition, the price of any particular input is the same for all producers, producers of different products will employ combinations of inputs with identical marginal physical productivity ratios. Hence the requirements of rule two are satisfied – output will be produced efficiently.

The requirements of rule three are satisfied because, in pure competition, individual firms will produce a level of output which equates the marginal cost of producing a particular product with the price of the product. That is, for any pair of products, the ratio of the marginal costs of the products will equal the ratio of product prices. In pure competition the ratio of marginal costs is the marginal rate of transformation (MRT) between the two goods in question. For example, assuming, for expositional convenience only, that labor is the only input which can be reallocated between different industries, the marginal cost of any product equals the wage of labor divided by the marginal physical productivity (MPP) of labor in the production of that product. The marginal cost ratio of two products X and Y is therefore the ratio of the MPP of labor in Y production to the MPP of labor in X production. This is the rate at which X can be transformed into Y by shifting resources from X production into Y production. From rule one, all consumers will equate the marginal rate of substitution (MRS) between two goods with the price ratio of those two goods. If the MRS between two goods equals the price ratio of those goods, and the ratio of their marginal costs (equals MRT) equals the price ratio of the goods, it follows that MRS equals MRT. That is, the rate at which every consumer is willing to exchange one good for the other is equal to the rate at which the products can be transformed into each other by shifting resources; therefore it is impossible, by shifting resources between products, to make anyone better off without making someone else worse off.

The preceding paragraphs demonstrate that the requirements of an optimal resource allocation mentioned in the first section of this chapter will be met by a purely competitive general equilibrium. It is necessary to add that the analysis ignores second-order conditions; that is, an allocation may satisfy the three rules of the section entitled Public Policy Objectives and yet not be optimal unless certain additional conditions, referred to as second-order conditions, are also satisfied. The three rules are necessary, but not sufficient, for maximizing the aggregate welfare of individuals in the community according to the Pareto criterion.

Apart from second-order conditions, the preceding analysis also ignores externalities, that is, benefits or costs that are not accurately reflected by money prices. If there are externalities, a purely competitive general equilibrium will not result in an optimal allocation of resources. Externalities may, however, also occur under monopoly or other

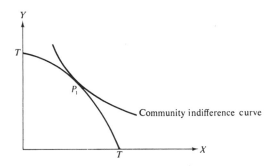

Figure 10–1. Diagrammatic representation of optimal resource allocation.

forms of market structure, and the analysis in this chapter will be confined to a comparison of pricing behavior under different market structures in the absence of externalities.

Importance of Income Distribution*

The relevance of income distribution, and the limitations of rule three, can be explained with the aid of Figure 10–1. *TT*, which is usually referred to as a production-possibility curve, represents the maximum alternative combinations of two goods, X and Y, which can be produced by a given amount of resources. The problem of securing an optimal allocation of resources between the production of X and Y is to select a point on *TT* which is the best point in some sense.

The slope at any point on the production-possibility curve equals the marginal rate of transformation (MRT) of X into Y. It indicates how many additional Y can be produced by reducing output of X by one unit and transferring resources to Y production. A point on *TT* which satisfies the condition that the MRS between X and Y of every member of society equals MRT can be depicted diagrammatically as a point at which a community indifference curve is tangent to that point, such as P_1 in Figure 10–1.

A community indifference curve (hereafter abbreviated to CIC) shows combinations of X and Y which yield unchanged amounts of satisfaction to all members of society. In order to understand fully the limitations of rule three, and the assumption which is implicit in any statement that P_1 is an optimal resource allocation, it is necessary to understand the way in which a CIC is related to income distribution.

The total output of X and Y implied by any given point P on *TT* can be allocated between members of society in many different ways. Assuming, for expositional convenience only, that there are two members of society, A and B, the preferences of the two can be exhibited by two sets of indifference curves, labeled $a_1, a_2 \ldots$ and $b_1, b_2 \ldots$, respectively. An indifference curve depicts different combinations of two goods yielding the same amount of satisfaction to an individual. Higher subscripts associated with any indifference curve denote higher levels of satisfaction for the individual concerned. Allocations of the output P between the two members which satisfy rule one are numerous. The locus of such allocations is called the contract curve. At any particular point on this curve the ratio of the marginal utilities of X and Y is the same for each member of society but this ratio generally differs in value at different points on the contract curve. The total

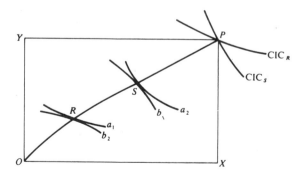

Figure 10–2. Total output, individual preferences, contract curve, and community indifference curves.

---

* The analysis in this section draws heavily on an illuminating article by Mishan (49).

output corresponding to some point P on TT, the preferences of A and B, and the contract curve are depicted diagrammatically in Figure 10–2.

Choosing a point P on the production possibility curve TT, we have dropped perpendiculars to both axes of the diagram, so that the sides of the rectangle represent the total amount of each good produced at point P. In the rectangle $OYPX$ are drawn two sets of indifference curves, those of A, relative to the origin O, and those of B, relative to the origin P. The contract curve, $ORSP$, is the locus of points of tangency between the indifference curves of A and B.

A CIC through P is derived by selecting a point on the contract curve and sliding B's individual indifference curve at that point up and down A's indifference curve at that point, ensuring that the B curve is at all times tangential to the A curve. The upper right-hand corner of the box diagram, which is fixed in relation to B's indifference curve, will trace out combinations of X and Y yielding the same satisfaction to each member as the combination P itself. That is, each point on a CIC curve is obtained by adding a combination of X and Y corresponding to a point on one of A's indifference curves to a combination of X and Y corresponding to a point on one of B's indifference curves, ensuring that the individual indifference curves have the same slope at the chosen points. Different points on the CIC curve correspond to differently sloped points on the two selected individual indifference curves. The slope of the CIC at any point will equal the slope of the mutually tangent individual indifference curves from which that point was derived; at P, for example, the slope of the CIC through P equals the slope of the mutually tangent individual indifference curves at the chosen point on the contract curve.

There will be a different CIC through P corresponding to every different point on the contract curve. Each of these CICs will pass through P at a different angle if, as is generally assumed to be the case, the slope of the mutually tangent individual indifference curves is different at different points on the contract curve.

Different points on the contract curve represent divisions of the total output of X and Y implied by point P which involve more of both goods for one member of the community and less of both goods for the other. Therefore, different points on the contract curve represent different levels of individual welfare for the members of society; a move along the contract curve makes one individual better off at the expense of the other. The level of welfare of each member of the community implied by a point on the contract curve is termed a welfare distribution. Since satisfaction is subjective and cannot be measured, one cannot compare different points on the contract curve, that is, different welfare distributions. A's loss (gain) of welfare resulting from a move along the contract curve cannot be compared with B's gain (loss). Therefore, in the absence of any generally agreed rule for the ranking of welfare distributions, no comparisons may be made between the CICs derived from different points on the contract curve, since each is associated with a different welfare distribution.

We return now to consider Figure 10–1. The slope of the CIC through P_1, the rate at which every member of the community would be willing to exchange one good for the other, depends upon the allocation of the total output P_1 between members of the community. Conversely, the fact that a particular CIC is tangent to TT at a particular point (such as P_1) implies a particular division of output P_1 between members of the group, and therefore a level of welfare for each member of the group. The income distribution will, for a community consisting of two members, correspond to that point on the contract curve where the slope of the members' individual indifference curves is equal to the slope of the CIC which is tangent at P_1. The level of individual welfare implicit in such an income distribution will be shown by the mutually tangent individual indifference curves at that point. Given the level of welfare for each member of society implied by this distribution of income, P_1 is the best point on TT – it is impossible by shifting resources to increase the satisfaction of any member of the community without reducing the satisfaction of some other member.

The assertion, however, that a point on TT such as P_1, at which a CIC is tangent, is the best allocation of resources implies a value judgement that the division of the output and resulting welfare distribution implicit in that CIC is the best. Changing the income distribution will change the slope of the CIC through P_1, and hence the optimality of the resource allocation at P_1. For each point on TT representing a combination of goods, there is a unique distribution of those goods among the members of the community which invests that point with the properties of an optimum, that is, which will result in a CIC being tangent to TT at that point. In Figure 10–3, for example, P_1, P_2, and P_3 are points on TT which satisfy rule three. Each of these points represents an optimal allocation of resources between the production of different goods, given the distribution of goods among members of the community and hence the level of individuals' welfare implied by the slope of the CIC at each point. Since the welfare distribution implicit in each CIC is different, that is, some people are better off and others worse off at the different points P_1, P_2, and P_3, the points themselves cannot be compared.

The preceding analysis enables us to point to another limitation of rule three. An allocation of resources which satisfies the requirements of rule three cannot be said to be superior to *any* allocation of resources which violates rule three. Two such allocations are

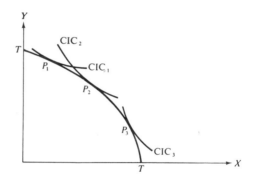

Figure 10–3. Optimal resource allocation with different welfare distributions.

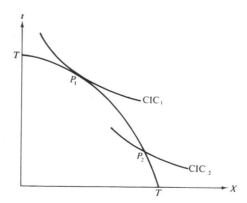

Figure 10–4. Incomparable resource allocations.

represented, respectively, by points P_1 and P_2 in Figure 10-4.

Of the point P_1, it may be asserted that, with the particular division of the output implied by the slope of CIC_1 at point P_1, it is impossible to increase the satisfaction of some members of the community without reducing that of other members, by shifting resources and producing a different combination of outputs. This statement, however, does not hold for point P_2, for by shifting resources from the production of X into the production of Y, hence moving from P_2 to some other point on TT, it would be possible to make some members of the community better off without making others worse off. Unless, however, the CICs through P_1 and P_2 reflect Pareto-comparable welfare distributions, the two resource allocations cannot be compared, and therefore P_1 cannot be said to be superior to P_2. The term 'Pareto-comparable' refers to welfare distributions which differ from each other merely in that some people are better off under one distribution than another, but no one is worse off.

Monopoly and Resource Allocation

Much discussion among economists about public policy directed against monopoly is based upon the implicit assumption that monopoly pricing behavior results in an allocation of resources which does not maximize welfare in the Pareto sense. It is appropriate, therefore, to investigate whether monopoly behavior violates the three rules outlined in the first section of this chapter.

Rule one will not be violated if monopolists charge the same price for any particular product to all consumers. Because each (maximizing) consumer chooses that combination of goods which equates his MRS between any pair of goods with the ratio of their prices, an economy, whether competitive or monopolistic, which charges the same price for each commodity to every consumer will equate the MRS of different consumers and therefore lead to an efficient allocation of output among consumers.

Rule one will be violated, however, if a monopolist charges a different price for the same commodity to different consumers. Because each maximizing consumer chooses that combination of goods which results in an equality between the ratio of marginal utilities of any two goods and the price ratio of those goods, different price ratios confronting different consumers as a result of monopoly price discrimination will mean that the ratio of marginal utilities of two goods differs for different consumers. That is, it would be possible for consumers to exchange products and thereby increase the total satisfaction they derive from a given total output.

If a monopolist in selling markets is also a monopsonist (single buyer) in input markets, so that the price which the monopolist has to pay for inputs is influenced by the scale of its input purchases, then it is likely that rule two will be violated. A purely competitive firm cannot influence the price it pays for inputs and in order to minimize the cost of producing its selected output level will select a combination of inputs which equates the ratio of the marginal physical productivities of each pair of inputs with the price ratio of the inputs. In contrast, in order to minimize the cost of producing any given level of output, a monopsonist will hire a combination of inputs which equates the ratio of the marginal physical productivities of any pair of inputs with the ratio of *marginal input costs*, not the ratio of input prices. Although, in equilibrium, all firms in the economy pay the same price per unit of any particular input, the ratio of marginal input costs to different firms will differ from the price ratio of the inputs, unless, by chance, the elasticity of supply of any input is the same for all firms. Apart from this last situation, it follows therefore that the ratio of the marginal physical productivities of any two inputs will be different in different firms, so that rule two is violated. The combination of inputs selected by the monopsonist will be inefficient in the sense that rule two is violated and, by using a different combination of inputs and reallocating inputs between firms, the same level of aggregate output could be produced with fewer resources.

It must be stressed that the above argument does not depend in any way upon a failure by the monopsonist to attempt to minimize the money cost of producing any particular level of output. A pure competitor must maximize profits in order to survive; a monopolist may pursue objectives other than profit maximization, such as sales-revenue maximization, for example. The pursuit of objectives other than profit maximization does not, however, imply absence of an attempt to minimize the cost of producing any given level of output. In the case of the sales-revenue maximizer, for example, it was pointed out in Chapter 1 that the need to make some profits acts as a constraint. A reduction in the cost of producing output and consequent increase in profits will enable the firm to satisfy the constraint and yet increase sales revenue. Hence, in order to show why monopolists should not be efficient in the sense of minimizing the total cost of producing any level of output they produce, it is not sufficient to point out that they pursue objectives other than profit maximization; instead it must be shown, for example, that the incentive to minimize costs is reduced.

Finally, we turn to rule three. The two preceding sections demonstrate that a system of pricing which results in output levels involving different price–marginal cost ratios for different products implies that the marginal rate of substitution in consumption is not equal to the marginal rate of transformation in production. Given the distribution of welfare implicit in such a price system and resulting allocation of resources, it would be possible to make some members of the community better off without making anyone worse off, by shifting resources from the production of those goods where the ratio of price to marginal cost is lowest to those goods where the ratio of price to marginal cost is highest.

A monopoly in an otherwise purely competitive economy therefore leads to a misallocation of resources. Likewise, even though no sectors of the economy are purely competitive, differences in price–marginal cost ratios imply a misallocation of resources in the Pareto sense. The reader might well wonder whether an economy composed of monopolies in final product markets, and where the ratio of price to marginal cost is the same in every industry, is just as efficient from the point of view of allocative efficiency as a purely competitive system in which price equals marginal cost in all sectors. Because the price ratio of each pair of goods will equal the ratio of the marginal costs of producing the goods, marginal rates of substitution in consumption will equal marginal rates of transformation in production *provided* the ratio of marginal costs of each pair of goods corresponds to the marginal rate at which one good can be transformed into the other by a reallocation of resources. This provision will be met only if the marginal cost of any particular input is the same to firms producing either of the goods in question. This, in turn, requires either that there is pure competition in factor markets so that input supply curves facing individual firms are horizontal, or that the elasticity of supply of any particular input is the same for all firms. Even if one of these conditions is satisfied, and marginal cost ratios reflect marginal rates of transformation, a world of monopolies with equal price–marginal cost ratios in final product markets is not quite as efficient from the point of view of allocative efficiency as a world of pure competition; there will be a misallocation of resources between the production of leisure and the production of all other goods. This can be explained as follows. Leisure is one of the commodities every individual can consume. Other goods are obtained by trading leisure (hours of work offered) for money incomes with which to buy other goods. In order to maximize satisfaction from consuming commodities and leisure, an individual must obtain as much satisfaction from the income earned as a result of his last (say) hour's effort as he obtains from the last hour of leisure. If this condition is violated, the individual can, by definition, increase his total satisfaction by working less (having more leisure), or the converse. This is the same as saying that the maximizing individual will equate the ratio of marginal utilities of income (other goods) and leisure with the ratio of their prices. Since the price of one unit of leisure is the wage forgone by having leisure, this condition can be expressed algebraically as

$$\frac{MU_{leisure}}{MU_{other\ goods}} = \frac{Wage}{P_{other\ goods}}$$

Firms, on the other hand, in order to maximize profits, will hire a quantity of labor which equates the marginal revenue from employing labor to the marginal cost of labor which, in the absence of monopsony in the labor market, equals the wage paid per unit of labor. Firms in pure competition will therefore hire a quantity of labor which satisfies the following condition:

$$Wage = MPP^{labor}_{other\ goods} \times P_{other\ goods}$$

that is,

$$\frac{Wage}{P_{og}} = MPP^{labor}_{other\ goods}$$

The expression $MPP^{labor}_{other\ goods}$ is the rate of transforming one unit of leisure into other goods – the marginal rate of technical transformation (MRT). Because $MPP^{labor}_{other\ goods}$ equals $Wage/P_{og}$, which in turn equals $MU_{leisure}/MU_{other\ goods}$, it follows that MRT = MRS, and rule three dealing with allocative efficiency is satisfied.

In a world of monopolies in final product markets, however, firms will, in order to maximize profits, hire a quantity of labor which satisfies the following condition:

$$Wage = MPP^{labor}_{other\ goods}\ Marginal\ revenue_{other\ goods}$$

that is,

$$\frac{Wage}{MR_{og}} = MPP^{labor}_{other\ goods}$$

Because $MPP^{labor}_{other\ goods}$ equals $Wage/MR_{og}$, which is greater than $Wage/P_{og}$, it follows that, in equilibrium, the rate at which leisure can be transformed into other goods (= MRT) exceeds the number of units of other goods for which consumers are willing to give up one unit of leisure (= MRS). The allocation of resources between leisure and the production of other goods is non-optimal since it is possible by shifting resources out of production of leisure into the production of other goods to make some people better off without making others worse off.

It must be stressed that the preceding arguments against monopoly in no way rest upon the argument that monopoly distorts income distribution. This argument, sometimes put forward against monopoly, is operationally meaningless in the absence of a universally acceptable criterion of ideal income distribution. The point of the preceding analysis is that under *any* income distribution, monopoly combined with pure competition, or uneven degrees of monopoly resulting in different price–marginal cost relationships, will result in a misallocation of resources in the Pareto sense. That is, it would be possible, *without altering the existing income distribution,* to make some members of the community better off without making anyone worse off, by reallocating resources and altering the distribution of output among members of the community.

Measurement of the Welfare Loss Attributable to Monopoly

The preceding sections indicate that a purely competitive general equilibrium simultaneously satisfies all the conditions necessary for a Pareto optimum, which is a situation in which it is impossible to increase the aggregate satisfaction of the community by changing the allocation of resources between different products. In contrast, a general equilibrium involving monopoly violates these necessary conditions because price will exceed marginal cost for some outputs, implying that marginal rates of substitution between products in consumption and production are not equal, as is required for a Pareto optimum.

If Pareto-optimal conditions are not satisfied, because, for example, price exceeds marginal cost in some industries, the crucial question is the *magnitude* of the potential gains to the community obtainable by moving to a Pareto optimum while holding the distribution of income unchanged in order to make the two situations comparable for reasons already explained. This question is relevant to the decision of whether to attempt to change existing conditions, because there may be costs of making such a change, such as the costs of administering and enforcing the antitrust policies required to achieve the change, and also to distinguish situations in which the potential gains are relatively small from situations in which the potential gains are of considerable magnitude. In order to answer this question, economists have devised the 'welfare loss' concept, which measures the change in satisfaction resulting from a change from one price–cost equilibrium position to another. The nature of this concept, and the logic underlying it, will be examined next.

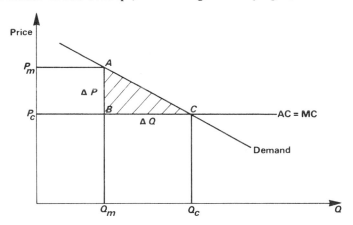

Figure 10–5. The allocative welfare loss attributable to monopoly.

Figure 10-5 exhibits the demand and cost conditions relating to the product of a particular industry; the assumption that marginal and average costs are constant as quantity changes is made purely for expositional convenience. Provided that price and marginal cost are equal in all other industries, the output level of Q_c where price equals marginal cost represents the optimal output of the industry from the point of view of maximizing the aggregate satisfaction of the community, because this output level will imply that Pareto optimum conditions are simultaneously satisfied in all sectors of the economy. Any other quantity of output, all other things remaining unchanged, involves a reduction in the aggregate satisfaction of the community compared with the level Q_c. If industry price and output under monopoly are P_m and Q_m, for example, the potential gain in satisfaction of the community, measured in money terms, of moving to P_c and Q_c is depicted by the shaded triangle ABC.

The logic underlying this conclusion can be explained in a number of different ways. One way is to use the concepts of consumers' surplus and producers' surplus, and to illustrate the changes in the magnitude of these two concepts which result from a change from the monopoly price to the purely competitive price. Consumers' surplus is defined as the excess of the amount which buyers would be willing to pay for a particular quantity of the product, over what they actually pay. Thus, at Q_m, total consumers' surplus is depicted diagrammatically by the area under the demand curve bounded by the price axis and the line $P_m A$, for this area represents the sum of the excess of the price which buyers would have been willing to pay (equal to the height of the demand curve) over the price they actually pay, for each consecutive unit of the product up to Q_m. If price were reduced from P_m to P_c, the area depicting consumers' surplus would increase by an amount equal to the rectangle $P_m ABP_c$ plus the triangle ABC. To this change in consumers' surplus must be added any change in producers' surplus caused by the change in price from P_m to P_c. Producers' surplus, also sometimes referred to as 'factor surplus' or 'economic rent' to factors of production, is defined as the excess of the earnings which producers receive for their product or services over the amount necessary to induce them to produce the product or services. The amount which factors must be paid in order to induce them to supply successive units of output is represented by the marginal cost schedule (which is the same as the average cost schedule in the example), since this represents the cost of the additional factor units which must be brought to the industry to increase output by that unit. Producers' surplus is therefore depicted by the rectangle $P_m ABP_c$ in Figure 10–5, which equals monopoly profits. If price is reduced to P_c, there will be no producers' surplus, because at P_c producers are obtaining an amount which just equals the amount necessary to induce factors to produce Q_c. In this case, therefore, the change in producers' surplus is a reduction, equal to the total monopoly profit, and the sum of the increase in consumers' surplus derived earlier plus this reduction in producers' surplus therefore equals the triangle ABC.

An alternative and perhaps easier way to view the logic underlying the welfare loss triangle ABC is as follows: a price reduction from P_m to P_c means that buyers pay less for the quantity Q_m, and sellers receive an equivalent amount less. That part of the change in consumers' surplus represented by $P_m ABP_c$, and the corresponding change in producers' surplus, in effect represents a transfer of income from producers to consumers. It has no net effect on aggregate satisfaction because, as already emphasized, in order to compare different equilibrium price–quantity situations, the income distribution in the economy must remain unchanged. Thus, the preceding income transfer must, implicitly, be reversed by some means or, alternatively, the suppliers of factors to the industry and buyers of its products must be the same people. The reduction in price from P_m to P_c also results in an increase in output of the product in question, equal to $Q_c - Q_m$. The value which buyers place on each successive additional unit of this output is shown by the height of the demand curve for the product. The added output of the product also implies a transfer of resources from other sectors, and a reduction in the output of other products. This reduction in the output of other products is the true 'opportunity cost', or alternative which is forgone by the community as a result of expansion of output in the industry being analyzed. Provided that price and marginal cost are equal in other sectors of the economy, the money costs of the added resources needed to expand output by Q_c-Q_m units, depicted by the area BCQ_cQ_m, equal the value which the community places on the alternative outputs which could be produced by these resources in other industries. The net gain in satisfaction of the community due to the increase in output of Q_c-Q_m equals the difference between the demand price and marginal cost of each successive unit of output, which is depicted diagrammatically by triangle ABC.

The welfare-loss triangle ABC in Figure 10–5 is equal in area to $1/2\Delta Q\Delta P$, where ΔQ and ΔP are the quantity and price differences between monopoly and competition. Since the price-elasticity of demand for a product is defined as $E_d = \dfrac{\Delta Q}{\Delta P}\cdot\dfrac{P}{Q}$, substitution for ΔQ in the preceding welfare-loss expression yields $1/2\,\Delta PE_d\dfrac{\Delta P}{P}\,Q$ and multiplying this by P/P yields the following expression for the area of welfare-loss triangle:

$$\text{Welfare Loss} = 1/2\,E_d\left(\frac{\Delta P}{P}\right)^2 PQ$$

where $\dfrac{\Delta P}{P}$ is the proportionate excess of price under monopoly over price under competition, E_d the price-elasticity of demand for the monopolist's product, and PQ the monopolist's sales revenue. The preceding expression indicates the magnitude of the welfare loss attributable to monopoly measures in money terms; dividing the expression by the dollar value of the output of the economy as a whole yields a measure of the welfare loss expressed as a percentage of the total value of output in the economy.

In a seminal article, A. C. Harberger (28) estimated the magnitude of the welfare loss attributable to monopoly in the U.S. economy using data for the period 1924–1928. His estimate of $59 million, or less than 1/10 of one per cent of the GNP would at first sight appear to relegate the importance of monopoly as a cause of resource misallocation to insignificance. The estimate is probably too low, however, for a number of reasons. First, Harberger used profit data for the manufacturing sector of the economy and in estimating the excess of monopoly price over competitive price used the average profit return on capital in manufacturing as a surrogate for the level of profit under competition. Since the average return on capital in manufacturing tends to be higher than the average return on capital in non-manufacturing sectors of the economy, this leads to an understatement of the monopoly-price distortions in the economy as a whole. Harberger's estimate of the price differential under monopoly and competition was only approximately four per cent. It is clear from the preceding welfare-loss formula that the magnitude of the price differential has important implications for the magnitude of the resulting welfare loss, since an increase in the price differential increases the welfare loss more than proportionately. A doubling of the Harberger price differential from four to eight per cent would increase $\left(\dfrac{\Delta P}{P}\right)^2$ by a factor of four, and an increase in the price differential from 4 to 20 per cent would increase $\left(\dfrac{\Delta P}{P}\right)^2$ 25 times, for example. Moreover, because profit-maximizing behavior implies that $(P - MC)/P = 1/E_d$, an optimal price–cost margin of 20 per cent implies an E_d of 5. The resulting welfare loss associated with a 20 per cent mark-up and price-elasticity of demand of 5 is 10 per cent of GNP, over a hundred times Harberger's estimate.

Harberger actually assumed that the price-elasticity of demand for the output of the monopoly sector equalled unity. This implies that profits are not being maximized in the monopoly sector, since the marginal revenue of industry output equals zero when E_d equals unity, and profit maximization requires equality of marginal revenue and marginal cost, which is positive. This assumption is not inconsistent with profit-maximizing behavior on the part of individual firms in the monopoly sector, however, since the price-elasticity of demand for the output of individual firms will equal price-elasticity of demand for industry output only when individual firms expect imitation of price changes by rivals, as explained in Chapter 3. Except in this case, the price-elasticity of demand for output of individual firms will be higher than industry price-elasticity. Despite this, Harberger's elasticity assumption may have been lower than the actual price-elasticity of demand for the output of the monopoly sector.

Finally, Harberger's welfare-loss estimate applied only to the manufacturing sector of the economy, which originated only about a quarter of the total output of the economy in 1924–1928. Monopoly distortions and associated welfare losses also exist in other sectors and, assuming that their relative importance is the same as in manufacturing, Harberger's welfare-loss estimate for the manufacturing sector alone must be multiplied by four to arrive at an economy-wide welfare-loss estimate.

Using data for 1956–1961 and statistically estimated industry price-elasticities, Professor David Kamerschen estimated the economy-wide welfare loss attributable to monopoly in the U.S. in an article published in 1966 (36). His welfare-loss estimates range from one to eight per cent of GNP, the most realistic estimate in his own opinion being roughly six per cent, considerably higher than Harberger's. An even more recent study of the welfare loss to monopoly in the U.S. for 1956–1969 by Dean Worcester (81) used disaggregated data for the largest 500 industrial firms in the U.S. to attempt to reveal monopoly welfare losses which in previous studies may have been hidden in wider industry groupings which included both profitable and unprofitable firms. He found that the degree of disaggregation has a small overall effect on the magnitude of the welfare loss attributable to the sector of the U.S. economy occupied by the 500 largest industrial firms, and that this loss in no year exceeded even one per cent of the GNP.

The debate concerning the magnitude of monopoly welfare losses in the U.S. economy continues, as recent articles by A. Bergson (6, 7) and subsequent replies by R. Carson (15) and Worcester (82) indicate. The main issues are the magnitude of price–cost margins and price-elasticities of demand in monopolized sectors of the economy. Most statistically estimated price-elasticities of demand for industry products are low. Moreover, although low elasticities imply high profit-maximizing price–cost mark-ups, actual price–cost mark-ups reflected by industry profit rates are low. This may reflect the fact that the price-elasticity of demand for the products of individual firms in an industry is much higher than the price-elasticity of industry demand. The argument that these higher elasticities should therefore be used in calculating monopoly welfare losses has been countered by the claim that industry elasticities are relevant because all firms in an industry generally adjust prices together in response to common influences facing the industry group.

For a selection of other notable contributions dealing with the concept and measurement of welfare losses attributable to monopoly, see Comanor and Leibenstein (16), Crew and Rowley (18), De Prano and Nugent (21), Green (26), Harberger (29, 30), Kamerschen (37, 38), Kasper (39), Mohring (50), Mueller (51), Schwartzman (64), Wallace (77) and Williamson (79, 80).

Even if the aggregate welfare loss attributable to monopoly in the U.S. economy is small, it may be high in particular industries, justifying antimonopoly measures in those sectors. J. J. Siegfried and T. K. Tiemann (69) found the total welfare loss in mining and manufacturing in the U.S. in 1963 to be very small, and similar to Harberger's original estimate. Their results showed that the bulk of the welfare loss attributable to monopoly was concentrated in five industries – plastic materials and synthetics, drugs, petroleum refining with extraction, office and computing machinery, and motor vehicles accounted for 67 per cent of the total estimated welfare loss. The motor vehicle alone was responsible for almost one half of the total loss – 44 per cent.

A common feature of all of the preceding studies, and the underlying welfare-loss concept, is that cost conditions under monopoly and competition are assumed to be the same. If, instead, the total and therefore average costs associated with any given output level were higher under monopoly than under competition, Figure 10–6 shows that the total welfare loss attributable to monopoly will be larger than was previously indicated, and will now equal the sum of triangle ADE and rectangle AC_mBDP_c. The triangle ADE, as before, is the gain in aggregate satisfaction of the community which would result from transferring resources from other sectors of the economy and increasing the output of the monopolized product to the competitive level. This is the 'allocative efficiency' component of the welfare loss attributable to monopoly. The rectangle AC_mBDP_c is the reduced total cost of producing the monopoly output level resulting from a change to competitive behavior in the industry, and reflects improved efficiency of factor use which frees resources for other uses. This is the 'technical efficiency' component of the welfare loss attributable to monopoly when costs are higher under monopoly than under competition.

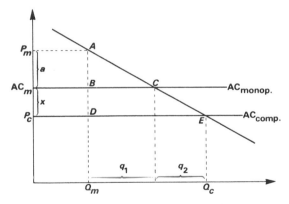

Figure 10–6. Allocative and technical welfare losses when costs are lower under competition than under monopoly.

The area of the allocative welfare loss triangle ADE could be expressed algebraically by means of a formula exactly like the one which was derived earlier in this section; the $\dfrac{\Delta P}{P}$ in the resulting formula would then represent the excess of price under monopoly over price under competition as before. Alternatively, it is also possible to express the welfare loss formula in terms of the excess of price under monopoly over cost under monopoly, and this procedure will be employed below, since it indicates the influence of the magnitude of cost differences under competition and monopoly on the magnitude of the welfare loss attributable to monopoly. Thus, the formula for that portion of the allocative welfare loss represented by triangle ABC in Figure 10–6, which would be the total welfare loss attributable to monopoly if costs were identical under monopoly and competition, and AC_m were the cost function, is as follows:

$$1/2\, E_d \left(\frac{\Delta P}{P}\right)^2 PQ$$

where $\Delta P/P$ stands for the excess of price over cost under monopoly. It can easily be shown * that the ratio of the area of triangle ADE to that of triangle ABC is $(1 + x/a)^2$, where x/a is the ratio of the cost increase under monopoly to the excess of price over cost under monopoly. Thus, the magnitude of the allocative welfare loss attributable to monopoly will be greater, the larger the cost reduction which can be achieved by changing to competition, and will increase more than proportionately with this cost reduction. For example, if unit costs are six per cent below price under monopoly, and costs could be reduced by a similar percentage under competition, $x/a = 1$ and the ratio of ADE to ABC will equal 4, implying that the allocative welfare loss attributable to monopoly is four times as large as it would have been if costs remained the same under competition as they are under monopoly. The sum of the allocative and technical efficiency welfare-loss components attributable to monopoly is therefore indicated by the following expression:

$$1/2\, E_d \left(\frac{\Delta P}{P}\right)^2 PQ(1 + x/a)^2 + x \cdot Q_m$$

where, as previously noted, $\dfrac{\Delta P}{P}$ represents the excess of price under monopoly over cost under monopoly.

If, in contrast to the preceding example, total and unit costs are higher under competition than under monopoly, the position of the AC_m and AC_c curves in Figure 10–6 would be reversed, and the rectangle xQ_m would represent a technical efficiency *gain*, instead of a loss as in the previous example, associated with monopoly. This technical efficiency gain would, accordingly, have to be *subtracted* from the allocative welfare loss associated with monopoly, which in these circumstances would be represented by the triangle ABC in Figure 10–6. The algebraic expression for the welfare loss attributable to monopoly would be as follows:

$$1/2\, E_d \left(\frac{\Delta P}{P}\right)^2 PQ - xQ_m$$

where $\dfrac{\Delta P}{P}$ represents the excess of price under monopoly over price under competition.

The above expression will be negative, indicating that on balance monopoly increases aggregate welfare compared to competition, when the technical efficiency effect exceeds the allocative efficiency effect. It is illuminating to consider the magnitude of the percentage

---

*Area $ABC = \dfrac{aq1}{2}$ Area $ADE = \dfrac{(q1 + q2)(a + x)}{2}$

$\dfrac{ADE}{ABC} = \dfrac{aq1 + aq2 + xq1 + xq2}{aq1} = 1 + \dfrac{q2}{q1} + \dfrac{x}{a} + \dfrac{xq2}{aq1}$

By similar triangles, $\dfrac{q2}{q1} = \dfrac{x}{a}$

Therefore $\dfrac{ADE}{ABC} = 1 + \dfrac{2x}{a} + \left(\dfrac{x}{a}\right)^2 = (1 + x/a)^2$

cost savings which would be necessary to justify monopoly by resulting in technical efficiency gains which exceeded the allocative welfare losses. From the preceding expression it follows that aggregate welfare will be higher under monopoly than under competition if the following condition is met:

$$Q_m \cdot x > \frac{E_d}{2}\left(\frac{\Delta P}{P}\right)^2 PQ \text{ or, alternatively, } \frac{x}{P_m} > \frac{E_d}{2}\left(\frac{\Delta P}{P}\right)^2$$

From this condition it is possible to determine the percentage cost reduction under monopoly which must accompany a price increase above the competitive price level in order to leave aggregate welfare higher under monopoly than under competition. The magnitude of E_d for the industry's product clearly plays a part in determining the answer, for it will influence the magnitude of the allocative component of the welfare loss associated with a price increase above the competitive level. Given E_d, however, it is also apparent that relatively modest reductions in cost are sufficient to compensate for relatively large increases in price. For example, if aggregate welfare is to remain unchanged on balance, a 20 per cent increase in price above the competitive level would require a cost reduction of four per cent when E_d is 2, and only two per cent if E_d equals unity.

Whether costs are higher under competition or monopoly is obviously a crucial issue in view of the resulting implications for the magnitude of welfare losses attributable to monopoly. As is usual in economics, hypotheses abound on both sides of the issue. The relative strength of pressures for technical efficiency, the ability of decision-makers to substitute other goals for profit maximization, and the relative magnitude of incentives to innovate under the two types of market structure are all relevant in this connection. As the discussion of these factors in Chapters 1, 2 and 6 suggests, no really convincing theoretical or empirical evidence has been presented to date to show that costs will be higher, or lower, under monopoly than under competition. Similarly, in a recent article Stephen Lofthouse (43) concluded that the argument that competition results in a lower degree of X-inefficiency than monopoly is supported by neither theory nor evidence. In contrast, using a related but slightly different diagrammatic analysis to that previously outlined in this section, Richard Posner has recently argued (56) that competition for the opportunity to earn monopoly profits will transform expected monopoly profits into higher costs, and that previous studies of the costs of monopoly may have grossly underestimated these costs. He also points out that the welfare loss due to public regulation may be greater in magnitude than the welfare cost of private monopoly. Whatever the final outcome of the debate over the magnitude of welfare losses, the analytical framework presented in this section provides a basis for dealing with public policy choices in situations in which allocative and technical efficiency considerations tend to conflict.

The allocative welfare-loss concept developed in this section so far is associated with a change in price and quantity from those existing under perfect competition to those existing under monopoly. The same methodology can also be applied to estimating the welfare effects of other changes in price and quantity. For example, it can be used to determine the allocative welfare loss associated with oligopoly which, except in the case of perfect collusion, results in a lower price and larger quantity of output than under monopoly. Alternatively, it can be used to estimate the welfare loss associated with monopoly compared to oligopoly. In the first case, the analysis and diagrammatics would be identical to that already employed in comparing competition and monopoly. In the second case, however, which is illustrated in Figure 10–7, there are two alternative ways to express the allocative welfare loss attributable to monopoly algebraically. This welfare

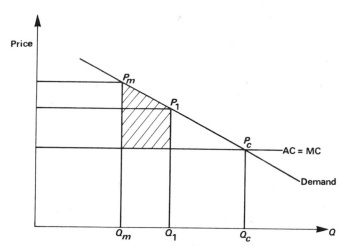

Figure 10–7. Allocative welfare loss when comparing monopoly and output levels below a purely competitive equilibrium.

loss, depicted by the shaded area in Figure 10–7, represents as before the excess of the value placed by the community on the increase in output resulting from a price reduction from P_m to P_1 over the marginal cost of increased output, which as before measures the value of the alternative uses of the resources required. The triangular portion of the shaded area is that part of the increase in consumers' surplus which is not offset by a reduction in producers' surplus on the initial output level Q_m, and the rectangular portion of the shaded area is the increase in producers' surplus associated with profits earned on each unit of increased output from Q_m to Q_1.

The preceding welfare loss can be expressed algebraically as

$$\tfrac{1}{2}\Delta P\Delta Q\left(1 - \frac{P_1 - P_c}{P_m - P_c}\right)$$

which can be rewritten as follows:

$$\frac{E_d}{2}\left(\frac{\Delta P}{P}\right)^2 PQ\left[1 - (k - 1)\frac{P_c}{\Delta P}\right]$$

where $k = P_1/P_c$, and ΔQ and ΔP are the difference between quantity and price under monopoly and competition. The preceding algebraic expression indicates that the allocative welfare loss based on a comparison of monopoly and competition must be *reduced* to the extent that monopoly is compared with industry pricing behavior involving a price above the competitive level.

Alternatively, if the change in price and quantity, ΔP and ΔQ, are defined as the difference between P_m and P_1, and between Q_m and Q_1, respectively, the appropriate algebraic formula for the allocative welfare loss depicted in Figure 10–7 is

$$\tfrac{1}{2}\Delta Q\Delta P + (P_1 - P_c)\Delta Q$$

which can be rewritten as follows:

$$E_d\frac{\Delta P}{P_1}\left[\frac{k}{2}\left(\frac{\Delta P}{P_1}\right) + (k - 1)\right]PQ$$

where $k = P_1/P_c$ as before. As the reader can easily verify, when $P_1 = P_c$, $k = 1$, and the usual allocative welfare loss formula applies in both cases.

Objections are sometimes raised to the welfare loss concept outlined in this section, and several of the major arguments raised against its use will be considered next. In a recent paper (53) Professors Parrish and Ng have argued that even if costs were higher under monopoly than under competition, the resulting technical efficiency loss ($x.Q_m$ in Figure 10–6) should not be added to the allocative efficiency loss when calculating the total loss of satisfaction of the community attributable to monopoly. This technical efficiency loss is offset, they argue, by an implicit gain in satisfaction accruing to managers of the monopoly as a result of the increased leisure which is the reason for the greater inefficiency in production under monopoly. Resolution of this argument is largely an empirical issue since, as was indicated in Chapter 2, costs of production may be higher than the minimum feasible level for reasons other than managerial utility maximization.

Another objection sometimes raised against the welfare-loss concept is that it is based on partial-equilibrium analysis, and fails to consider the effect of the price change analyzed on demand and cost conditions in other industries. This argument can be rejected, however, for the following reasons (see A. C. Harberger (30) for a reply similar to this line of reasoning): even though the demand and cost conditions in other sectors of the economy may be shifted as a consequence of the change in price and quantity in the market being analyzed, the measure of the resulting welfare change is unaffected by such shifts provided that price equals marginal cost in all other sectors both before and after the price change. These shifts may change the optimal prices and quantities in other markets; however, the effect of such changes on aggregate satisfaction will be reflected in the welfare-loss triangle in the market under consideration. The only proviso is that the industry demand curve being analyzed must be the 'total' demand curve which takes account of all such indirect effects which a change in price and quantity of the good being analyzed would have on the demand price of the good. The assumption that price equals marginal cost in all other sectors is, however, critical in this connection; as will be explained in the next section dealing with the theory of second-best, when this assumption is relaxed, the welfare effects in the market under analysis do not indicate the total welfare effects of a change in price and quantity in that market. The analysis of the present section is merely extended to incorporate this change, however, in a manner to be indicated in the following section.

A more fundamental type of objection to the welfare-loss concept is concerned with the consumers' surplus concept which underlies the welfare-loss measure. The purpose of a welfare-loss measure is to indicate the magnitude of the change in satisfaction experienced by individuals as a result of a change in equilibrium prices and quantities. The consumers' surplus concept, depicted by the area to the left of a demand curve between two prices, is a *monetary evaluation* of the change in satisfaction experienced by the individual to which the demand curve applies. The change in satisfaction itself will equal this monetary evaluation *multiplied by the individual's marginal utility of income*. Only if the marginal utility of income is constant at all income levels will the area to the left of an individual's demand curve be proportional to the change in satisfaction experienced by the individual. Similarly, areas under the demand of different individuals cannot be mechanically added together unless the marginal utility of income is the same for different individuals. Neither of these conditions will generally be satisfied. Nonetheless, this does not invalidate welfare-loss measures based on the consumers' surplus concept; it merely means that the monetary evaluation of a change in satisfaction should be weighted by individuals' marginal utility of income to arrive at a measure of the change in satisfaction itself.

When a change in only one price is under consideration, the monetary evaluation of the resulting change in satisfaction is uniquely defined because there is only one path of adjustment in the sense of the order in which prices are changed in moving to the new equilibrium price set. When the welfare effect of changes in more than one equilibrium price is under consideration, an added problem arises in applying the consumers' surplus concept which is not present when a single price change is contemplated. When more than one equilibrium price changes, there is an infinite number of possible adjustment paths of prices and quantities between two equilibrium situations. The marginal utility of income can take on a different range of values along each different adjustment path, depending on the precise order in which the prices are changed in moving from one equilibrium price set to another. This means that the money value placed on the change in satisfaction associated with a particular price change can vary, depending on the precise order in which prices are changed. The magnitude of the monetary evaluation of the change in satisfaction, obtained by summing the consumers' surplus measures associated with successive price changes, is therefore dependent on the precise order in which prices are changed, and there is a different consumers' surplus measure for each possible adjustment path of prices between two equilibrium positions. The 'equivalent' and 'compensating' variation concepts of conventional demand theory are but two of the possible consumers' surplus measures, each associated with a different path of adjustment between two equilibrium positions. These two consumers' surplus measures do, however, define the upper and lower limits to the money value placed on a change in an equilibrium price, and are therefore perhaps more important than many of the other innumerable possible adjustment paths and associated consumers' surplus measures. Moreover, by considering an example utilizing the equivalent and compensating variation of consumers' surplus measures, it is possible to show that the maximum possible difference between the different money values of a given change in satisfaction associated with different adjustment paths of prices is likely to be slight.

Therefore, for most practical purposes, the variability of the money value measure of a given change in satisfaction according to the precise path of adjustment of prices is likely to be of greater theoretical interest than practical importance. Bearing in mind that the money value measure of a particular change in satisfaction can vary with the adjustment path of prices between two equilibria, and that the money value measure of consumers' surplus itself does not indicate the change in satisfaction itself, the consumers' surplus concept (or the many consumers' surplus concepts) are valid and useful constructs, and the welfare-loss concepts based on them are not invalidated by the preceding factors. The preceding comments on the consumers' surplus concept apply equally to the producers' surplus concept, which also underlies the welfare-loss concept discussed in this section. For further analysis of the concepts of consumers' and producers' surplus, see Berry (8), Burns (14), Currie, Murphy and Schnitz (20) and Silberberg (70).

The Theory of Second-Best and Welfare-Maximizing Pricing Rules

In order to maximize allocative efficiency in an economy, resources must be allocated between the production of different products in such a manner that it is impossible, by transferring resources from one product to another, to increase the level of aggregate satisfaction in the community. In the second section of this chapter it was explained that if price equals marginal cost for every product produced in an economy, the ratios of price and marginal cost of any two products will be equal, and allocative efficiency will be maximized for the following reasons: price ratios indicate people's relative evaluation, expressed in money terms, of the benefits they receive from marginal units of the two goods, while ratios of marginal cost indicate the rate of transforming one product into another by switching resources from the production of a unit of one good to production of the other. Unless price ratios equalled the rate of transforming one product into the other, it follows that by shifting some resources from the production of one product to the other it would be possible to increase, on balance, the total satisfaction of the community. For example, suppose that resources producing a marginal unit of X can produce an additional unit of Y. If the price of Y (which indicates the added satisfaction, expressed in money terms, derived from an added unit of Y) exceeds the price of X (which indicates the loss of satisfaction associated with a unit reduction in output of X), aggregate satisfaction in the community can be increased by reducing X output by one unit and shifting the resources to Y production. This process can continue to raise aggregate satisfaction as long as the price ratio and rate of transformation are not equal. This is the logic underlying the conclusion that pricing at marginal cost in all sectors of the economy leads to an optimal allocation of resources between different sectors.

The theory of second-best is concerned with the nature of welfare-maximizing pricing rules in situations in which any constraint exists which prevents price from equalling marginal cost in all sectors of the economy simultaneously. For seminal articles on the theory see Baumol and Bradford (5), Fleming (24) and Lipsey and Lancaster (42).

At first sight, the appropriate pricing rule for allocative efficiency in these circumstances seems obvious, namely to set price–marginal cost ratios in every sector equal, since this would again imply that price ratios and marginal cost ratios would be equal in all sectors; that is,

if $P_1/MC_1 = P_2/MC_2$, then $P_1/P_2 = MC_1/MC_2$ even if $P_1 \neq MC_1$ and $P_2 \neq MC_2$.

The theory of second-best indicates that this view is generally incorrect, however, because it ignores the nature of the constraint and the reasons *why* prices cannot equal marginal cost in all sectors of the economy simultaneously. In the presence of any such constraint, the general condition which must be satisfied in order to achieve a welfare-maximizing allocation of resources between different sectors is as follows: the ratio of the marginal benefits which two goods yield to the community, expressed in money terms as the ratio of their prices, must now equal the ratio of the marginal effects of changes in the output levels of the two goods *on the constraint*, instead of equalling the ratio of their marginal costs as is the case in the absence of the constraint. The logic underlying this optimal 'second-best' condition is quite simple: if the ratio of the marginal benefits which two goods yield the community were not equal to the ratio of their marginal effects on the constraint, it follows automatically that it is possible to increase the total satisfaction of the community while continuing to meet the constraint. This can be accomplished by switching some resources from production of the good where the ratio between the marginal benefit (price) and the marginal effect of the good on the constraint is lower, to production of the good where this ratio is higher. Only when the marginal effects of different products on the constraint are proportional to their respective marginal costs will this second-best condition lead to a situation where allocative efficiency is maximized by equating price ratios and marginal cost ratios or, what is the same thing, by equating price ratios and marginal rates of transformation in production.

Although the preceding second-best allocative efficiency condition is perfectly general, the precise relationship between price and marginal cost in different firms which is necessary in order to satisfy this condition will obviously depend on the precise nature of the constraint which prevents price from equalling marginal cost in all sectors simultaneously. *Generalizations* concerning the price–marginal cost relationship required for allocative efficiency are therefore impossible in these circumstances, since different optimal price–marginal cost relationships will be appropriate for different constraints.

However, many of the constraints such as taxes and the existence of decreasing-cost industries, which make it impossible in practice to set price equal to marginal cost in all sectors of the economy simultaneously, result in very similar optimal second-best pricing conditions. The nature of these optimal pricing conditions will now be illustrated.

One way to approach the issue of optimal pricing rules for allocative efficiency is as follows: if the crucial pricing condition necessary in order to secure allocative efficiency appears to be setting $P = MC$ in all markets, why not achieve this directly by passing a law requiring such behavior in all industries? If, in one or more industries in the economy, cost conditions exhibit declining unit costs with scale of output, the marginal cost of any output rate will be less than the corresponding cost per unit of output. In other words, pricing at marginal cost will automatically mean that the firm's total sales revenue will be less than the firm's total costs. Since a firm cannot continue to operate for long without covering its total costs, either the firm must be subsidized, or it must price above marginal cost in order to cover its total costs from its own sales revenue. If it is subsidized, however, taxes would have to be imposed on some other products produced in the economy in order to raise the revenues required for subsidization; this would then imply that prices would have to exceed marginal costs in some other sectors of the economy. Both of the two preceding alternatives therefore involve a second-best situation, since price cannot equal marginal cost in all sectors of the economy simultaneously. In these circumstances, should the decreasing-cost firms price above marginal cost and cover their own total costs, or should they price at marginal cost and be subsidized? The answer is that neither of these two alternatives will, in general, be optimal from the point of view of maximizing allocative efficiency; as indicated below, the optimal solution will generally involve pricing above marginal costs but below average cost in decreasing-cost industries, so that some subsidization occurs.

In the presence of decreasing unit cost with scale of output in one or more sectors of the economy, total costs of all firms must be covered, either from their own sales revenues or from subsidies raised by taxing other products. The constraint which renders this a second-best situation therefore takes the form of a requirement that total tax revenues equal total subsidies required for firms which price below average cost. The effect of a change in the output level of any particular product on the constraint therefore equals the effect of the output change on tax revenues. Imposing a tax on a product X produced in a non-decreasing cost industry in effect raises price relative to marginal cost, as previously noted. The resulting effect on tax revenues is shown by the shaded area $ABCD$ in

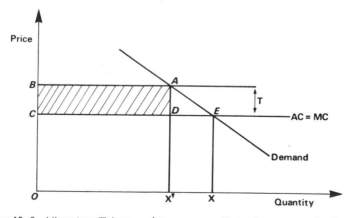

Figure 10–8. Allocative efficiency and tax revenue effects of a tax per unit of output.

Figure 10–8, where unit costs are assumed to be constant at different output rates merely for expositional convenience. The reduction in output from X to X' caused by this tax and price rise from OC to OB results in a reduction in aggregate satisfaction of the community which is measured in money terms by the triangle ADE, which is the familiar allocative 'welfare-loss triangle' analyzed in the preceding section. Assume, for the present, that cross-elasticities of demand and supply between different products are zero, so that changes in the price of one product will not change the quantities of other products demanded in the economy. The ratio of triangle ABC to the rectangle $ABCD$ therefore represents the ratio between the effect of the change in X output on aggregate satisfaction in the community and its effect on the economy-wide tax-revenue constraint. As indicated earlier, this ratio must be the same for all products produced in the economy in order for allocative efficiency to be maximized; in other words, taxes must be imposed on other non-decreasing cost industries such that the resulting price–marginal cost discrepancy in each sector results in the same ratio between the effect of the output change in each of those sectors on aggregate satisfaction and the effect on tax revenues.

These propositions, and their implications for welfare-maximizing price–marginal cost differences, can be clarified with the aid of some simple algebra: the triangle $ADE = (P - MC)\Delta Q/2$. A moment's reflection will indicate that the rectangle $ABCD$, which represents the tax revenues associated with the imposition of a tax, is also equivalent to the increase in profits which would result in a rise in price from OC to OB. This increase in profits is also equal to the expression $(MR - MC)\Delta Q$, where MR represents the marginal revenue associated with the firm's output level. In order for allocative efficiency to be maximized in the economy in the preceding example, it follows that the ratio $\dfrac{(P - MC)\Delta Q/2}{(MR - MC)\Delta Q}$, or $\dfrac{(P - MC)}{(MR - MC)}$, must be the same in all sectors of the economy, equal to some number λ. λ will depend on the total economy-wide level of tax revenues to be raised.

If cross-elasticities of demand and supply between different products are zero, as assumed, the relationship between the price and marginal revenue of any product is as follows:

$$MR = P(1 - 1/E_d)$$

where E_d is the price-elasticity of demand for the product in question. The welfare-maximizing allocative efficiency condition can therefore be expressed as follows:

$$\frac{(P - MC)}{P(1 - 1/E_d) - MC} = \lambda$$ in all sectors of the economy, and this rearranges to the following

condition:

$$\frac{P - MC}{P} = \left(\frac{\lambda}{\lambda + 1}\right) \cdot \frac{1}{E_d}$$

The preceding expression indicates that the welfare-maximizing price–marginal cost ratio in any sector depends on the price-elasticity of demand for that sector's product. Several implications of this condition are immediately apparent:

1. Setting prices proportionate to marginal cost in all sectors will only maximize allocative efficiency if price-elasticities of demand are equal in every sector.
2. Setting price equal to marginal cost is only optimal when price-elasticity of demand is infinity.

3. The excess of price over marginal cost should be higher in markets where price-elasticity of demand is lower. This proposition can be illustrated diagrammatically with the aid of Figure 10–9 which shows the demand conditions associated with two products which have the same cost conditions. If the same sized tax per unit of output is imposed on both products, the price of both products rises from OP to OP'. It is clear from the diagram that the triangle representing the allocative welfare loss associated with demand curve D_1 is larger than that associated with demand curve D_2. It is equally clear from the diagram that the same sized tax will bring in less tax revenues from product 1 than from product 2. The ratio between the allocative welfare loss and the tax revenues associated with the tax will therefore necessarily be greater for product 1 than for product 2, which violates the requirement for allocative efficiency in a second-best situation. The same total tax revenue could be achieved, and aggregate satisfaction increased, by raising the size of the tax on product 2 and reducing the size of the tax on product 1. In other words, the welfare-maximizing price–marginal cost ratio will be higher for product 2, the product with the lowest price-elasticity of demand.

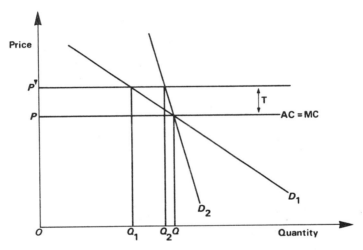

Figure 10–9. Influence of price-elasticity of demand on allocative efficiency and tax revenue effects in different markets.

Returning to our initial problem of determining optimal price–marginal cost relationships in the presence of decreasing-cost industries in an economy, the implications of the preceding analysis are as follows: if cross-elasticities of demand and supply between different products in the economy are zero, optimal prices will exceed marginal costs in all firms (including the decreasing-cost firms) except those with infinitely price-elastic demand. Since this implies positive taxes, and given the zero economy-wide tax revenue constraint initially posited, it follows that the optimal solution will involve some subsidization of the decreasing-cost firm(s). This in turn implies that price will exceed marginal cost in the decreasing-cost firm(s) by less than the amount necessary to cover the firm's total costs from its own sales revenues.

In the preceding example of a second-best situation, due to the existence of decreasing-cost industries, there was no net resource withdrawal from the private sector as a result of taxes. Since the tax proceeds were used to subsidize the decreasing-cost industries, a mere reallocation of resources within the private sector was involved, which resulted in a welfare-maximizing allocation of resources between the different industries. If there are no decreasing-cost industries, but taxes must be imposed somewhere in the economy in order to withdraw resources from the private sector, the preceding principles equally apply. Essentially, the problem is how to secure a given overall reduction in private sector resource use with minimum reduction in aggregate satisfaction of the community. Taxes on any product raise the price of the product, reduce demand for the product, and result in a reduction in private sector resource use. Again, unless the reduction in aggregate satisfaction per dollar of tax revenue raised is the same in all sectors, it follows that a different structure of taxes, and therefore price–marginal cost relationships, can produce the same total resource withdrawal with a smaller reduction in aggregate satisfaction. Assuming cross-elasticities of demand and supply are zero, price–marginal cost relationships must again be set in relation to price-elasticities of demand in each sector. The only possible difference between this case and the decreasing-cost industry example initially considered lies in the magnitude of the total tax revenue constraint. The larger the amount of tax revenues to be raised, the higher the absolute excess of price over marginal cost in every industry. The *relative* level of prices in different sectors, which depends on price-elasticities of demand, will remain unchanged, however.

It is appropriate to comment briefly on the consequences of relaxing the assumption that cross-elasticities of demand and supply between different products are zero. This will not change the general second-best allocative efficiency condition, which requires that the ratio between the effect of an output change on aggregate satisfaction in the community and the effect on the relevant second-best constraint be the same for all products produced in the economy. However, the optimal relationship between price and marginal cost in each sector which achieves this condition will now depend not only on the price elasticity of demand in each sector, but also on cross-elasticities of demand and supply between different products. When cross-elasticities of demand and supply are zero, the effect of a change in the price and quantity of an individual product on the satisfaction of the community is measured by the marginal net benefit $(P - MC)$ of the product in question multiplied by the change in its output level. In contrast, as explained in the preceding section, when cross-elasticities of demand and supply are not zero, the effect of a change in the price and quantity of an individual product on the satisfaction of the community is measured by this amount *plus* the sum of the marginal net benefit $(P - MC)$ associated with other products multiplied by changes in their quantities produced as a result of the change in price and output of the first product. When the quantities of other products increase in response to an increase in the quantity of a particular product, a 'complementary' relationship is said to exist between the products. The marginal effect of a change in the output of a such a good on the satisfaction of the community will clearly be larger than when cross-elasticities are zero. When the quantities of other products decrease in response to an increase in the quantity of a particular good, a 'substitute' relationship is said to exist between the products. In this case the marginal effect of a change in the quantity of such a good on aggregate satisfaction will be smaller than when cross-elasticities are zero.

Apart from influencing the magnitude of the effects of a change in output of individual products on aggregate satisfaction, non-zero cross-elasticities may also affect the magnitude of the effect of the change in output on the relevant second-best constraint also. This would happen, for example, in the case of a tax-revenue constraint. If cross-elasticities are not zero, the effect of a change in one type of output on tax revenues will depend not only on tax revenues raised from that product, but also on the resulting changes in output levels of other products, multiplied by their taxes per unit of product.

To summarize: since non-zero cross-elasticities of demand and supply affect the magnitude of the marginal effect of changes in the quantities of individual products on aggregate satisfaction and also possibly on the second-best constraint, they are also obviously relevant in determining the relationship between the price and marginal cost of individual products which is necessary in order to achieve allocative efficiency by equating the ratio of marginal social benefit to marginal effect on constraint for different products.

The consequences of non-zero cross-elasticities of demand for the algebraic second-best pricing rules outlined earlier are as follows: the expression $(P - MC)/(MR - MC)$ represented the ratio between the effect of a change in output of a product X on aggregate satisfaction and the effect on tax revenues when no other output levels changed. When other output levels Y, Z change also as a result of complementary or substitute relationships between X and Y and Z, the $(P - MC)/(MR - MC)$ ratios associated with Y and Z must be added to the one for X, in order to obtain the *total* effects of the change in X output on aggregate satisfaction and on tax revenues. The $(P - MC)/(MR - MC)$ ratios for Y and Z may be either negative or positive, depending on whether Y and Z are substitutes or complements. It can be shown that the welfare-maximizing price–marginal cost relationship for each product is as follows:

$$\frac{P - MC}{P} = \left(\frac{\lambda}{\lambda + 1}\right) \cdot \left(\frac{1}{E_d} + \Sigma CE\right)$$

where ΣCE represents the sum of cross-elasticities of demand between the product in question and other products.

When cross-elasticities of demand are zero, as initially assumed in our example, the above condition implies that optimal prices will exceed marginal costs in all firms whose price-elasticity of demand is less than infinitely large, with the magnitude of the excess varying between firms in accordance with differences in price-elasticity of demand. With non-zero cross-elasticities of demand, the optimal excess of price over marginal cost will be higher for products where a substitute relationship with other products is dominant so that the sum of cross-elasticities is a positive number. When a complementary relationship with other products is dominant, so that the sum of cross-elasticities of demand is negative, the optimal excess of price over marginal cost is lower. In fact, as the above optimal pricing formula indicates, if the complementary relationship is sufficiently strong, a firm may have to price *below* marginal cost in order to achieve allocative efficiency in the economy as a whole. The intuitive logic of this possibility is quite straightforward, especially when viewed within the diagrammatic framework of the welfare-loss measurement analysis contained in the previous section: although pricing below marginal cost implies a 'welfare-loss triangle' associated with the partial-equilibrium diagram of demand and cost conditions for the product in question, the increased satisfaction resulting from the increased quantities of complementary products may be large enough to result in a net increase in total satisfaction of the community.

The theory of second-best also has important implications for the problem of measuring the allocative welfare losses or gains associated with changes in the output level of individual products. A crucial assumption underlying the entire analysis of this problem contained in the preceding section is that price equals marginal cost in all sectors of the economy other than the market being analyzed. The significance of this assumption is that all the allocative welfare effects of a change in output in the market under consideration are captured by the demand and cost conditions in that market. Thus, for example, when cross-elasticities of demand and supply are non-zero, changes in price and output in the market under consideration will change demand and cost conditions, and therefore output levels, in other sectors of the economy. However, the net change in aggregate satisfaction associated with these output changes in other sectors, which equals the change in output in each sector multiplied by $(P - MC)$ in that sector, will be zero when price equals marginal cost in those sectors. In contrast, when price is not equal to marginal cost in all other sectors, which by definition will always be the case in a second-best situation, there are two major implications for welfare-loss concepts and measures: the first is that the allocative welfare effects of a change in output in the market under consideration are not entirely reflected by the demand and cost conditions in that market. The change in aggregate satisfaction of the community due to changes in resource allocation is then equal to the following expression:

$$(P - MC)\Delta Q_i + \Sigma(P - MC)\Delta Q_j$$

where the ΔQ_js can be positive or negative depending on whether the goods are complements or substitutes for the ith product. It is clear from this expression that the term following the plus sign, which indicates the allocative welfare affects in other sectors associated with a change in price and output in the market for the ith good, will only be zero when price equals marginal cost in all other sectors. Diagrammatically, the expression preceding the plus sign represents the familiar 'welfare-change triangle' analyzed in the preceding section, while the expression following the plus sign is the algebraic sum of areas like $ABCE$ in Figure 10–10, which equals $(P - MC)\Delta Q$ in another sector.

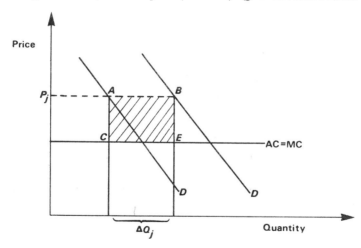

Figure 10–10. Allocative efficiency effects in other markets.

Another way to view the matter is as follows: when price equals marginal cost in all other sectors, the marginal cost of resources used in the market under consideration measures the value placed by the community on alternative outputs which must be forgone in order to expand output in that market. When prices exceed marginal cost in other sectors, however, the marginal cost of resources in the market under consideration understates the value placed by the community on alternative outputs forgone. The excess of price over marginal cost in other sectors where output reduction occurs when resources are transferred into the market under consideration must be subtracted from the conventional welfare-loss triangle representing the difference between price and marginal cost of output in the market under consideration. Similarly, excess of price over marginal cost in other sectors experiencing an increase in output when output in the market under consideration increases, as a result of a complementary relationship in demand and supply between the two goods, must be added to the conventional welfare-loss triangle.

The second major implication for welfare-loss measurement of prices not equalling marginal cost in sectors other than the market under consideration concerns the price–marginal cost relationship in different sectors which maximizes allocative efficiency. When prices exceed marginal cost in all sectors, it is tempting to conclude that prices should exceed marginal cost by a proportionate amount in all sectors in order to maximize allocative efficiency. This ignores two considerations: first, when cross-elasticities of demand and supply are not zero, the price–marginal cost difference in any particular sector does not measure the total effect of a change in output in that sector on aggregate welfare, for reasons already outlined. Even if cross-elasticities of demand and supply were equal, however, so that price–marginal cost differences in any sector did measure the allocative welfare effects of changes in output in that sector, there is an additional consideration which is relevant in determining welfare-maximizing price–marginal cost relationships: namely, the *reason why* prices exceed marginal cost in other sectors. If the reason is merely the existence of unavoidable monopoly elements in other sectors, then equalizing the effect of a change in each type of output on aggregate satisfaction is necessary for maximizing allocative efficiency; if cross-elasticities of demand and supply are zero this *will* imply setting prices proportional to marginal costs in different sectors. If, however, the reason why prices exceed marginal cost in other sectors is the existence of taxes, and the need to raise a certain amount of tax revenues for public-sector purposes, the optimal condition for allocative efficiency requires that the ratio between the effect of a change in output on aggregate satisfaction *and the effect on the tax revenue constraint* be equal for different types of output. In these circumstances, allocative efficiency consideration requires that one take into account not only the effect of output changes on aggregate satisfaction, but *also* the resulting effects on the relevant second-best constraint. This last aspect has been largely overlooked in the literature dealing with concepts and measures of allocative welfare losses and gains.

Before concluding this section, it must be emphasized that the points just discussed do not mean that the welfare loss and gain measures outlined in the preceding section must be discarded. Rather, they must be extended to incorporate two added considerations: welfare effects occurring in other markets as a result of output changes in the market under consideration, and the existence and nature of any relevant second-best constraint. Because the welfare effects in other sectors will depend on cross-elasticity of demand and supply between different products, this will of course greatly increase the information required to calculate the welfare losses and gains associated with a change in output levels of individual products. Also, as in the case of a second-best tax revenue constraint, the effect of an output change in the constraint may also depend on the cross-elasticities of demand and supply.

Allocating Antitrust Resources Optimally

Both the welfare-loss concept and the theory of second-best have important implications for the quantity and utilization of resources allocated to regulatory agencies which attempt to influence industrial structure and conduct. The activities of regulatory agencies, such as the Department of Justice and the Federal Trade Commission in the United States and the Monopolies and Mergers Commission and Restrictive Practices Court in the United Kingdom, use scarce manpower and other resources. The total amount of resources devoted to regulatory agencies should be expanded up to the point at which the resulting incremental gains to the community, in the form of increases in technical and allocative efficiency attributable to the activities of the agencies, equal the opportunity cost, measured in terms of the alternative outputs forgone by using resources for regulatory activities. In addition, any given level of regulatory resources, whether the optimal level or not, should be allocated between different types of regulatory activity in such a manner that the largest possible increase in aggregate satisfaction of the community is obtained from their employment. This requires that the marginal returns, measured in terms of the resulting improvements in technical and allocative efficiency, per unit of expenditure on each type of regulatory activity be the same. Obviously, if they are not equal, a reallocation of regulatory resources from activities which yield low marginal improvements in technical and allocative efficiency towards those regulatory activities which yield higher marginal returns will increase total satisfaction in the community.

In order to apply the preceding principles underlying the optimal allocation of regulatory agency resources, it is absolutely essential to measure the magnitude of technical and allocative welfare gains associated with changes in various aspects of industrial behavior. Ideally, what is required in this connection is a detailed inventory of potential welfare gains and losses associated with changes in the behavior of individual industries, individual firms in those industries, and different types of behavior. Initial steps in this direction are beginning to emerge from research conducted both within and outside regulatory agencies in the United States. For example, W. G. Shepherd attempted to estimate the gains which would result from changing the market shares of individual giant U.S. firms (66), while another study by J. J. Siegfried and T. K. Tiemann attempted to allocate the total welfare loss attributable to monopoly in the United States between different industries (69). Studies such as these are a promising beginning, but much more effort will be required both in refining welfare loss and gain concepts themselves and in estimating their magnitude for different types of industrial behavior in addition to pricing, before really significant progress can be made in improving the allocation of regulatory agency resources.

In addition to the magnitude of the potential gains in technical and allocative efficiency associated with specific changes in industrial behavior, the probability of regulatory activities securing the required change in industrial behavior is *also* relevant in determining the benefits resulting from regulatory activities. Clearly, no matter how large the gains associated with a particular change in industrial behavior, if the probability of success in securing that change in behavior by means of regulatory policies is very small, the expected gain from regulatory policy will be correspondingly small. The probability that regulatory policies will result in a particular change in industrial behavior depends mainly on the existence of appropriate remedies, and especially on the magnitude of the penalties which the agencies are able to apply to non-complying firms. Any firm confronted by the possibility of regulatory action as a result of certain types of behavior will in principle compare the benefits to the firm of not complying with regulatory policy with the penalties which the regulatory agencies are able to apply in the event of non-compliance. Unless the penalties for non-compliance are sufficiently large to offset the benefits to the firm resulting from failure to comply with the regulatory requirements, regulatory policies will be ineffective in securing the desired changes in industrial behavior. Until recently, this aspect of regulatory policy has been neglected by economists and regulatory agencies alike. For an analysis of alternative types of penalties for antitrust violations, and a proposal that emphasis be placed solely on a (revised) system of fines, see K. G. Elzinga and W. Breit (23).

Although the magnitude of potential technical and allocative efficiency gains resulting from specific changes in industrial behavior is not, by itself, sufficient to determine the probable gains to society from regulatory policies, for the reasons just outlined, information regarding the existence and magnitude of such gains *is* necessary in order to determine which industries or firms, or which types of behavior, are likely to be fruitful subjects for regulatory action, and also the nature of the appropriate remedies and penalties required. Moreover, the same information may itself highlight areas of regulatory activity where changes in methods are necessary to increase the probability of success in influencing industrial behavior. For example, even if appropriate penalties for antitrust violations exist, their application requires the expenditure of regulatory resources for monitoring the behavior of firms in order to detect violations and secure compliance. These monitoring costs may differ significantly for different types of behavior. For example, it may be much more difficult and costly to monitor whether socially desirable input mixes and output mixes are being achieved within a firm than whether the firm's market share exceeds a certain size. Apart from highlighting aspects of industrial behavior where monitoring costs are worth while, information on the magnitude of potential gains in technical and allocative efficiency is important in determining the optimal level of monitoring costs and probability of antitrust success itself. In principle, antitrust monitoring costs connected with any particular type of industrial behavior should be expanded to the level where the marginal monitoring cost equals the product of the resulting marginal change in probability of success multiplied by the potential gain in allocative and technical efficiency.

The principles expounded in this section are not new to economists; they are, however, unfamiliar to the majority of antitrust agency personnel, who are lawyers and who generally view winning antitrust cases as an end in itself rather than as a means to an end. A recent study by L. W. Weiss (78) dealing with the allocation of resources in the Justice Department Antitrust Division (see the article by R. A. Posner (55) too) suggests that the overall level of antitrust resources is too low, since measures of only some of the gains to society from antitrust actions tend to exceed the marginal costs of the antitrust resources employed. In view of the small size of the annual budget of the nation's antitrust agencies, compared to even the smallest estimates of technical and allocative efficiency losses existing in the United States, this conclusion is hardly surprising. As one would also expect, the evidence in Weiss's study suggests the existence of a misallocation of resources between different antitrust activities. For example, Weiss finds that the large emphasis on civil collusion and horizontal merger cases seems well justified, but that the heavy resource use by the Antitrust Division in dealing with potential entry mergers, pure conglomerate mergers, and leverage cases is questionable.

The following sections will consider the rationale underlying existing public policy with regard to individual aspects of industrial behavior, including pricing, mergers, advertising activities, and research and development activities. Although these aspects of behavior are treated separately, the reader should remember that rational allocation of antitrust resources between activities designed to influence these aspects of behavior requires that the potential gains to society associated with the respective behavior changes be estimated empirically and compared.

Public Policy and Pricing Behavior

The philosophy underlying public policy towards industry is not always clear; nonetheless, it is undoubtedly influenced by economic theory. There seems to be a presumption that monopoly pricing behavior results in a misallocation of resources; this presumption is based largely upon orthodox economic theory, as already outlined in the preceding sections.

A group of independent firms may, perhaps by colluding, price or determine output as though the industry they form were a monopoly. There is, in general, a presumption that agreements between independent firms with respect to prices, terms, quantities, or markets served, are against the public interest. In the United States, for example, price agreements are illegal per se. In Great Britain, a slightly different approach is taken; price agreements have to be registered and are presumed to be against the public interest unless the parties to the agreement can demonstrate, to the satisfaction of the Restrictive Practices Court, that the agreement is in the public interest.

Instead of agreeing explicitly on prices or other terms, independent firms may be parties to open prices or price information agreements. In these circumstances the firms agree to notify each other of prices and conditions of sale and changes therein, and often agree to supply other relevant information such as costs and turnover. An important question facing public policy makers is how these agreements are likely to affect the behavior of the firms who are parties to the agreement.

A number of economists have attempted to show that such agreements can improve competition. It has been argued, for example, that the exchange of price information avoids 'phantom competition', the quoting by customers of other firms' prices at lower levels than the true ones in order to persuade the seller to reduce his price; in reply, other economists have argued that far less information than is usually provided under information agreements is needed to overcome this problem. Some writers have claimed that information agreements reduce uncertainty and permit more orderly investment planning; in reply, others have pointed out that although reduced uncertainty may permit more efficient but less flexible machinery to be installed, for example, it may also, by reducing the profitability of a price cut, deter investment in more efficient methods of production. Finally, some economists have suggested that information agreements will help to avoid the misdirection of competitive efforts; it can also be argued, however, that uncertainty about rivals' reactions may foster concern by entrepreneurs with more efficient methods. The threat of price competition may strengthen the incentive to innovate, for example.

The most important effect of the exchange of price or other information by sellers is that, by providing firms with information about which they would otherwise have been in doubt, the expected reaction of a firm's rivals is made more certain. In Chapter 3 it was pointed out that the pricing behavior of a firm will be influenced by the firm's expectations regarding the reactions of its rivals to its own policies. At one extreme, if a firm believes that its rivals are unaware of its prices, then it will be less likely to consider their reactions to its pricing decision than if it knows that they are fully informed. Under a price-information agreement, secret changes are by definition ruled out, hence the expected reaction must be considered.

Although there is much controversy about the economic consequences of price-information agreements, most observers agree that collusion becomes easier where price or other information is exchanged; however, whether it is more likely to occur remains controversial. The United States has a tradition of per se condemnation of explicit price agreements, but the circulation of prices is not condemned per se. The American approach is one of attempting to discover whether collusion actually exists with respect to the price charged. The courts have been reluctant to infer collusion from mere uniformity of prices charged; other factors suggesting collusion must usually be present, such as express agreement not to deviate from published prices, or meetings to discuss price and output policies.

It must be stressed, however, that price-information agreements may affect pricing behavior even though there is no collusion whatever between the parties to the information agreement. The mere fact of dissemination may affect pricing behavior; all that is required is that the information agreement change a firm's expectations regarding rivals' reactions. As explained in Chapters 3 and 7, monopoly pricing by firms in a particular industry can occur without collusion of any kind. By entering into a price-information agreement, firms voluntarily give up the advantage of surprise attack in return for similar assurances from their rivals. In these circumstances, retaliation can be immediate, and a firm will only cut price when it believes that other firms will not do so, or that even though they do, it will not help them. For further analysis of information agreements, see the article by D. P. O'Brien and D. Swann (52).

The relation of prices to costs is one important aspect of industry behavior; the rapidity of the response of prices to changes in supply and demand conditions is a related matter. Changes in tastes, or technology, will mean that the optimal allocation of resources changes through time. Price agreements, or price-information agreements, may reduce the flexibility of prices in response to such changes, and therefore hinder the achievement of an optimal resource allocation.

Before leaving the subject of public policy and pricing behavior, we shall analyze price-discrimination practices in order to illustrate the complications involved in attempting to apply economic analysis to particular problems of public policy: if different consumers pay different prices for the same good, the ratio of marginal utilities of that good and other goods will differ for different consumers and rule one, the rule of distributive efficiency, will be violated. Can it be concluded that abolition of price discrimination would be an unambiguous improvement in the situation? The answer is no. Let us assume, for the moment, that abolition of price discrimination will not change the level of output. Although it is true that it would be *possible* to improve the welfare of some members of the community without making others worse off, it cannot be assumed that this would occur merely as a result of making price discrimination illegal. The resulting price changes will probably change income distribution, and therefore welfare distribution. If the total market is originally divided into two submarkets, abolition of price discrimination will increase price in the market where demand is more elastic. In the absence of any other changes, the real income, and therefore welfare, of buyers in that market will be reduced. Additional policies, such as redistributions of money income, are necessary in order to ensure that no one suffers a reduction in welfare. Second, it is possible that abolition of price discrimination will change the level of output of the product. In these circumstances, price discrimination can only be judged by comparing the output mix with and without price discrimination. The problem cannot be solved by invoking rule one only. Suppose, for example, that output is greater with price discrimination than without price discrimination, and that in the absence of price discrimination the ratio of price to marginal cost is higher in this industry than elsewhere in the economy. Given the existing welfare distribution, this might imply that the allocation of resources could be improved by increasing the output of the product – that is, discriminating monopoly may move resource allocation closer to optimal than absence of price discrimination, despite the fact that it would be possible to allocate the output mix resulting under discrimination more efficiently between members of the community.

Public Policy and Mergers

A number of countries have adopted public policy measures which restrict merger between formerly independent firms in certain circumstances. In the United States, for example, Section 7 of the Clayton Act, as amended by the 1950 Celler–Kefauver Antimerger Act, forbids mergers which tend to lessen competition substantially, or tend to create a monopoly, in any line of commerce. The Clayton Act applies not only to so-called horizontal mergers between firms operating at the same stage in the production and distribution of a particular product, but also to vertical mergers between firms at successive stages in the production of a particular product, and to conglomerate mergers between firms producing different products. Similarly, in the United Kingdom, mergers between firms which result in control, locally or nationally, of a quarter of the supply of any category of goods or services, or which result in combined assets exceeding £5 million, may be referred to the Monopolies and Mergers Commission, and may be prohibited if found to operate against the public interest.

We shall not be concerned with how the courts and regulatory agencies have interpreted and applied the law affecting mergers, but instead consider briefly the underlying economic rationale of merger policy, distinguishing between horizontal, vertical, and conglomerate mergers.

In order to judge whether a particular merger is likely to lessen competition substantially in practice, the relevant market must be defined, because whether behavior will be influenced depends upon the number and size distribution of firms operating in the relevant market. As indicated in Chapter 5, if one is interested in the behavior of firms, the relevant market should be defined to include products of firms whose behavior is likely to affect each other significantly and whose behavior will therefore be interrelated.

Apart from the problem of defining the relevant market, answering the question of whether merger will lessen competition is not without its problems. Horizontal merger between two firms operating in the same market reduces the number of firms in that market, and this may influence industry behavior. Confining ourselves for the moment to pricing behavior, a priori theory does not, however, indicate that industry behavior will necessarily be worsened by a reduction in the number of firms in an industry. Smaller numbers may make firms more aware of interdependence and therefore lead to more monopolistic pricing behavior; on the other hand it may not do so. The number of firms in the market will of course be an important determinant of whether this is likely to be the case. With very small numbers, interdependence may already have been recognized and taken into account prior to merger, and merger may therefore have no effect upon industry behavior. With very large numbers, behavior may also be unaffected if the number of firms remaining after merger is still large enough to lead firms to ignore each other in their individual policymaking. Apart from the effect on numbers, the effect of merger on the size distribution of firms in an industry may be a more important determinant of industry behavior in certain circumstances, and a reduction in numbers may be accompanied by a change in size distribution which improves industry pricing performance despite increased awareness of interdependence. Merger between two small firms, for example, may enable them to compete more effectively with larger firms dominating the relevant market.

The effect of vertical mergers upon pricing behavior at each stage of the productive process has been discussed at length in Chapter 8, and will not be repeated here. It is sufficient to remind the reader that vertical integration may either increase or reduce the price of the final product and that it is impossible to generalize about the effect of vertical integration by merger on industry pricing performance.

Finally, we turn to the question of how conglomerate mergers between firms producing different products are likely to influence behavior in individual product markets. As explained in Chapter 9, whether industry behavior will be changed by such mergers depends upon whether the merged firms will act in a different manner from the manner in which they acted individually prior to merger, or whether other firms in individual product markets expect them to act differently. The belief is widely held that a diversified firm, by virtue of its multiplicity of geographic and product markets, has a competitive advantage over a firm producing and selling in only one of those markets. This belief seems to be founded upon the notion that a diversified firm can subsidize the cost of products sold in some markets out of the profits earned in other markets, thereby placing the firms operating only in the subsidized markets at a competitive disadvantage and either driving them out of business or reducing their profits and growth rate. Unless capital requirement or other entry barriers exist to prevent a single-product firm from diversifying into the subsidizing markets, however, it is difficult to see how any competitive advantage can exist for diversified firms.

The preceding discussion has been confined to analyzing the influence of merger on industry pricing performance. Even if the pricing performance is worsened by merger, smaller numbers may mean an increase in other forms of competition, and an improvement in other dimensions of industry performance, such as R&D or other aspects of product policy. Unfortunately, for reasons explained in the following sections, we lack criteria for judging these other aspects of industry performance; for the present, therefore, public policy must necessarily confine itself to evaluating the effect of merger on pricing performance only.

A number of arguments are sometimes put forward in defense of mergers. One defense of merger is limited to those cases in which bankruptcy or liquidation seem imminent. The so-called failing company defense, recognized by the United States courts, is based upon the idea that if a firm is failing, it is no longer a vital competitive factor in the market. There are obvious problems involved in trying to apply such a doctrine. What is the appropriate criterion, for example, for judging whether a company has failed enough to justify a merger? A firm may even be failing precisely because of the predatory tactics of another firm wishing to take it over.

Another prominent defense of merger is the argument that merger may increase efficiency and reduce the cost of producing an industry's output either by permitting scale economies to be reaped or by eliminating other inefficiencies. Profits depend upon costs in addition to revenues, and even though merger may not affect the level of industry price and revenue, it may increase efficiency and industry profits. If merger were the only way to achieve economies in cost, the merger might also change industry pricing behavior and worsen allocative efficiency even though it improved technical efficiency, and the public-policy maker would be confronted with the problem of choosing between these two aspects of economic efficiency. Some economists have argued that such a conflict need not arise because if increased efficiency is really the motive for merger it can be achieved through internal expansion of a single firm, and that any important economies attained through merger can instead be gained through internal growth. Other economists have questioned the presumption that internal expansion is as efficient as merger (see K. Retwisch (60), for example). Also, it should be emphasized that in order to improve the efficiency with which a particular level of industry output is produced by means of internal expansion of one firm, other firms must contract their output and/or be eliminated from the industry. Price competition by the expanding firm is a means of accomplishing this. In some circumstances, however, there may be no incentive to eliminate inefficiencies through internal expansion. In the case of an oligopolistic industry composed of a few strong firms and characterized by absence of price competition, for example, merger may be the only means of eliminating inefficiencies, since expansion and price competition initiated by one firm is unlikely to occur.

A more recent defense (see H. G. Manne (45)) of mergers consists of the argument that mergers are a device safeguarding shareholders' interests by forcing managers to be efficient and maximize profits. The market price of a firm's shares will, it is argued, be correlated with the profits earned by the firm. If a firm is poorly managed, in the sense of not making as great a return for the shareholders as could be accomplished under other feasible managements, the market price of the shares will be low relative to the market price of shares of other firms in the same industry or relative to the market as a whole. The lower the share price, relative to what it could be with other more efficient management, the more attractive a take-over becomes to those who believe that they can manage the firm more efficiently. The threat of take-over will, it is argued, act as a spur to management efficiency.

Furthermore, it can be argued that the managers of *competing* firms are likely to have more information crucial to take-over decisions, such as cost conditions in their own firms. Reliable information is also available to a firm's suppliers and customers. For these reasons, many horizontal and vertical mergers may be of this control take-over variety rather than the foreclosure of competitors or scale economies type.

While this argument is a plausible hypothesis, the problem confronting the public-policy maker is that of devising methods for distinguishing mergers motivated by a quest for monopoly profits from those merely trying to establish efficient management in poorly run companies. Industry profits depend not only upon costs, but also upon revenues. Higher profits may be anticipated, not because of increased efficiency and lower costs in the firm taken over, but because of higher anticipated revenues resulting from more monopolistic industry pricing after merger than existed in the industry prior to merger. Alternatively, anticipated profits may be increased for both reasons, in which case the dilemma of choosing between greater technical efficiency at the expense of less allocative efficiency confronts the public-policy maker once again.

Public Policy and Advertising Activities

In Chapter 4, advertising was introduced into the analysis of a firm's behavior as an input that affects the demand for the firm's product. While public policy towards pricing behavior is based, at least in part, upon conclusions derived from economic theory, the same cannot be said of policy towards advertising. Economic theory provides no clear public policy guidelines in the case of advertising. Few people would deny that a clear case can be made for laws to protect consumers against false or misleading advertising; what, however, can be said regarding levels of advertising which do not fall into this category?

Advertising is frequently treated with hostility by laymen and economists alike. See J. Bachman (3) and J. H. Reilly (59) for examples of contrary views on advertising. The argument that advertising outlays are too high in particular industries, such as the pharmaceutical industry, is frequently heard. Distrust of advertising stems from comparative neglect, fostered by economic theory itself, of the benefits of advertising from the point of view of buyers of advertised products, as opposed to the benefits to sellers of these products. Traditional economic theory assumes that knowledge is perfect – that consumers are fully aware of the nature of all products offered by producers, and the prices of the products. This assumption is not a valid description of the real world. Information regarding available products is not a free good, automatically available to anyone and everyone. In the absence of advertising, buyers must acquire information in other ways, ways which might conceivably be more costly, from the buyer's point of view, than the cost of resources devoted to advertising, which must be recouped in the prices of advertised products. Referring back to the rules of optimal resource and product allocation in the first section of this chapter, advertising may be a means of achieving these optimal conditions by providing buyers with information regarding available products and their terms of sale, at lower cost than alternative methods of obtaining information.

A distinction is sometimes made between informative and persuasive advertising, the implication being that the former is desirable while the latter is undesirable. Unfortunately, this provides no additional guidelines for public policy, for it is impossible to give any operationally significant meaning to the two terms. Conceptually, the difference between the two types of advertising is that informative advertising enables buyers to satisfy existing preferences by informing them of available alternatives, while persuasive advertising changes preferences. In practice, however, preferences are necessarily formed on the basis of information; whether such information is informative or persuasive is a matter of semantics. Nor is it possible to evaluate the level of advertising associated with particular products with reference to whether the price of the product is reduced or increased. In Chapter 4 it was explained that advertising might either increase price or, by permitting firms to reap economies of scale in production, might reduce the price of a product. Even though price is increased, however, the cost of the product plus the cost of obtaining information regarding the nature of the product may be lower to buyers than in the absence of advertising.

Advertising itself uses resources; viewed in this context the problem of evaluating levels of advertising becomes a special case in the problem of resource allocation. The relevant question, then, is whether the benefits of advertising, from the point of view of the members of the community, at least equal the benefits that could be obtained if the resources used in advertising were used for other purposes. An answer to this question requires that the benefits of advertising be measured and compared with the benefits resulting from alternative uses of resources devoted to advertising. Unfortunately, the problem of defining and measuring the benefits of advertising has not yet been solved. As a result, the problem of determining how many resources to devote to advertising is a question which, in its current state, economic theory cannot answer. Some questions relating to advertising may not, however, require the measurement of actual benefits associated with the information provided. For example, it may be possible to determine whether the same information provided by current levels of advertising could be provided more efficiently, in terms of resources used, by other methods, while leaving the question of how many resources to devote to providing information until such time as the analytical tools required to provide an answer to this question have been forged.

Although economic theory provides no clear guidelines for public policy towards advertising itself, what can be said of the relationship between advertising and other aspects of firms' behavior, such as pricing and price–cost relationships? Some empirical evidence (L. Telser (74), for example) reveals that the prices of advertised goods tend to be higher than those of unadvertised goods. However, as already explained, the cost of the advertised product, including information, may be lower for buyers of these products than in the absence of advertising. If this were not so, there would seem little reason why advertised products should survive in competition with unadvertised brands. A more important consideration than the height of price is the relationship between advertising and price–cost margins. Does advertising, for example, foster monopoly by creating barriers to entry which permit monopoly pricing? Advertising may increase barriers to entry into an industry if, in order to enter the industry, potential entrants must spend more on advertising per unit of output than established firms spend, because this implies an absolute cost disadvantage to potential entrants compared to established firms. Alternatively, advertising can increase entry barriers if advertising is characterized by economies of scale, or if the funds to finance advertising can only be obtained at a higher interest rate than that paid by established firms.

Empirical evidence relating to these matters is still scarce, and by no means conclusive. As the discussion in the section of Chapter 6 which deals with advertising and concentration indicated, industry advertising and seller concentration do not appear to be systematically related. Some of the empirical evidence also suggests that there is negative correlation between changes in advertising and industrial concentration; this is consistent with a situation in which new firms break into an industry by advertising, and some economists have stressed that advertising expenditures may be a means by which new competitors can establish themselves, rather than a barrier to entry. None of this evidence, however, is inconsistent with the hypothesis that advertising is a barrier to entry and permits monopoly pricing by established firms in an industry. The influence of concentration on price–cost relationships is analytically distinct from that of entry barriers. On the other hand, a priori theory indicates that, other things being equal, higher concentration may be expected to lead to higher industry profit rates; on the other hand, as the analysis in Chapter 7 indicates, price cannot exceed average cost in the long run by more than the height of entry barriers. The relevant question at issue is whether advertising and profit rates are related, not whether advertising and concentration are related.

The evidence presented in a number of statistical studies (see W. S. Comanor and T. A. Wilson (17) and J. M. Vernon and R. E. M. Nourse (76), and the references cited therein) suggests that profits rates and advertising are positively associated. If this positive relationship is a long-run characteristic, this evidence is consistent with the hypothesis that advertising creates entry barriers and permits monopoly pricing. In interpreting these studies it must be remembered that the height of entry barriers depends also on other factors in addition to advertising, such as the extent of production economies of scale relative to the size of the market, the absolute amount of capital required to operate a plant of minimum efficient scale, and other absolute production cost disadvantages of new entrants compared to established firms. The issue of whether advertising creates entry barriers is dealt with in detail in the section of Chapter 7 entitled Non-Price Aspects of Entry Barrier Theory.

The conclusion that advertising may act as a barrier to entry and permit more monopolistic pricing in particular industries is not altered by the finding of some studies that brand shares within industries are less stable, the higher the level of industry advertising, implying that advertising is a means of competition. That is, competition between firms in an industry through advertising is still compatible with poor industry pricing performance as indicated by price–cost relationships.

If advertising is a substitute for price competition, the problem confronting the policy maker is that of choosing between better pricing performance and lower advertising. In the current state of our knowledge, there are no grounds for preferring good pricing performance to more advertising. That is, there is no reason, in a world of imperfect knowledge and changes in tastes and technology, to believe that price competition is more desirable than advertising. In certain circumstances, advertising may amount to price competition; if, for example, some buyers are purchasing a product at a price higher than the price charged by another firm about which they are uninformed, advertising which provides this information may reduce the price of the product to these buyers. Even if products were not changing in character with the passage of time, the population of buyers is changing over time, and advertising may be the most efficient means of informing them of alternatives available. Similarly, even if the composition of the buying population were not changing, information regarding changes in the nature of seller's products resulting from technical progress must be transmitted to buyers, and might be transmitted to them most efficiently by advertising messages. Unfortunately, as already mentioned, we are lacking an operational criterion of good advertising performance; in the absence of such a criterion, it is impossible to choose objectively between good pricing behavior and more advertising.

Public Policy and Research and Development Activities

The preceding sections indicate that there is a general presumption in favor of low concentration as a structural goal on the grounds that this is more likely to result in price–cost relationships compatible with efficient resource allocation.

There is disagreement among economists on the question of which form of market structure is most conducive to research activity and technological progress. Some argue that firms with monopoly power are more likely to undertake technological research than firms in highly competitive industries; this argument is based upon the notion that the prospective returns to R&D activities will be higher in the case of firms in the former category, and/or that such firms will have higher profits and hence a larger supply of funds for financing R&D activities. Supporters of the contrary view argue that the competitive influences of atomistic industries will spur the quest for technological advances whereas monopolies, even if they possess greater investment funds, need not employ them in the quest for new technology, and are less likely to do so since competitive pressures are less. Other economists have argued that oligopoly is the market structure most likely to encourage innovation, for such a structure, it is argued, combines the funds to finance R&D with competitive pressures that will cause firms to use the funds to innovate.

What does empirical evidence concerning market structure and R&D activities indicate? A considerable amount of empirical evidence has been gathered concerning the relationship between firm size and innovational input and output. It is undoubtedly true that most R&D is performed by the larger firms in an economy. In part this may be accounted for by the indivisibilities of expensive R&D inputs, already discussed in Chapter 4 in the section entitled Research and Development Activities. However, looking at those firms which carry out R&D, the evidence suggests that beyond a certain size level, the ratio of R&D expenditures to some index of firm size does not increase significantly with firm size, and may even decline. Up to that size level, which varies from industry to industry, innovational effort appears to increase more than proportionately with size. Uncertainty concerning the precise relationship between R&D and firm size among the largest firms in a particular industry is largely attributable to the small number of firms in this category in most industries. The results of any particular statistical study will be greatly influenced by the treatment accorded to each individual observation; different statistical approaches, such as differences in how firms not engaging in R&D activities are dealt with, are capable of yielding different results in terms of the relationship between large firm size and R&D activities.

Large absolute size is not, of course, the same thing as large market power, which depends instead upon absolute size in relation to market size. The available statistical evidence concerning the relationship between market power, measured by concentration, and R&D activities is still rather inconclusive. Industrial research, whether measured by R&D expenditures, employment of scientific and technical personnel, or patented inventions, is heavily concentrated in industries which have moderate to high levels of concentration. However, the industries of relatively high concentration are also the industries in which technological opportunity is greater. That is, the advance of science opens up more possibilities in these industries, and greater technological opportunity, rather than higher concentration, might conceivably account for the greater apparent progressiveness of these industries. The important question is whether, in industries with similar technological opportunity, R&D activities are greater in the more concentrated industries. A recent statistical study by F. M. Scherer (63) suggests that even after interindustry technological opportunity differences are taken into account, there remains a tendency for R&D input, measured by scientific and technical personnel, to increase with concentration at low levels of concentration. This tendency appears to be absent, however, at high levels of concentration; the same study found that when the four-firm concentration ratio exceeds 50 or 55 per cent, additional concentration is not associated with increases in R&D input, and may even be associated with a decline in this variable. The main public policy implication of these findings is that policies designed to reduce very high levels of concentration on grounds of promoting pricing behavior compatible with efficient resource allocation are unlikely to reduce the level of inventive and innovative activity in the economy. R&D inputs will be reduced only if desirable pricing behavior requires a level of concentration lower than the level at which R&D inputs cease to increase with increases in concentration.

Even if the evidence suggested that reduced concentration would reduce R&D activities, this would not necessarily imply that public policies which are designed to reduce concentration should be abandoned, and that the dilemma confronting the public-policy maker should always be resolved in favour of more R&D. It cannot be argued that more R&D is in all circumstances better than less R&D. R&D activities require resources which could be used for alternative purposes, and it is impossible to speak meaningfully of technological progress being too slow or too fast without first making quite explicit the general principle by which the distribution of resources between innovational uses and other uses is to be decided. Since the problem is precisely analogous to that of securing an optimal allocation of resources – merely a special case of this problem – it is not immediately obvious that principles similar to those employed in orthodox economic theory and discussed in the first section of this chapter should be rejected. See D. Usher (75) for more on this point. We reject entirely the view of some economists who have argued that aspects of economic performance such as economic progress have nothing to do with the efficiency of use of scarce resources.

These issues are, however, still extremely controversial and a number of problems remain to be solved. In order to devise public policy with respect to R&D activities, it is necessary to show what principles must be applied to determine the right amount of R&D and resulting rate of technological progress in a particular industry, and what kinds of market structure will lead to these optimal levels of R&D. Until these problems have been solved, the goal of adequate progressiveness will continue to lack operational meaning for purposes of policy making.

In view of the preceding comments, it is appropriate to mention briefly the rationale of the patent system which, whatever its actual effects, is intended to encourage R&D investment and the disclosure of new knowledge by giving to firms exclusive rights to commercial exploitation of inventions and innovations resulting from their R&D efforts. This policy, it must be explained, is not based upon the assumption that more R&D is always better than less. It is based to a large extent upon the assumption that there are externalities associated with the production and dissemination of new knowledge and that this will result in a lower level of R&D and dissemination activities than the community desires, whatever the market structure a firm happens to operate in, unless patent protection is granted. Reference has already been made in the section of this chapter entitled Pure Competition and Resource Allocation to the concept of externalities, defined as benefits or costs not reflected by prices or money costs. The argument in support of patent protection, in brief, is as follows.

The total potential benefits of a given amount of new knowledge, in the form of resource savings and new and improved products, may be spread over a wide area of the economy. These benefits can be realized only if potential users are aware of the new knowledge. In the absence of legal property rights over new knowledge, however, a firm has no incentive to disseminate new knowledge once it exists, and may have little incentive to produce new knowledge by investing in R&D activities.

The level of R&D investment financed and undertaken by a firm will depend upon the money value of the benefits of new knowledge that the firm expects to be able to recoup for itself. In the absence of legal property rights over new knowledge, the magnitude of such recoupable benefits is determined largely by the firm's ability to keep new knowledge secret. Some limit on the unrestricted ability of other firms to use the new knowledge is necessary in order to enable the firm to recoup part of the benefits of new knowledge for itself. If products or processes embodying new knowledge can be imitated immediately by other firms, product prices might be driven down to current production costs, preventing the firm from reaping any of the benefits of the new knowledge and from recouping the R&D outlay which produced the new knowledge.

Even if the ability to keep the new knowledge secret for a time results in a situation in which the expected return on R&D investment is sufficient to induce a firm to invest in R&D activities, the potential benefits of the resulting knowledge may be far in excess of the realized benefits. In addition to benefits from the application of new knowledge in the firm's own immediate market area, new knowledge may have applications in a much wider and unanticipated area. These benefits cannot be realized unless potential users are aware of the new knowledge, but the firm has no incentive to disseminate the new knowledge resulting from its R&D activities; as already indicated, secrecy is essential in order to enable the firm to reap benefits in the absence of legal property rights over the new knowledge.

These considerations suggest that, in the absence of property rights over new knowledge, the level of R&D investment will be below the level for which consumers would be willing to pay; patent protection, it is argued, will encourage R&D investment and the disclosure of new knowledge in circumstances in which it would otherwise be kept secret, and will move the output of new knowledge closer to the level that consumers desire.

Concluding Comments

This section summarizes briefly some of the problems that remain to be solved in developing a logically consistent body of public policy measures designed to influence industrial structure.

Existing public policy relies heavily upon economic theory concerning the determinants of pricing behavior. There is, however, much scope for broadening our understanding of the determinants of firms' pricing behavior. Economic theory in its present state is still highly inadequate for purposes of generalizing on such traditional variables as price and level of output in situations involving oligopoly, vertical integration, and conglomerate mergers. The nature of other variables, in addition to cost conditions and concentration, which influence firms' pricing behavior, is another area requiring further study.

The current state of economic theory concerning the determinants of other aspects of firms' behavior, including advertising, product policies, and R&D, is far less satisfactory than current theory concerning the determinants of pricing behavior. There are numerous deficiencies in the theoretical and empirical knowledge concerning the determinants of, and relationship between, the various aspects of non-price competition. However, much work is currently being undertaken in this field, particularly in the area of R&D activities. Although the individual studies usually treat aspects of firms' behavior in isolation, it is to be hoped that from this work will stem a more general theory of firms' behavior encompassing the relationship between different aspects of a firm's behavior. Development of such a theory is essential in order to permit one to predict the effect of particular public policy measures on different dimensions of a firm's behavior. There is, for example, the problem of possible undesirable side effects on progressiveness, selling costs, and other product policies, of measures designed to eliminate monopolistic pricing performance. The interdependence of various aspects of a firm's behavior makes predictions based upon a neglect of this interdependence extremely hazardous.

The implications of alternative objectives, in addition to profit-maximization, for the behavior of firms is also a potential area for further study and refinement of existing knowledge. As indicated in Chapter 1, although profit maximization may provide an adequate description of behavior for purposes of predicting the sign of changes in variables in response to public policy measures, it may not be adequate when interested in the levels and characteristics of firms' activities corresponding to certain public policy parameters in the economic system.

Even if the determinants of all aspects of firms' behavior were known precisely, the application of public policy requires standards against which existing behavior, or changes in behavior, can be compared. Unfortunately, apart from pricing, we lack standards for judging aspects of firms' behavior, particularly standards for evaluating advertising and product policy performance including durability, product variety, and R&D activities. See the references by Auld (2), Bishop (9), Hunter (33), McCain (46) and Wright (83) for analyses of the appropriate variety of products in an economy. While the ideal type of pricing performance from the point of view of maximizing the aggregate welfare of individuals in the community, has been more or less clearly defined and is backed by a respectable body of analysis, the other types of ideal performance have not yet been defined. In the current state of knowledge, there is no way of ascertaining whether the R&D activities of firms in a particular industry constitute good or bad performance in a given situation. Similarly, a definitive and empirically applicable distinction between desirable and excessive or deficient selling costs is not yet available. Both goals therefore have little current operational meaning for purposes of public policy, and much work remains to be done in these areas.

Appendix I: Substantive Provisions of the United States Antitrust Laws

There are three principal antitrust statutes in the United States: the Sherman Act, the Federal Trade Commission Act, and the Clayton Act. Their major provisions, and those of subsequent amending Acts, are outlined briefly below.

The Sherman Act

Enacted in 1890, the Sherman Act has two major provisions:

Section 1. 'Every contract, combination in the form of a trust or otherwise, or conspiracy, in restraint of trade or commerce among the several States, or with foreign nations, is hereby declared to be illegal . . .'

Section 2. 'Every person who shall monopolize, or attempt to monopolize, or combine or conspire with any other person or persons, to monopolize any part of the trade or commerce among the several States, or with foreign nations, shall be guilty of a misdemeanor . . .'

In 1937 Section 1 of the Sherman Act was amended by the *Miller–Tydings Act*, which provides exemption for resale price agreements between manufacturers of products identified by a brand name or trademark and suppliers in states which have their own 'fair trade' laws sanctioning resale price agreements.

The Federal Trade Commission Act

This Act, passed in 1914, established the Federal Trade Commission to strengthen the observance and enforcement of the antitrust laws. Section 5 of the Act contained a general prohibition of unfair methods of competition in commerce.

In 1938 the *Wheeler–Lea Act* was passed to extend the Commission's jurisdiction to include not only unfair methods of competition which injured competitors, but also deceptive or unfair acts in which no competitors were harmed but the public was injured. Section 5 of the Federal Trade Commission Act, as amended, provides in part that:

'Unfair methods of competition in commerce, and unfair or deceptive acts or practices in commerce, are hereby declared illegal.'

In 1952 the *McGuire Act* was passed to exempt from Section 5 and allow enforcement of 'nonsigners' clauses where the 'fair trade' laws of a state permit such clauses in resale price agreements between parties of different states. A 'nonsigners' clause requires all retailers in a state, even those who did not sign a contract, to follow the manufacturer's resale price maintenance program once one retailer signs the contract and the other retailers are served notice of this fact.

The Clayton Act

In contrast to the general prohibition against unfair methods of competition which was contained in the Federal Trade Commission Act, the Clayton Act, which was also enacted in 1914, outlawed four specific types of conduct: price discrimination, exclusive and tying contracts, intercorporate acquisitions and mergers, and interlocking directorates.

(i) Section 2: Price discrimination. Section 2 of the Clayton Act prohibits sellers from discriminating in price between different purchasers, except where differences in the grade, quality, or quantity of the commodity exist and the resulting lower prices make due allowance only for differences in the cost of selling or transportation, and are offered in good faith to meet competition, where the effect may be substantially to lessen competition or tend to create a monopoly. The original section was designed primarily to prevent large manufacturers from eliminating smaller rivals by temporarily cutting prices in some markets while maintaining prices in other markets.

Section 2 was amended in 1936 by the *Robinson–Patman Act*, which was passed in response to the demands of independent wholesalers for added restrictions on the freedom of suppliers to discriminate, and the complaint that chain stores were obtaining from their suppliers advantages in the form of lower prices, greater advertising allowances, and larger discounts, than were warranted by lower costs associated with the large volume purchased by chain stores. Section 2 of the Robinson–Patman Act provides in part that:

'It shall be unlawful for any person engaged in commerce, in the course of such commerce, either directly or indirectly, to discriminate in price between different purchasers of commodities of like grade and quality, where either or any of the purchasers involved in such discrimination are in commerce, where such commodities are sold for use, consumption, or resale within the United States . . . and where the effect of such discrimination may be substantially to lessen competition or tend to create a monopoly in any line of commerce, or to injure, destroy, or prevent competition with any person who either grants or knowingly receives the benefit of such discrimination, or with customers of either of them . . .'

Like Section 2 of the Clayton Act, Section 2 of the Robinson–Patman Act allows price differentials which make due allowance only for differences in cost of manufacture, sale, or delivery, and also permits price discrimination if it is justified by the necessity of a seller to meet in good faith the equally low price of a competitor. Other parts of Section 2 of the Robinson–Patman Act are directed against arrangements whereby buyers exact price discrimination disguised as brokerage commissions, against discrimination in promotional allowances and services made available to purchasers who buy for resale, and against buyers who use their buying power to extract more favorable treatment from their suppliers than is allowed under the terms of Section 2.

(ii) Section 3: Tying Arrangements and Exclusive Dealing. The Clayton Act prohibits tying sales where the purchase of one good is made conditional upon the purchase of other goods, exclusive dealing where the purchaser cannot handle competing lines, and requirements contracts which require the purchaser to obtain all or most of his needs from a single supplier, where the effect of such restraints may substantially lessen competition or tend to create a monopoly. Section 3 provides in part that:

'It shall be unlawful for any person engaged in commerce, in the course of such commerce, to lease or make a sale or contract for sale of goods, wares, merchandise, machinery, supplies, or other commodities . . . on the condition, agreement, or understanding that the lessee or purchaser thereof shall not use or deal in the goods, wares, merchandise, machinery, supplies, or other commodities of a competitor or competitors of the lessor or seller, where the effect of such lease, sale, or contract for sale or such condition, agreement, or understanding may be to substantially lessen competition or tend to create a monopoly in any line of commerce.'

(iii) Section 7: Corporate Acquisitions and Mergers. Section 7 of the Clayton Act forbade any corporation to acquire the shares of competing corporations where the effect may be to substantially lessen competition or tend to create a monopoly. The effectiveness of Section 7 was impaired by subsequent decisions of the Supreme Court, which effectively barred Section 7 from applying in the case of acquisitions of assets, rather than shares, of a competing corporation. In 1950 the *Celler–Kefauver Act* amended Section 7 of the Clayton Act and broadened this section to cover mergers accomplished through asset purchases as well as share purchases. As amended by the Celler-Kefauver Act, Section 7 provides in part that:

'No corporation engaged in commerce shall acquire, directly or indirectly, the whole or any part of the stock or other share capital and no corporation subject to the jurisdiction of the Federal Trade Commission shall acquire the whole or any part of the assets of another corporation engaged also in commerce, where in any line of commerce in any section of the country, the effect of such acquisition may be substantially to lessen competition, or tend to create a monopoly.'

(iv) Section 8: Interlocking Directorates. Section 8 of the Clayton Act prohibited interlocking directorates between corporations engaged in commerce where one of them has a capital and surplus of more than $1 million and where the elimination of competition between them would constitute a violation of any of the provisions of the antitrust laws.

Appendix II: Summary of Substantive Provisions of the United Kingdom Anti-monopoly Legislation *

Monopolies and Restrictive Practices Act 1948

Defined monopoly as a situation in which at least one third of a given category of output was supplied by a single firm or by two or more firms acting in concert with the effect of restricting competition. The Board of Trade was empowered to refer to any such monopoly situation it believed existed to a Monopoly and Restrictive Practices Commission, which was charged with deciding whether a monopoly situation did in fact exist, and whether it operated or could be expected to operate against the public interest. In the latter event, the Commission was empowered to suggest remedies, but the Board of Trade was not obliged to accept them.

Monopolies and Restrictive Practices Commission Act 1953

Increased the maximum size of the Monopolies and Restrictive Practices Commission from 10 to 25 members, and empowered it to sit in divisions instead of a single body, in order to speed up and increase the capacity of its operations.

Restrictive Trade Practices Act 1956

Removed restrictive agreements from the scope of the existing Commission, which was renamed the Monopolies Commission, and established a new branch of the High Court, the Restrictive Practices Court, for the purpose of hearing cases brought before it by a newly created Registrar of Restrictive Trade Practices.

The Act required certain specified categories of restrictive agreements to be registered, including agreements on prices and other terms of sale, quantities or types of goods and services to be supplied, processes of manufacture to be used, and restrictions on persons or areas to be supplied. These registerable agreements were presumed to be against the public interest unless it could be established before the Court that the restrictions resulted in one or more of seven categories of benefit specified in the Act.

---

*For more detailed discussion the reader is referred to the readings dealing with these laws listed at the end of this chapter.

Resale Prices Act 1964

Created a general presumption that resale price maintenance is contrary to the public interest and the practice was legally prohibited unless exemption was granted by the Registrar of Restrictive Trade Practices on the grounds of one or more of five categories of justification.

Monopolies and Mergers Act 1965

Gave the Board of Trade power to refer to the Monopolies Commission any merger that might lead to a monopoly situation as defined in the 1948 Act, or which involved assets totalling £5 million or more. Prior to this Act, there was no provision for inquiry into proposed mergers to see whether they would result in a monopoly situation which operated against the public interest.

Restrictive Trade Practices Act 1968

Brought agreements to exchange information between firms within the scope of the 1956 Act by making them registerable with the Registrar of Restrictive Trade Practices.

Fair Trading Act 1973

Amended the Restrictive Trade Practices Acts of 1956 and 1968, and replaces the Monopolies and Mergers Acts of 1948 and 1965, incorporating much of the existing legislation but also revising some of its provisions. The Act also created two new institutions, a Consumer Protection Advisory Committee and the office of Director General of Fair Trading, who took over the functions of the Registrar of Restrictive Practices.

The Monopolies Commission was renamed the Monopolies and Mergers Commission, and the definition of monopoly was changed from a situation in which at least one third of a given category of output is supplied by a single source, or subject to a collective agreement, to one in which at least a quarter of a given category of ouput is so supplied. Also, the relevant market may be defined as a specific geographic area, thus enabling local monopolies to be referred to the Commission.

RECOMMENDED READINGS

1. Asch, P., The determinants and effects of antitrust activity, *Journal of Law and Economics*, October 1975.
2. Auld, D. A., A note on consumer welfare and product differentiation, *Quarterly Review of Economics and Business*, Winter 1971.
3. Bachman, J., Is advertising wasteful? *Journal of Marketing*, January 1968.
4. Bator, F. M., The simple analytics of welfare maximization, *American Economic Review*, March 1957. Reprinted in Breit, W. and Hochman, H. M. (Eds.) *Readings in Microeconomics* (New York: Holt, Rinehart and Winston, Inc., 1968).
5. Baumol, W. J. and Bradford, D. F., Optimal departures from marginal-cost pricing, *American Economic Review*, June 1970.
6. Bergson, A., On monopoly and welfare losses, *American Economic Review*, September 1973.
7. Bergson, A., On monopoly and welfare losses, *American Economic Review*, December 1973.
8. Berry, R. A., A review of problems in the interpretation of producers' surplus, *Southern Economic Journal*, July 1972.
9. Bishop, R. L., Monopolistic competition and welfare economics. In Kuenne, R. E. (Ed.) *Monopolistic Competition Theory: Studies in Impact* (New York: John Wiley & Sons, Inc., 1967).
10. Boyle, S. E., A blueprint for competition: restructuring the motor vehicle industry, *Journal of Economic Issues*, June 1975.
11. Brock, Catherine, *The Control of Restrictive Practices from 1956: A Study of The Restrictive Practices Court* (London: McGraw-Hill, 1966).
12. Brodley, J. F., Industrial deconcentration and legal feasibility: the efficiencies defence, *Journal of Economic Issues*, June 1975.
13. Buchanan, J. M. and Tullock, G., The dead hand of monopoly, *Antitrust Law and Economics Review*, Summer 1968.
14. Burns, M. E., A note on the concept of consumers' surplus, *American Economic Review*, June 1973.

15. Carson, R., On monopoly welfare losses: comment, *American Economic Review*, December 1975.
16. Comanor, W. S. and Leibenstein, H., Allocative efficiency, X-efficiency, and the measurement of welfare losses, *Economica*, August 1969.
17. Comanor, W. S. and Wilson, T. A., Advertising, market structure and performance, *Review of Economics and Statistics*, November 1967.
18. Crew, M. A. and Rowley, C. K., On allocative efficiency, X-efficiency, and the measurement of welfare loss, *Economica*, May 1971.
19. Crew, M. and Rowley, C. K., A note on X-efficiency, *Economic Journal*, December 1972.
20. Currie, J. M., Murphy, J. and Schnitz, A., The concept of economic surplus and its use in economic analysis, *Economic Journal*, December 1971.
21. De Prano, M. E. and Nugent, J. B., Economics as an antitrust defense: comment, *American Economic Review*, December 1969; *and* Reply by Williamson, O. E.
22. Edwards, C. D., Policy towards big business: what lessons after forty years? *Journal of Economic Issues*, June 1975.
23. Elzinga, K. G. and Breit, W., *The Antitrust Penalties: A Study in Law and Economics* (New Haven, Connecticut: Yale University Press, 1976).
24. Fleming, M., Optimal production with fixed profits, *Economica*, August 1953.
25. Goldschmidt, H. J., Mann, H. M. and Weston, J. F. (Eds.) *Industrial Concentration: The New Learning* (Boston: Little, Brown & Co., 1974), Chapter 7.
26. Green, J. R., Welfare losses from monopoly in the drug industry: the Oklahoma Antisubstitution Law, *Antitrust Law and Economics Review*, Spring 1972.
27. Grether, E. T., Competition policy in the United States: looking ahead, *California Management Review*, Summer 1974.
28. Harberger, A. C., Monopoly and resource allocation, *American Economic Review*, May 1954.
29. Harberger, A. C., The measurement of waste, *American Economic Review, Papers and Proceedings*, May 1964.
30. Harberger, A. C., Three basic postulates for applied welfare economics, *Journal of Economic Literature*, September 1971.
31. Hause, J. C., The theory of welfare cost measurement, *Journal of Political Economy*, December 1975.
32. Holahan, W. L., The welfare effects of spatial price discrimination, *American Economic Review*, June 1975.
33. Hunter, A., Product differentiation and welfare economics, *Quarterly Journal of Economics*, November 1955.
34. Hunter, A., *Competition and the Law* (London: Allen & Unwin, 1966).
35. Jacoby, N. H., Antitrust of pro-competition? *California Management Review*, Summer 1974.
36. Kamerschen, D. R., An estimation of the welfare losses from monopoly in the American economy, *Western Economic Journal*, Summer 1966.
37. Kamerschen, D. R., Monopoly and welfare, *Zeitschrift für Nationalökonomie*, Vol. 31, 1971.
38. Kamerschen, D. R. and Wallace, R. L., The costs of monopoly, *Antitrust Bulletin*, Summer 1972; *and* Note by Goldberg, V. P.
39. Kasper, H., The measures of economic costs, *Bell Journal of Economics and Management Science*, Spring 1971.
40. Kenen, P. B., On the geometry of welfare economics, *Quarterly Journal of Economics*, August 1957.
41. Levin, H. J. (Ed.) *Business Organization and Public Policy: A Book of Readings* (New York: Holt, Rinehart and Winston, Inc., 1963).
42. Lipsey, R. G. and Lancaster, K., The general theory of second best, *Review of Economic Studies*, December 1956.
43. Lofthouse, S., Recent literature relating to the X-efficiency and market structure relationship, *Zeitschrift für Nationalökonomie*, 34, 1974, pp. 409–423.
44. Long, W. F., Schramm, R. and Tollison, R., The economic determinants of antitrust activity, *Journal of Law and Economics*, October 1973.
45. Manne, H. G., Mergers and the market for corporate control, *Journal of Political Economy*, April 1965.
46. McCain, R. A., Consumer welfare and product differentiation: an agnostic comment; *and* Reply by Goddard, F. O., *Quarterly Review of Economics and Business*, Summer 1973.
47. McKean, R. N. and Minasian, J. R., On achieving Pareto optimality regardless of cost, *Western Economic Journal*, December 1966.
48. Menzies, B. J., The Robinson–Patman Act: current developments, *Antitrust Bulletin*, Winter 1969.
49. Mishan, E. J., The principle of compensation reconsidered, *Journal of Political Economy*, August 1952, pp. 314–317 only.
50. Mohring, H., Alternative welfare gain and loss measures, *Western Economic Journal*, December 1971.
51. Mueller, C. E., Lawyers' guide to the welfare loss concept: an introduction, *Antitrust Law and Economics Review*, Spring 1972.

52. O'Brien, D. P. and Swann, D., Information agreements – a problem in search of a policy, *Manchester School of Economics and Social Studies*, September 1966.
53. Parrish, R. and Ng, Y.K., Monopoly, X-efficiency and the measurement of welfare loss, *Economica*, August 1972.
54. Parzych, K. M., A restructuring of U.S. antitrust policy: the Industrial Reorganization Act, *Rivista Internazionale de Scienze Economiche e Commerciali*, October 1975.
55. Posner, R. A., A statistical study of antitrust enforcement, *Journal of Law and Economics*, October 1970.
56. Posner, R. A., The social costs of monopoly and regulation, *Journal of Political Economy*, August 1975.
57. Posner, R. A., *Antitrust Law: An Economic Perspective* (Chicago: Chicago University Press, 1976).
58. Preston, Lee E., Is it time for industrial reorganization? *California Management Review*, Summer 1974.
59. Reilly, J. H., A welfare critique of advertising, *American Journal of Economics and Sociology*, July 1972.
60. Retwisch, K., A note on the presumed desirability of internal over external growth, *Antitrust Bulletin*, Winter 1969.
61. Rowley, C. K., *The British Monopolies Commission* (London: Allen & Unwin, 1966).
62. Samuels, W. J., The Industrial Reorganization Bill: the burden of the future, *Journal of Economic Issues*, June 1975.
63. Scherer, F. M., Market structure and the employment of scientists and engineers, *American Economic Review*, June 1967.
64. Schwartzman, D., The effect of monopoly on price, *Journal of Political Economy*, August 1959.
65. Shepherd, A. R., The social welfare loss due to monopoly: comment; *and* Reply by Koo, Shou-Eng, *Southern Economic Journal*, January 1972.
66. Shepherd, W. G., The yields from abating market power, *Industrial Organization Review*, Vol. 1, Spring 1973.
67. Sherman, R., Competition over competition, *Public Policy*, Fall 1972.
68. Siegfried, J. J., The determinants of antitrust activity, *Journal of Law and Economics*, October 1975.
69. Siegfried, J. J. and Tiemann, T. K., The welfare cost of monopoly: an interindustry analysis, *Economic Inquiry*, June 1974; *and* Comment by Cocks, D. L.; *and* Further Comments by Siegfried and Tiemann, *Economic Inquiry*, December 1975.
70. Silberberg, E., Duality and the many consumers' surpluses, *American Economic Review*, December 1972.
71. Stelzer, I. M., *Selected Antitrust Cases: Landmark Decisions*, 5th edn (Homewood, Illinois: Irwin, 1976).
72. Stevens, R. B. and Yamey, B. S., *The Restrictive Practices Court* (London: Weidenfeld & Nicholson, 1965).
73. Sutherland, A., *The Monopolies Commission in Action* (Cambridge: University of Cambridge Dept of Applied Economics, Occasional Paper 21, 1970).
74. Telser, L., Advertising and competition, *Journal of Political Economy*, December 1964.
75. Usher, D., The welfare economics of invention, *Economica*, August 1964.
76. Vernon, J. M. and Nourse, R. E. M., Profit rates and market share of advertising intensive firms, *Journal of Industrial Economics*, September 1973.
77. Wallace, T. D., Measures of social costs of agricultural programs, *Journal of Farm Economics*, May 1962.
78. Weiss, L. W., An analysis of the allocation of antitrust division resources, *Benefit-Cost and Policy Analysis, 1973* (Chicago: Aldine, 1974), pp. 330–355.
79. Williamson, O. E., Economics as an antitrust defense: the welfare tradeoffs, *American Economic Review*, March 1968; *and* Correction *and* Reply, *American Economic Review*, December 1968.
80. Williamson, O. E., Allocative efficiency and the limits of antitrust, *American Economic Review, Papers and Proceedings*, May 1969.
81. Worcester, D. A. Jr, New estimates of the welfare loss to monopoly in the United States, 1956–69, *Southern Economic Journal*, October 1973.
82. Worcester, D. A. Jr, On monopoly welfare losses, *American Economic Review*, December 1975.
83. Wright, J. C. G., Products and welfare, *Australian Economic Papers*, December 1969.
84. Yamey, B., Monopolistic price discrimination and economic welfare, *Journal of Law and Economics*, October 1974.

CHAPTER ELEVEN

THE ECONOMICS OF
PUBLICLY REGULATED INDUSTRIES

Overview of the Behavior and Rationale of Regulated Firms

The behavior of unregulated firms is determined by the objectives of the decision-makers controlling them and the constraints confronting these decision-makers. Some of the relevant constraints, such as demand conditions facing a firm, depend on the behavior of buyers and rival sellers, while other constraints such as cost conditions depend on technology and the behavior of inputs used by the firm. Still other constraints on the behavior of a firm's decision-makers will be determined by capital market factors and the behavior of the firm's owners and creditors.

The preceding summary of the determinants of the behavior of unregulated firms provides a useful starting point in analyzing and understanding the behavior of regulated industrial enterprises. A regulated firm faces two other types of constraint in addition to those just enumerated, in the form of (i) legislative constraints contained either in the legislation which created the regulated status of the industry in question or in subsequent statutory amendments, and (ii) the behavior of regulatory agencies entrusted with the task of monitoring the industry's performance and enforcing the legislative mandate. Legislation may establish prescribed rules of conduct, such as an obligation for regulated firms to cover their total costs, or to earn a certain rate of return on capital, for example. A good (past) example of such guidelines for the nationalized industries of the United Kingdom can be found in H.M.S.O. (39). In addition to influencing conduct, regulatory legislation may also affect industry structure directly, by requiring licensing or similar restrictions on entry into the industry, for instance; oil exploration is an obvious example of this. The regulatory agency charged with ensuring that the industry meets these statutorily imposed obligations will generally add its own rules and procedures governing the conduct or structure of the regulated industry as the need emerges to interpret general legislative guidelines in particular circumstances.

In most countries, the regulated sector of the economy encompasses basic energy, transportation, and communication industries. In some countries, regulated industries are also publicly owned; in the United Kingdom, for example, a number of basic industries were 'nationalized' after the Second World War. Public ownership is not necessary, however, in order to regulate industries; public utilities and the railways in Britain were highly regulated by statute for many years before they were nationalized. Also, although the Boards of Management of the various nationalized industries in the United Kingdom operate under the influence of Ministers of the British government, instead of being under the control of a regulatory commission as in the United States, this difference is less important from the point of view of the resulting effects of regulation on industry behavior than differences in the type of regulatory constraint applied by the respective regulatory agencies. This chapter will not describe or compare particular regulated industries in different countries; instead, the intent is to provide the reader with a framework for understanding the effects of public regulation on firms' behavior in any country.

There are many possible types of regulatory constraint, including constraints on a firm's total profits, on rates of return on capital, and on the prices of individual goods and services. In subsequent sections of this chapter we shall investigate the nature and consequences for firms' behavior of some typical regulatory constraints. First, however, it is necessary to emphasize two important points which need to be borne in mind when analyzing the behavior of regulated enterprises: the effects of regulation on the behavior of any particular firm depend on the precise form of the regulatory constraint itself, and even slight variations in this constraint may result in very different implications for the regulated firm's behavior; second, the effect of any particular form of the regulatory constraint on the behavior of a firm will depend also on the objectives of the firm's decision-makers and the nature of all the other constraints confronting the firm. Differences in these objectives or other constraints between firms or industries can produce very different behavior despite the existence of similar regulatory constraints. Similarly, the effects of regulatory constraints will change with changes in these other objectives and constraints, so that a form of regulation which is appropriate at one time may cease to be appropriate with the passage of time. This point is stressed by P. MacAvoy (53).

The remainder of this section will consider the reasons for the existence of regulatory constraints. For a useful overview of different approaches to the rationale of utility regulation see R. A. Posner (68). One view is that regulation is a means of avoiding the twin evils of either monopoly or excessive duplication of resources which would otherwise occur in some industries due to certain characteristics of demand or cost conditions, such as decreasing unit costs with scale of output, or easy entry. According to this view, regulation is imposed upon an industry, the objective being to increase the satisfaction of the community due to the resulting implications for the allocation of resources between different sectors of the economy. This is the traditional view of public regulation which permeates most texts dealing with public utility economics and the pronouncements of regulated industries and regulatory commissions.

A very different view is offered by Professor G. Stigler (86), who argues that as a rule regulation is not thrust upon an unwilling industry, but instead is generally actively sought by the industry itself, and is designed and operated primarily for the industry's benefit, rather than in the interests of the whole community. (See also the references by Demsetz (28, 29), Telser (89), Green and Nader (35), Koller (48), Posner (67, 68) and Westfield (100) on the rationale of utility regulation.) An industry can gain from various forms of regulation such as subsidization, control of entry into the industry, restriction of competition from substitutes and encouragement of demand for complements, price fixing and the elimination of competition within the industry. Which of these forms of regulation an industry will demand depends on conditions in the industry in question. Subsidization will not be beneficial if entry is easy so that the subsidy is dissipated among a growing number of firms, for example. Regulation results from the legislative process, with the industry demanding regulation opposed by those members of the community who are likely to be adversely affected by regulation, including buyers, potential entrants or producers of substitute products, and certain inputs purchased by the industry. The actual outcome of the legislative process, which determines whether the demand for regulation is successful or not, will depend on the relative magnitude of the votes and resources which the two opposing sides are able to offer the political decision-makers who make the legislative decisions.

The view that regulation is operated primarily for the benefit of the regulated industry is also articulated by G. Hilton (36), who focuses on the factors which determine how regulatory commissions interpret and apply their legislative mandate. Hilton argues that since most commission members are at some time employed by the industry, the system of rewards and penalties confronting members of regulatory commissions encourages decisions which are in favor of the industry. The constraint which confronts regulators, in the form of a mandate to operate in the public interest will be met, Hilton argues, by allowing the industry to exploit its original monopoly position while simultaneously encouraging other marginally unprofitable or inefficient activities in order to keep the regulated firm's overall profit position within the legislative guidelines. In other words, in Hilton's view the allocative inefficiency which regulation is often intended to eliminate will be compounded by additional allocative inefficiency as regulated firms are encouraged to expand into activities with low marginal social benefit, or are permitted to operate with technical inefficiency, in order to reduce the firms' apparent overall profit to acceptable levels.

Traditionally, economic analysis of public regulation has focused on the effects of specific types of regulatory constraint on the behavior of public utilities themselves, generally omitting consideration of the legislative or regulatory processes. Fortunately, though rather belatedly, the interest of economists in these other aspects of regulation is now increasing, as the previously cited articles by Stigler and Hilton indicate. As another example, a recent article by P. L. Joskow (42) has attempted to determine what factors affect the allowed rate of return set by a regulatory commission in practice. A better understanding of how the regulatory decision process operates in practice is absolutely essential to progress in the regulated utility area. Even if the effects of alternative regulatory constraints on the behavior of public utilities were clearly understood, and ideal types of constraint from the point of view of maximizing the community's satisfaction were known, they could only be implemented in practice if this process is also understood, so that appropriate constraints could be applied to the behavior of regulators themselves where necessary to ensure the application of the desired regulatory constraint. There is little point in directing intensive research efforts towards discovery of an ideal form of regulatory constraint if regulators are unlikely to apply this constraint in practice. Similarly, the outcome of any particular regulatory constraint in practice may be very different from that predicted by a theory which omits the behavior of regulatory commissions. If Hilton's argument is correct, for example, then in addition to the technical inefficiency usually attributed to rate of return on capital regulation, allocative efficiency within the regulated sector may be worsened by regulation, rather than improved as is usually concluded by conventional economic analysis.

Effects of Regulation on Input Mixes: the A–J Effect

As already explained in Chapter 10, firms' input mixes influence the level of aggregate satisfaction in the community. It was shown that unless the ratio of the marginal physical products of any two inputs is the same in different firms, it is possible to produce the same output levels with fewer resources, by using different input mixes. Input mixes which minimize the total cost of producing a firm's selected output level will equate the ratio of the marginal physical product of any two inputs with the ratio of the marginal costs of those inputs to the firm. Therefore, provided that the ratio of marginal input costs is the same for different firms, total cost minimization by individual firms will also minimize the amount of resources required to produce any given mixture of outputs produced in the economy.

In a seminal article, Professors H. Averch and L. L. Johnson (2) demonstrated that if the amount of profit which a regulated firm is allowed to earn is dependent on the amount of capital used by the firm, incentives are created for the firm to use an inefficient input mix involving more capital and fewer other inputs than the input mix which would minimize the total cost of producing its output. The remainder of this section will be devoted to explaining the reasoning underlying this conclusion, emphasizing the conditions which are necessary for this 'A–J Effect' to be present, and reviewing the empirical evidence on the extent to which it is found in practice. For a selection of useful contributions to the implications of regulation for input mixes and technical efficiency, see Bailey and Coleman (5), Baumol and Klevorick (8), Corey (18), Courville (19), Davis (27), Hodiri and Takayama (40), Johnson (41), Klevorick (46, 47), Pressman and Carol (70), Spann (82), Takayama (88) and Zajac (106).

Assuming for expositional convenience that a firm uses two inputs, labor and capital, the firm's profit is equal to the difference between the total revenue earned from selling the resulting output and the firm's expenditure on labor and capital. This may be expressed symbolically as follows:

$$\text{Profit} = pq - (wL + iK)$$

where w and i are the prices per unit of labor and capital respectively. The firm's profit opportunities can be expressed as a function of the quantities of labor and capital used by the firm. Diagrammatically, holding L constant at any arbitrary level, increases in the quantity of capital, K, used by the firm will increase the firm's output level. The demand conditions facing the firm will determine at what price any resulting quantity of output can be sold, and therefore the total sales revenue associated with alternative levels of K. As

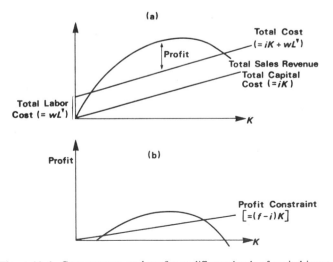

Figure 11–1. Cost, revenue, and profits at different levels of capital input.

shown in Figure 11–1(a), when K is increased total revenue first rises but eventually falls when the price-elasticity of demand for the firm's product falls below unity, implying that increased output can be sold only if price is reduced more than proportionately. The firm's total costs at each level of K are the sum of total expenditure on labor and capital. Given the assumption that L does not vary, the total cost of labor is constant and, given the price of capital, the total cost of capital is proportional to the amount of capital used by the firm, as shown in Figure 11–1(a). Subtracting total cost from total revenue yields the profit associated with each alternative level of K, as indicated in Figure 11–1(b).

If the preceding process is repeated for different levels of L, the result will be a profit 'surface', or 'hill', as demonstrated in Figure 11–2. An unregulated profit-maximizing firm

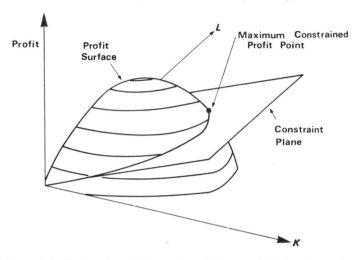

Figure 11–2. Total and permitted profits at different capital–labor input mixes.

would select the capital–labor mix associated with the highest point on the profit surface. A regulated firm will generally be prevented from selecting that point, due to the adverse allocative implications of the associated output level. Precisely which other point a profit-maximizing regulated firm will select depends on the nature of the regulatory constraint. If the manner in which the firm is regulated is by setting a maximum rate of return on capital employed by the firm, the regulatory constraint on profits will be expressed symbolically as follows:

$$\frac{pq - wL}{K} = f$$

where f is the permitted rate of return on capital. Multiplying the preceding expression by K and using the earlier expression for the firm's profits, the regulatory constraint can also be expressed alternatively as follows:

Permitted profit $= (f - i)K$

The second form of the profit constraint indicates clearly that the firm's total permitted profit increases proportionately with K, by $(f - i)$ per unit of capital employed, as shown in Figure 11–1(b). Also, since at any particular level of K the firm's permitted profit is the same irrespective of the level of L, it follows that the three-dimensional profit constraint is a flat surface, or plane, which is hinged at the L-axis and slices through the profit hill as shown in Figure 11–2. The slope of this plane will be greater, the larger is f, the permitted rate of return on capital.

Since the firm is not allowed to make more profits than the amount shown by points on the constraint plane, it will select a combination of capital and labor yielding the highest total profit compatible with the constraint.

This will obviously be the point with the largest K along the intersection of the constraint plane and the profit hill. However, in order to understand why this input mix will be an inefficient method of producing the resulting output level, it is useful to view the same situation from a slightly different perspective. Thus, Figure 11–3 depicts the locus of capital–labor combinations along the intersection of the constraint plane and profit hill.

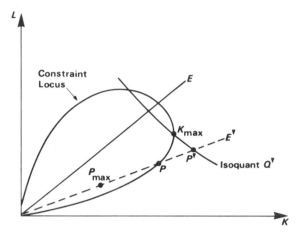

Figure 11–3. Relationship between the firm's expansion path and the K_{max} point.

The point on this constraint locus which yields the firm the maximum amount of permitted profit is $K_{max.}$. Alternative input mixes which result in the same output levels as K_{max} are depicted by the isoquant Q'. K_{max} will not be the most efficient method of producing the output level Q', from the point of view of minimizing the total cost of producing Q', for the following reasons: if K_{max} were the total-cost minimizing method of producing Q', a move away from K_{max} in either direction along the isoquant Q' would increase total cost and, since output and therefore total revenue are unchanged, reduce the firm's total profit. This would imply that K_{max} were the unconstrained profit-maximizing point in Figure 11–2, for only at this point does a move along an isoquant in either direction lead to a fall in the height of the profit hill. Since the reason for regulation is usually to prevent a firm from being at the unconstrained profit-maximizing point, it can be concluded that K_{max} will not be the total-cost minimizing method of producing the output level Q'. This means that K_{max} does not lie on the firm's 'expansion path' which, as already explained in Chapter 2, is defined as the locus of input mixes which minimize the total cost of various alternative output levels. Proving that K_{max} does not lie on the firm's expansion path does not prove the existence of an A–J effect, however. An A–J effect will exist only if K_{max} lies below the firm's expansion path, indicating that the firm uses more capital and less labor to produce any given level of output than the total-cost minimizing input mix. If K_{max} lies above the firm's expansion path, this would imply that the firm uses more labor and less capital than the cost minimizing mix, the exact opposite of an A–J effect. The existence of an A–J effect can be demonstrated by showing that a logical contradiction arises if K_{max} were to lie above the firm's expansion path. Thus, if the dashed line labeled E' in Figure 11–3 were the firm's expansion path, a move along E' from the origin of the diagram results in rising profit until the unconstrained profit-maximizing point P_{max}, which lies somewhere inside the constraint locus, is reached. Continuing further along E' will imply a monotonically declining profit level as one descends the profit hill, so that profit at P on the constraint locus exceeds profit at P' where the isoquant through K_{max} intersects E'. Profit at P' will in turn exceed profit at K_{max} because both points involve the same output level and total revenue but P' involves a lower total cost of producing that output level than K_{max}. This would then imply that profit at K_{max} is less than profit at P, a possibility which is clearly contradicted and ruled out by the level of profit at various points along the intersection of the constraint plane and profit hill in Figure 11–2. It follows that in order to avoid this logical contradiction the firm's expansion path must pass *above* K_{max}, like the solid line E in Figure 11–3, and that a firm regulated by return on capital will therefore use more capital and less labor to produce its output than the cost-minimizing input mix.

It should be noted that the firm's expansion path is drawn as a straight line only for expositional convenience. The shape of the expansion path depends on the precise nature of the firm's production function and will only be a straight line when there are 'constant returns to scale' in production, which means that a proportionate change in the quantities of all the firm's inputs produces a proportionate change in total output. The expansion path will generally slope up from left to right, however, indicating that increases in output require more of both inputs, and none of the conclusions reached in the present analysis will be altered if the expansion path is not a straight line.

Some of the conditions which are necessary in order to generate the preceding A–J effect require emphasis, since regulating the return on capital will not produce this effect in all circumstances. The two most important underlying assumptions are concerned with the magnitude of f relative to i, and the objectives of managers of the regulated firm. The analysis assumes that f, the permitted return on capital, exceeds i, the cost of capital to the firm. If, as frequently occurs in practice, regulators attempt to set f equal to i, the constraint plane coincides with the K-axis in Figure 11–2, and all points on the constraint locus in Figure 11–3 will involve zero total profit. To choose between such points, it would be necessary for decision-makers to use some decision criterion other than profit maximization, and whether or not an inefficient input mix, or an A–J effect, will result in these circumstances depends on the precise nature of the objective which is pursued.

For example, if the regulated firm's decision-makers attempt to maximize sales revenue subject to the zero-profit constraint, they will attempt to minimize the total cost of any output level produced. If the total cost of producing an output level were not minimized, an opportunity would exist to purchase additional inputs with the cost savings, thereby raising total sales revenue without violating the profit constraint. Therefore, sales-revenue maximizing firms will select the point where the firm's expansion path E intersects the constraint locus, S_{max} in Figure 11–4(a) and the firm's output level will be produced efficiently.

Alternatively, if the objective of the regulated firm's decision-makers is output maximization, the selected point on the constraint locus will be where an isoquant is tangent to the constraint locus, as shown by Q_{max} in Figure 11–4(b). The slope of the constraint locus equals the ratio of changes in K and L which leave the firm's return on capital unchanged at the permitted level. This slope will differ at different points on the constraint locus since it depends on the marginal physical productivities of the two inputs as well as on input prices and the permitted rate of return on capital. At the point of tangency between an isoquant and the constraint locus, however, it can be shown that the slope of the two curves equals f/w. When $f = i$, this point of tangency will also lie on the

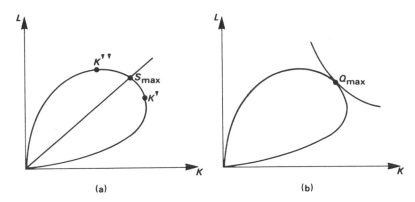

Figure 11–4. Optimal points on the constraint locus under alternative objectives.

firm's expansion path, since as explained in Chapter 2 the expansion path is the locus of points of tangency between isoquants representing different output levels and the ratio of input prices i/w. In other words, when $f = i$, S_{max} and Q_{max}, the points on the constraint locus which would be selected by sales-revenue maximizers and output maximizers, respectively, coincide.

As a final example, managerial utility maximization will lead a regulated firm's decision-makers to select an inefficient point on the constraint locus if either capital or labor themselves yield positive satisfaction to the firm's decision-makers. If managerial utility depends on capital, a point such as K' in Figure 11–4 will be selected; although this point will in general differ from the A–J point K_{max}, both will involve an inefficient input mix involving excessive capital. In contrast, if managerial utility depends on labor rather than capital inputs, a point such as K'' in Figure 11–4 will be selected; such a point will also be inefficient, but will involve excessive labor relative to capital, the opposite result to that present in the case of the A–J effect.

Even when f exceeds i, there may be no A–J effect if the objective of the regulated firm's decision-makers is not profit maximization. If their objective is constrained sales-revenue maximization, for example, the point where the firm's expansion path intersects the constraint locus will be selected, for reasons previously explained. Similarly, if managerial utility maximization is the objective, and managerial utility depends on labor rather than on capital inputs, the selected point on the constraint locus will lie above the expansion path and involve excessive labor rather than excessive capital. Also, in the case of output-maximization objectives, when f exceeds i the point on the constraint curve which will be selected by the firm's decision-makers will not involve an efficient input mix. Instead, Q_{max} will lie *above* the point where the firm's expansion path intersects the constraint locus, again implying excessive use of labor compared to the cost-minimizing method of producing the associated output level. The reason for this is that the slope of the tangent curves at Q_{max}, which equals f/w, will in this case exceed i/w, which is the slope of the isoquant at the cost-minimizing input mix on the firm's expansion path.

Even when the regulated firm's decision-makers pursue the goal of profit maximization, and f exceeds i, the existence of uncertainty concerning demand conditions facing the firm can also modify the conclusion that there will be an A–J effect under rate of return on capital regulation. If demand conditions are not known, this implies that the location and shape of the profit hill in Figure 11–2, and of the constraint locus in Figure 11–3 which represents the intersection of the profit hill and constraint plane, will also not be known. The precise nature of the rules of thumb adopted by the regulated firm's decision-makers to cope with this uncertainty will play a major role in determining whether or not there will be an A–J effect. For example, they may minimize the cost of producing output, operating initially on the expansion path inside the constraint locus, and responding to regulatory commission requests to reduce the rate of return on capital to the permitted level by reducing the price of the product. The firm will then move along its expansion path to its point of intersection with the constraint locus, where an equilibrium would be reached which would not involve inefficiency in production. Although the K_{max} point on the constraint locus would yield the firm more profits, by assumption the firm does not know the location of this point. Alternatively, the firm may adopt a strategy of producing any level of output it selects with an input mix which satisfies the regulatory constraint on permitted rate of return, thereby operating initially somewhere on the underside of the constraint locus. It may then search for the K_{max} point by requesting permission to reduce the price of its output, and producing the increased output level demanded with an input mix which makes the resulting profit–capital ratio meet the regulatory constraint. By continuing this process as long as price reductions result in increased output, capital, and profits, the firm will move along the constraint locus and eventually reach K_{max}.

This second strategy results in an A–J effect during the process of adjustment towards equilibrium as well as in equilibrium, whereas the first strategy does not. Still a third possibility is that an A–J effect may exist in equilibrium, but not during part of the adjustment towards equilibrium. This would occur, for example, if a firm combined the two types of adjustment process previously outlined, first cutting the price of its product and moving along the expansion path until the resulting reduction in profits and rise in capital established the permitted rate of return represented by the point where the expansion path meets the constraint locus. At that point the firm might attempt to raise its permitted profits further by raising the price of its product and producing the output demanded using an inefficient input mix involving the excessive amount of capital which is needed to meet the permitted rate of return constraint.

Since an A–J effect need not necessarily result from regulating firms' return on capital, for one or more of the reasons just outlined, empirical investigation of the existence and magnitude of this effect in practice is clearly warranted. Very few studies of this nature have been undertaken to date, however. Two very recent examples will be mentioned briefly here. R. M. Spann used data relating to regulated electric utilities in the United States to test the A–J thesis, and concluded in a 1974 article (82) that the evidence appears to indicate the existence of an A–J effect. In the same issue of the same journal, L. Courville (19) presented results of an investigation of a cross section of steam-generated electricity plants, concluding that the proposition that rate of return regulation induces firms to operate inefficiently is strongly confirmed. Courville also presented estimates of the magnitude of the regulation-induced inefficiency by computing the percentage deviation of actual cost from estimated cost. He found that in spite of the fact that overcapitalization in the plants studied was strongly confirmed, the actual deviation from minimum cost is relatively small, being only 12 per cent of actual total production costs. Using this estimate of the deviation from minimum cost, the total saving in cost which would have occurred in 1962 from efficient production of electricity in steam power plants was estimated to be only $436.6 million.

In appraising the results of empirical estimates of the existence and magnitude of the A–J effect, several points need to be borne in mind. First, an observed failure of regulated firms to minimize total costs and a tendency to use excessive capital inputs can result from factors other than rate of return regulation itself, such as decision-maker objectives, for example. Eliminating rate of return regulation will not therefore necessarily eliminate such inefficiency. Second, it must be emphasized that failure to minimize the total money cost of producing a firm's output results in reduced output and satisfaction in the economy as a whole *only* if it implies that ratios of marginal physical productivity (MPP) of any two inputs are not the same in different uses. As explained in Chapter 10, if individual firms minimize total costs by equating the ratio of MPP of any two inputs with the ratio of the marginal input costs to the firm, *provided* that the ratio of marginal input costs is the same for different firms, this will imply that the ratio of MPP is the same in different firms, as is required if any given total output in the economy as a whole is to be produced with as few resources as possible. On the other hand, if the ratio of MPP of any two inputs in other sectors is *not* equal to the ratio of the marginal costs of those inputs to a firm, either because other sectors fail to minimize their total costs or because the ratio of marginal input costs differs for different firms due to input-market imperfections, minimizing total cost in the firm in question will not equate the ratio of MPP of two inputs in all sectors. That is, a firm's input mix may not minimize the total cost of its output, and yet may still be an optimal input mix from the point of view of the economy as a whole. This result is yet another example of the theory of second-best. Decision-maker objectives which conflict with cost minimization, or input-market imperfections, are added constraints not considered in the conventional analysis of Pareto optimal conditions for maximizing aggregate satisfaction in an economy. In the presence of these added constraints, although equating the ratio of MPPs of any two inputs in different uses is still necessary in order to maximize aggregate satisfaction in the economy, the conditions within individual firms which must be satisfied in order to achieve this result may not involve total-cost minimization. Before the reader concludes that this is an excuse permitting any and every type of inefficiency within firms, it should be hastily added that precise welfare-maximizing conditions will exist corresponding to any constraints which are added to the conventional analysis of Pareto optimality, and a firm's performance can still be evaluated with respect to these conditions. For example, in order to justify failure to minimize total costs by overcapitalization, it would be necessary to show that added constraints exist in the economy which tend to lead all firms to overcapitalize, given input prices; also, there would be an optimal degree of overcapitalization for individual firms, necessary in order to equate the MPP of capital and non-capital inputs in different uses.

A third point which needs to be borne in mind in appraising the A–J effect is that, even if it exists and is of considerable magnitude, this does not necessarily mean that total satisfaction in the economy is reduced by rate of return regulation. Regulation also affects the firm's output level, and the net effect on aggregate satisfaction in the economy depends on the allocative efficiency implications of the resulting output effects as well as on the technical efficiency effects.

The optimal level of the permitted rate of return on capital can itself be determined by reference to these two effects. The optimal level of the permitted rate of return on capital would be achieved when the effect of a change in this rate on allocative efficiency and the effect on technical efficiency are equal in magnitude. The determination of this optimal rate of return on capital can be depicted diagrammatically in a manner exactly analogous to the analysis of conflicting allocative and technical efficiency effects contained in the section of Chapter 10 entitled Measurement of Welfare Loss Attributable to Monopoly.

Although rate of return on capital regulation is compatible with an increase in aggregate satisfaction in the community despite the existence of A–J effects, it is appropriate to consider briefly how the A–J effects could be avoided while retaining the beneficial allocative effects of regulation. Some economists have suggested that the appropriate method is to make the permitted rate of return on capital vary with different levels of capital utilized by a firm, declining as the amount of capital increases. As other economists have shown, however, this will not eliminate the A–J effect. Diagrammatically, it will turn the constraint plane into a curved surface which is convex upwards, but the surface will be hinged at the L-axis and an A–J effect will still occur as long as permitted profit depends on K only. The real solution is to make the allowed profit rate depend on the firm's total expenditure on labor and capital. This will avoid creating an inducement for the firm to substitute capital for labor in order to increase permitted profits. If this approach is adopted, the constraint plane is no longer hinged at the L-axis and instead will slope upwards in the labor-profit dimension as well as in the capital-profit dimension. The intersection of this constraint plane and the profit hill will again be represented by a constraint locus; the difference between this constraint locus and the one previously analyzed in connection with the A–J effect being that its slope depends on the marginal physical productivities of the inputs and their respective prices, instead of on the price of labor and the permitted rate of return on capital, as is the case with the A–J constraint locus.

A profit-maximizing firm will select the point on this constraint locus which maximizes the firm's total outlay on labor and capital, since this will maximize permitted profits. This point will be where a budget-line showing alternative combinations of labor and capital which can be purchased with a given amount of expenditure is just tangent to the constraint locus, as indicated by point O in Figure 11–5. Since the slope of this budget line will equal the ratio of input prices confronting the firm, it follows that the slope of the constraint locus at the selected point will equal the ratio of input prices. It can also be shown that an isoquant will be tangent to the constraint locus at this same point. Therefore, the selected point will lie on the firm's expansion path and will be efficient, in the sense of minimizing the total cost of the output level produced by the firm.

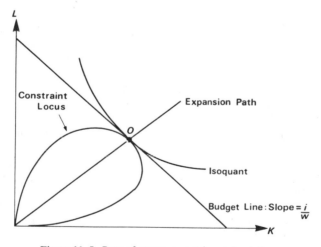

Figure 11–5. Rate of return on total cost regulation.

Before concluding this section, it is appropriate to mention briefly the problem of rate-base padding, or 'gold-plating', which relates to the use of unproductive capital by the firm, rather than simply to excessive capital utilization associated with the existence of an A–J effect. If a firm's permitted profit depends only on the amount of capital utilized, the question arises as to whether an incentive will exist for the firm to 'pad', or enlarge, its rate base by using unproductive capital. E. Zajac (107) has shown that such an incentive will not generally exist, for the following reasons: if a firm was operating at a constrained profit maximum with some unproductive capital, it could exchange this capital for an equal amount of productive capital and at the same time reduce labor input so as to keep output unchanged. This would leave the firm's total revenues and rate base unchanged, but profit would increase due to the reduced expenditure on labor. To prevent the profit constraint from being violated, the firm could then move along the isoquant to its intersection with the constraint locus by substituting additional productive capital for labor; this would expand the firm's rate base and hence its permitted profits would be higher than originally. Once on the constraint curve, the firm could realize still higher permitted profit by moving to the K_{max} point in Figure 11–3. The existence of an A–J effect does not therefore generally imply the use of unproductive capital by the firm. Padding the rate base with unproductive capital is optimal only if the regulated firm has exhausted all positive-income-producing investment opportunities and must resort to negative-income-producing investments to being down its rate of return to that allowed.

Effects of Regulation on Output Levels: Pricing Rules for Regulated Firms

In the previous section, attention was focused on the effects of regulation on the regulated firm's input mix and on the resulting implications for efficiency within the firm and in the economy as a whole. It was noted that regulation also affects the firm's output level and therefore has implications for allocative efficiency. These implications can be illuminated by directing attention to the firm's pricing behavior. Thus, as explained in Chapter 3, for example, a profit-maximizing firm will select a price and resulting output level which equates the marginal revenue and marginal cost of the firm's output and establishes the following relationship:

$$(P - MC)/P = 1/E_d$$

An additional constraint limiting the firm's rate of return on capital will affect the firm's marginal revenue and marginal cost and change the above profit-maximizing pricing condition. It is easy to demonstrate that the optimal level of price relative to marginal cost is lowered, implying a larger output level for the firm. It must be emphasized again, however, that as in the case of input-mix effects, the precise effect of regulation on a firm's output level will depend not only on the nature of the regulatory constraint itself, but also on the nature of the objectives pursued by the firm's decision-makers and on other constraints confronting them.

In this section, instead of examining the effects of alternative forms of regulation, decision-maker objectives, and other relevant constraints on the pricing behavior of regulated firms, attention will be focused on the characteristics of welfare-maximizing pricing conditions themselves. For more on the nature of optimal pricing rules and output-level behavior for regulated enterprises, however, see Acharya (1), Bergson (9), Boiteux (11), Cross (25), Kafoglis (45), Klevorick (47), Kolm (49), Rees (71), Turvey (92) and Vickrey (95, 96). Knowledge of the nature and underlying logic of these conditions is obviously necessary in order to develop prescriptive rules of behavior or targets for the regulatory process, and for devising appropriate regulatory constraints designed to achieve these conditions under any given set of decision-maker objectives and other relevant constraints.

A pricing rule which is frequently advocated for public utilities and other regulated firms is that of setting product prices equal to the marginal cost of the products. *If price and marginal cost are equal in all other firms in the economy*, pricing at marginal cost in the public utility will ensure that the ratios of price and marginal cost of any two products produced in the economy are equal. As explained in Chapter 10, price ratios indicate peoples' relative evaluation of the marginal benefits placed on the two goods, while ratios of marginal cost indicate the rate of transforming one product into another by switching resources from the production of one good to the production of the other. If prices equal marginal costs everywhere, marginal rates of transformation in production will therefore equal the ratio of the community's evaluation of marginal benefits yielded by the products in question, as is required in order to maximize allocative efficiency.

If prices do not equal marginal costs in other sectors of the economy, setting the price of public utility products equal to their marginal cost will not maximize allocative efficiency. At first sight, the appropriate pricing rule seems obvious, namely to set the public utility's price–marginal cost ratio or, what is the same thing, $(P - \text{MC})/P$, equal to the ratio existing in other sectors of the economy, since this will again imply that price ratios and marginal cost ratios are equal. Even if the price–marginal cost ratio in all other sectors of the economy were the same, so that no problem of deciding *which* sector's price–marginal cost ratio to use as a pricing guide should exist, this view is generally incorrect because it ignores the reasons *why* prices differ from marginal cost in other sectors. When a constraint exists which prevents price from equalling marginal cost in all sectors of the economy simultaneously, the correct pricing rule for allocative efficiency was indicated in Chapter 10 in the section dealing with the theory of second-best. It is that the ratio of the marginal benefits which any two goods yield to the community must equal the ratio of their marginal effects *on the constraint*, instead of the ratio of their marginal effects on total cost as is the case in absence of the constraint. The logic underlying this optimal 'second-best' condition is quite simple: if the ratio of the marginal benefits which two goods yield the community are not equal to the ratio of their marginal effects on the constraint, it follows automatically that it is possible to increase the total satisfaction of the community while continuing to meet the constraint. This can be accomplished by switching some resources from production of the good where the ratio between the marginal benefit and the effect on the constraint is lower, to production of the good where this ratio is higher. Only when the marginal effects of different products on the constraint are proportional to their respective marginal costs will this second-best pricing rule lead to a situation where allocative efficiency is maximized by equating price ratios and marginal cost ratios or, what is the same thing, by equating price ratios and marginal rates of transformation in production.

Although the preceding second-best allocative efficiency condition is perfectly general, the precise relationship between price and marginal cost in different firms which is necessary in order to satisfy this condition will obviously depend on the nature of the constraint which prevents price from equalling marginal cost in all sectors simultaneously. Generalizations concerning the price–marginal cost relationship required for allocative efficiency are therefore impossible in these circumstances, since different price–marginal cost relationships will be appropriate for different constraints. In addition, it must be emphasized that, whatever the constraint, the marginal effect of individual products on the satisfaction of the community, and therefore the optimal second-best price–marginal cost relationship in different firms, also depends on the nature of the demand and cost interrelationships which exist between different products.

This last proposition can be illustrated by reference to the examples of optimal second-best pricing conditions contained in Chapter 10. It was explained there that if price and marginal cost are not equal in other sectors of the economy due to taxes imposed on products produced in other sectors, and the second-best constraint takes the form of an economy-wide level of required tax revenues, allocative efficiency requires that price–marginal cost ratios in individual firms be set in relation to the price-elasticity of demand for individual products. The logic underlying this conclusion was explained in some detail in Chapter 10 and will not be repeated here. It was emphasized, however, that this pricing rule is optimal only if the cross-elasticities of demand and supply between different products are zero, so that changes in the prices and quantities of individual products do not cause changes in the quantities of other products demanded or supplied. In these circumstances, the effect of a change in the price and quantity of individual products on the satisfaction of the community is measured by the marginal net benefit (P − MC) of the product in question multiplied by the change in its output level. In contrast, when cross-elasticities of demand and supply are not zero, the effect of a change in the price and quantity of individual products on the satisfaction of the community is measured by this amount *plus* the sum of the marginal net benefit (P − MC) associated with other products multiplied by changes in their quantities produced as a result of the change in output of the first product. When the quantities of other goods increase in response to an increase in the quantity of a particular product, a 'complementary' relationship is said to exist between the products: the marginal effect of a change in the output of such a good on the satisfaction of the community will clearly be larger than when cross-elasticities are zero. When the quantities of other goods decrease in response to an increase in the quantity of a particular good, a 'substitute' relationship is said to exist between the products; in this case the marginal effect of a change in the quantity of such a good on aggregate satisfaction will be smaller than when cross-elasticities are zero. Since non-zero cross-elasticities of demand and supply affect the magnitude of the marginal effect of changes in the quantities of individual products on the satisfaction of the community, they are obviously relevant in determining the relationship between the price and marginal cost of individual products which is necessary in order to achieve allocative efficiency by equating the ratio of marginal benefit to marginal effect on constraint for different products. As indicated in Chapter 10, price–marginal cost relationships which achieve allocative efficiency subject to the tax-revenue constraint satisfy the following condition:

$$\frac{P - \mathrm{MC}}{P} = \frac{\lambda}{\lambda + 1} \cdot \left(\frac{1}{E_d} + \Sigma CE \right)$$

When cross-elasticities are zero, the above condition implies that optimal prices will exceed marginal costs in all firms whose price-elasticity of demand is less than infinitely large, with the magnitude of the excess varying between firms in accordance with differences in price-elasticity of demand. With non-zero cross-elasticities of demand and supply, the optimal excess of price over marginal cost will be higher for products where a substitute relationship with other products is dominant so that the sum of cross-elasticities is a positive number. When a complementary relationship with other products is dominant, so that the sum of cross-elasticities is negative, the optimal excess of price over marginal cost will be lower. In fact, as the preceding optimal pricing formula indicates, if the complementary relationship is sufficiently strong, a firm may have to price *below* marginal cost in order to achieve allocative efficiency in the economy as a whole. The intuitive logic of this result is quite straightforward, especially when viewed within the diagrammatic framework of the welfare-loss measurement analysis contained in Chapter 10: although pricing below marginal cost implies a 'welfare-loss triangle' associated with the partial-equilibrium diagram of demand and cost conditions for the product in question, the increased satisfaction resulting from the increased quantities of complementary products may be large enough to result in a net increase in total satisfaction for the community.

The possibility that some products may have to be priced below marginal cost in order to achieve allocative efficiency is worth stressing in the present context, because many public utilities produce products, such as electricity and transportation, to name but two examples, which are inputs in many other production processes and exhibit strong complementary relationships with many other products. Before the reader concludes that pricing below marginal cost is optimal for public utilities, however, it must be remembered that public utility products are also sometimes substitutes for other products. Apart from the assumption regarding the nature of the second-best constraint which is implicit in the preceding optimal pricing condition, empirical evidence on the magnitude of all cross-elasticity relationships between public utility and other products would be needed in order to reach a definite conclusion on this score.

To this point, the discussion of appropriate public utility pricing rules for allocative efficiency has assumed that constraints exist which prevent prices from equalling marginal costs outside the public utility sector. Even if prices and marginal costs were equal in other sectors, however, constraints internal to the public utility itself may prevent prices from equalling marginal costs in all sectors of the economy simultaneously. A notable example, also discussed already in Chapter 10, is the existence of cost conditions exhibiting declining unit costs with scale of output. If unit costs of producing public utility output decline with scale of the firm's output rate, the marginal cost of any output rate will be less than the corresponding cost per unit of output, so that pricing at marginal cost will mean that the firm's total sales revenue is less than the firm's total costs. Since a firm cannot continue to operate for long without covering its total costs, either the firm must be subsidized, or it must price above marginal cost in order to cover its total costs from its sales revenue. If it is subsidized, however, taxes would have to be imposed on some other activities in the economy in order to raise the revenues required for subsidization; this would then imply that prices would have to exceed marginal cost in some other sectors of the economy. Either of the preceding alternatives, therefore, involves a second-best situation, since price cannot equal marginal cost in all sectors simultaneously. In these circumstances, should the decreasing-cost firm price above marginal cost and cover its own total costs, or should it price at marginal cost and be subsidized? The answer is that neither of these two alternatives will, in general, be optimal from the point of view of securing allocative efficiency. The optimal solution depends, as always, on the exact nature of the constraint. If the constraint is that the total costs of all firms must be covered, either from their own sales revenues or from subsidies raised by taxing other products, the problem is again that of the optimal structure of price–marginal cost relationships subject to a total tax revenue constraint. The optimal price–marginal cost condition is virtually the same as that outlined earlier in this section; price–marginal cost relationships must be set in relation to price- and cross-elasticities of demand facing individual firms. The only difference would lie in the absolute magnitude of the price–marginal cost discrepancy across all sectors, which will be lower when the net amount of tax revenues raised is zero, as occurs when total taxes equal total subsidies, than when the net amount of tax revenues to be raised is positive.

Some of the resulting implications of the optimal solution are interesting and worth illuminating. If cross-elasticities of demand and supply between products are zero, optimal prices will exceed marginal costs in all firms except those with infinitely elastic demand. Since this implies positive taxes, and given the zero total-revenue constraint assumed, it follows that the optimal solution will involve some subsidization of the decreasing-cost firm(s). This in turn implies that price will exceed marginal cost in the decreasing-cost firm by less than the amount necessary to cover the firm's total costs from its own sales revenues. This conclusion would be modified in the presence of non-zero cross-elasticities of demand or supply; as already explained, sufficiently strong complementary re-lationships between public utility product and other products could even result in pricing at less than marginal cost in the public utility.

As the preceding discussion indicates, knowledge of price, and of cross-elasticities of demand and supply between different products in the economic system, will generally be required in order to determine the price–marginal cost relationships which are necessary to achieve allocative efficiency in different firms. Cross-elasticities of demand and supply could be ignored only if prices and marginal costs were everywhere equal, for then changes in quantities in other sectors due to product interdependence would have no net effect on the level of total satisfaction in the community. While cross-elasticities of demand depend on buyer behavior, cross-elasticities of supply depend on both price and non-price reactions of rival sellers, and such information is obviously not easily obtained. In addition, when a public utility produces multiple products, apart from information on cross-elasticities of demand and supply between its products and those of other sectors, similar information relating to its own products is also required in order to determine the price–marginal cost structure of its various products which maximizes allocative efficiency in any given set of circumstances. Finally, even when the characteristics of optimal price–marginal cost relationships from the point of view of allocative efficiency in the economy are determined, the problem of devising appropriate constraints on the behavior of decision-makers in order to ensure implementation of these pricing conditions must also be solved.

The costs of gathering information needed to determine optimal pricing rules, and the costs of implementing desired pricing behavior, are really an additional constraint which is frequently ignored in discussions of optimal pricing behavior, whether best or second-best. At least one noted economist, Ralph Turvey, who has spent a good portion of his career attempting to devise and implement rational pricing systems in the public utility sector, has gone as far as to suggest that when these information and implementation costs are taken into account, pricing at marginal cost may still be optimal even in second-best situations. This view is probably too extreme, however. The same logic could be used to suggest, for example, that where difficulties exist in determining a firm's marginal cost, pricing at average cost, or some other more easily obtainable measure, is appropriate. The correct principle, in deciding whether or not to attempt to apply particular pricing principles designed to serve any objective such as allocative efficiency, is whether the cost in terms of the necessary information-gathering and implementation techniques is greater or less than the potential gain in the level of the community's satisfaction which results from the application of particular pricing rules. Turvey offers no real evidence (92) to indicate that the added costs of attempting to apply more sophisticated pricing rules than pricing at marginal cost exceed the potential benefits to the community in terms of the resulting increase in allocative efficiency. Nor has anyone else provided evidence to suggest the contrary. The important point, in the present context, is that none of these issues can be settled without evidence concerning economic performance under alternative pricing systems. This requires practical experimentation to determine the consequences, for allocative and other types of efficiency, of alternative pricing systems. At a theoretical level, emphasis is still mainly on the nature of optimal equilibrium second-best pricing conditions themselves, rather than on alternative methods of achieving them. While this information is obviously necessary in order to provide a target for regulatory processes, the development of pricing rules of thumb which are simpler than the static optimal pricing conditions, and which are dynamically efficient in the sense of causing resource allocation to converge rapidly towards an optimum, may also be potentially rewarding in terms of increasing total satisfaction in the community. This view is strengthened once one remembers that price- and cross-elasticities of demand and supply are continually changing.

Peak-Load Pricing Problems and Regulation

If the demand for a firm's product varies in strength from one period of time to another, as occurs with transportation, electricity, and telephone calls, for example, there exists what is termed a 'peak-load problem'. Different writers stress different aspects of this problem, some focusing on the problem of how to price a product in different time periods in the face of fluctuating demand (the pricing problem), while others focus on the question of how much 'capacity' to install to meet fluctuating demands. These different aspects are related, however, and solutions to all aspects of the problem are interdependent and simultaneously determined. This section explains the nature of the peak-load problem, its solution, and the effect of regulation on the solutions to the problem. For a selection of prominent contributions to the literature on this problem, see Bailey (4), Baumol (7), Boiteux (10), Crew and Kleindorfer (22, 23), Littlechild (52), Minasian (56), Mohring (57), Officer (61), Pressman (69), Turvey (90), White (102) and Wilson (105).

Much of the unnecessary mystique and confusion which often surrounds discussions of the peak-load problem can be avoided if it is recognized at the outset that the problem is merely a special case of a firm's general pricing problem, with two characteristics which are generally analyzed separately combined together. Since one of the characteristics of the peak-load problem is that demand in different periods differs, the demand situation is similar to that found in the traditional treatment of price discrimination already discussed in Chapter 3. The only difference, as far as demand conditions facing the firm are concerned, is that in the case of price discrimination the firm is confronted simultaneously in time by demands which differ in different markets, whereas the different demands confronting the firm in the peak-load problem situation are associated with different time periods. This difference leads to another element which is not present in the traditional analysis of price discrimination: whereas the output sold in different markets in the price-discrimination analysis is produced by different units of input, in the peak-load problem output sold in different time periods is produced sequentially by the same capacity. Thus, the peak-load problem is similar to the price-discrimination framework, but differs in that it also includes the 'joint-product' problem discussed in Chapter 2.

The optimal solution to any pricing problem depends on the objectives pursued; whatever the nature of the objectives, however, optimal pricing always requires that price be set in some specific relationship to the marginal cost of output. Thus, for example, maximization of the satisfaction of the community requires that prices be set equal to marginal costs, while profit maximization requires that the price–marginal cost relationship be such as to equate marginal cost and marginal revenue, which generally requires that price exceed marginal cost. Whatever objectives are pursued, therefore, it is always necessary to determine the marginal cost of output sold in any market, or time period, in order to implement the required optimal pricing rules. The marginal cost of output depends on the marginal cost of the inputs required to produce a marginal unity of output. In the case of a peak-load problem, the same units of some inputs – 'capacity' as they are usually referred to – produce output in different periods, so that the output produced and sold in different periods is a joint product of capacity. The key to the solution of all peak-load pricing problems therefore lies in determining the appropriate marginal-capacity cost of output produced in different periods.

The analysis of joint-product costing contained in Chapter 2 is applicable in this connection, and provides the appropriate marginal cost of capacity concepts required for a solution to any peak-load pricing problem. It was explained there that when an input produces joint products, the proper marginal-cost concept for individual products is an 'opportunity cost', equal to the total marginal cost of the input minus the marginal contribution *of all other outputs* to the decision-maker's objectives. If the objective is profit maximization, the marginal cost of any individual joint product equals the total marginal cost of the input required to produce it minus the sum of the marginal revenues of the other joint products which are produced. When this marginal-cost concept is equated to the marginal revenue from the product in question, it follows automatically that the sum of marginal revenues from all joint products equals the total marginal cost of the input which produces them, as is necessary in order for the level of the input to be at a profit-maximizing level. Similarly, if the objective is maximization of the community's satisfaction, the marginal opportunity cost of one joint product equals the total marginal cost of the input required to produce it minus the sum of the marginal demand prices of the other joint products. When this marginal-cost concept is equal to the demand price of the product in question, it follows that the marginal cost of the input equals the sum of society's marginal evaluations of all the joint products, as is required for input and output levels which maximize the community's satisfaction.

Provided that certain assumptions are made about demand and cost conditions, the optimal solution to a peak-load pricing problem can be depicted diagrammatically. Thus, curves D^1 and D^2 in Figure 11–6 represent the demand for a product in two different time

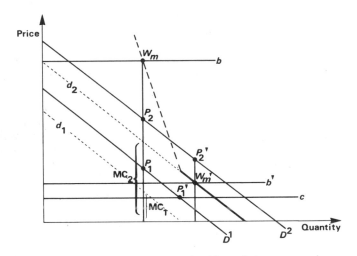

Figure 11–6. Peak-load pricing solutions.

periods of equal length. Quantity demanded at any price is greater in period 2 than in period 1, and demand in each period is assumed to be independent of the price charged in the other period. Total operating costs in each period are assumed to increase in proportion to output, so that average and marginal operating costs are constant and equal to c in both periods. Total capacity costs are also assumed to increase in proportion to the output rate in any period so that average and marginal capacity costs per unit of output are constant; as shown by the solid line labeled b. If the objective is maximizing the community's satisfaction, and assuming that price equals marginal cost in all other sectors of the economy, the price of output produced in each period must be set equal to the marginal cost of output in that period. The steps involved in the diagrammatic solution to this peak-load pricing problem may be summarized as follows:

1. The vertical distance between the demand curve and operating cost curve in each

period represents that period's effective demand for capacity per unit of output, at different output rates. These effective demand for capacity curves are shown by the dotted lines labeled d_1 and d_2.

2. By adding *vertically* the demand for capacity curves in each period, one obtains the total effective demand for capacity which is used to produce a given output rate in all periods. This total effective demand for capacity curve is shown by the dashed line in Figure 11–6; it lies above d_2 for output rates where the effective demand for capacity of period 1 is positive, and coincides with d_2 at output rates where the effective demand for capacity in period 1 is zero or negative. It should be noted at this stage that the assumption that the two time periods are of equal length is made purely for expositional convenience. As O. E. Williamson has pointed out, if the periods to which the demand for output curves apply are of different lengths, the effective demand for capacity curve associated with each period must be weighted according to their relative length before the vertical summation of these curves occurs. The reason can be illustrated by a simple example: with two identical demand for output curves, if one related to a period one half the length of the other, the total output and capacity associated with any given output rate would be one half that of the other period.

3. The optimal (welfare-maximizing) level of capacity is determined by the intersection of the vertical summation of the demand for capacity curves associated with individual periods and the marginal cost of capacity curve. At this point, labeled W_m in Figure 11–6, the total value placed by buyers of output in all periods on the level of capacity is equal to the marginal cost of capacity, which represents the value in alternative uses of the resources required to produce additional capacity.

4. The portion of the total marginal cost of capacity which is allocated to output produced in any periods should equal the marginal opportunity cost of capacity in that period, defined as the difference between the total marginal cost of capacity and the effective demand for that level of capacity in other periods. Clearly, at the optimal level of capacity, the marginal opportunity cost of capacity in each period will equal the period's effective demand for the optimal level of capacity. When total marginal capacity cost equals b, the marginal cost of capacity in period 1 therefore equals MC_1 in Figure 11–6, and the marginal cost of capacity in period 2 equals MC_2.

5. The optimal level of price and output in each period are found by adding the marginal operating cost to the period's marginal cost of capacity. When marginal capacity cost equals b, the optimal prices of output in periods 1 and 2 are P_1 and P_2, and output rates are the same in both periods. As indicated below, however, output rates need not always be the same in the different periods.

The essence of the preceding welfare-maximizing solution to the peak-load pricing problem is that prices equal marginal cost of output produced in each period, and that the capacity-cost component of marginal cost of output is an opportunity-cost concept. Several other characteristics of the welfare-maximizing solution should also be noted, before considering the consequences of relaxing some of the assumptions regarding demand and cost conditions which underlie the solution. First, as regards output levels and capacity utilization in different periods, the optimal level of capacity is fully utilized in every time period where the effective demand price of that capacity level is positive. If there are periods where the effective demand price of the optimal level of capacity is zero, no part of the marginal cost of capacity is allocated to output produced and sold in these periods. The marginal opportunity cost of the optimal capacity level in these periods is zero, since the effective demand for that capacity level in other periods exceeds its total marginal cost. The fact that buyers in these periods pay nothing towards the marginal cost of capacity will not, however, encourage overexpansion of capacity, for the very reason that they are not charged is that they will not use the optimal capacity fully. In such periods, the output rate and level of capacity utilization will be determined by the intersection of the marginal operating cost curve and the demand for output curve. Thus, for example, if the marginal cost of capacity curve is b' in Figure 11–6, optimal capacity is determined by the intersection of the vertically summed effective demand for capacity curve and b' at W_m'. The optimal prices of output in each period are P_1', which covers marginal operating cost only, and P_2', which covers operating and total marginal capacity cost. In this case, the output rate and capacity utilization in the off-peak period is lower than in the peak period.

Turning next to the pricing implications of the preceding solution, controversy exists in the literature as to whether the solution to the peak-load pricing problem involves price discrimination. In his original seminal contribution, P. O. Steiner (85) claimed that the welfare-maximizing solution involves price discrimination. As O. E. Williamson (103, 104) and J. Hirschleifer (37) both subsequently pointed out, the welfare-maximizing prices are not discriminatory because they reflect the difference in marginal cost, defined in an opportunity cost sense, of serving the markets in different periods. As explained in Chapter 3, price discrimination is present when prices are not proportional to marginal costs in different markets. It must be added, however, that a *profit-maximizing* solution to the peak-load pricing problem *will* generally involve price discrimination. This is because whereas welfare maximization requires equality of price and marginal cost of output sold in different periods, profit maximization requires equality of marginal revenue and marginal cost in each period. The relationship between price and marginal revenue in any market depends on the magnitude of price-elasticity of demand for the product, as explained in Chapter 3. Only if price-elasticity of demand is the same in different markets, or periods, will price–marginal revenue relationships, and therefore profit-maximizing price–marginal cost relationships, be the same in different markets. The profit-maximizing solution to the peak-load pricing problem can also be explained diagrammatically by reference to Figure 11–6. Instead of demand curves for output and effective demand for capacity curves, what is required if the objective is profit maximization are the marginal revenue curves associated with output in different periods, and marginal-revenue-of-capacity curves obtained by subtracting marginal operating cost curves from marginal revenue curves in each period. From this point the diagrammatic procedure is the same as in the welfare-maximizing solution: the marginal-revenue-of-capacity curves for each period are summed vertically, and their intersection with the marginal-cost-of-capacity curve determines the optimal (profit-maximizing) level of capacity. The marginal opportunity cost of capacity in each period is now the difference between the total marginal cost of capacity and the sum of marginal revenue of capacity in all other periods, instead of the sum of effective demands for capacity in other periods as in the case of welfare maximization. The optimal output levels in each period are obtained by adding the marginal opportunity cost of capacity for each period to the marginal operating cost and equating this with the marginal revenue of output in each period. The point on the demand for output curve for each period which corresponds to the output rate determined in the preceding manner indicates the optimal output price for the period.

The preceding remarks indicate that the pursuit of objectives other than welfare maximization may result in optimal solutions to the peak-load pricing problem which involve non-proportional price–marginal cost relationships in different periods, and therefore result in price discrimination. It should also be noted that even when welfare maximization is the objective, the existence of a constraint which prevents prices from equalling marginal costs in all markets in the economy simultaneously can also result in welfare-maximizing price–marginal cost relationships in different periods which involve price discrimination. This will occur whenever the effects of changes in output produced in different periods on the constraint are not proportional to the effects of the output changes on total costs or, what is the same, to marginal costs of output in different periods.

The logic underlying this conclusion may be stated briefly as follows: it was explained in the previous section that welfare-maximizing second-best pricing rules require that the marginal effect of each type of output on aggregate satisfaction in the community be proportional to the marginal effect of each type of output on the constraint which is responsible for the existence of a second-best situation. Price–marginal cost differences are a measure of the effect of output changes on aggregate satisfaction, as explained. When price–marginal cost differences are proportional to effects of output change on the second-best constraint, it follows automatically that only if marginal costs of output are proportional to marginal effects of output on the constraint will welfare-maximizing price–marginal cost differences be proportional for different products.

An example where this requirement will not generally be met occurs when the second-best constraint takes the form of a maximum total profit level for the public utility, or an economy-wide tax-revenue constraint. In the presence of such a constraint, as was explained earlier in Chapter 10 and again in a previous section of the present chapter, the welfare-maximizing price–marginal cost difference for any product is proportional to price- and cross-elasticities of demand and supply. It follows that only if price- and cross-elasticities of demand for all products were identical (in which case the products are in effect identical) will the welfare-maximizing price–marginal cost relationship be the same for different products. In view of the apparent similarity between the second-best pricing rule in this example and profit-maximizing pricing rules, it is appropriate to point out the difference between them. Although both situations require that price–marginal cost differences for different products be proportional to price- and cross-elasticities of demand and supply, the *absolute* magnitude of the price–marginal cost difference for all products will differ, being lower in the case of welfare maximization than in the case of profit-maximization. Only if the second-best constraint took the form of a requirement that the public utility maximize its profits would the welfare-maximizing and profit-maximizing solutions be identical.

The issue of whether a solution to the peak-load pricing problem involves price discrimination is concerned with the relationship between price and marginal cost of output sold in different periods. Also of interest is a comparison of the absolute level of price itself in different periods. The diagrammatic solution to the peak-load problem illustrated in Figure 11–6 shows that price in the period of peak demand exceeds price in the off-peak period. This will always be the case when welfare maximization requires equality of price and marginal cost in any period, and when marginal operating and capacity costs are the same at all output levels and in all periods. When demand at any price is greater in one period than another, the peak period's effective demand for capacity, and therefore the period's optimal marginal opportunity cost of capacity, will be higher. Only if marginal operating costs were higher in the off-peak period than in the peak period, and this difference in operating cost exceeded the difference in marginal capacity costs of the two periods, could price in the off-peak period exceed that of the peak period.

When a constraint prevents price from being equal to marginal cost in every period, however, the conclusion that welfare-maximizing prices will be higher in the peak period than in the off-peak period may be reversed, even when operating costs are the same in both periods. This can be illustrated by using the earlier example where the optimal second-best price–marginal cost differences are proportional to price- and cross-elasticities of demand. Assuming, for expositional convenience, that cross-elasticities of demand and supply between different products are zero, and that the effective demand in the off-peak period for the optimal level of capacity is zero so that the marginal opportunity cost of capacity in the off-peak period is zero, the welfare-maximizing second-best pricing conditions for the off-peak and peak periods are, respectively,

$$\frac{p-c}{p} = \frac{\lambda}{(1+\lambda)} \cdot \frac{1}{E_o} \quad \text{and} \quad \frac{P-(c+k)}{P} = \frac{\lambda}{(1+\lambda)} \cdot \frac{1}{E_p}$$

where the symbols c and k represent, respectively, marginal operating cost and total marginal capacity cost, E_o and E_p are the price-elasticities of demand in the off-peak and peak periods, and λ represents the marginal effect of a change in the second-best constraint on the level of aggregate satisfaction in the community. Although the marginal cost of output produced in the peak period clearly exceeds that of output produced in the off-peak period (p), it is possible for the optimal level of price in the off-peak period to exceed price in the peak periods (P) both in absolute terms and in relation to the period's marginal cost. For this to occur, price-elasticity of demand for output in the off-peak period must be sufficiently lower than in the peak period so as to compensate for the larger marginal costs attributable to output in the peak period. It is also apparent from the above relationships that the size of k relative to c is also important in determining the relative level of price in each period. When total marginal capacity costs (k) are large relative to marginal operating costs (c), it is less likely that price will be higher in the off-peak period than in the peak period.

The pursuit of objectives other than welfare maximization can also reverse the conclusion that price in the peak period will exceed price in the off-peak period. If profit maximization is the objective, optimal price–marginal cost relationships in any period again depend on price- and cross-elasticities of demand as in the preceding second-best welfare-maximizing example. The only difference between the second-best pricing conditions just outlined and the profit-maximizing pricing conditions in the off-peak and peak periods would be the absence of the $\dfrac{\lambda}{(1+\lambda)}$ term from the preceding conditions in the case of profit maximization. This means that the absolute level of price–marginal cost differences will be greater for all products under profit maximization than under welfare maximization, but in both cases optimal price–marginal cost relationships will depend on price-elasticities of demand. A sufficiently low price-elasticity of demand for output in the off-peak period can therefore result in a higher price of output in the off-peak period than in the peak period under profit maximization also. So-called 'price reversals' can also occur under certain types of regulatory constraint, as will be explained later in this section.

Before considering the impact of regulation on solutions to the peak-load pricing problem, it is appropriate to consider briefly the consequences of changing the assumptions regarding demand and cost conditions which underlie the diagrammatic solution depicted earlier and the ensuing discussion of its implications. The assumption that demand for output in any period is independent of the price and quantity of output produced in other periods may be adequate for some purposes; for others, however, it may be more realistic to assume that buyers regard output in different periods to be either substitutable or complementary to some degree, so that the demand conditions in different periods are interdependent. In these circumstances, the principles involved in solving the peak-load pricing problem expounded earlier, particularly the concept of the marginal cost of capacity in different periods, remain unchanged, but diagrammatic exposition of the solution becomes very difficult. The consequences of demand interdependence for the solution to the peak-load pricing problem are relatively easy to explain in algebraic terms, however. Demand interdependence merely means that cross-elasticities of demand will now enter into the algebraic expressions which indicate optimal price–marginal cost relationships in different periods. Demand and cost interdependence is another possibility not considered in the earlier diagrammatic solution. The mix of capacity and other inputs which minimizes the total cost of producing any particular output rate depends on the total volume of output to be produced in all periods in the future. The expected volume of output and its distribution between different time periods depend on demand conditions anticipated in those periods. Thus, cost conditions may depend on demand conditions, resulting in a situation exhibiting cost and demand interdependence. Even if demand conditions in different periods are themselves independent, this again greatly complicates diagrammatic exposition of the peak-load pricing problem. Again, however, the cost and demand interdependence will appear in the algebraic optimal pricing conditions describing the solution, and does not change the principles involved.

Another assumption relating to cost conditions themselves was that marginal operating and capacity costs were both constant, indicating that the firm's total operating costs and total capacity costs both increase proportionately with the output rate produced in any period. If marginal capacity costs were to decline with scale of output, for example, pricing at marginal cost in every period would not enable the firm to cover its total costs. As a result, pricing at marginal cost in all sectors of the economy simultaneously would not be possible, and a second-best pricing solution would be appropriate if the objective of the firm were welfare maximization. In other words, the welfare-maximizing price–marginal cost relationship in each period would no longer involve equality of price and marginal cost, in contrast to the welfare-maximizing diagrammatic solution to the peak-load pricing problem depicted earlier. Once again, however, the principles involved in calculating the marginal opportunity cost of capacity in each period remain unchanged.

Traditionally, the literature dealing with the peak-load pricing problem has focused upon the welfare-maximizing solution. While this is appropriate if one is seeking guidelines for regulatory and similar public policy, it is also obviously necessary to determine the effect of different forms of regulation on solutions to the peak-load pricing problem in order to select the appropriate form of regulatory constraint. This last aspect of the peak-load problem has been largely ignored in the literature until very recently, but the essential principles involved will be indicated briefly at this stage, together with several illustrative examples.

At the outset, it should always be remembered that the effect of regulation on a firm's behavior depends not only on the nature of the regulatory constraint itself, but also on the objectives of the firm's decision-makers and the nature of other constraints confronting them. In the context of the peak-load pricing problem, this means that the precise nature of the optimal price–marginal cost relationships in different periods, which represent the solution to a peak-load pricing problem in the absence of regulation, can vary depending on the objectives of the firm's decision-makers and the nature of other constraints such as demand and cost conditions. The addition of a regulatory constraint will change these optimal pricing conditions in some or all periods, the exact nature of the resulting changes will depend on the objectives and other constraints facing the firm's decision-makers, however, and no generalizations independent of these factors are possible.

The second point of major importance is that the effect of regulation on solutions to the peak-load pricing problem will depend on the nature of the regulatory constraint itself. In two recent papers, for example, E. Bailey (4) and L. J. White (102) have shown that in the case of a profit-maximizing firm, regulation limiting the rate of return on capital investment lowers prices charged in the peak period only; in contrast, when regulation limits profit per unit of output, or return on total cost, prices are reduced in peak and off-peak periods. It is appropriate to consider the reasoning which underlies these conclusions within the analytical framework developed in this section: in the Bailey and White peak-load pricing models, the effective marginal revenue associated with the optimal level of capacity in the off-peak period is zero, so that the marginal opportunity cost of capacity in the off-peak period is zero. As explained earlier in this section, the optimal pricing rules for the unregulated profit-maximizing firm require that the sum of marginal operating cost plus marginal opportunity cost of capacity be equated with the marginal revenue from output sold in each period. Regulating the rate of return on capital in effect reduces the total marginal cost of capacity, which will increase the optimal level of capacity where the sum of effective marginal revenue from capacity in every period equals the total marginal cost of capacity. It follows that output will be greater, and price lower, in the peak period. Since the effective marginal revenue associated with capacity in the off-peak period was already zero, no part of the total marginal cost of the new higher optimal level of capacity is attributed to the off-peak period, so that output and price in the off-peak period remain the same as in the absence of regulation. It was explained earlier that off-peak price could be lower than peak price in an unregulated profit-maximizing firm, provided that the price-elasticity of off-peak demand is sufficiently small relative to that of the peak period. Under rate-of-return-on-capital regulation, the likelihood of this occurring is clearly increased.

It must be emphasized that the preceding conclusion, that the off-peak price and output level remain unchanged under rate-of-return-on-capital regulation, is based upon the assumption of zero cross-elasticity of demand between different periods. When cross-elasticities are not zero, a change in the price and output level of the peak period changes the demand conditions for the product in the off-peak period, and will therefore result in a change in the price and output of that period. If a complementary relationship exists between demand in each period, the lower peak-period price will increase demand in the off-peak period, while the opposite will be the case if there is a substitute relationship between demand in each period. In either case, whether the optimal output level in the off-peak period is increased or reduced depends on the precise manner in which demand at all prices is changed, since this will determine the effect on marginal revenue at different output levels, and no generalizations are possible. Another point which needs to be borne in mind is the assumption that the marginal revenue associated with capacity in the off-peak period is zero. Whenever this condition is not met, so that the marginal opportunity cost of capacity in the off-peak period is positive instead of zero, a reduction in the total marginal cost of capacity will result in a reduction in the marginal opportunity cost of capacity in the off-peak period also, causing an increase in output and a reduction in price in the off-peak period also.

The implications of rate-of-return-on-capital regulation for the optimal level of capacity are also interesting, as Bailey and White have demonstrated. Is it possible, for example, for the increase in capacity under this form of regulation to result in a larger level of capacity and output in the peak period than the level which maximizes allocative efficiency in the economy?* An affirmative answer to this question is indicated by the analysis of Bailey and White, who show that the optimal level of capacity will exceed the level required for allocative efficiency whenever off-peak-period profits are large enough to require losses in the peak period. When this condition is not met, the regulated firm will provide a capacity and peak output level larger than would a profit-maximizing firm, but lower than the level required for allocative efficiency.

---

* This is a different issue from that of whether return-on-capital regulation causes technical efficiency due to the existence of an A–J effect. The latter issue deals with the question of whether, whatever the firm's output level, the input mix used to produce it minimizes the total cost of that output level. In contrast, the present issue is whether the output rate itself exceeds the level required for allocative efficiency.

The conclusion that capacity may exceed the welfare-maximizing level can be explained intuitively as follows: since price and output in the off-peak period are unchanged, given the assumptions of zero cross-elasticities of demand and zero effective marginal revenue in the off-peak period, profits earned in the off-peak period will also remain unchanged. This means that the level of peak capacity and output selected by the firm must be such as to make the ratio of peak plus off-peak profits to capacity meet the regulatory constraint. Given the allowed return on capital, the larger the off-peak profits, the larger will be the capacity and output level in the peak period which is necessary to meet the constraint. Also, the lower the excess of allowed rate of return over the firm's cost of capital, the larger the capacity and output level in the peak period which will be necessary to meet the regulatory constraint. As Bailey and White demonstrate, when the peak capacity and output level required to meet the constraint result in losses in the peak period, capacity will be in excess of the level required for allocative efficiency. The two crucial variables which determine whether or not the peak capacity level exceeds the level required for allocative efficiency are therefore the size of off-peak profits and the margin between the allowed rate of return on capital and the firm's cost of capital.

Another possibility demonstrated by Bailey and White, which contrasts markedly with one of the conclusions reached in the analysis of the A–J effect in the second section of this chapter, is that the firm may employ unproductive capital in order to bring its overall profits in line with the regulatory constraint. If, in order to absorb its off-peak profits and meet the regulatory constraint, a firm must expand capacity beyond the point where marginal revenue from the output in the peak period equals marginal operating cost, the best way of expanding capital further is to add capital that is not used productively. The addition of unproductive capital does not increase output and lower price further, whereas adding productive capacity would mean that the price and marginal revenue on peak-period operations have to drop further, resulting in a situation in which the firm's marginal expenditure on operating costs exceeds the additional revenue it brings in.

Regulation limiting profit per unit of output produces different results from return-on-capital regulation. In effect, the marginal cost of any unit of output, whether produced in the peak or off-peak period, is reduced by an amount equal to the amount of profit allowed per unit of output. Output will be higher and price will be lower, in both the peak and off-peak period, than in the unregulated profit-maximizing firm. As before, optimal capacity will be increased, and marginal capacity costs will be attributed to output produced in the peak period only. Regulation limiting a firm's rate of return on total cost produces results which are very similar to regulation of profit per unit of output. There is in effect a proportional reduction of the marginal cost of output produced in each period, instead of an equal absolute reduction as occurred under regulation limiting profit per unit of output. The result, again, is an increase in output in both the peak and off-peak periods.

Optimal Depreciation Policy and Regulation

At this stage it is convenient to consider the subject of depreciation policy, since the nature of the depreciation problem and its solution are very similar to the peak-load pricing problem discussed in the preceding section. Depreciation policy refers to the manner in which the cost of long-lived assets such as items of capital equipment is allocated between different periods of time during the economic life of the equipment (see Baumol (7) on the subject). Since the output produced by an item of capital equipment in each of the number of consecutive periods of time may be viewed as joint products of the equipment, the problem of depreciation is equivalent to the problem of allocating the cost of an input among a number of joint products.

As already explained in Chapter 3 and again in the two preceding sections of the present chapter, whatever the objectives pursued by a firm's decision-makers, optimal pricing behavior requires that the price of output sold in any period be set in some fixed relationship to the marginal cost of producing output in that period. Choice of a depreciation policy, since it determines the fraction of the cost of equipment which is allocated to output produced in any period, is therefore equivalent to choice of an intertemporal pattern of prices of the firm's output. Also, although depreciation rules are often treated as an ex-post phenomenon, of relevance after an item of capital equipment has been acquired, it must be emphasized that depreciation policy is itself vitally important to the decision of how much to invest in capital equipment. This is because, given demand conditions anticipated in future periods, the intertemporal pattern of revenues resulting from the use of the equipment, which determines whether the present value of the stream of income anticipated from using the equipment will exceed its cost, depends on the prices charged for output in each future period. In other words, investment decisions, which deal with input levels, and pricing decisions, which deal with output levels, are interdependent and jointly determined.

Viewed as a problem of allocating the cost of an input among a number of joint products, the solution to a firm's depreciation problem is analogous to the peak-load pricing solution discussed in the preceding section. As in the peak-load problem, the optimal level of the capital input in question will itself depend on the objectives pursued by the firm's decision-makers. Under profit-maximization, for example, the optimal level of the input will be where the marginal cost of equipment equals the combined sum of the marginal revenues (net of operating costs) associated with capacity in different periods of time. In contrast, the welfare-maximizing level of the input will be larger, corresponding to the level where the marginal cost of the capital equipment equals the combined sum of the effective demands for capacity in different time periods. The rule that price equal marginal cost for welfare maximization will of course be modified to the extent that prices cannot equal marginal cost in all sectors of the economy simultaneously, and the appropriate price–marginal cost relationship for welfare maximization then depends on the nature of the constraint which prevents price from equalling marginal cost everywhere.

Whatever the objective which is being pursued, however, the portion of the marginal cost of capital equipment and therefore the depreciation charge which is attributable to any period of time is determined by demand conditions, and is an opportunity-cost concept. As in the peak-load problem, the marginal cost of capacity in any particular period equals the total marginal cost of capacity minus the sum of the marginal contribution of capacity to the firm's objectives in all other periods. In the case of profit-maximizing objectives, for example, the marginal contribution of capacity to the firm's objectives is represented by the sum of the marginal revenues (net of operating costs) associated with the existing level of capacity in each period and, at a profit-maximizing level of the capital input, the marginal cost of the input equals the sum of these marginal revenues. It follows automatically that the marginal opportunity cost of the optimal level of capacity in any period, and accordingly the optimal depreciation charge for the period, will equal the marginal revenue (net of operating cost) associated with the optimal level of capacity in that period. In the case of welfare-maximizing objectives, the marginal contribution of a capital input to the firm's objectives equals the sum of effective demands (net of operating costs) associated with the existing level of the input in each period, and at a welfare-maximizing level of capacity this sum equals the marginal cost of capacity. In this case, therefore, the marginal opportunity cost of the optimal level of capacity in any period, and the corresponding optimal depreciation charge, will equal the effective demand (net of operating cost) for the optimal level of capacity in that period.

Applying the preceding cost-allocation rules for optimal pricing to the problem of determining the appropriate depreciation charge for any period of time, it follows that in periods where capacity is not fully utilized when product prices are set at levels which equate marginal revenue from output with marginal operating cost (or when product prices are set equal to marginal operating cost, as in the case of welfare-maximizing objectives), the marginal cost of output equals only marginal operating cost and includes absolutely no depreciation charge contributing towards the marginal cost of capacity. In all other periods a depreciation charge will be attributed to output produced; under profit maximization the depreciation charge equals the marginal revenue (net of operating cost) associated with the optimal level of capacity in each period, while under welfare maximization the charge equals the demand price (net of operating cost) of the optimal level of capacity in each period.

Under either objective, optimal product prices in each of these periods will be at levels which result in full utilization of the optimal level of capacity, and output will be the same in these periods. Optimal product prices, and the depreciation charge attributed to output produced in each period under any given objective, will not be the same unless demand conditions are identical in different periods of time, however. Also, it is illuminating to compare the depreciation policy under profit maximization and welfare maximization. The optimal level of capacity and output in each period will be higher under welfare maximization than under profit maximization; however, if the marginal cost of capacity is independent of the output levels produced by a firm, marginal capacity costs will be the same under either objective. This means that the marginal cost of capacity which is to be allocated between different periods, and the corresponding depreciation charge which is to be allocated between output produced in different periods, are the same under either objective. Under welfare maximization this cost is allocated between periods in proportion to each period's demand for the optimal level of capacity, while under profit maximization it is allocated between periods in proportion to the marginal revenue associated with the optimal capacity level in each period. It follows that the depreciation charge allocated to any given period will be the same under profit and welfare maximization only if the ratio of the demand price and marginal revenue from capacity is the same in different periods. Since the relationship between price and marginal revenue depends on price- and cross-elasticities of demand, it follows that only if these elasticities are the same in different periods of time will optimal depreciation policy be the same under profit and welfare maximization. For example, whereas the depreciation charge for two periods with equal effective demand for capacity will be the same under welfare maximization, if price-elasticities of demand differ in the two periods, the ratio of demand and marginal revenue will differ in each period and under profit maximization the depreciation charges for the two periods will differ. The period with lower price-elasticity of demand at the optimal capacity level will be attributed a lower depreciation charge under profit maximization because marginal revenue will be lower relative to demand price in that period. The depreciation charge in the period with higher price-elasticity of demand at the optimal level of capacity will be higher under profit maximization because marginal revenue will be higher relative to demand price in the period.

The preceding comparison of optimal depreciation policy under profit and welfare maximization is based upon the assumption that welfare maximization requires equality of price and marginal cost of output produced in each period. If some constraint prevents price from equalling marginal cost in all sectors of the economy simultaneously, welfare-maximization no longer requires equality of price and marginal cost, as already explained in the section of Chapter 10 dealing with the theory of second-best. The welfare-maximizing price–marginal cost relationship then depends on the nature of the constraint in question, as was explained. However, for a number of constraints of practical relevance, such as economy-wide tax-revenue constraints, or the requirement that a firm cover its total costs from its own sales revenues or achieve some target level of profit, the welfare-maximizing price–marginal cost relationship was shown to depend on price- and cross-elasticities of demand. In these circumstances, assuming zero cross-elasticities of demand for expositional convenience, the welfare-maximizing price of output will exceed marginal cost in all periods, and at the optimal level of capacity the sum of effective demand for capacity in each period will exceed the marginal cost of capacity. The marginal opportunity cost of the optimal level of capacity in each period, and therefore the optimal depreciation charge for each period, will now be less than the period's effective demand for the optimal capacity level, in contrast to the unconstrained welfare-maximizing case, but will exceed the marginal revenue associated with the optimal capacity level. The precise amount by which the marginal opportunity cost of optimal capacity exceeds marginal revenue associated with capacity in any period depends on the price-elasticity of demand for output in the period, being higher the larger the price-elasticity of demand. The allocation of the marginal cost of optimal capacity between different periods in this constrained welfare-maximizing case, because it depends on price-elasticities of demand for output in different periods, is therefore very similar to the optimal depreciation policy of a profit-maximizing firm. In fact, the two optimal depreciation policies are identical if the marginal cost of capacity does not vary with the level of capacity so that the optimal marginal cost of capacity is the same under either objective. In such circumstances the only difference between a profit-maximizing firm and a welfare-maximizing firm will be that capacity and output in each period will be larger in the latter firm, reflecting the fact that the optimal excess of product price over marginal cost is lower for welfare maximization than for profit maximization. For profit maximization, price exceeds marginal cost by an amount which ensures equality between marginal revenue and marginal cost of output in every period; in contrast, the welfare-maximizing excess of price over marginal cost results in a situation where marginal revenue is less than marginal cost of output in every period. However, although the *absolute* level of price in every period is higher in the profit-maximizing firm, the *relative* levels of price in different periods are the same under profit maximization and the preceding constrained welfare-maximization example, because in both cases they depend on the price-elasticities of demand in different periods.

Before concluding this section on depreciation policy, it is appropriate to point out the implications of the preceding discussion for the issue of whether the optimal depreciation charges allocated to different periods will add up to the total cost of capacity. If the marginal cost of capacity does not vary with the level of capacity installed by a firm, average or unit capacity costs and marginal capacity costs are identical. In these circumstances, it is obvious that the sum of the optimal depreciation charges allocated to different periods, which equal the marginal cost of capacity per unit of output, will also cover the unit and total costs of capacity. In contrast, if the unit cost of capacity to a firm is lower the larger the number of units of capacity installed, the cost per unit of capacity will exceed the marginal cost of capacity, and the marginal cost of capacity which is allocated between different periods for optimal pricing purposes will not cover the cost of the marginal unit of capacity. In these circumstances, pricing at marginal cost of output in any period would imply that the firm's total costs would not be covered by the resulting revenues earned, and this is one of the reasons why pricing above marginal cost may be necessary for welfare maximization. In the presence of a constraint requiring that the firm cover its total costs, the constrained welfare-maximizing pricing rules, optimal level of capacity, and optimal marginal opportunity cost of capacity in different time periods which are applicable are the same as those described in the preceding paragraph.

Regulation and Non-Price Aspects of Firms' Behavior

As the preceding sections of this chapter indicate, the effect of various forms of regulatory constraint on a firm's input mix and price and output level policies has received considerable attention from economists. In contrast, very little attention has been directed towards determining the effect of regulation on other aspects of a firm's operations, such as the durability and other characteristics of output or the level and nature of advertising and R&D activities. Moreover, even where some attention has been focused upon these other dimensions of a firm's activities, the analyses are partial equilibrium in nature since they generally ignore the interdependence which exists between optimal levels of price and non-price decision variables. This neglect is serious, for the following reasons: as the analysis contained in Chapter 5 and some sections of Chapter 6 indicates, the optimal levels of all the various decision variables within a firm are interdependent and simultaneously determined by the objectives and all constraints facing the firm's decision-makers. Changes in optimal price and output-level conditions will imply changes in the optimal conditions relating to other aspects of behavior also. If regulation affects a firm's optimal price–marginal cost relationship, it will also change the optimal advertising–sales and R&D–sales relationships, for example, since in part these conditions depend on the relationship between the price and marginal cost of the firm's output. This will generally cause changes in the optimal levels of these non-price decision variables, which in turn will imply changes in the demand conditions facing the regulated firm. Despite this, the demand conditions facing a regulated firm are usually assumed to remain unchanged in analyses of the effect of regulation of firm's input mix and price and output level behavior. When the consequences of regulatory constraints for non-price dimensions of a firm's behavior are taken into consideration, together with the interdependence between price and non-price dimensions of behavior, the resulting implications for the traditional conclusions regarding the effect of regulation on input mixes and output levels in the regulated firm could be quite suprising. For example, if a regulatory constraint which reduced the optimal excess of price over marginal cost of the firm's output also reduced the optimal level of the firm's non-price decision variables such as advertising, leading to reduced demand for the firm's product at any price, the traditional conclusion that the output level of the regulated firm will be higher than in absence of regulation may no longer be valid. It should be noted that the preceding example is not the only possible outcome, however. Thus, regulation may not affect the optimal price–marginal cost relationship, but may affect a firm's expectations regarding its rivals' non-price reactions. As explained in Chapter 6 in the section dealing with seller concentration and R&D behavior, a change in the optimal price–marginal cost relationship in one direction is compatible with a rise, or a fall, or no change, in the optimal sales (or advertising–sales) ratio of the firm, depending on whether and how the firm's expectations regarding its rivals' non-price behavior are affected.

As the preceding comments suggest, no generalizations are possible concerning the effect of regulation on optimal levels of non-price decision variables. The effect depends on how regulation affects the optimal conditions relating to each of the firm's decision variables, and on the precise nature of the interdependence which exists between different decision variables in any particular case. Also, as usual, the effect of regulation will depend on the nature of the regulatory constraint itself. If, for example, advertising expenditures are included in the allowed rate base under rate of return on capital regulation, a different effect on the firm's optimal advertising condition will be obtained than if these expenditures are excluded from the rate base. Another point to bear in mind is that there will in general be more than one regulatory constraint exerting an influence on the regulated firm's behavior; in addition to a return-on-capital constraint, there may, for example, be legislative constraints which create or reduce entry barriers into the regulated industry and influence the firm's expectations regarding the behavior of rival firms. Unfortunately, given the current limited state of economic knowledge and analysis of non-price aspects of firms' behavior in general, we can do little more in a book of this nature than point out the appropriate directions in which attention needs to be directed in order to develop a more comprehensive and satisfactory framework for analyzing, and choosing between, alternative types of regulatory policy.

RECOMMENDED READINGS

1. Acharya, S. N., Public enterprise pricing and social benefit-cost analysis, *Oxford Economic Papers*, March 1972.
2. Averch, H. and Johnson, L. L., Behavior of the firm under regulatory constraints, *American Economic Review*, December 1962.
3. Bailey, E. E., Innovation and regulation, *Journal of Public Economics*, August 1974.
4. Bailey, E. J., Peak-load pricing under regulatory constraint, *Journal of Political Economy*, July–August 1972.
5. Bailey, E. and Coleman, R. D., The effect of lagged regulation in an A–J model, *Bell Journal of Economics and Management Science*, Spring 1971.
6. Bailey, E. and Malone, J. C., Resource allocation in the regulated firm, *Bell Journal of Economics and Management Science*, Spring 1970.
7. Baumol, W. J., Optimal depreciation policy: pricing the products of durable assets, *Bell Journal of Economics and Management Science*, Autumn 1971.
8. Baumol, W. J. and Klevorick, A. K., The A–J thesis: input choices and rate of return regulation: an overview of the discussion, *Bell Journal of Economics and Management Science*, Autumn 1970.
9. Bergson, A., Optimal pricing for a public enterprise, *Quarterly Journal of Economics*, November 1972.
10. Boiteux, M., Peak-load pricing, *Journal of Business*, April 1960.
11. Boiteux, M., On the management of public monopolies subject to budgetary constraints, *Journal of Economic Theory*, September 1971.
12. Boyes, W. J., An empirical examination of the Averch–Johnson effect, *Economic Inquiry*, March 1976.
13. Breen, W. J. and Lerner, E. M., On the use of B in regulatory proceedings, *Bell Journal of Economics and Management Science*, Autumn 1972.
14. Callen, J., Mathewson, G. F. and Mohring, H., The benefits and costs of rate of return regulation, *American Economic Review*, June 1976.
15. Caves, R. E., Direct regulation and market performance in the American economy, *American Economic Review*, May 1964.
16. Coase, R. H., The theory of public utility pricing, *Bell Journal of Economics and Management Science*, Spring 1970.
17. Cootner, P. H. and Holland, D. M., Rate of return and business risk, *Bell Journal of Economics and Management Science*, Autumn 1970.
18. Corey, G. R., The A–J proposition: a critical analysis, *Bell Journal of Economics and Management Science*, Spring 1971.
19. Courville, L., Regulation and efficiency in the electric utility industry, *Bell Journal of Economics and Management Science*, Spring 1974.
20. Craven, J., On the choice of optimal time periods for a surplus-maximizing utility subject to fluctuating demand, *Bell Journal of Economics and Management Science*, Autumn 1971.
21. Craven, J., Space–time pricing for public utilities, *Bell Journal of Economics and Management Science*, Spring 1974.
22. Crew, M. A. and Kleindorfer, P., Marshall and Turvey on peak load or joint product pricing, *Journal of Political Economy*, November–December 1971.
23. Crew, M. A. and Kleindorfer, P., Recent contributions to the problem of marginal cost pricing: the problem of peak loads, *Economic Journal*, December 1971.

24. Crew, M. A. and Kleindorfer, P. R., On off-peak pricing: an alternative technological solution, *Kyklos*, Vol. 28(1), 1975, pp. 80–93.
25. Cross, J. G., Incentive pricing and utility regulation, *Quarterly Journal of Economics*, May 1970; *and* Comment by Jaffee, B.; *and* Reply by Cross, *Quarterly Journal of Economics*, February 1972.
26. Davis, B. E., Investment and the rate of return for the regulated firm, *Bell Journal of Economics and Management Science*, Autumn 1970.
27. Davis, E. G., A dynamic model of the regulated firm with a price adjustment mechanism, *Bell Journal of Economics and Management Science*, Spring 1973.
28. Demsetz, H., Why regulate utilities? *Journal of Law and Economics*, April 1968.
29. Demsetz, H., On the regulation of industry: a reply, *Journal of Political Economy*, March–April 1971.
30. De Vany, A. S., Capacity utilization under alternative regulatory restraints: an analysis of taxi markets, *Journal of Political Economy*, February 1975.
31. De Vany, A. S., The effects of price and entry regulation on airline output capacity and efficiency, *Bell Journal of Economics and Management Science*, Spring 1975.
32. Edelson, N. M., Resource allocation and the regulated firm, *Bell Journal of Economics and Management Science*, Spring 1971.
33. Elton, E. J. and Gruber, M. J., Valuation and the cost of capital for regulated industries, *Journal of Finance*, June 1971.
34. Goddard, F. O., On the effectiveness of regulation of electric utility prices: comment, *Southern Economic Journal*, July 1971.
35. Green, M. and Nader, R., Economic regulation vs. competition: Uncle Sam the monopoly man, *Yale Law Journal*, April 1973.
36. Hilton, G. W., The basic behavior of regulatory commissions, *American Economic Review, Papers and Proceedings*, May 1972.
37. Hirshleifer, J., Peak loads and efficient pricing: comment, *Quarterly Journal of Economics*, August 1958.
38. H.M.S.O., United Kingdom, *The Financial and Economic Objectives of the Nationalised Industries* (1961), Cmnd 1337.
39. H.M.S.O., United Kingdom, *Nationalised Industries: A Review of Economic and Financial Objectives* (1967), Cmnd 3437.
40. Hodiri, M.E. and Takayama, A., Behavior of the firm under regulatory constraint: clarifications, *American Economic Review*, May 1973.
41. Johnson, L. L., Behavior of the firm under regulatory constraint: a reassessment, *American Economic Review, Papers and Proceedings*, May 1973.
42. Joskow, P. L., The determination of the allowed rate of return in a formal regulatory hearing, *Bell Journal of Economics and Management Science*, Autumn 1972.
43. Joskow, P. L., Pricing decisions in regulated firms: a behavioral approach, *Bell Journal of Economics and Management Science*, Spring 1973.
44. Joskow, P. L., Crew, M., Kleindorfer, P. R. and Wenders, J. T., Symposium on peak-load pricing, *Bell Journal of Economics and Management Science*, Spring 1976.
45. Kafoglis, M. Z., Output of the restrained firm, *American Economic Review*, September 1969; *and* Comment.
46. Klevorick, A., The graduated fair return: a regulatory proposal, *American Economic Review*, June 1966; *and* Comments by Kahn, A. E., March 1968, and by Wichers, C. R., with further comment by Klevorick, September 1971 (all in *American Economic Review*).
47. Klevorick, A., The optimal fair rate of return, *Bell Journal of Economics and Management Science*, Spring 1971.
48. Koller, R. H. II, Why regulate utilities? To control price discrimination, *Journal of Law and Economics*, April 1973.
49. Kolm, S., Footnotes to Boiteux's value-constrained second-best, *Journal of Economic Theory*, September 1971.
50. Landon, J. H., Pricing in combined gas and electric utilities: comment; *and* Reply by Owen, B. M., *Antitrust Bulletin*, Spring 1973.
51. Littlechild, S. C., Marginal cost pricing with joint costs, *Economic Journal*, June 1970.
52. Littlechild, S. C., Peak-load pricing of telephone calls, *Bell Journal of Economics and Management Science*, Autumn 1970.
53. MacAvoy, P. W. (Ed.) *The Crisis of the Regulatory Commissions* (New York: W. W. Norton, 1970).
54. Mann, P. C. and Siegfried, E. J., Pricing in the case of publicly owned electric industries, *Quarterly Review of Economics and Business*, Summer 1972.
55. Miller, M. H. and Modigliani, F., Some estimates of the cost of capital to the electric utility industry, 1954–57, *American Economic Review*, June 1966.
56. Minasian, J. R., Ambiguities in the theory of peak-load pricing and application of the theory of queues, *Land Economics*, August 1966.

57. Mohring, H., The peak-load problem with increasing returns and pricing constraints, *American Economic Review*, September 1970.

58. Moore, C. G., Has electricity regulation resulted in higher prices? *Economic Inquiry*, June 1975.

59. Moore, T. G., The effectiveness of regulation of electric utility prices, *Southern Economic Journal*, April 1970.

60. Needy, C. W., Social cost of the A–J–W output distortion, *Southern Economic Journal*, January 1976.

61. Officer, L. H., The optimality of pure competition in the capacity problem, *Quarterly Journal of Economics*, November 1966; *and* Comment by Buchanan, J. M., November 1967; *and* Reply by Officer, November 1967; *and* Further comment by Crew, M. A., May 1969 (all in *Quarterly Journal of Economics*).

62. Owen, B. M., Monopoly pricing in combined gas and electric utilities, *Antitrust Bulletin*, Winter 1970.

63. Pace, J. D., Relevant markets and the nature of competition in the electric utility industry, *Antitrust Bulletin*, Winter 1971.

64. Pelzman, S., Pricing in public and private enterprises: electric utilities in the U.S., *Journal of Law and Economics*, April 1971.

65. Peterson, H. C., An empirical test of regulatory effects, *Bell Journal of Economics and Management Science*, Spring 1975.

66. Phillips, A. (Ed.) *Promoting Competition in Regulated Markets* (Washington D.C.: The Brookings Institution, 1975).

67. Posner, R. A., Taxation by regulation, *Bell Journal of Economics and Management Science*, Spring 1971.

68. Posner, R. A., Theories of economic regulation, *Bell Journal of Economics and Management Science*, Autumn 1974.

69. Pressman, I., A mathematical formulation of the peak-load pricing problem, *Bell Journal of Economics and Management Science*, Autumn 1970.

70. Pressman, I. and Carol, A., Behavior of the firm under regulatory constraint: note, *American Economic Review*, March 1971.

71. Rees, R., Second best rules for public enterprise pricing, *Economics*, August 1968.

72. Reid, G. L. and Allen, K. (Eds.) *Nationalized Industries* (Harmondsworth, England: Penguin Books, 1970).

73. Robichek, A. A., Higgins, R. C. and Kinsman, M., The effect of leverage on the cost of capital of electric utility firms, *Journal of Finance*, May 1973.

74. Rosoff, P., Application of traditional theory to a regulated firm, *Business Economics*, January 1969.

75. Russel, M. and Shelton, R. B., A model of regulatory agency behavior, *Public Choice*, Winter 1974.

76. Sampson, R. J., Inherent advantage under regulation, *American Economic Review*, Papers and Proceedings, May 1972.

77. Schmalensee, R., Regulation and the durability of goods, *Bell Journal of Economics and Management Science*, Spring 1970.

78. Schmalensee, R., Estimating the costs and benefits of utility regulation, *Quarterly Review of Economics and Business*, Summer 1974.

79. Seneca, R. S., Inherent advantage, costs and resource allocation in the transportation industry, *American Economic Review*, December 1973.

80. Sheshinski, E., Welfare aspects of a regulatory constraint: note, *American Economic Review*, March 1971.

81. Soloman, E., Alternative rate of return concepts and their implications for utility regulation, *Bell Journal of Economics and Management Science*, Spring 1970.

82. Spann, R. M., Rate of return regulation and efficiency in production: an empirical test of the A.J. thesis, *Bell Journal of Economics and Management Science*, Spring 1974.

83. Spence, A. M., Monopoly quality and regulation, *Bell Journal of Economics and Management Science*, Autumn 1975.

84. Stein, J. L. and Borts, G., Behavior of the firm under regulatory constraint, *American Economic Review*, December 1972.

85. Steiner, P. O., Peak loads and efficient pricing, *Quarterly Journal of Economics*, November 1957; *and* Comments by Hirschleifer, J., August 1958, and by Buchanan, J. M., August 1964 (both in *Quarterly Journal of Economics*).

86. Stigler, G. J., The theory of economic regulation, *Bell Journal of Economics and Management Science*, Spring 1971.

87. Swan, P. L., The durability of goods and regulation of monopoly, *Bell Journal of Economics and Management Science*, Spring 1971.

88. Takayama, A., Behavior of the firm under regulatory constraint, *American Economic Review*, June 1969.

89. Telser, L., On the regulation of industry: a note, *Journal of Political Economy*, November 1969; *and* Reply by Demsetz, H., *and* Rejoinder by Telser, March–April 1971; *and* A Correction by Telser, July–August 1971 (all in *Journal of Political Economy*).

90. Turvey, R., Peak-load pricing, *Journal of Political Economy*, January–February 1968.

91. Turvey, R. (Ed.) *Public Enterprise* (Harmondsworth, England: Penguin Books, 1968).

92. Turvey, R., The second-best case for marginal cost pricing. In Margolis, J. and Guitton, H. (Eds.) *Public Economics* (New York: St Martin's Press, 1969).

93. Turvey, R., *Economic Analysis and Public Enterprise* (London: Allen & Unwin, 1971).

94. Ulveling, E. F., Regulated firms and optimal resource allocation, *Rivista Internationale di Scienze Economiche e Commerciali*, Vol. 19, March 1972.

95. Vickrey, W., Responsive pricing of public utility services, *Bell Journal of Economics and Management Science*, Spring 1971.

96. Vickrey, W., Maximum output or maximum welfare? More on the off-peak pricing problem, *Kyklos*, March 1971.

97. Waverman, L., Peak-load pricing under regulatory constraint: a proof of inefficiency, *Journal of Political Economy*, June 1975.

98. Weintraub, S., Rate making and an incentive rate of return, *Public Utilities Fortnightly*, April 1968.

99. Wellisz, S. H., Regulation of natural gas pipeline companies: an economic analysis, *Journal of Political Economy*, February 1963.

100. Westfield, F. M., Methodology of evaluating economic regulation, *American Economic Review, Papers and Proceedings*, May 1971.

101. Whinston, A. and Loehman, E., A new theory of pricing and decision making for public investment, *Bell Journal of Economics and Management Science*, Autumn 1971.

102. White, L. J., Reversals in peak and off-peak prices, *Bell Journal of Economics and Management Science*, Spring 1974.

103. Williamson, O. E., Peak-load pricing and optimal capacity under indivisibility constraints, *American Economic Review*, September 1966.

104. Williamson, O. E., Peak-load pricing: some further remarks, *Bell Journal of Economics and Management Science*, Spring 1974.

105. Wilson, G. W., The theory of peak-load pricing: a final note, *Bell Journal of Economics and Management Science*, Spring 1972.

106. Zajac, E. E., Geometric treatment of Averch–Johnson's behavior of the firm under regulatory constraint, *American Economic Review*, March 1970; *and* Comment by Stonebraker, R. J. *and* Reply by Zajac, *American Economic Review*, March 1972.

107. Zajac, E. E., A note on 'gold plating' or 'rate-base padding', *Bell Journal of Economics and Management Science*, Spring 1972.

AUTHOR INDEX

SUBJECT INDEX